SIXTH EDITION

STRATEGIC MANAGEMENT IN ACTION

Mary Coulter

Missouri State University

PEARSON

Boston   Columbus   Indianapolis   New York   San Francisco   Upper Saddle River
Amsterdam   Cape Town   Dubai   London   Madrid   Milan   Munich   Paris   Montréal   Toronto
Delhi   Mexico City   São Paulo   Sydney   Hong Kong   Seoul   Singapore   Taipei   Tokyo

Editor in Chief: Stephanie Wall
Senior Acquisitions Editor: April Cole
Editorial Project Manager:
    Claudia Fernandes
Director of Marketing: Maggie Moylan
Senior Marketing Manager: Nikki Ayana Jones
Marketing Assistant: Gianna Sandri
Senior Managing Editor: Judy Leale
Production Project Manager: Kelly Warsak
Senior Operations Supervisor: Arnold Vila
Operations Specialist: Cathleen Petersen
Creative Director: Blair Brown
Senior Art Director: Kenny Beck

Text Designer: LCI Design
Cover Designer: LCI Design
Cover Art: Svetoslav Iliev/Shutterstock.com
Permission Specialist: Brooks Hill-Whilton
Media Project Manager, Production:
    Lisa Rinaldi
Senior Media Project Manager,
    Editorial: Denise Vaughn
Full-Service Project Management and
    Composition: Integra
Printer/Binder: RRD/Willard
Cover Printer: Lehigh-Phoenix Color
Text Font: 10/12, Times LT Std

Credits and acknowledgments borrowed from other sources and reproduced, with permission, in this textbook appear on appropriate page within text.

Library of Congress Cataloging-in-Publication Data
Coulter, Mary K.
    Strategic management in action / Mary Coulter.—6th ed.
        p. cm.
    Includes index.
    ISBN 978-0-13-262067-3
    1. Strategic planning.   I. Title.
HD30.28.C696 2010
658.4'012—dc23
                                    2012021727

10 9 8 7 6 5 4 3 2 1

ISBN 10:   0-13-262067-7
ISBN 13: 978-0-13-262067-3

To my husband, Ron!

Brief Contents

Contents

Preface

Strategy Theory + Strategy Practice = Strategic Management in Action, Sixth Edition

Competitive advantage. It's a concept that's fundamental to the study of strategic management—and one you'll be quite familiar with after reading this text. What is competitive advantage? It refers to what sets something (an organization, a team, a job applicant, a book, etc.) apart. And what sets this text apart? What is its competitive advantage? This is a strategic management text that effectively integrates strategy theory and strategy practice. As one professor who uses the text so clearly said, "It's the right stuff compactly and clearly presented." The sixth edition of Strategic Management in Action continues to do what it does best—presenting current strategic management theories and practices in an interesting, engaging, and easy-to-read format. And now, we've added color and photos—making it even more fun to read!

New to the Sixth Edition

Here is a chapter-by-chapter list of the changes in the sixth edition.

Chapter 1
- New opening case on Zynga
- Today's economic climate
- Boxed material includes *Think About* or *To Do* assignments
- Updated and new boxes, examples, and cases

Chapter 2
- New opening case on Kodak
- New case on Gap
- Boxed material includes *Think About* or *To Do* assignments
- Updated and new boxes, examples, and cases

Chapter 3
- Boxed material includes *Think About* or *To Do* assignments
- Updated and new boxes, examples, and cases

Chapter 4
- New opening case on Avon
- Boxed material includes *Think About* or *To Do* assignments
- New case on Coca-Cola
- Updated and new boxes, examples, and cases

Chapter 5
- Condensed material on functional strategies combined with competitive strategies
- Boxed material includes *Think About* or *To Do* assignments
- Updated and new boxes, examples, and cases

Chapter 6
- New opening case on Under Armour
- New box on "thinking small"
- Boxed material includes *Think About* or *To Do* assignments
- Updated and new boxes, examples, and cases

Chapter 7
- New chapter devoted to international strategies
- New case on Nokia
- New case on Nomura Holdings
- Updated and new boxes, examples, and cases

Module
- New module devoted to strategies for entrepreneurial ventures and not-for-profits
- Updated and new information on job creation, start-ups, and Global Entrepreneurship Monitor

Finally, this edition continues to discuss contemporary strategic management theories and practices including, for example, corporate reputations, the ethics of profits, global corporate governance, offshoring versus outsourcing, employee layoff strategies, the hourglass phenomenon, workers' rights, and global trade. Of course, traditional strategy concepts such as competitive advantage, SWOT analysis, corporate growth, and strategy implementation are covered as well.

Emphasizes Strategy in Action

This text illustrates strategic managers and strategic management in action. How? By describing real managers and real organizations using strategic management. These strategy in action examples are featured throughout the chapters in the various boxed features. For instance, the Strategic Management in Action boxes describe organizations (all types and all sizes) and the unique strategies they're using. The Strategic Management in Action—Global Perspective boxes describe global organizations and the unique challenges they're facing and the unique strategies they're using. Additionally, strategic management concepts discussed throughout the various chapters are "brought to life" through descriptions of organizations using those concepts as they do what they're in business to do.

Opportunities to Practice Strategic Management

I believe everyone in an organization—not just the top management team—deals with strategy and as such needs to know what's involved with strategic management. What better way to do that than by "practicing" it? And this text provides several opportunities for students to do that.

Case analysis is an important part of most strategy courses, but not every case assignment needs to be a comprehensive case for students to learn something from it. At the beginning of each chapter, there's a Strategic Management in Action mini-case, which describes a company facing a strategic decision. (Some of these companies are Zynga, Zara, Under Armour, Kodak, and Avon.) Using the discussion questions posed at the end of the chapter, students can analyze this company. It's a way for them to "practice" strategic management by evaluating what these companies have done, as well as a way to practice different parts of the strategic management process. In addition, two or three other mini-cases and discussion questions are found at the end of each chapter. With these mini-cases at the end of every chapter, there's ample opportunity for students to work with the concepts and theories that are presented in each chapter and to apply them to an organizational situation.

In addition, all chapter boxes have suggestions for further research, review, or discussion. Another chapter feature—The Grey Zone—emphasizes the ethical dilemmas that strategic decision makers often face and asks students to come up with suggestions about how they would handle that dilemma.

Finally, at the end of each chapter, there are several "You As Strategic Decision Maker: Building Your Skills" exercises that provide students with opportunities to practice strategic management by doing additional research, analysis, and writing.

Discussion of Strategies

When strategic decision makers must change the strategic direction of an organization and choose a different strategy, making that decision isn't enough. There are more steps to the process. That strategy also needs to be put into action (implemented) and the results of the strategy evaluated. This strategy text discusses that process of formulation, implementation, and evaluation as each strategy level (functional, competitive, and corporate) is presented. So, for instance, when discussing competitive strategies, you'll find information on what strategies strategic decision makers can choose from (for instance, cost leadership, differentiation, etc.), how those strategies are implemented (by using the organization's resources and capabilities and by using offensive and defensive moves), and how results are evaluated (what performance measures might be used to evaluate the effectiveness of the competitive strategies). This approach makes sense because students need to see all the aspects of a strategy from start to finish—from formulation to implementation to evaluation.

Writing Style

An academic text doesn't have to be boring. This text is unique in the market because it isn't boring. Its conversational and highly readable writing style makes learning about strategic management interesting and fun. Although an author's writing style is difficult to describe (especially your own!), I did write this text in a way that I hope makes the concepts and theories of strategy and strategic management clear and understandable—yet enjoyable! My teaching philosophy—and I taught for over 30 years, won teaching awards at my university, and was consistently ranked toward the top of my department based on student evaluations—has been that learning can be fun. So, I write like I teach. But only you, the reader, can ultimately judge how well I've written the material.

Instructor Supplements

Instructor Resource Center

At http://www.pearsonhighered.com/irc, instructors can access a variety of print, digital, and presentation resources available with this text in downloadable format. Registration is simple and gives you immediate access to new titles and new editions. As a registered faculty member, you can download resource files and receive immediate access to and instructions for installing course management content on your campus server. In case you ever need assistance, our dedicated technical support team is ready to help with the media supplements that accompany this text. Visit http://247.pearsoned.com for answers to frequently asked questions and toll-free user support phone numbers. The following supplements are available for download to adopting instructors:

- Instructor's Resource Manual
- Test Bank
- TestGen® Computerized Test Bank (test-generating program)
- PowerPoint Presentations

Student Supplements

CourseSmart eTextbook

CourseSmart eTextbooks were developed for students looking to save on required or recommended textbooks. Students simply select their eText by title or author and purchase immediate access to the content for the duration of the course using any major credit card. With a CourseSmart eText, students can search for specific keywords or page numbers, take notes online, print out reading assignments that incorporate lecture notes, and bookmark important passages for later review. For more information or to purchase a CourseSmart eTextbook, visit www.coursesmart.com.

Acknowledgments

I need to thank a number of people for their contributions to this text. Without them, you wouldn't be holding *Strategic Management in Action,* Sixth Edition in front of you. First of all, my students. Through my experiences teaching our Strategic Management course (most of them enjoyable!), I developed my own personal philosophy of what seemed to work and what didn't. I learned things every semester from my students and loved when they challenged me on topics (even if I was the textbook author!). And I hope they learned from me—and e-mails I get from former students seem to suggest that they did learn important concepts.

I would also like to recognize the individuals who provided me with thoughtful, intelligent, and thorough reviews of the first five editions of this text. I appreciate your willingness to provide your comments and ideas. I know the sixth edition is better because of the suggestions you have provided. Thank you. These individuals are:

Dr. Augustus Abbey, Morgan State University
Moses Acquaah, University of North Carolina at Greensboro
Dr. Yusaf H. Akbar, Southern New Hampshire University
Hamid Akbari, Northeastern Illinois University
Dr. A. D. Amar, Seton Hall University
Dr. William P. Anthony, Florida State University
Dr. Richard D. Babcock, University of San Francisco
Eugene Baten, Central Connecticut State University
Laquita Blockson, University of Northern Iowa
David T. Cadden, Quinnipiac University
Laurie Dahlin, Worcester State College
Fred Dorn, University of Mississippi
Michael Fratantuono, Dickinson College
Robert Goldberg, Northeastern University
Roy D. Iraggi, New York City College of Technology
David R. King, Marquette University
Dr. Jeryl L. Nelson, Wayne State College
Don Otto, Lindenwood University
Louis P. Panetta, California State University Monterey Bay
Richard Potter, University of Illinois at Chicago
Clint Relyea, Arkansas State University
Frederick R. Richards, Sacred Heart University
David F. Robinson, Indiana State University
Patrick L. Schultz, Texas Tech University
Ram Subramanian, Montclair State University
Jerry Thomas, Arapahoe Community College
Marvin Washington, Texas Tech University
Jack Wheeler, Indiana Wesleyan University
Andrzej Wlodarczyk, Concordia College

I'd also like to thank the management team at Pearson Education. As usual, all of you have been super to work with. A big THANK YOU to Claudia Fernandes, Project Manager. Claudia, thanks for all you do to make my writing easier. You are truly amazing and just a joy to work with. Thank you Claudia for all you do. Then, there's the person who is responsible for the marketing of my text, Nikki Jones. Nikki...you're so creative and so energetic. Thank you for all of your hard work. Some of the other people who have been important to making this text come to life include Kelly Warsak, Kenny Beck, and Allison Campbell. Thank you to all for all your diligent efforts in making this text what it is!

Next, I'd like to say a special thank you to a good friend and outstanding mentor—Steve Robbins, a textbook author icon. Steve, your friendship and advice continue to mean a lot to me. As I've said before, thanks for taking a chance on me and for showing me the ropes of textbook publishing. I know I'm a better writer because of you. Thanks!

Finally, I can't forget the people in my life who mean the world to me—my wonderful and truly supportive husband Ron, and my now expanded family that includes two sons-in-law and two adorable grandchildren: Katie, Matt, Brooklynn, and Blake; and Sarah and James. Sarah and Katie, you have become the most amazing young women and I am so proud of you as I am of your husbands! Although it's hard for a mom to "turn loose" of her kids—even adult "kids"—I couldn't ask for two better young men to be part of our family. And to Brooklynn and Blake—I love being "gammy" to two amazing kids! I love you very much and love every moment we get to spend together! To all of you...thank you for being patient with me when I was focused on writing and for not complaining about the many take-out meals we've consumed and the many times I've not been able to go do something because I had a deadline. You all provide that much-needed balance to my life. And what I've been able to do is because of you...my family. Thank you, and I love you all!

Mary Coulter
Emeritus Professor of Management, Missouri State University

INTRODUCING THE CONCEPTS

LEARNING OUTCOMES

1.1 Explain why strategic management is important.

1.2 Explain what strategic management is.

1.3 Explain who's involved with strategic management.

1.4 Discuss the three important factors impacting strategic management today.

CASE #1 Virtual Worlds, Real Profits

Farmville. Cityville. Words with Friends. Mafia Wars 2. These are some of the more popular online games created by Zynga and available for free on Facebook, Myspace, Yahoo!, and as apps on iPads and iPhones.[1] Founded by CEO Mark Pincus in 2007, Zynga (named after his late dog, Zinga) is one of the world's leading social game developers and one of the tech industry's hottest companies. The company's goal is to enable users to build social connections through online games. But how do you build a viable business getting people "to buy a bunch of things that don't exist?"

While sifting through data that Zynga collects when people play its online games, product managers for a game called FishVille discovered something quite interesting. Players were buying "a translucent anglerfish at six times the rate of other sea creatures, using an imaginary currency people get by playing the game." So they quickly had company artists create "a set of similar imaginary sea creatures with translucent fins and other distinctive features." One difference—this time they charged real money for the virtual fish. Players snapped them up at $3 to $4 each. Although 95 percent of Zynga's game players never spend any real money on its games, its audience of unique monthly users (around 150 million) is so large that the small percentage that actually buys imaginary chickens and imaginary skyscrapers and imaginary fish generate big bucks. In fact, some players—Zynga calls them "whales," the same name used for casino high rollers—spend hundreds or even thousands of dollars a month. Zynga's revenues were nearly $600 million in 2010, with profits of $91 million. With the continuing economic uncertainties, the first half of 2011 was more challenging as sales activity fell for the first time in company history.

Despite these challenges, Zynga continues to transform the game industry with its strategies. While other traditional video game companies create games they think players will want and then sell those

David J. Green–Lifestyle/Alamy

1

games, Zynga's strategy has been to offer free games through social networks, such as Facebook, and then study data on how its audience plays them. Using these findings, it figures out ways to get people to play longer, to tell friends about the games, and to buy more virtual goods. Zynga's unique ability is analyzing reams of data on how players are reacting to games. The company's vice president in charge of the data analysis team says, "We're an analytics company masquerading as a games company." Data analysis has been and continues to be a key part of Zynga's strategy.

This chapter-opening case illustrates many of the complexities and challenges that today's managers face in strategic management, that is, in *managing strategically.* Zynga's strategic initiatives will affect what its managers and employees do. Even managers at other entertainment and game design companies have to decide whether and how to respond to Zynga's strategic moves. Such strategic decisions are common in today's competitive environment for all types and sizes of organizations. Understanding the how and why of strategic management is what this book is about. By studying strategic management, you can begin to understand how employees manage various strategic issues. Then, whether you're an art director in Austin, Texas, an engineering manager in Bangalore, India, or a data analyst in San Francisco, you'll be able to recognize and understand strategic decisions. What kinds of changes might be needed? How might these changes affect my work or my team?

In this introductory chapter, you'll get a taste of what strategic management is about. It's divided into three major sections: why is strategic management important, what is strategic management, and who's involved with it. The one thing not included is the *how* aspect. Don't worry! That's what the rest of the text covers—how you actually *do* strategic management. First, though, we want to look at why strategic management is important.

LEARNING OUTCOME 1.1

Explain Why Strategic Management Is Important

You may be asking yourself, "Why is this stuff important to organizations and, even more to the point, why is it important to me? I'm majoring in accounting, and my goal is to make partner in an accounting firm. What do I care about strategic management?" Or, you may be a computer graphics major who wants to design e-business applications for an online retailer. You may feel that strategic management and managing strategically have little to do with you. However, one of the assumptions we make in this book is that *every*one in an organization plays a role in managing strategically. Because life after school for most of you means finding a job in order to have an income, this means you'll be working for some organization. (Even if you choose the entrepreneurial path, managing strategically is important, as we'll discuss in the special topics module.) The very fact that you'll be working in some organization means you'll need to know about strategic management. Why? Because understanding how and why strategic decisions are made is important so you can do your job well and have your work valued and rewarded accordingly. But, strategic management also is important for other reasons that pertain more directly to the organization.

One significant reason why strategic management is important is that it does appear to make a difference in how well an organization performs. The most fundamental questions in strategy are why firms succeed or fail and why firms have varying levels of performance. These questions have guided strategic management researchers for years.[2] Do we have answers to those questions? Does strategic management make a difference? Yes, it appears to! Studies have shown that organizations that use strategic management tend to have higher levels of performance, usually measured as the "bottom line" or profits.[3] So, if it affects organizational performance, that would seem to be an important reason to know something about strategic management.

FOR YOUR INFORMATION
Corporate Reputations

The decade of the 2010s has been called the "reputation" one. Is having a good corporate reputation important? Research suggests that in this brave new world, "it's not only what you sell, but also what you stand for and how you conduct business that matter most." And, according to a global survey of financial analysts, having a good reputation is important. More than 90 percent agreed that if a company doesn't take care of the reputational aspects of its performance, it will suffer financially. These reputational aspects of performance included executing company strategy, transparent disclosure of information, and strong corporate governance. So which companies have "good" corporate reputations?

An annual survey conducted by the Reputation Institute assesses the reputations of the world's largest companies and identifies those with the best corporate reputations. The top 10 from the latest list (2011) of the world's 100 most reputable companies includes Google (USA), Apple (USA), Walt Disney Company (USA), BMW (Germany), LEGO (Denmark), Sony (Japan), Daimler (Germany), Canon (Japan), Intel (USA), and Volkswagen (Germany).

THINK ABOUT

- Considering there are thousands of businesses around the world, how did these companies "make this list"? What will keep them there?
- Although they do many things well, strategic management is one thing these companies excel at. Select one of these companies and research what it does and how it manages strategically.

Sources: Reputation Institute, "The Global RepTrak™ 100: A Study of the World's Most Reputable Companies in 2011," [www. reputationinstitute.com]; D. J. Flanagan, K. C. O'Shaughnessy, "Re-Assessing the Relationship Between the Fortune Reputation Data and Financial Performance: Overwhelming Influence or Just a Part of the Puzzle?" *Corporation Reputation Review*, Spring 2011, pp. 3–14; R. G. Eccles, S. C. Newquist, and R. Schatz, "Reputation and Its Risks," *Harvard Business Review*, February 2007, pp. 104–114; and D. K. Basdeo, K. G. Smith, C. M. Grimm, V. P. Rindova, and P. J. Derfus, "The Impact of Market Actions on Firm Reputation," *Strategic Management Journal*, December 2006, pp. 1205–1219.

Another reason for studying strategic management is that organizations of all types and sizes face continually changing situations both externally and internally. Being able to cope with these uncertainties *and* achieve expected levels of performance is a real challenge. However, this is where strategic management comes in. The deliberate structure of the strategic management process guides organizational decision makers in examining important issues to determine the most appropriate strategic decisions and actions. In fact, studies of the strategy decision process suggest that the *way* strategy is developed can make a difference in performance. For instance, one study found that strategic decision makers who collected information and used analytical techniques made more effective strategic decisions than those who did not.[4] And that's what strategic management is all about—analyzing the situation and then developing and implementing appropriate strategies. Another study found that organizations that used several approaches to developing strategy outperformed those that used a single approach.[5] These studies show that having a structured, systematic approach—that is, the strategic management process—to cope with uncertain environments can positively affect organizational performance.

The final reason strategic management is important is because an organization's various divisions, departments, and work activities need to be coordinated and focused on achieving the organization's goals. The strategic management process fills this purpose. Employees from any organizational area—operations, marketing, accounting, and so on—*and* from any level or location formulate, implement, and evaluate strategies they believe will help the organization perform at desired levels. Strategic management can ensure that their actions are coordinated.

Although strategic management is important, it may not solve all of an organization's problems. Yet, given the fact that it's increasingly difficult to achieve high performance levels, the structured nature of the strategic management process forces organizational decision makers to at least think about relevant variables.

- State four reasons why strategic management is important.
- Describe what studies have shown about the relationship between strategic management and an organization's performance.

LEARNING OUTCOME 1.2

Explain What Strategic Management Is

The study of strategic management *is* one of the most exciting of all the traditional business areas! That's because everything done by an organization's employees has strategic implications. Whether it's the National Basketball Association looking to expand its market reach globally, Kodak's attempts to compete with digital technology, your local library's decision to use self-checkout procedures like those used in Wal-Mart, or Zynga's data analysis plans, strategic management is involved. But, what *is* strategic management? Let's take a closer look.

The Basics of Strategy and Strategic Management

To begin to understand the basics of strategy and strategic management, simply look at the discount retail industry. Two of the industry's competitors—Wal-Mart and Kmart—have battled for market dominance since 1962, the year both companies were founded. The two chains have other similarities as well: names, store atmosphere, markets served, and organizational purpose. Yet, Wal-Mart's performance (financial and otherwise) has far surpassed that of Kmart. Wal-Mart is the world's largest and most successful retailer, and Kmart was the largest retailer ever to seek Chapter 11 bankruptcy protection (from which it emerged in 2003). Why the difference in performance? Remember our earlier statement of the two fundamental questions in strategy: why firms succeed or fail and why firms have varying levels of performance. Although researchers have examined different factors in trying to answer these questions, it boils down to the fact that organizations vary in how well they perform *because of differences in their strategic positions and differences in how they've used strategic management.*[6]

STRATEGIC MANAGEMENT IN ACTION

IDEO, the design firm based in Palo Alto, California, is well known for its design innovations created for some of corporate America's best-known companies—the first computer mouse for Apple, the Leap chair for Steelcase, a needle-free vaccine patch for biotech company Iomai, and the Swiffer CarpetFlick and stand-up toothpaste tube for Procter & Gamble, to name a few. And the company consistently wins global design awards for its innovative products. One strategy IDEO uses to keep the innovative design ideas flowing is an unusual lending library called "the tech box, a freezer-size chest of drawers" where designers can find gadgets, materials, textiles, and artifacts to help them brainstorm and to come up with applications or materials they may not have thought of. The cocreators of the tech box, Dennis Boyle and Rickson Sun, say, "It's not a typical lending library,

but people will use the tech box to cross-pollinate every new project."

THINK ABOUT

- In today's globally competitive environment, what might other companies learn from IDEO's unusual strategic approach?

Sources: Based on J. Guthrie, "David Kelly of IDEO Raises Level of Design," *San Francisco Chronicle,* October 23, 2011 [www.sfgate.com]; C. T. Greer, "Innovation 101," *Wall Street Journal,* October 17, 2011 [online.wsj.com]; L. Tischler, "A Designer Takes on His Biggest Challenge," *Fast Company,* February 2009, pp. 78+; P. Dvorak, "Businesses Take a Page from Design Firms," *Wall Street Journal,* November 10, 2008, p. B4; and J. Wiscombe, "IDEO: The Innovation Factory," *Workforce Management Online,* February 13, 2007 [www.workforce.com].

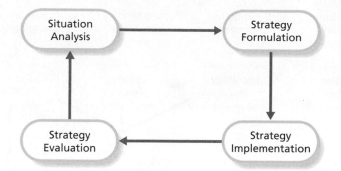

FIGURE 1.1

Basic Activities of
Strategic Management

Definition of Strategy

Strategy has been defined in various ways. Early efforts ranged from defining strategies as integrated decisions, actions, or plans designed to set and achieve organizational goals to defining strategy as simply the outcome of the strategy formulation process.[7] We're defining **strategies** as an organization's goal-directed plans and actions that align ("match") its capabilities and resources with the opportunities and threats in its environment. Let's look at some key parts of this definition. First of all, strategy involves an organization's goals. The chosen strategy (or strategies) should help an organization achieve its goals. But just deciding on (formulating) a goal-directed strategy isn't enough. Strategy also involves goal-directed actions—that is, implementing the strategy. In other words, an organization's strategy involves not only *what* it wants to do, but *doing* it. Finally, the organization's strategies should take into account its key internal strengths (capabilities and resources) and external opportunities and threats. We consider this "matching" idea important to the concept of strategy and strategic management, and you'll see it frequently referred to throughout the book.

Definition of Strategic Management

Strategic management is a process of analyzing the current situation, developing appropriate strategies, putting those strategies into action, and evaluating and changing those strategies as needed. We call these activities situation analysis, strategy formulation, strategy implementation, and strategy evaluation. (See Figure 1.1.)

Strategic management has four characteristics. First, it is, by nature, *interdisciplinary.*[8] It doesn't focus on any one specific organizational area—such as human resources or production or marketing—but instead encompasses all the functional areas. Second, strategic management has an *external focus,* that is, it involves the interactions of the organization with its external environment. As organizational employees manage strategically, they look at the external environment to see how factors such as the economy, competitors, or market demographics might impact strategic decisions and actions. The third characteristic of strategic management is that it also has an *internal focus,* meaning it involves assessing the organization's resources and capabilities. Again, as organizational employees manage strategically, they're looking at the resources the organization has or doesn't have and at its capabilities—what it does or doesn't do well. Finally, strategic management involves the *future direction* of the organization. That "future" can mean weekly manufacturing decisions, yearly financial planning cycles, or significant long-term shifts in the organization's products and markets. Now, let's look closer at how organizational employees do strategic management.

The Strategic Management Process

A process implies sequential and interrelated activities leading to some outcome. In the strategic management process, the interrelated activities—situation analysis, strategy formulation, strategy implementation, and strategy evaluation—result in a set of strategies the organization

FIGURE 1.2

Strategic Management
in Action

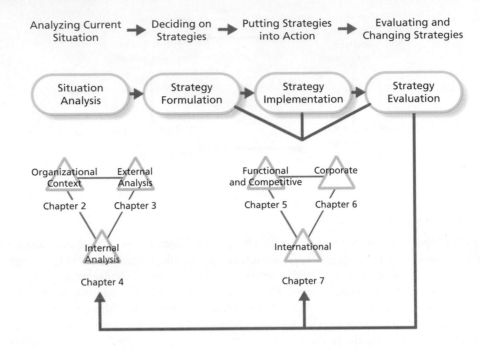

uses in doing its business. Figure 1.2 illustrates this process. As organizational members manage strategically, these are the activities they're doing. What's involved with each?

Situation Analysis

Before deciding on an appropriate strategic direction or response, organizational employees need to analyze the current situation. A **situation analysis** involves scanning and evaluating the current organizational context, external environment, and organizational environment. In Chapter 2, we'll explore the organizational context by looking at the new economy, the role

STRATEGIC MANAGEMENT IN ACTION

"We know one thing for sure: Our strategy works." When CEO Julia Stewart first took over the top spot at IHOP, she led several strategic changes that contributed to a successful turnaround of a struggling company. Then, when IHOP acquired the world's largest casual dining chain—Applebee's—in late 2007, Stewart, who used to be president of Applebee's before taking on the top job at IHOP, had another struggling company to rebuild. Using many of the same strategies used in the IHOP transformation—better food, better advertising, and better atmosphere—she revived Applebee's brand and reputation. Today, the combined companies operating under the corporate name DineEquity, Inc. is one of the leading chain restaurant companies in the United States.

list of these strategies and be prepared to share your list with the class.
- What do you think of these strategies?

Source: Based on DineEquity Annual Report 2010, [www.dineequity.com], pp. 2–3; B. Horovitz, "IHOP Goes Self-Service for Speed, Hip Factor," *USA Today*, November 17, 2011, p. 3B; S. Smith, "Julia Stewart Loves Franchising: And She Thinks You Should Too," *Restaurant Business*, February 2011, pp. 14–15; J. Stewart, "I'm Standing Up for the Industry. Are You?" *Restaurant Business*, February 2011, pp. 36–37; "How It Works: DineEquity Franchisees' Purchasing Co-Op," *Restaurant Business*, February 2011, p. 82; "Iconic Brands Combine to Create Full-Service Restaurant Company," *Franchising World*, May 2010, p. 91; and B. Horovitz, "New CEO Puts Comeback on the Menu at Applebee's," *USA Today*, April 28, 2008, pp. 1B+.

TO DO
- Go to DineEquity's Web site [**www.dineequity.com**], and do some research on its strategies. Make a bulleted

of stakeholders, the dynamics of change, and the role of organizational culture and mission. In Chapter 3, we'll look at what an external analysis is and how it's done. Finally, in Chapter 4, we'll study the steps involved in doing an internal analysis and look at an organization's resources, distinctive capabilities, and core competencies. Each of these—the context, the external environment, and the internal environment—provides important clues to the organization's current situation.

Strategy Formulation

Strategy formulation is developing and then choosing appropriate strategies (as guided by the results of the situation analysis). Figure 1.3 summarizes the three main types of strategies.

Functional strategies (also called **operational strategies**) are the goal-directed plans and actions of the organization's functional areas. The most common functional areas include production-operations (manufacturing), marketing, research and development, human resources, financial-accounting, and information systems technology and support. But keep in mind that each organization has its own unique functions. For instance, your school's functional areas might include academics, student services, financial services, facilities management, alumni relations, and athletics. A retail store's functional areas might include purchasing, merchandising display, floor sales, personnel, and store operations. We'll briefly look at functional strategies in Chapter 5.

Competitive strategies (also called **business strategies**) are the goal-directed plans and actions concerned with how an organization competes in a specific business or industry. For instance, Abercrombie & Fitch has strategies to compete with American Eagle Outfitters, Gap, J. Crew, and other specialty clothing retailers. Look back at our chapter-opening case and consider how Disney might compete with other entertainment and media companies. The competitive strategies address the competitive advantages an organization currently has or wants to develop. All aspects of competitive strategies and actions are also discussed in Chapter 5.

Corporate strategies are goal-directed plans and actions concerned with the choices of what business(es) to be in and what to do with those businesses. For instance, FedEx's decision to acquire Kinko's is an example of a corporate strategy. Other examples would be decisions PepsiCo makes regarding its various divisions—PepsiCo Americas Beverage (beverages including Pepsi, Aquafina Tropicana, Gatorade, and so forth), PepsiCo International, Frito-Lay North America (snack foods), Quaker Foods North America (prepared foods), and Latin America Foods. When PepsiCo changed its portfolio of businesses—as it did when it spun off its fast-food division (Taco Bell, Pizza Hut, and KFC) as a separate business or when it acquired sparkling beverage companies IZZE and Naked Juice—these actions involved corporate strategy. But what

FIGURE 1.3

Types of Strategies

Corporate
(What direction are we going and what business(es) are we in or do we want to be in?)

Competitive
(How are we going to compete in our chosen business(es)?)

Functional
(What resources and capabilities do we have to support the corporate and competitive strategies?)

STRATEGIC MANAGEMENT IN ACTION

The grocery industry is extremely competitive! From online grocery stores to "destination supermarkets" to the aggressive pricing strategies of the world's largest retailer (Wal-Mart), each industry competitor is looking for the strategic approaches that will keep customers browsing the aisles and filling the cash registers. Talk about the need for some effective competitive strategies! And no one knows that better than The Kroger Company [**www.kroger.com**], the nation's largest "pure" grocery chain.

TO DO

• Go to Kroger's Web site and find the "About the Company" section. Browse through the information for the various store formats, company beliefs, mission, and so on. What types of things is Kroger doing to compete in the grocery industry? Make a bulleted list describing its strategies.

about organizations like Pepsi's major competitor, the Coca-Cola Company, that don't have a portfolio of different businesses? What do their corporate strategies entail? In those instances, corporate strategy isn't so much concerned with the optimal mix of business(es) as it is with plans and actions regarding the future direction of the organization. Corporate strategy will be discussed in Chapter 6.

Strategy Implementation

It's not enough to formulate great strategies. Those strategies have to be implemented. **Strategy implementation** is putting the various strategies into action. Because *how* a strategy is implemented should be considered as it's formulated, we'll be looking at that as we discuss each type of strategy.

Strategy Evaluation

Strategy evaluation involves evaluating both the outcomes of the strategies and how they've been implemented. If they don't measure up to expectations or strategic goals, then the strategy itself or its implementation may need to be modified. We'll also cover evaluation as we discuss each type of strategy.

Strategic Management Process in Action

You need to understand that although we've described the strategic management process by isolating each step in order to study it, in reality it's a continual cycle that may not always follow a normal sequence. That usually only happens when strategic decision makers pursue an entirely different strategy or new strategic direction. Otherwise, strategic management in action

---

FOR YOUR INFORMATION
Making It Last

DuPont & Company was founded in 1802, the Proctor & Gamble Company in 1837, and the Coca-Cola Company in 1886. What have these (and other companies) done to "make it last"? How have they endured through the vast changes that have happened?

One organizational researcher who has studied company longevity says that such companies have distinguishing characteristics that include maintaining a continual focus on value and profitability; keeping strategy simple by understanding key priorities; remaining committed to effective communication, which starts at the top levels of the organization; having a performance-oriented culture; sharing decision making; quickly obtaining and filtering important information from key stakeholders; and rapidly adapting to change. He says, "These qualities provide agile businesses with an edge that allows them to react to market changes in a way that fosters continual cost and growth refinement, thereby creating an environment to achieve consistent measured growth and sustained profitability."

Another perspective on companies that have endured for years can be found in the best-selling book, *Built to Last: Successful Habits of Visionary Companies,* by James C. Collins and Jerry I. Porras. These authors noted that key elements of these companies were, "Good old-fashioned hard work, dedication to improvement, and continually building for the future." In addition, Collins and Porras said that these long-lasting companies articulated a core ideology comprised of core values and a purpose that extended beyond simply making money. This core ideology had not changed or been altered by changing times and changing strategies. As Collins stated in the introduction to the 2008 list of the *Fortune 500,* "The best corporate leaders never point out the window to blame external conditions; they look in the mirror and say 'We are responsible for our results!'"

TO DO

- Research the strategies of one of these enduringly great companies—Procter & Gamble, Johnson & Johnson, the Coca-Cola Company, General Electric, Nucor Corporation, or Xerox—and describe them in a short paper.

Sources: Based on J. Collins, "The Secret of Enduring Greatness," *Fortune,* May 5, 2008, pp. 72–76; J. Jusko, "Secrets to Longevity," *Industry Week,* March 2003, pp. 24–27; and J. C. Collins and J. I. Porras, *Built to Last: Successful Habits of Visionary Companies* (New York: Harper Business, 1994).

involves adjustments to organizational strategies currently in effect. That may mean evaluating the strategy first, then analyzing the situation before formulating and implementing a new strategy. The point is that the way organizations actually do strategic management doesn't always happen according to a prescribed sequence, but that doesn't minimize the importance of the specific steps in the process.

Looking at Strategic Management's Past

We look at the history of strategic management to help us better understand how and why today's managers do strategic management and perhaps even for clues as to why organizational performance levels vary. Strategic management's history is quite interesting, ranging from great military battles to current research to better understand why firms succeed or fail.

Strategy's Military Roots

Strategy can be seen in historical decisions and actions used by military organizations. (The word *strategy* itself comes from the Greek word *strategos,* or military commander.) Historical accounts tell us that a country's military decision makers designed battlefield strategies to gain an edge on the enemy. They would try to exploit the enemy's weak spots and attack them where they were most vulnerable, thus giving the aggressor the best chance of succeeding. Even today, military historians enjoy analyzing great battles in terms of the strategies that each side used

---

FOR YOUR INFORMATION
Principles of War

The United States' leading military academies teach the "nine principles of war." These principles have stood the test of time even though the environment of war has changed dramatically. The marketplace is often viewed as a "battleground," meaning these principles might be useful in developing an organization's competitive strategy. What are these nine principles?

- **The objective:** Direct every operation toward a clearly defined, decisive, and attainable objective.
- **The offensive:** Seize, retain, and exploit the initiative.
- **Unity of command:** Forces must be under one commander with full authority and responsibility.
- **Mass:** Concentrate combat power at the decisive place and time.
- **Economy of force:** Allocate only the essential minimum of forces to secondary efforts.
- **Maneuver:** Place the enemy in a position of disadvantage through the flexible application of combat power.
- **Surprise:** Strike at the enemy at a time or a place that's unexpected.
- **Security:** Never allow the enemy to acquire an unexpected advantage.
- **Simplicity:** Prepare clear, uncomplicated plans and clear, concise orders to ensure thorough understanding.

There has been some debate within the American military establishment to add "flexibility" as the tenth principle. However, experts say that flexibility is a "given" since it pervades all aspects of each of the nine principles.

THINK ABOUT

- Relate these nine "war" principles to what an organization does as it "battles" in the marketplace. Can they be applied? Explain.
- Do you think "flexibility" needs to be added as a principle of war especially when considering today's environment?

Sources: Based on Department of Military Science, Worcester Polytechnic Institute [http://www.wpi.edu/Academics/Depts/MilSci/Resources/prinwar.html], "Nine Principles of War," December 30, 2008; Lt. Cmdr. C. E. van Avery, "12 New Principles of War," *Armed Forces Journal* [http://www.armedforcesjournal.com], July 2007; W. C. Finnie, "A Four Cycle Approach to Strategy Development and Implementation," *Strategy & Leadership,* January/February 1997, p. 28; and C. von Clausewitz, *The Most Important Principles of the Art of War to Complete My Course of Instruction for His Royal Highness the Crown Prince* (German: *Die wichtigsten Grundsätze des Kriegführens zur Ergänzung meines Unterrichts bei Sr. Königlichen Hoheit dem Kronprinzen*), 1812; translated and edited by Hans W. Gatzke as "Principles of War," September 1942, The Military Service Publishing Company.

and trying to interpret why some were successful whereas others failed. And popular games such as Battleship, chess, tic-tac-toe, and checkers are based on the idea of a "strategy." Most involve figuring out what your opponent is doing and taking actions based on that information. The process of analyzing the situation and crafting, implementing, and evaluating an appropriate response is common, although we may not specifically think of it in strategy terms.

Academic Origins of Strategic Management[9]

As a field of study, strategic management is relatively young. Much of its theoretical foundation comes from economics and organization studies. Although mainstream economic theory, with its emphasis on rationality, predictability, and similarity, may not quite fit the realities of strategic management, it has provided a way to explore the role of management decisions and strategic choices. In addition, early organizational studies by Frederick Taylor (scientific management), Max Weber (bureaucratic organizations), and Chester Barnard (administrative functions and the organization as an open system) provided important knowledge about efficient and effective organizations and the role that managers played.

Strategic Planning and Strategic Management Emerge[10]

During the 1960s, organization theorists searched for explanations of organizational differences in functioning and performance. The belief that there was one correct way to manage in all situations was replaced by contingency approaches, which proposed that each organizational situation was different and that the best way of managing depended on the situation. Also, during this time, three classic strategy books—Alfred Chandler's *Strategy and Structure*, Igor Ansoff's *Corporate Strategy*, and a Harvard textbook, *Business Policy: Text and Cases* by Learned, Christensen, Andrews, and Guth—were instrumental in establishing many basic concepts of strategic management and in distinguishing strategic management as a separate academic field.

A dichotomy developed during the 1970s and 1980s as researchers tried to understand and describe strategic management.[11] Process researchers studied strategic management from the perspective of "how" strategy is formed, that is, the process. Content researchers studied the "what," or the content, of a strategic decision. Despite their differences in perspective, both process and content researchers continue to try to understand the relationship between strategic decisions and organizational performance.

STRATEGIC MANAGEMENT IN ACTION
The Global Perspective

As the world's largest beauty products company, L'Oréal SA creates cosmetics, perfume, and hair and skin care items. However, as the global economy continued down a fluctuating and uncertain path, the French company found itself with stagnating sales. According to company officials, one contributing factor was higher raw materials costs that have hit many companies, including L'Oréal, which uses oil in its products and packaging. However, weak consumer demand and currency fluctuations played a major role in the sales slowdown. In an effort to reduce its dependence on mature consumer markets such as Europe and the United States, L'Oréal's strategy is to recruit millions of new consumers in emerging markets from Africa to Asia.

THINK ABOUT

- What do you think of L'Oréal's strategies in light of today's environment?
- How might strategic management be useful?

Sources: Based on C. Passariello, "Heiress Loses L'Oréal Family Fight," *Wall Street Journal*, October 18, 2011, p. B8; C. Passariello and Noémie Bisserbe, "Uncertainty Colors L'Oréal," *Wall Street Journal*, August 31, 2011, p. B4; and C. Passariello, "Sales Stagnate at L'Oréal," *Wall Street Journal*, July 13, 2011, p. B4.

LEARNING REVIEW LEARNING OUTCOME 1.2

- Define strategy and strategic management.
- Describe the strategic management process.
- Describe the three types of organizational strategies.
- Explain the historical evolution of strategic management.

As we said earlier, one assumption we make is that strategic management isn't simply the responsibility of an organization's top managers. Strategic thinking techniques are needed at all levels of an organization.[12] People at *all* organizational levels play a role in developing, implementing, and changing strategy. Strategic management is just as important for the bank teller at a drive-through facility as it is for the bank's executive vice president who's in charge of commercial loans. Think back to our definition of strategic management—analyzing the current situation, deciding strategies, putting those strategies into action, evaluating those strategies, and then modifying or changing those strategies as needed—and you can begin to see how each and every person is involved. The difference is the scope of the individual's strategic actions. For instance, the bank teller is concerned with issues (functional strategies) that arise at the drive-through facility; the bank's executive vice president is more concerned with strategic issues that arise at the competitive or corporate level (or both). Let's look at the three main groups that play key roles in the strategic management process: the board of directors, the top management team, and other strategic managers and organizational employees.

LEARNING OUTCOME 1.3

Explain Who's Involved with Strategic Management

The Board of Directors

The **board of directors** is an elected group that represents a company's shareholders. A board's legal obligation is to represent the shareholders (stockholders) and protect their interests. It is empowered to act on the shareholders' behalf in overseeing the management of the company and plays a significant role in corporate governance—that is, in governing the decisions and actions of the organization. Because this is an important issue for today's strategic managers, we'll discuss it extensively in the last section of this chapter. Table 1.1 lists some of the responsibilities of a board of directors. Even not-for-profit organizations often have a board of

TABLE 1.1 Typical Board Responsibilities

- Review and approve strategic goals and plans.
- Review and approve organization's financial standards and policies.
- Ensure integrity of organization's financial controls and reporting system.
- Approve an organizational philosophy.
- Monitor organizational performance and regularly review performance results.
- Select, evaluate, and compensate top-level managers.
- Develop management succession plans.
- Review and approve capital allocations and expenditures.
- Monitor relations with shareholders and other key stakeholders.

Other responsibilities may be assigned depending on the unique culture and needs of the organization.

Source: Based on K. McG. Sullivan and H. J. Gregory, "Board Self-Assessment," *The Corporate Board,* November–December 1995, p. 7.

advisers. In fact, your college may have a governing board that evaluates top management decisions and perhaps even makes recommendations as far as future strategic decisions and actions.

How much a board is involved in formulating and implementing strategy has always been a thorny issue.[13] The board's role has been approached from two opposing perspectives. In those organizations in which the board acted in an *approving role,* the top management team would keep board members informed of strategies, on which the board might have given limited input, but the board's role was primarily to "approve" the strategies. However, that's not what we're seeing with today's boards. Significant changes in legal mandates, investor activism, and corporate strategy have changed the role of many boards in the strategic management process. Today's board members often find themselves taking a much more *involved role* in the strategic management process by initiating strategies as well as overseeing the implementation and evaluation of the strategies.

The Role of Top Management

There's no doubt that an organization's top managers play a significant role in the strategic management process. An organization's top manager is typically the chief executive officer (CEO). This person (Mark Pincus in our chapter-opening case) usually works with a top management team that includes other executive or senior managers such as a chief operating officer (COO), chief financial officer (CFO), chief information officer (CIO), and other individuals who may have various titles. Traditional descriptions of the CEO's role in strategic management include being the "chief" strategist, structural architect, and developer of the organization's information/control systems.[14] Other descriptions of the strategic role of the chief executive include key decision maker, visionary leader, political actor, monitor and interpreter of environment changes, and strategy designer.[15] The job of the top manager continues to be of interest to researchers. A recent book identified five qualities essential for success as a CEO: passionate curiosity, battle-hardened confidence, team smarts, a simple mindset, and fearlessness.[16]

No matter how the top management's job is described, you can be certain that from their perspective at the organization's upper levels, it's like no other job in the organization. By definition, top managers are ultimately responsible for every decision and action of every organizational employee. One important role that top managers play is that of strategic

---

STRATEGIC MANAGEMENT IN ACTION

"Heat shield." That's the new role of Bonnie G. Hill, the longest-serving director on Home Depot's board. Company shareholders had been quite vocal about their unhappiness with the previous CEO's pay and performance. Upon his departure, Hill met with dozens of stockholders, listened to them, and eased their anger by persuading fellow directors to link the pay of current CEO Frank Blake more closely to the company's performance. Hill's approach characterizes an emerging breed of directors who want a closer connection with shareholders. Board members at Pfizer, Hewlett-Packard, and UnitedHealth Group, among other companies, have also taken similar approaches. Some executives still think that such increased dialogue is a bad idea as board members "run the risk of having discussions that undermine the CEO." However, with increased shareholder activism and changed corporate governance, such arguments may not carry much weight.

THINK ABOUT

- What do you think of the idea of directors reaching out to shareholders?
- What advantages and drawbacks might there be from such a practice for both the company and board members?

Sources: Based on J. S. Lublin, "Lead Directors Gain Clout to Counterbalance Strong CEOs," *Wall Street Journal,* September 13, 2010, p. B11; J. S. Lublin, "New Breed of Directors Reaches Out to Shareholders," *Wall Street Journal,* July 21, 2008, p. B4; and J. Weber, R. O. Crockett, M. Arndt, B. Grow, and N. Byrnes, "How the Best Boards Stay Clued In," *BusinessWeek,* June 27, 2005, p. 40.

FIGURE 1.4

Effective Strategic
Leadership

Source: Based on
R. D. Ireland and
M.A. Hill, *"Achieving
and Maintaining Strategic
Competitiveness in the
21st Century: The Role
of Strategic Leadership."*
Academy of Management
Executive, February 1999,
pp. 43–57.

leader. As you're probably well aware, leadership is a perennially popular management topic. Libraries and bookstores have numerous books on the subject. Type *leadership* in a Web search engine and you'll get millions of hits (101 million at Google). Organizational research-ers study leadership in relation to strategic management because an organization's top manag-ers must provide effective strategic leadership. What is **strategic leadership?** It's the ability to anticipate, envision, maintain flexibility, think strategically, and work with others in the organization to initiate changes that will create a viable and valuable future for the organiza-tion.[17] How can top managers provide effective strategic leadership? Six key dimensions have been identified.[18] (See Figure 1.4.) These dimensions include determining the organization's purpose or vision, exploiting and maintaining the organization's core competencies, develop-ing the organization's human capital, creating and sustaining a strong organizational culture, emphasizing ethical organizational decisions and practices, and establishing appropriately balanced organizational controls. Each dimension describes an important part of the strategic management process.

Other Managers and Organizational Employees

Although an organization's top managers have several important strategic leadership responsi-bilities in the strategic management process, managers and employees at other levels throughout the organization also are important to the process. What are some of their strategic responsibili-ties?[19] One is strategy implementation. They're the individuals putting the strategies into action. They might be supervising or managing the work of others and even may be personally doing work as well. For example, think back to our opening case. Someone had to write the code for Words with Friends. Someone had to design the farm characters in Farmville. And, someone had to hire employees for the Frankfurt and Bangalore locations. As Zynga continues to adjust to its changing environment, new strategies will have to be put into action. That's another role of managers and organizational employees.

The other thing that these individuals likely do is evaluating whether the strategies are working. If the strategies aren't helping an organization achieve its goals, then they need to be changed. Although top management may establish the guidelines for evaluating performance, it's often the managers and organizational employees who do the evaluating and follow-up.

LEARNING REVIEW   LEARNING OUTCOME 1.3

- Explain the role of the board of directors in strategic management.
- Discuss how top managers can be effective strategic leaders.
- Describe the role of other managers and organizational employees in strategy.

LEARNING OUTCOME 1.4

Discuss Two Important Factors Impacting Strategic Management Today

Managing strategically in today's world isn't easy! We want to look at two important issues affecting strategic management. These include the global economy and globalization and corporate governance.

The Global Economy and Globalization

Over the last quarter century, globalization has been an important component of many company's strategies. (So important, in fact, that you'll find an entire chapter—Chapter 7—devoted to global issues and strategies.) National borders have become irrelevant. For instance, more than two-thirds of Avon's revenues come from outside North America. Nissan, a Japanese firm, makes cars in the United States and in Mexico. Lend Lease Corporation, Australia's leading real-estate company, built the Bluewater shopping complex in Kent, England and contracted with Coca-Cola to build all its bottling plants in Southeast Asia. McDonald's, a U.S. business, plans to double its outlets in China to 2,000 by the year 2013. Korea's largest car company, Hyundai, chose to build its first American plant in Georgia. Swiss company ABB Ltd. constructed power-generating plants in Malaysia, South Korea, China, and Indonesia. Although globalization has offered significant business opportunities, today's economic climate is challenging even the best-managed global companies. Doing business globally has never been easy, but the next few years are likely to be even more difficult as countries continued to face an uncertain economic environment. Financial problems in Greece, Italy, and Spain are challenging the European continent as well as the United States, a major banking and trading partner with Europe.[20] In addition to the challenges of managing strategically in an economic climate fraught with reduced consumer demand, restricted access to capital, and severe pressures to cut costs, strategic decision makers face two additional ones: the openness of globalization and significant cultural differences.

THE GREY ZONE

How much profit is too much profit? Is it okay that ExxonMobil earned more than $41 billion in 2011, $30 billion in 2010, $19 billion in 2009, and $45 billion in 2008? Does it make a difference that the global economy was precariously sputtering and that consumers were paying high prices at the gas pump? How much can—and should—a company ethically earn?

THINK ABOUT

- As a business student, what do you think?
- How would you explain this to your friends who are not business students or to the "Occupy" protesters?
- How about to society or to your community?

The push to go global has been widespread. Advocates praise the economic and social benefits that come from globalization. Yet, it has created challenges because of the openness that's necessary for it to work. For instance, the public outcry when a Dubai company proposed acquiring certain U.S. ports highlighted the concerns and fears (real or perceived) that having an open economy and open borders entails.[21] Some have wondered whether the "openness" of globalization has made people more sensitive to political and cultural differences and thus increased the threats of attack by those who misunderstand or disagree. Although globalization is meant to open up trade and to break down the geographical barriers separating countries, opening up means just that—being open to the good *and* the bad. Current realities illustrate another challenge from the openness of globalization— the economic interdependence of trading countries. When one country's economy falters, it can have a domino effect on other countries with which it does business. There are mechanisms in place for dealing with such situations, but they may not always be able to prevent a crisis. One such mechanism is the **World Trade Organization (WTO),** a global organization of 153 countries whose goal is to help organizations conduct business by enacting trade agreements negotiated and ratified by the vast majority of the world's trading nations.[22] Another is the **World Bank Group,** a cooperative of 187 member countries that provides vital financial and technical assistance to developing countries around the world. The goal of the World Bank Group is to promote long-term economic development and poverty reduction by providing members with technical and financial support.[23] Finally, the **International Monetary Fund (IMF)** is an organization of 187 countries that promotes international monetary cooperation and provides member countries with policy advice, temporary loans, and technical assistance to establish and maintain financial stability and strengthen economies.[24]

The challenges from openness aren't the only ones that strategic managers face globally. Serious challenges also come from fundamental cultural differences between countries— differences that encompass traditions, history, religious beliefs, and deep-seated values. Capitalism's emphasis on profits, efficiency, and growth may be generally accepted in the United States, Australia, and Hong Kong, but isn't nearly as popular in places like France, the Middle East, or the Scandinavian countries. There are those who think that globalization is simply a euphemism for "Americanization"—that is, U.S. cultural values and business philosophy slowly taking over the world.[25] Proponents of Americanization hope others see how progressive, efficient,

STRATEGIC MANAGEMENT IN ACTION
The Global Perspective

As the world's number one food company, Switzerland-based Nestlé has revenues of more than $100 billion a year from the global sales of its 8,000+ brands—ranging from Nescafé instant coffee and Alpo dog food to KitKat candy bars and Jenny Craig weight loss centers. Nestlé's global strategy has been to concentrate on value-added products. In addition, Chairman Peter Brabeck-Letmathe has implemented some strategic changes including streamlining worldwide operations by improving information technology and centralizing purchasing and other corporate activities; strengthening key segments by acquiring competitors such as Finnish dairy company Valid's Valiojääteloö's ice cream business and Greece's Delta Ice Cream; eliminating less profitable activities such as tomato canning and pasta production and cocoa processing; and developing new products such as nutritionally enhanced cosmetics and toothpastes. Brabeck hopes these strategies will deliver robust sales growth and cost savings that will give Nestlé stronger operating margins.

THINK ABOUT

- As a global company, what types of strategic challenges might Brabeck face in today's economic climate?

- Another challenge Brabeck faces is the "intersection of food, politics, and environment." What do you think he's referring to? (Hint: Think of biofuels, GMOs— genetically modified crops—and demographics.) Why are these issues so important to his company's future?

Sources: Based on J. Revill, "Nestlé Lifts Full-Year Outlook," *Wall Street Journal Online,* October 20, 2011; B. M. Carney, "Can the World Still Feed Itself?" *Wall Street Journal Online,* September 3, 2011; "World's Largest Corporations," *Fortune,* July 25, 2011, pp. 161+; and J. Revill, "Nestlé Pressured in Emerging Markets," *Wall Street Journal,* June 14, 2011.

industrious, and free U.S. society and businesses are and want to emulate that way of doing things. However, critics claim that this attitude of the "almighty American dollar wanting to spread the American way to every single country" has created many problems.[26] Although history is filled with clashes between civilizations, what's unique about this time period is the speed and ease with which misunderstandings and disagreements erupt and escalate. The Internet, television and other media, and global air travel have brought the good and bad of American entertainment, products, and behaviors to every corner of the globe. For those who don't like what Americans do, say, or believe, this may lead to resentment, dislike, distrust, and even outright hatred. Successful strategic management under such conditions requires being sensitive to cultural and political differences. Strategic decision makers need to be aware of how their decisions and actions will be viewed, not only by those who may agree, but more important, by those who may disagree. Organizations are likely to have to adjust their strategies to accommodate increasingly diverse views.

Corporate Governance

Enron. Tyco. Worldcom. These are just a few of the more notorious names from the corporate financial scandals that destroyed billions of dollars in shareholder value during a timespan of approximately 18 months in 2001 and 2002. Because directors at these companies missed or ignored organizational problems, many involving fraudulent accounting schemes, U.S. legislators vowed to reform corporate governance. A significant part of this reform was the passage of the **Sarbanes-Oxley Act,** a U.S. law designed to protect investors by improving the accuracy and reliability of corporate disclosures.

What is **corporate governance?** It's the way a corporation is governed or the "determination of the broad uses to which organizational resources will be deployed and the resolution of conflicts among the myriad participants in organizations."[27] In other words, corporate governance involves how a corporation uses its resources and protects stakeholders' interests. Sarbanes-Oxley mandated two areas of corporate governance reform: the role of the board of directors and the type and scope of financial reporting.

The Role of Boards of Directors

The original purpose of a corporate board of directors was to ensure that a group, independent from management, looked out for the interests of the owners (i.e., the shareholders) who were not involved in the day-to-day operations of the corporation. What actually happened in too many organizations was that board members often enjoyed a cozy relationship in which board members "took care" of the CEO and the CEO "took care" of board members. With the passage of Sarbanes-Oxley, this arrangement changed, and demands on board members of publicly traded companies increased considerably.[28] The Business Roundtable, an association of CEOs of leading corporations, outlined

STRATEGIC MANAGEMENT IN ACTION
The Global Perspective

Corporate governance isn't a concern just for U.S. companies. Governance Metrics International (GMI), a corporate governance research and ratings agency [**www.gmiratings.com**], rates countries on their governance structures and procedures. It uses six broad categories of analysis: board accountability, financial disclosure and internal controls, executive compensation, shareholder rights, ownership base, and takeover provisions. In addition, GMI looks at corporate behavior and social responsibility. What countries were rated on top? The United Kingdom had the highest overall average rating, followed by Canada, Ireland, the United States, and New Zealand. Chile had the lowest overall average rating, preceded by Mexico, Indonesia, Japan, and China.

Source: Based on GMI, *GMI Country Rankings,* Governance Metrics International (New York), September 27, 2010 [www.gmiratings.com].

TABLE 1.2 Guiding Principles of Corporate Governance

1. The primary duty of a board of directors is to *select a CEO* and to *oversee the CEO and senior management* in the competent and ethical operation of the corporation on a day-to-day basis.

2. It is the responsibility of management to *operate the corporation in an effective and ethical manner* to produce long-term value for shareholders.

3. It is the responsibility of management to *develop and implement the corporation's strategic plans and to identify, evaluate, and manage the risks inherent in the corporation's strategy.*

4. It is the responsibility of management to *produce in a timely manner financial statements that fairly represent* the financial condition and results of corporate operations.

5. It is the responsibility of the board to *engage an independent accounting firm to audit the financial statements,* issue an opinion that those statements are in accordance with Generally Accepted Accounting Principles, and oversee the corporation's relationship with the outside auditor.

6. It is the responsibility of the board to *play a leadership role in shaping the corporate governance of the corporation.*

7. It is the responsibility of the board to *adopt and oversee the implementation of compensation* policies, establish goals for performance-based compensation, and determine the compensation of the CEO and senior management.

8. It is the responsibility of the board to *respond appropriately to shareholders' concerns.*

9. It is the responsibility of the corporation to *deal with its employees, customers, suppliers, and other constituencies* in a fair and equitable manner.

Source: Based on Principles of Corporate Governance, *Business Roundtable* (Washington, DC), April 2010.

a set of governance principles for boards and top managers (see Table 1.2) that are critical "to the functioning of the modern public corporation and the integrity of the public markets."[29]

Financial Reporting

In addition to expanding the role of board members, Sarbanes-Oxley also called for more disclosure and transparency of financial information. One requirement was the certification of the accuracy of financial statements, which senior managers now must do by signing off on them. Another aspect of the financial reporting requirement, which has created some special problems for companies (especially smaller public companies), is Section 404.[30] This brief passage (a mere 168 words) deals with the establishment and auditing of internal financial controls. Creating the control systems and hiring independent auditors to attest to managers' internal controls have proved very expensive. Businesses claim that countless employee hours and millions of dollars have been spent documenting things that many felt had nothing to do with the integrity of their financial statements. In response to a push by business lobbyists, securities and accounting regulators established more flexible guidelines to help companies and auditors interpret Section 404 in a way that saves them time and money.[31]

Concluding Thought

No matter where in an organization you work or what your job is, you'll find yourself involved in some way with strategic management. Whether your career goal is to be part of a top management team or whether you plan to apply your academic training in some functional area of the organization, you'll be affected by and have an effect on the organization's strategic management process. This chapter is just the beginning of your exciting journey to understand strategic management!

LEARNING REVIEW   LEARNING OUTCOME 1.4

- Discuss how the global economy and globalization affect strategic management.
- Explain the concept of corporate governance and how it impacts strategic management.

The Bottom Line

Learning Outcome 1.1: Explain why strategic management is important.

- *Individually:* you will be evaluated on and rewarded for doing your job well, which means understanding how and why strategic decisions are made.
- *Organizationally:* can make a difference in how well an organization performs; helps deal with continually changing situations; and helps in coordinating various divisions, functions, and work activities.

Learning Outcome 1.2: Explain what strategic management is.

- *Strategies*: an organization's goal-directed plans and actions that align its capabilities and resources with the opportunities and threats in its environment.
- *Strategic management*: a process of analyzing the current situation; developing appropriate strategies; putting the strategies into action; and evaluating, modifying, or changing the strategies as needed.
- *Four characteristics:* interdisciplinary, external focus, internal focus, and future-oriented.
- *Strategic management process: situation analysis* (scanning and evaluating the current organizational context and external and internal environments); *strategy formulation* (developing and then choosing appropriate strategies); *strategy implementation* (putting strategies into action); and *strategy evaluation* (evaluating the implementation and outcomes of strategies).
- *Types of organizational strategies: functional* or *operational* (goal-directed plans and actions of the organization's functional areas); *competitive* or *business* (goal-directed plans and actions concerned with how an organization competes); and *corporate* (goal-directed plans and actions concerned with the choices of what businesses to be in and what to do with those businesses).
- *Reality:* process may not always follow the stated sequence, but activities are still completed.
- *Background:* military strategies (exploiting enemy's weak spots and attacking them where most vulnerable); academic origins (economics and organizational theory).
- *Emergence of strategic planning and strategic management:* 1960s, when researchers began looking for explanations of organizational differences in performance and functioning; 1970s and 1980s, with focus on process (how strategies were formed) and content (relationship between strategic choices and performance).

Learning Outcome 1.3: Explain who's involved with strategic management.

- *Assumption:* everyone in an organization plays an important role.
- *Three main groups: board of directors* (elected group that represents a company's shareholders), whose involvement ranges from approving strategy to initiating strategy; top management, whose role involves *strategic leadership* (the ability to anticipate, envision, maintain flexibility, think strategically, and work with others in the organization to initiate changes that will create a viable and valuable future for the organization); and other managers and organizational employees, whose primary tasks include strategy implementation and strategy evaluation.
- *Six key dimensions of strategic leadership:* determining the organization's purpose or vision; exploiting and maintaining the organization's core competencies; developing the organization's human capital; creating and sustaining a strong organizational culture; emphasizing ethical organizational decisions and practices; and establishing appropriately balanced controls.

Learning Outcome 1.4: Discuss two important factors impacting strategic management today.

- *Global economy and globalization:* provides both economic and social benefits; challenges come from current state of global economy; from openness, which has made countries more vulnerable to political and cultural differences; and from economic interdependence of trading nations.
- *Challenges of openness and economic interdependence have been countered by:* the *World Trade Organization* (a global organization of 153 countries that deals with monitoring and facilitating the rules of trade among nations); the *World Bank Group* (a cooperative of 185 member countries that provides financial and technical assistance to developing countries); and the *International Monetary Fund* (an organization of 185 member countries that promotes international monetary cooperation and provides financial advice, temporary loans, and technical assistance).
- *Challenges of cultural and political differences:* requires sensitivity to those differences.
- *Corporate governance* (the way a corporation is governed or the "determination of the broad uses to which organizational resources will be deployed and the resolution of conflicts among the myriad participants in organizations"): reform brought about by *Sarbanes-Oxley Act* (a U.S. federal law designed to protect investors by improving the accuracy and reliability of corporate disclosures); reform mandated in two areas—role of boards of directors and financial reporting.

YOU as strategic decision maker: building your skills

1. Research the strategic leader(s) of Pepsi-Cola, Amazon.com, and Toyota Motor Company. Use paper-based sources (business periodicals, books, etc.) or Web-based information. In a brief paper, describe how each of these strategic leaders fulfills the characteristics of effective strategic leadership (see Figure 1.4).

2. "Making strategy, once an event, is now a continuous process." Explain what you think this statement means.

3. Boards of directors and top managers are being scrutinized more than ever. Complete the following assignments having to do with these two groups of strategic decision makers.

   a. *Fortune* publishes an annual ranking of the most admired companies, both globally and in the United States. Choose either ranking and get the most recent listing of the top 10. Look up financial information on the top three companies on the list. Look up information on the boards of directors of these companies. Report what you find. What conclusions might you draw about the role of the board in the strategic management of these most admired companies?

   b. Top executive compensation has been a controversial topic recently because of floundering company performance. Do some research on executive pay. What issues are being raised? How do you feel about these issues? What things are happening in response to these issues?

4. "With respect to business, the Internet represents one of the most important innovations of this generation for firms to cut costs, improve services, and expand markets." Do you agree with this statement? Why or why not? What are the implications for strategic decision makers?

5. The term *business model* became extremely popular during the dot-com craze—everyone was searching for that Web-based business model that promised unimaginable profits. However, as the dot-com craze imploded, the concept lost its luster. But we shouldn't be so quick to dismiss it. A good **business model,** which is simply a strategic design for how a company intends to profit from its broad array of strategies, processes, and activities, should answer four questions: (1) Who is our customer? (2) What does the customer value? (3) How do we make money in this business? and (4) What underlying economic logic explains how we can deliver value to customers at an appropriate cost?

   With this in mind, describe the business model each of the following companies is using: eBay, Carnival Cruise Lines, Domino's Pizza, and Dell Computer.

CASES

CASE #1 Virtual Worlds, Real Profits

This Strategic Management in Action case can be found at the beginning of Chapter 1.

1. What is Zynga's goal? How will that goal affect the way strategies are pursued? Try to be as specific as possible.
2. How *do* you build a viable business getting people "to buy a bunch of things that don't exist?"
3. What do you think it will take to be successful in the game industry? What challenges does this industry face?
4. How might Pincus and his top management team use the strategic management process to continue making real profits in virtual worlds?

David J. Green–Lifestyle/Alamy

CASE #2 Making Magic Happen

Magic happens at the happiest place on earth. At least that's what the folks at the Walt Disney Company (Disney) work hard to make us believe. In fact, when Walt Disney, the company's founder and namesake, dedicated the original Disneyland on July 17, 1955, his first words were, "To all who come to this happy place, welcome." And that heartfelt "welcome" to guests, customers, and audiences encompasses its four major business units: studio entertainment, parks and resorts, consumer products, and media networks. The difficult business climate in 2008 and 2009 challenged Disney, as it did many other well-managed companies; however, CEO Bob Iger and his top management team conjured up their own magic and found ways to strategically maneuver the company to prosper despite the environmental uncertainties.

As the world's largest media conglomerate, Disney has had a long record of successes. From the *High School Musical, Hannah Montana,* and *Jonas Brothers* phenomena to the ever-popular Mickey Mouse characters, the "Disney Difference" is noticeably apparent. What is the Disney Difference? It's "high-quality creative content, backed up by a clear strategy for maximizing that content's value across platforms and markets." From books, toys, and games to online media, soundtracks, and DVDs, Disney exploits its rich legacy of products through quality creative content and exceptional storytelling. Some of these products include, among many others, *The Lion King, Toy Story, Snow White and the Seven Dwarfs, The Jungle Book, Cars,* Disney-ABC Television, and ESPN programming. Although Disney is a U.S.-based company, its businesses span the globe, with operations in North America, Europe, Asia-Pacific, and Latin America. In Russia, a large untapped market, Disney is introducing a nationally broadcast version of the Disney Channel. The president of Walt Disney International says, "We believe there is vast growth to come out of this market, despite the near-term economic turmoil." The company's latest push, however, is China, where it's opened more than 20 English language instruction academies. English proficiency will be a plus for the

opening sometime in 2015 or 2016 of the $4.4 billion Shanghai Disney Resort. Despite its magical touch on all these different products and markets, just a few short years ago, Disney wasn't such a happy place.

When Bob Iger was named CEO in 2005, analysts believed that the Disney brand had become outdated. The perception: too much Disney product in the marketplace lacking the quality people expected. Iger said, "That combination—lack of quality and too much product—was really deadly." At that time also, the Disney brand was more tied to its history than it was to being contemporary and innovative. And, there was this sense that Disney's target audience was young and that its products couldn't possibly be of interest to older kids. Iger, who views himself as the steward of the entire Disney brand, immediately recognized the importance of leveraging the company's vast media content on different platforms. His strategic approach—the Disney Difference—had been working well until the economy slowed. The decline in global consumer spending made 2008 and 2009 extremely tough years and 2010 a difficult one. Iger and his top management team will have to use all the strategic tools they have to guide the company and keep the magic coming. One additional future challenge is that Iger announced he will be stepping down as CEO in 2015.

Discussion Questions

1. What is the Disney Difference, and how does it affect the company's corporate, competitive, and functional strategies?
2. What challenges do you think Disney might face in doing business in Russia? In China? How could Iger and his top management team best prepare for those challenges?
3. "The steward of the entire Disney brand." What do you think it means that Iger views himself as this? Is this part of being an effective strategic leader? Explain. How might it affect the company's strategy formulation, implementation, and evaluation?

4. How might Iger and his top management team use the strategic management process to "keep the magic coming" in the current economic climate?

5. Do some research on CEO succession. What advice might you have for Disney's board of directors as they prepare for this event?

Sources: B. Barnes, "Disney Channel to Be Introduced in Russia," *New York Times Online*, October 27, 2011; E. Smith, "Disney's Iger Plans Exit," *Wall Street Journal*, October 8–9, 2011, p. B3; A. Ignatius,

"Technology, Tradition & The Mouse: An Interview with Robert A. Iger," *Harvard Business Review*, July–August, 2011, pp. 112–117; M. Wei and M. Conley, "Some Chinese Kids' First English Word: Mickey," *Bloomberg BusinessWeek*, June 13–June 19, 2011, pp. 24–25; K. Swisher, "Proliferating Platforms," *Wall Street Journal*, June 6, 2011, p. R2; C. Rose, "Charlie Rose Talks to Bob Iger," *Bloomberg BusinessWeek*, March 14–March 20, 2011, p. 26; E. Smith, "Ad Rates, Parks Fuel Disney Profit," *Wall Street Journal*, February 9, 2011, p. B3; B. Barnes, "Disney Looking Into Cradle for Customers," *New York Times Online*, February 6, 2011; 2010 Annual Report, Walt Disney Company, January 2011; and R. Siklos, "Q&A: The Iger Difference," *Fortune*, April 28, 2008, pp. 90–94.

CASE #3 MTV's New Reality

MTV. Is there any college student today who hasn't at least heard of MTV? The cable TV icon has "proved one thing over time…it knows where the kids are." In its early years (the company was founded in 1981), MTV was a radical newcomer in an industry filled with conventional approaches. With its suggestive language and racy images, teens and young adults loved the edgy content and presentation. Then, in 1992, the company pioneered reality television with *The Real World*, in which seven young adult strangers lived together in a house and had their lives—the good, the bad, and the downright weird—videotaped. MTV's cutting-edge, real-life programming has been, and still is, widely copied. Although ratings for the MTV channel have stagnated for years, its audience is massive. In 1981, it had 2.1 million subscribers. Thirty years later, it has more than 100 million. The network remains "far and away the premier address for advertisers seeking to reach its coveted 18–34-year-old audience." And in 2010, MTV's ratings in that core audience rose 16 percent, the biggest annual increase since 1999. As a subsidiary of Viacom (the film production and cable television company), MTV Networks owns and operates cable networks MTV, VH1, Nickelodeon, CMT (Country Music Television), Spike TV, and other channels, including Comedy Central, TV Land, and LOGO. It also operates MTV Films in conjunction with Paramount Pictures, another subsidiary of Viacom. MTV Networks continues to be the "financial engine" of Viacom. It accounted for some 61 percent of the company's annual revenue in 2011 and most of its operating profit. Despite its long history of knowing what an elusive and fickle audience finds interesting, the executive team must continually juggle the strategic challenges of guiding this company as it looks for ways to continue its success. "As a brand, MTV has moved beyond durable, managing to reinvent itself continuously and in doing so presenting a fast-moving target that left many would-be rivals in its wake." Today, the primary challenges are the company's digital and global strategies.

Pointing to the popularity of social networking sites such as Facebook and Twitter, industry analysts criticized MTV's digital strategy, claiming that its "lock" on the youth culture was in danger. Those criticisms escalated when MTV didn't buy MySpace when it was for sale. It made other blunders in digital media as well. Its Web video site (Overdrive) never really took off nor did its digital music store (Urge). However, MTV managers countered those criticisms by noting the company's plans to "mine deep vertical slices of pop culture, rather than attempting to build wide horizontal platforms." For instance, at the Web site dance.mtv.com, which is based on the show *America's Best Dance Crew*, amateur dancers can upload videos showing off their moves. One analyst said: "What they're doing with these smaller properties is very smart. And the way they market it with a chance to get on TV is a huge draw." So far, the results of its digital online strategy seem to have been working. The number of unique users for MTV Networks' Web sites grew by 13 percent during the first half of 2008, and the average time spent at the sites grew by 20 percent to almost half an hour. Then, there's Twitter. When Twitter first came on the scene in 2007, MTV's VP of wireless saw its potential for MTV's audience of early adopters. He felt it could be "the perfect way to give fans more access to the juicy backstories of touring, performing, and being famous." By the 2010 VMAs (Video Music Awards show), both celebrities and the public were Twitter-literate, and Twitter became part of the main event. "The team had to create an entirely new aesthetic that would work online, as part of the preshow TV programming, but also theatrically as part of a live, on-stage event." Creating a seamless relationship between what was happening on TV and on Twitter wasn't easy, but it worked and worked well. During the show, some 2.3 million tweets came in and 11.4 million viewers tuned in, up 27 percent from 2009. Even as the media business continues to change, MTV will need to continually keep moving forward with its digital strategy.

MTV Networks has an extensive global presence, reaching more than 520 million households in 160 countries. Using a first-in-the-market strategy that focuses on channels with broad appeal (such as MTV Asia, MTV Latin America, MTV Turkey, MTV India, and MTV Arabia), MTV is the world's most ubiquitous TV network with more than 120 channels worldwide. Now the company is expanding in key global markets with more MTV Networks brands, like Nickelodeon, by using a range of technologies such as cable, satellite, and cell phones. Analysts caution that the key to MTV's global strategy, however, is "sticking with a winning approach that mixes universal youth sensibilities with local tastes. That way the company won't come across as a cultural imperialist." Despite MTV's far-ranging global reach and a 20 percent annual international growth rate, the U.S. division still accounts for 73 percent of overall revenue, which means there's still a lot of upside potential in the global market. The executive team must be ready to tackle the strategic challenges of both the global and the digital media environments. And they'll have to do it without the guidance and insights of long-time CEO, Judy McGrath, who had been with the company from day one, starting first as a copywriter in MTV's promotions department. Her resignation in May 2011 came as a surprise to many and ended the tenure of one of the most powerful women in television. "The change marks the end of an era at MTV, which had been run largely by home-grown veterans since its creation in 1981." Viacom's press release said Ms. McGrath's resignation was due to a "desire to seek a new career direction." However, several executives connected to the company said that Ms. McGrath was put into a position to resign by the president of Viacom after he made her an offer that would have changed her duties. With McGrath's departure, MTV's strategic decisions and directions became the responsibility of the president of Viacom.

Discussion Questions

1. Explain how strategic management and the strategic management process are illustrated in this case.

2. What challenges do you think MTV might face in crafting future digital and global strategies?

3. What are some performance measures that MTV's strategic decision makers might use as they evaluate the results of their digital and global strategies?

4. What challenges might a change in strategic leadership bring to a company? How might this affect the strategic management process?

Sources: Based on Viacom 10-K, [hoovers.com], November 15, 2011; B. Braiker, "MTV Book Surfs the Channel's History," *USA Today*, November 15, 2011, p. 3D; "I Got My MTV," *Time*, August 8, 2011, pp. 56–57; "30th Anniversary of MTV," *Fast Company*, July/August 2011, pp. 22–23; S. Schechner and L. A. E. Schuker, "MTV Networks Chief Resigns," *Wall Street Journal*, May 6, 2011, p. B3; B. Carter, "Head of MTV Networks Resigns Abruptly," *New York Times Online*, May 5, 2011; S. Elliott, "MTV Strives to Keep Up With Young Viewers," *New York Times Online*, January 30, 2011; R. Levine, "MTV's Digital Makeover," *Fast Company*, November 2008, pp. 67–70; and D. Carr, "Do They Still Want Their MTV?" *New York Times Online*, February 10, 2007.

CASE #4 Fighting Grime

Look in your pantry, your laundry room, your bathroom, or under your kitchen sink. Chances are, you have at least one of the Clorox Company's many cleaning products in your household. The Clorox Company [www.thecloroxcompany.com], a $5.2 billion company, manufactures and markets household cleaning and grocery products in more than 100 countries around the globe. Some of its most recognizable product names include Clorox Bleach, Glad bags, Soft Scrub bathroom cleaner, Tilex shower cleaner, Rain Dance car care products, Kingsford charcoal, Brita water filters, S.O.S. cleaning pads, Hidden Valley Ranch dressings, and many others. It's the worldwide leader in the bleach market and added to that lead with its purchase of Colgate-Palmolive's bleach businesses. Despite its name being synonymous with bleach, that isn't even the company's biggest brand. That distinction belongs to its Glad line of food storage and disposal products. Like many consumer-products companies that have large product lines, Clorox found that close to 30 percent of its products were falling short of their sales and profit goals. Company executives responded by developing a formal product evaluation process to help them decide which products to cut. The outcome? Nearly 90 percent of Clorox's products now meet volume and profit goals. Despite the success of this strategic initiative, Clorox executives have to walk a fine line. They don't want to discontinue products that customers want, so product lines are frequently reviewed with customers.

The Clorox Company is facing other strategic challenges. A critical one is commodity costs (primarily oil and chemicals), which have risen significantly. To offset these costs, Clorox increased prices of many of its products; however, market risks are associated with continually raising prices. In addition, when

one of your biggest customers is the world's largest and most powerful retailer, you're vulnerable to its strategic changes. When Wal-Mart decided to "adjust" its inventories, several consumer-products giants took a hit—including Clorox. One analyst noted, however, that Wal-Mart actually may have done those companies a favor by making them more efficient and thus more competitive globally. Finally, Clorox had to deal with the unexpected retirement of its popular CEO (Jerry Johnston) who suffered a heart attack in early 2006. During his tenure, Jerry had set the bar high. He challenged the entire organization to understand its connection to the consumer and to recognize this as its most significant source of competitive advantage. The current CEO, Donald Knauss (who was previously head of Coke's North American business), is the first outsider to run Clorox and has continued pushing the company in new directions, the most important of which is a "going green" strategy. In late 2007, Clorox bought Burt's Bees, the company that produces lip balms and soaps from natural ingredients. In addition, Knauss oversaw the launch of a collection of natural-cleaning products called Green Works. This product line has been one of the most successful product launches in recent memory.

However, challenges still remain. In mid-2011, activist investor Carl Icahn (who owns about 7 percent of the company) wanted to replace Clorox's board with his own nominees and then proceed to sell the company to a strategic buyer. Analysts said the bid for the company that will reach 100 years in 2013 underscored how the company had missed out on acquisitions and international expansion strategies that other leaders of the consumer-products industry pursued. However, Icahn dropped his effort to win control of Clorox's board after other major shareholders said they would not sell, believing that the economic and financial environments were too precarious. (Mr. Icahn has a long history of building up big stakes in companies and then pushing for changes in strategy or an outright sale.) So, in addition to the rising commodity costs and intensified competition from much bigger rivals such as Unilever PLC (more than $59 billion in revenues) and Procter & Gamble (more than $83 billion in revenues), the company has that threat hanging over them. However, Clorox's board believes that Knauss's global and big-brand expertise and his strong bonds with major retailers continue to help the company's global and product expansion. Knauss said he was "attracted by Clorox's market-leading brands and an ambition to lead a public company." He said that global markets would be a "key area of focus because there's a tremendous amount of growth potential there." In addition, Knauss hoped to continue exploiting Clorox's strong brand portfolio—nearly 90 percent of its brands rank number 1 or number 2 in market share—by maintaining its commitment to innovation. He said, "I think there is a unique opportunity at Clorox to focus on consumer trends and to broaden the footprint of an already great stable of brands."

Yes, these are strategic challenges that Knauss and the management team at the Clorox Company welcome. After all, if they can effectively fight the grime and dirt found in some customers' homes, the marketplace wars might not seem so bad after all!

Discussion Questions

1. Do you think strategic management has contributed to the Clorox Company's success? Why or why not?
2. Given the information included in this mini-case about the Clorox Company, at what step in the strategic management process do you think it excels? Explain your choice.
3. How might Donald Knauss use strategic management to manage the challenges facing his company?
4. Update the information on the Clorox Company by logging on to the company's Web site. How big is Clorox now in terms of sales? In terms of number of employees? What new strategies is it pursuing, if any?

Sources: Based on 2011 Annual Report, The Clorox Company, [www.thecloroxcompany.com], November 15, 2011; P. Ziobro, "Icahn Ends Bid to Gain Control of Clorox," *Wall Street Journal,* September 24–25, 2011, p. B3; E. Byron and G. Zuckerman, "Icahn Puts Clorox in Play," *Wall Street Journal,* July 16–17, 2011, pp. B1+; A. Kamenetz, "Cleaning Solution," *Fast Company,* November 2008, pp. 120–125; L. Story, "Can Burt's Bees Turn Clorox Green?" *New York Times Online,* January 6, 2008; J. S. Lublin and E. Byron, "Clorox Picks a Top Coke Officer as New Leader," *Wall Street Journal,* August 31, 2006, p. A3.

Endnotes

1. A. Shahani, "Farmville Makers Putting Stock in Virtual Goods," [www.npr.org], November 6, 2011; S. Raice, "Zynga Devises a New Plan to Break Its Facebook Habit, *Wall Street Journal,* October 12, 2011, p. B1; J. Swartz, "Zynga Goes on a Big Game Blitz," *USA Today,* October 12, 2011, p. 1B; D. Streitfield, "Zynga Releases New Games and a New Platform," *New York Times Online,* October 11, 2011; F. Manjdoo, "The Zynga Conundrum," *Fast Company,* October 2011, p. 54; C. Nuttall, "Zynga IPO Odds Lengthen As Profits Fall," *Financial Times Blog,* September 22, 2011; N. Wingfield, "Virtual Products, Real Profits," *Wall Street Journal,* September 9, 2011, pp. A1+; N. Wingfield, "Zynga Secures $1 Billion Cushion," *Wall Street Journal,* August 12, 2011, p. B4; D. MacMillan and B. Stone, "Zynga's Little-Known Addiction: 'Whales,'" *Bloomberg BusinessWeek,* July 11–July17, 2011, pp. 37–38; and N. Wingfield and L. Cowan, "Virtual Farms, Rich Harvest," *Wall Street Journal,* July 2–3, 2011, pp. B1+.

2. T. C. Powell, "Varieties of Competitive Parity," *Strategic Management Journal,* January 2003, pp. 61–86; M. Farjoun, "Towards an Organic Perspective on Strategy," *Strategic Management Journal,* July 2002, pp. 561–594.

3. M. Song, S. Im, H. van der Bij, and L. Z. Song, "Does Strategic Planning Enhance or Impede Innovation and Firm Performance?" *Journal of Product Innovation Management,* July 2011, pp. 503–520; C. Zott and R. Amit, "The Fit Between Product Market Strategy and Business Model: Implications for Firm Performance," *Strategic Management Journal,* January 2008, pp. 1–26; J. C. Short, D. J. Ketchen, Jr., T. B. Palmer, and G. T. M. Hult, "Firm, Strategic Group, and Industry Influences on Performance," *Strategic Management Journal,* February 2007, pp. 147–167; F. T. Rothaermel, M. A. Hitt, and L. A. Jobe, "Balancing Vertical Integration and Strategic Outsourcing: Effects on Product Portfolio, Product Success, and Firm Performance," *Strategic Management Journal,* November 2006, pp. 1033–1056; D. J. Miller, "Technological Diversity, Related Diversification, and Firm Performance," *Strategic Management Journal,* July 2006, pp. 601–619; J. J. Ebben and A. C. Johnson, "Efficiency, Flexibility, or Both? Evidence Linking Strategy to Performance in Small Firms," *Strategic Management Journal,* December 2005, pp. 1249–1259; C. B. Shrader, T. I. Chacko, P. Herrmann, and C. Mulford, "Planning and Firm Performance: Effects of Multiple Planning Activities and Technology Policy," *International Journal of Management and Decision Making,* vol. 5, no. 2/3, 2004, pp. 171–195; A. B. Desai, "Does Strategic Planning Create Value? The Stock Market's Belief," *Management Decision,* December 2000, pp. 685–693; P. J. Brews and M. R. Hunt, "Learning to Plan and Planning to Learn: Resolving the Planning School/Learning School Debate," *Strategic Management Journal,* vol. 20, 1999, pp. 889–913; D. J. Ketchen, Jr., J. B. Thomas, and R. R. McDaniel, Jr., "Process, Content and Context: Synergistic Effects on Performance," *Journal of Management,* vol. 22, no.2, 1996, pp. 231–257; C. C. Miller and L. B. Cardinal, "Strategic Planning and Firm Performance: A Synthesis of More Than Two Decades of Research," *Academy of Management Journal,* December 1994, pp. 1649–1665; and N. Capon, J. U. Farley, and J. M. Hulbert, "Strategic Planning and Financial Performance: More Evidence," *Journal of Management Studies,* January 1994, pp. 105–110.

4. J. W. Dean, Jr. and M. P. Sharfman, "Does Decision Process Matter? A Study of Strategic Decision-Making Effectiveness," *Academy of Management Journal,* April 1996, pp. 368–396.

5. S. Hart and C. Banbury, "How Strategy-Making Processes Can Make a Difference," *Strategic Management Journal,* May 1994, pp. 251–269.

6. W. P. Barnett, H. R. Greve, and D. Y. Park, "An Evolutionary Model of Organizational Performance," *Strategic Management Journal,* Winter 1994, pp. 11–28.

7. A. D. Chandler, Jr., *Strategy and Structure: Chapters in the History of the Industrial Enterprise* (Cambridge, MA: MIT Press, 1962); and C. W. Hofer and D. Schendel, *Strategy Formulation: Analytical Concepts* (St. Paul, MN: West, 1978).

8. O. E. Williamson, "Strategy Research: Governance and Competence Perspectives," *Strategic Management Journal,* 20, 1999, pp. 1087–1108.

9. S. P. Nerur, A. A. Rasheed, and V. Natarajan, "The Intellectual Structure of the Strategic Management Field: An Author Co-Citation Analysis," *Strategic Management Journal,* March 2008, pp. 319–336; D. C. Hambrick and M-J Chen, "New Academic Fields as Admittance-Seeking Social Movements: The Case of Strategic Management," *Academy of Management Review,* January 2008, pp. 32–54; R. Nag, D. C. Hambrick, and M-J Chen, "What Is Strategic Management, Really? Inductive Derivation of a Consensus Definition of the Field," *Strategic Management Journal,* September 2007, pp. 935–955; B. K. Boyd, S. Finkelstein, and S. Gove, "How Advanced Is the Strategy Paradigm? The Role of Particularism and Universalism in Shaping Research

Outcomes," *Strategic Management Journal,* September 2005, pp. 841–854; and R. P. Rumelt, D. E. Schendel, and D. J. Teece, "Fundamental Issues in Strategy," in R. P. Rumelt, D. E. Schendel, and D. J. Teece, (eds.), *Fundamental Issues in Strategy: A Research Agenda* (Boston, MA: Harvard Business School Press, 1994), pp. 9–47.

10. R. E. Hoskisson, M. A. Hitt, W. P. Wan, and D. Yiu, "Theory and Research in Strategic Management: Swings of a Pendulum," *Journal of Management,* vol. 25, no. 3, 1999, pp. 417–456; and R. P. Rumelt, D. E. Schendel, and D. J. Teece, 1994.

11. D. J. Ketchen, J. B. Thomas, and R. R. McDaniel, Jr., 1996.

12. J. Fowler and J. Savage, "Ask 'What,' Not 'How'," *HR Magazine,* August 2011, pp. 85–86.

13. K. Whitehouse, "Move Over CEO: Here Come the Directors," *Wall Street Journal,* October 9, 2006, pp. R1+; J. S. Lublin and E. White, "Drama in the Boardroom," *Wall Street Journal,* October 2, 2006, pp. B1+; J. Jusko, "Beefed Up Boards," *Industry Week,* August 2005, pp. 53–56; D. A. Nadler, "Building Better Boards," *Harvard Business Review,* May 2004, pp. 102–111; E. Iwata, "Judges Signal Boards to Take Duties Seriously," *USA Today,* March 29, 2004, p. 1B; and N. Donaldson, "A New Tool for Boards: The Strategic Audit," *Harvard Business Review,* July–August 1995, pp. 99–107.

14. S. Ghoshal and C. A. Bartlett, "Changing the Role of Top Management: Beyond Structure to Process," *Harvard Business Review,* January–February 1995, pp. 86–96.

15. R. Calori, G. Johnson, and P. Sarnin, "CEO's Cognitive Maps and the Scope of the Organization," *Strategic Management Journal,* July 1994, pp. 437–457.

16. A. Bryant, "Distilling the Wisdom of C.E.O.'s," *New York Times Online,* April 16, 2011.

17. R. D. Ireland and M. A. Hitt, "Achieving and Maintaining Strategic Competitiveness in the 21st Century: The Role of Strategic Leadership," *Academy of Management Executive,* February 1999, pp. 43–57.

18. Ibid.

19. J. Fowler and J. Savage, August 2011; and S. W. Floyd and P. J. Lane, "Strategizing Throughout the Organization: Managing Role Conflict in Strategic Renewal," *Academy of Management Review,* January 2000, pp. 154–177.

20. L. Alderman and J. Ewing, "In Europe, Signs of 2nd Recession With Wide Reach," *New York Times Online,* October 4, 2011; L. Story and M. Saltmarsh, "Europeans Talk of Sharp Changes in Fiscal Affairs," *New York Times Online,* September 5, 2011; and L. Alderman and J. Kanter, "European Bankers Urge Leaders to Move Quickly on Debt Crisis," *New York Times Online,* September 5, 2011.

21. D. J. Lynch, "Some Would Like to Build a Wall Around U.S. Economy," *USA Today,* March 16, 2006, p. 1B+; D. E. Sanger, "A Bush Alarm: Urging U.S. to Shun Isolationism," *New York Times Online* [www.nytimes.com], March 13, 2006; G. Ip and N. King Jr., "Ports Deal Shows Roadblocks for Globalization," *Wall Street Journal,* March 11, 2006, p. A1+; and M. A. Stein, "A Big Deal Overshadowed by the Politics of Ports," *New York Times Online* [www.nytimes.com], March 11, 2006.

22. World Trade Organization Web site [www.wto.org], November 7, 2011.

23. World Bank Group Web site [www.worldbank.org], November 7, 2011.

24. International Monetary Fund Web site [www.imf.org], November 7, 2011.

25. P. Gumbel, "Branding America," *Time,* March 2005, pp. A13–A14; T. Purdum, "Survival of the Fittest," *Industry Week,* October 2003, pp. 23–25; D. Yergin, "Globalization Opens Door to New Dangers," *USA Today,* May 28, 2003, p. 11A; K. Lowrey Miller, "Is It Globaloney?" *Newsweek,* December 16, 2002, pp. E4–E8; L. Gomes, "Globalization Is Now a Two-Way Street—Good News for the U.S.," *Wall Street Journal,* December 9, 2002, p. B1; J. Kurlantzick and J. T. Allen, "The Trouble With Globalism," *U.S. News and World Report,* February 11, 2002, pp. 38–41; and J. Guyon, "The American Way," *Fortune,* November 26, 2001, pp. 114–120.

26. Guyon, "The American Way."

27. C. M. Daily, D. R. Dalton, and A. A. Cannella, Jr., "Corporate Governance: Decades of Dialogue and Data," *Academy of Management Review,* July 2003, p. 371.

28. S. Liebs, "New Terrain," *CFO,* February 2004, pp. 40–47; C. Hymowitz and J. S. Lublin, "Boardrooms Under Renovation," *Wall Street Journal,* July 22, 2003, pp. B1+; and D. Salierno, "Boards Face Increased Responsibility," *Internal Auditor,* June 2003, pp. 14–15.

29. *Principles of Corporate Governance 2005,* Business Roundtable (Washington, DC), November 2005, p. 3.

30. D. Raths, "Backlash Against Sarbanes-Oxley," *CRO,* Winter 2006, pp. 40–41; K. Scannell and D. Solomon, "Business Wins Its Battle to Ease a Costly Sarbanes-Oxley Rule," *Wall Street Journal,* November 10, 2006, pp. A1+; S. Labaton, "Panel to Propose Exceptions to Governance Rules," *New York Times Online,* April 19, 2006; A. Borrus, "Learning to Love Sarbanes-Oxley," *BusinessWeek,* November 21, 2005, pp. 126–128; "Special Report on Corporate Governance," *Wall Street Journal,* October 17, 2005, pp. R1+; and T. Reason, "Feeling the Pain: Are the Benefits of Sarbanes-Oxley Worth the Cost?" *CFO,* May 2005, pp. 50–60.

31. Scannell and Solomon, ibid.

LEARNING OUTCOMES

2.1 **Describe the different perspectives on competitive advantage.**

2.2 **Explain the driving forces, implications, and critical success factors of the business environment.**

2.3 **Discuss two organizational elements that guide strategic decision makers in managing strategically in today's context.**

STRATEGIC MANAGEMENT IN ACTION

CASE #1 Out of Focus

Eastman Kodak Co. (most people call the company by the shortened name, Kodak) is struggling to "stay in the picture" in a changed world.[1] Founded in 1884 (yes, you read that right, 1884), Kodak was once the premier maker of photographic film. Many of us probably have snapshots tucked in a box or photo album that were taken with film bearing that unmistakable yellow-and-red K logo. A senior market intelligence analyst who worked for the company in the 1980s said, "You could look up and see that yellow sign all over the world—no matter where you went, people depended on that for their memory-recording." For decades, Kodak profited from that one high-margin product: film. "Kodak's affordable film and cameras transformed photography from a highly skilled pursuit to a pastime of the everyman." Those were truly the glory days for the company. Then, everything in the picture began to change.

By the 1980s, foreign film competitors began slicing away at Kodak's market share. For instance, Japan's Fujifilm with its green-and-white branded film canisters and single-use cameras soon became a common fixture sold right next to Kodak's yellow-and-red products. Although the new competition was a wake-up call, it wasn't the major blow to the company's iconic brand—digital technologies were. Kodak has said it invented the world's first digital camera in 1975 and spent millions of dollars developing digital technology, but the fear of cannibalizing highly profitable film sales paralyzed the company from taking anything new to the market. However, others weren't as reluctant, and it wasn't long before digital cameras that didn't need film were everywhere—and the value of Kodak's photographic film brand began to decline. The knockout punch, however, probably came in 1994 when the first cell phone/camera product appeared. Although these first phone cameras weren't anything great—the photos were low quality—the all-important "rules of the game" had changed

Amir Kaljikovic/Fotolia.com

for Kodak. By 2007, when Apple's first iPhone was introduced, the "game" was essentially over. Today's phone cameras take quality photos that can be shared instantaneously with friends and family on social media Web sites or via e-mail. Sales of photographic film continue to plummet. According to the Photo Marketing Association, only some 20 million rolls of film were purchased in 2011, down from a high of 786 million in the late 1990s. Now, Kodak struggles to adjust its strategies to the changed context.

The challenges faced by Kodak is a good example of why it's important to consider, understand, and interpret the context in which an organization's employees do strategic management. Strategic decision makers need to know their competitive advantage *and* the dynamic context they're operating in. Why? Because the context determines the "rules" of the game and what actions are likely to work best. Just as the coach of a baseball team analyzes the specific context (looking at factors such as the condition of the playing field, the team's cohesiveness, player injuries, or maybe even the team's current rankings) in deciding what game strategies might work best, so too should organizational decision makers. You can see how the context of managing strategically fits into the overall strategic management process in Figure 2.1.

LEARNING OUTCOME 2.1

Describe the Different Perspectives on Competitive Advantage

Managing strategically means formulating and implementing strategies that allow an organization to develop and maintain a **competitive advantage**—what sets an organization apart or what is its competitive edge. When an organization has a competitive advantage, it has something that competitors don't, it does something better than other organizations do, or it does something that others can't. A key concept in strategic management, competitive advantage is necessary for an organization's long-term success and survival. Even not-for-profit organizations (such as governmental agencies, educational institutions, community arts organizations, or social service groups) need something that sets them apart—something unique that they offer in order to keep their programs and services going. Getting and keeping competitive advantage is what

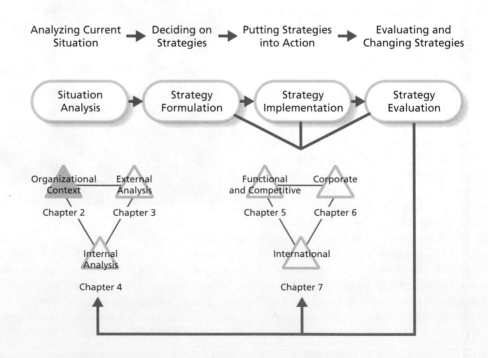

FIGURE 2.1

Strategic Management in Action

STRATEGIC MANAGEMENT IN ACTION

As women everywhere will attest—pantyhose are not a wardrobe must-have. According to industry analysts, sales of pantyhose started declining in the mid-1990s. Reasons for the declining popularity include relaxed office dress codes, more natural-looking and affordable self-tanning sprays and creams, the uncomfortable feel when wearing them, and popular media attention—also known as "the *Sex and the City* effect" because the show's four women helped make going without pantyhose fashionable. One industry competitor, Hanesbrands Inc., has seen declines in its hosiery segment for a couple of years. However, Hanes and other pantyhose makers aren't walking away. After several years of flat sales, executives at legwear and sock firms are feeling bullish. Although rising labor and raw materials costs have affected companies, executives say that there's been no major toll. There's also a belief that legwear, especially sheers, are making a comeback. Run-resistant technology, as well as the popularity of leggings, are positive signs. The designer of Hanes Legwear predicted a "bounce-back for legwear." The president of the Hosiery Association (an industry trade group) says, "The industry is not dead. Forward-thinking companies are diversifying their product offerings."

THINK ABOUT

- What might the I/O view say about the pantyhose industry?
- Where might competitive advantage come from in this industry? Go to Hanesbrands' Web site **[www.hanesbrands.com]**. What strategies is it pursuing to get and keep a competitive advantage in this industry?

Sources: Based on Hanesbrands Investor Presentation, 2011 [www.hanesbrands.com]; K. Monget, "Runway Looks to Generate Momentum," *Women's Wear Daily,* November 29, 2010, p. 11–1; L. Petrecca, "Hope for Sagging Pantyhose Sales?" *USA Today,* January 2, 2007, p. 3B; "Bare-Legs Trend Still Making Strides," *Springfield, Missouri, News-Leader,* January 2, 2007, p. 5B; and I. M. Augstums, "Pantyhose Sales Sag As Trends Change," *BusinessWeek Online* (Associated Press), December 10, 2006.

managing strategically is all about. It's not easy to do, and an organization will either succeed or fail at it. Most managers would prefer that their organizations succeed; they don't deliberately choose to fail. Instead, failure usually can be traced to not recognizing the impact of important external factors or not capitalizing on organizational resources and capabilities. Both represent different perspectives on what it takes to capture competitive advantage—that is, to manage strategically. The first view suggests organizations look at the impact of external factors and is called the industrial organization (I/O) view.[2] The second perspective—the resource-based view (RBV)—emphasizes exploiting organizational resources in order to develop and maintain competitive advantage.[3] In addition to these two traditional approaches, another, more contemporary perspective is the guerrilla view of competitive advantage, so called because it proposes that an organization's competitive advantage is temporary and can be gained only by peppering the competitive marketplace with rapid radical surprises.[4] Because you need to understand where an organization's competitive advantage comes from, we're going to look more closely at these three perspectives. Table 2.1 summarizes the main points of each view.

TABLE 2.1 Comparing the I/O, Resource-Based, and Guerrilla Views of Competitive Advantage

	I/O View	RBV	Guerrilla View
Competitive Advantage	Positioning in industry	Possessing unique organizational assets or capabilities	Temporary
Determinants of Profitability	Characteristics of industry, firm's position within industry	Type, amount, and nature of firm's resources	Ability to change and radically surprise competitors with strategic actions
Focus of Analysis	External	Internal	External and internal
Major Concern	Competition	Resources–capabilities	Continual, radical, and chaotic conditions
Strategic Choices	Choosing attractive industry; appropriate position	Developing unique resources and distinctive capabilities	Rapidly and repeatedly disrupting current situation and surprising competitors

The I/O View

The **I/O view** focuses on the structural forces within an industry, the competitive environment of firms, and how these influence competitive advantage. Most of what we know about the I/O approach comes from Michael Porter of the Harvard Business School. According to Porter, five industry forces (which we'll cover in detail in Chapter 3) determine the average profitability of an industry, which in turn influences the profitability of firms within the industry. His approach emphasizes choosing the "best" industries and, within those industries, the most advantageous (or competitive) positions.

The I/O approach proposes that getting and keeping competitive advantage means analyzing external forces and basing strategic decisions on that analysis. Thus, the focus of strategic analysis in the I/O view is external. Because all firms within an industry face essentially the same external forces, a major concern of the I/O view is how the firm stacks up against its competitors. Keep in mind the I/O view proposes that competitive advantage relates to competitive positioning in the industry. Also, the I/O view suggests that both a firm's position within the industry and the underlying industry characteristics determine its potential profitability. If there are significant negative forces in the industry or if the firm has a weak position within the industry, then its profitability will be lower than average. But if the industry is characterized by significant opportunities or if the firm has a strong position within the industry, then its profitability will be above average. According to the I/O view, managers make sound strategic choices by understanding what makes an industry attractive, choosing an attractive industry in which to compete, and then choosing an appropriate competitive position within that industry.

The I/O view makes important contributions to understanding how to manage strategically, but critics say it doesn't tell the whole story. Although Porter's ideas don't ignore the characteristics of individual companies, the emphasis is clearly on understanding what is happening at the industry level. Several researchers believed that a complete understanding of competitive advantage also required looking at the role a firm's resources played.

Resource-Based View

The **RBV** says that a firm's resources are most important in getting and keeping a competitive advantage. It sees organizations as different collections of assets and capabilities; that is, none have had the same set of experiences, acquired the same assets or capabilities, or built the same organizational cultures. According to the RBV, there are some key assets (resources) that can give a firm a competitive advantage. Therefore, an organization will be positioned to succeed if it has the best and most appropriate resources for its business.

Managing strategically, according to the RBV, involves developing and exploiting an organization's unique resources and capabilities. But, what exactly are "resources"—and what makes them "unique"?

Resources include all of the financial, physical, human, intangible, and structural/cultural assets used by an organization to develop, produce, and deliver products or services to its customers.[5] Financial assets include the financial holdings of an organization (cash reserves, investments, etc.), the actual and available debt and equity used by the organization, and any retained earnings. Physical assets include an organization's equipment, office buildings, manufacturing or sales facilities, raw materials, or other tangible materials. Human resources include the experiences, characteristics, knowledge, judgment, wisdom, skills, abilities, and competencies of an organization's employees. Intangible assets include such things as brand names, patents, reputation, trademarks, copyrights, registered designs, and databases. Finally, structural/cultural assets include an organization's history, culture, work systems, organizational policies, working relationships, level of employee trust, and the formal structure in use.

Although every organization has resources it needs and uses to do its work, not all those resources will lead to a sustainable competitive advantage. The RBV suggests that resources must

STRATEGIC MANAGEMENT IN ACTION

As a pioneer of Internet TV, Hulu is one of the most-watched on-line video properties in the United States. Hulu operates a Web site that features video from more than 225 content providers. Offerings include TV shows from ABC, Fox, and NBC as well as from cable channels and films from studios including Sony and MGM. Most of the content is streamed free eight days after its broadcast debut. Viewers can watch shows earlier through a premium subscription service called Hulu Plus. Hulu.com attracts some 26 million visitors a month. Hulu is owned by entertainment and broadcasting powerhouses, including NBC Universal, Comcast, News Corp., and Walt Disney Co., and by a private equity firm. However, it now faces a challenging environment in which consumers have a growing number of options on where and how to access content. Hulu's owners had been exploring a sale of the online video venture but decided in late 2011 not to sell the company. Now they have to figure out what to do with it.

THINK ABOUT

- What do you think Hulu's owners should do now?
- What is it about this situation context that's so challenging?
- What type of resource(s) does Hulu have? Would you call it unique? Explain.

Sources: Based on S. Schechner, "Hulu Puts Owners in New Quandary," *Wall Street Journal*, October 17, 2011, p. B1; S. Schechner, "Hulu's Owners End Efforts to Sell Streaming-TV Website," *Wall Street Journal*, October 14, 2011, p. B3; S. Schechner and J. E. Vascellaro, "Hulu Reworks Its Script As Digital Change Hits TV," *Wall Street Journal*, January 27, 2011, pp. A1+; and A. Palazzo, "Hulu Says It Will Reach 1 Million Paid-User Goal in 3 Months," *Bloomberg BusinessWeek Online*, July 6, 2011.

be unique to be a source of potential competitive advantage. Figure 2.2 illustrates what makes resources unique. Because these characteristics are important, let's look at them more closely.

Value

An organizational resource is unique if it adds value. Adding value means that the resource can be used to exploit external circumstances likely to bring in organizational revenues or that it can be used to neutralize negative external situations likely to keep revenue from flowing in. An organization's resources aren't valuable by themselves but only when they exploit those external opportunities or neutralize the threats. As environmental factors such as customer tastes or technology change, resources can become more valuable or less valuable. So, a resource is valuable in the context of what's happening in the external environment.

FIGURE 2.2

What Makes Organizational Resources Unique?

Source: Based on Jay B. Barney, "Looking Inside for Competitive Advantage," *Academy of Management Executive,* November 1995, pp. 49–61.

Rarity

For a resource to be rare, ideally no competing firms should already possess it. If more competitors acquire certain resources that have been a source of competitive advantage, then it becomes a less likely source of sustainable competitive advantage for an organization. Keep in mind, though, that even commonly held resources may be valuable if for no other reason than the firm's survival in a competitive environment. But, in order to gain a competitive advantage, a resource should be both valuable *and* rare.

Difficult to Imitate (Duplicate) and Substitute

Obviously, if a resource can't be imitated or substituted by a competitor, then any revenues it generates are more likely to continue flowing in. Organizations want resources that are hard to imitate and substitute. Imitation (duplication) is when a competitor builds the same kind of resource as the firm it's imitating. Substitution is when a firm substitutes an alternative resource for the specific resource currently used to gain competitive advantage and achieves the same results. So, in order to keep resources unique, you want them to be hard to imitate and substitute. Some resources are harder to imitate and substitute—for instance, such things as company reputation, employee trust, teamwork, and organizational culture.

Ability to Exploit

Not only must organizational resources be valuable, rare, and hard to imitate or substitute, the organization must be able to exploit them. Are the formal structure, systems, policies, procedures, and processes in place to use the resources it has to develop a sustainable competitive advantage? In other words, is it able to exploit the full competitive potential of its resources? Without these abilities, it will be difficult for an organization to create and maintain a competitive advantage.

All four of these characteristics are important indicators of a resource's ability to be a source of sustainable competitive advantage. The popular business press is filled with stories of companies that have unique and valuable resources they're able to exploit. But, there are also many examples of organizations that have not been able to get and keep a competitive edge because they have no unique resources or they haven't been able to exploit the unique resources they do have. According to the RBV, managing strategically means continually building and maintaining organizational resources—capitalizing on the "crown jewels" of the firm. However, a question facing strategic decision makers is this: Do the unique resources that are sources of competitive advantage today remain so over time? According to the next view, not always.

STRATEGIC MANAGEMENT IN ACTION

W. L. Gore & Associates **[www.gore. com]** is known for its high-quality and revolutionary outdoor wear products and was recently named one of *Fortune* magazine's 100 Best Companies to Work For (for the fifteenth consecutive year). The kinds of innovative efforts exhibited by Gore's associates (they're not called employees) are made possible by a unique organizational culture that unleashes creativity and fosters teamwork. Being an associate at Gore requires a commitment to four basic principles articulated by company founder Bill Gore: fairness to each other and everyone you come in contact with; freedom to encourage, help, and allow other associates to grow in knowledge, skill, and scope of responsibility; the ability to make your own commitments and keep them; and consulting with other associates before undertaking actions that could impact the reputation of the company.

TO DO

- Go to the company's Web site. What other examples of resources do you see?
- Do you think any of these resources are unique? Explain.

Sources: Based on W. L. Gore & Associates [www.gore.com], December 5, 2011; and M. Moskowitz, R. Levering, C. Tkaczyk, C. Keating, A. Konrad, A. Vandermey, and C. Kapelke "The 100 Best Companies to Work For," *Fortune*, February 6, 2012, pp. 117+.

Guerrilla View

What do you think of when you hear the term *guerrilla?* Do you envision brief and covert attacks on an enemy position by a well-trained, competent, and skilled unit? That's the analogy behind the **guerrilla view,** which is the view that an organization's competitive advantage is temporary. Why? Because the environment is characterized by continual and often revolutionary changes. For instance, disruptions in technology, market instabilities, and other types of significant, but unpredictable changes challenge strategic managers' attempts at creating a sustainable competitive advantage. For instance, think about the environment the recorded music industry faced over the past few years and how difficult it has been to get and keep a competitive advantage. According to the guerrilla view, successful organizations must rapidly and repeatedly disrupt the current situation and radically surprise competitors with strategic actions designed to keep them off balance—in other words, act like a guerrilla unit. Successful organizations will repeatedly create new competitive advantages based on how the context is changing.

Which View Is Best?

We know competitive advantage is important to how an organization ultimately performs, so which view is best? Each brings a unique perspective to understanding competitive advantage. The I/O view addresses the need to look at the external environment, particularly the industry and competitors, and emphasizes the importance of understanding competitive positioning. The RBV considers the need to look inside the organization for the unique resources and capabilities that can be exploited. And, the guerrilla view forces strategic decision makers to recognize that the dynamic nature of the external environment can affect what is considered a competitive advantage and how long that competitive advantage can last.

Managing strategically involves looking both externally and internally to come up with strategies that have a chance of creating a sustainable competitive advantage, even if for only a brief period of time. In this way, unique resources and capabilities can be "matched" to changing

---

STRATEGIC MANAGEMENT IN ACTION

What if customers said they no longer needed packages shipped "absolutely, positively overnight?" That's the position FedEx, the world's largest express transport company and a company that prided itself for being consistently on the cutting edge of product delivery, found itself in. Overnight, its market turned upside down, and the competitive advantage FedEx had developed was no longer valuable. Customers no longer wanted fast, but pricey, delivery service. External changes such as instantaneous e-mail delivery of information, discount carriers that provided package tracking information online, and competitive rivals that copied FedEx's elaborate information system that once distinguished the company have all contributed to its strategic management challenges. The company's strategic decision makers aren't just sitting back, however. To bolster the number of package pick-up locations and to give them a stronger retail presence, they acquired copy company Kinko's (now FedEx Office). In addition, the company is focusing more on long-haul global and domestic cargo markets by buying new planes and acquiring a domestic trucking company.

TO DO

- Take a look at the company's Web site. What other strategic options are they pursuing, especially in light of rising fuel costs and retail slump (meaning fewer packages delivered)?
- Do FedEx's actions reflect the guerrilla view of competitive advantage? Discuss.

Sources: Based on W. B. Cassidy, "FedEx Ground Delivers Profits," *The Journal of Commerce,* October 3, 2011, pp. 45–46; P. McDougall, "FedEx Adapts From Overnight to Over Net," *Information Week,* September 19, 2011, p. 80; S. Schaefer, "RBC Slashes FedEx Forecast on Shaky Economic Outlook," *Forbes.com,* September 13, 2011, p. 13; "FedEx Invests in Fuel-Efficient Vehicles," *Commercial Carrier Journal,* August 2011, p. 26; and C. Dade and S. Tibken, "FedEx Swings to a Rare Loss On Fuel Costs, Retail Slump," *Wall Street Journal,* June 19, 2008, p. B1.

external circumstances. Because the external environment is continually changing (new competitors come and go, customers' tastes change, technology changes, current competitors start a price war, etc.), the source of sustainable competitive advantage *is* probably found in different places at different points in time. So, how can strategic decision makers ever hope to develop a sustainable competitive advantage—that is, manage strategically? The answer is by continually analyzing both the external and internal organizational environments and then taking advantage of any positive changes (or buffering against negative changes) with the organization's unique resources and capabilities. One of the most important changes strategic managers must contend with is the business environment. That's what we'll look at next.

LEARNING REVIEW   LEARNING OUTCOME 2.1

- Define competitive advantage and explain why it's important.
- Describe the different perspectives on competitive advantage.
- Explain what makes a resource unique.

LEARNING OUTCOME 2.2

Explain the Driving Forces, Implications, and Critical Success Factors of the Business Environment

The business context or environment that organizations operate in today is a lot different than what it used to be. Even not-for-profit organizations feel the impact of the changing context because they, too, need resources such as labor, technology, and funding to operate. We need to examine important characteristics of this business environment: What forces are "driving" it? What are the implications? And, what will it take to be successful in this context? Figure 2.3 provides an overview.

Drivers of the Business Environment

Three critical driving forces in this new business environment are: (1) the information revolution, (2) technology, and (3) globalization. Let's discuss each more thoroughly.[6]

FIGURE 2.3

The New Business Environment

The Information Revolution

If one driving force has set the tone for this business environment, it's the information revolution. This revolution is not just continuing—it's accelerating. A recent study showed that the amount of information created and replicated worldwide surpassed 1.8 zettabytes (1.8 trillion gigabytes). That's the equivalent of every U.S. citizen writing 3 tweets per minute for 26,976 years. Another study showed that the amount of new information saved in a single year alone would fill half a million libraries the size of the Library of Congress. And another showed that the amount of digital information is 3 million times all the books ever written.[7] Any way you look at it, that's a lot of information! And this information is readily available to practically anyone from anywhere on the globe at any hour of the day and pretty much in any format. The instant availability of information has radically changed the nature of the business environment, which, in turn, affects the context of strategic management.

Information (knowledge) has always been used in producing goods and services, primarily to design work tools, organizational processes, management systems, and products, as organizations searched for ways to be more efficient and effective. However, a fundamental shift has occurred in which information is now *the* essential resource of production, not simply a means to an end. Knowledge is no longer viewed only as a way to make sure other resources are used efficiently. Land, labor, and capital have become supporting, not the main, factors in production.[8] This means that organizations can no longer rely on the traditional factors of production to provide a sustainable competitive advantage but must look to how information and knowledge can be exploited. In addition to knowledge, technology is also one of the driving forces of this business environment.

Technology

All organizations use some form of technology to do their work. What is **technology?** It's using equipment, materials, knowledge, and experience to perform tasks. Some industries are more technology intensive than others (for instance, think of electronics, software, telecommunications, and pharmaceuticals). But even organizations such as the American Red Cross, your neighborhood grocery store, utility companies, and steel mills use technology. Technology significantly changed the nature of competition in the last part of the twentieth century. Work approaches and tools

---

FOR YOUR INFORMATION
All Service All the Time

"The war between the tangible and intangible sectors of the U.S. economy is over, and the intangibles have won." When Wal-Mart Stores first topped the list of *Fortune's* Global 500 in 2002 (and has been number one for 8 of the last 10 years), it was the culmination of a major economic shift that had been taking place for years—that is, the shift from producing goods to producing services. Manufacturing's share of U.S. employment, which peaked in 1953 at 35 percent, has steadily declined ever since and now stands at less than 12 percent. This is also true in all other developed economies (Germany, Canada, Japan, etc.) as well. The Bureau of Labor Statistics predicts that through the year 2014, production jobs will continue to decline while occupations in service-providing industries will continue to expand. Or put another way, the service-providing industries are expected to account for approximately 18.7 million of the 18.9 million new wage and salary jobs generated. One explanation for this shift is that as Americans got richer, consumption got more sophisticated. With more income to spend, people started purchasing more services—movies and travel, massages and facials, mortgages to buy houses, insurance to protect those houses and possessions, and so on. Economists call this a shift in the demand pattern. It's also a reason why so many top global companies are service companies.

THINK ABOUT

- How has the information revolution impacted service businesses?

Sources: J. Mitchell, "Manufacturing Slows Outside U.S.," *Wall Street Journal,* December 2, 2011, p. A12; L. Uchitelle, "Is Manufacturing Falling Off the Radar?" *New York Times Online,* September 10, 2011; and M. Mandel, "They Make Jobs, Not Widgets," *BusinessWeek,* December 22, 2008, p. 32.

STRATEGIC MANAGEMENT IN ACTION
The Global Perspective

Safe. Secure. Reliable. Dependable. Impenetrable. Powerful. All things we think of when we think about information technology. However, even IT can't escape a natural disaster. Rewind to late December 2006. Computer screens at Reuters financial information company in Singapore suddenly went blank. International telephone conversations suddenly went silent. Access to international Web sites was spotty. Even international transactions at automated teller machines were lost. An "earthquake off Taiwan had damaged undersea cables, jamming Internet services as voice and data traffic vied for space on smaller cables and slower satellite links." Because most of Asia is separated by water, the most efficient option for carrying data is undersea cable systems. This earthquake took out six of seven existing systems. The service disruption was most directly experienced in Taiwan, Singapore, Hong Kong, South Korea, and Japan, but it didn't take long for a "ripple effect" to be felt in other parts of the world. Even those businesses so reliant on technology that they had a backup source found that a backup was useless when it was gone, too. As one reporter said, this "disruption exposed our global networks' fragility." Executives at some telecommunication companies said the problems highlighted a need to "beef up their backup systems even more."

THINK ABOUT

- What does this scenario tell us about the importance of knowing the context?

Sources: D. Greenlee and W. Arnold, "Asia Scrambles to Repair Quake Damage to Data Cables," *New York Times Online*, December 29, 2006; C. Hang-Sun and W. Arnold, "Asian Quake Disrupts Data Traffic," *New York Times Online*, December 28, 2006; and J. Dean, "Asian Quake's Telecom Disruption Exposes Global Networks' Fragility," *Wall Street Journal*, December 28, 2006, p. A1+.

that may have been effective in the past weren't anymore and new ones were rapidly developed. Technology continues to have far-reaching effects on how organizations do their work—effects we can see in three different areas: innovation, bottom-up capability, and organizational performance.

Technology impacts **innovation,** which we define as turning a creative idea into a product or process that can be used or sold. Innovation *is* more than just being creative—it's developing, making, and marketing something that can generate revenue. At a global innovation conference, IBM's Chairman Sam Palmisano once said, "The way you will thrive in this environment is by innovating—innovating in technologies, innovating in strategies, innovating in business models."[9] So how important is innovation to companies? In a new study of business and government executives, 98 percent said that innovation will be critical to the success of their organizations over the next five years. [10] Earlier research on the most innovative companies in the world found that these innovators have achieved a profit margin growth of 3.4 percent a year since 1995, compared to 0.4 percent growth for a company on Standard & Poor's Global 1200 list.[11] Although the majority of these "masters" of innovation were U.S. companies, recent statistics show that while the United States still leads the world in scientific research, five countries now devote a larger share of their GDP to R&D spending, leading some experts to sound a cautionary note regarding future breakthroughs.[12]

Another area where technology has had an impact on organizations is in terms of what can be called a "bottom-up" or mass collaboration capability. Through technology such as the Internet, personal messaging systems, and social networks, power is shifting from institutions to individuals. Take, for example, the popularity of Fox Network's reality show *American Idol,* in which the audience decides who "wins." Or look at what eBay has done. The company's founder said that managers don't control the brand or customer experience—the customers do.

One final area technology affects is organizational performance. High-performance companies (e.g., Wal-Mart, McDonald's, Southwest Airlines, Samsung, and IKEA) are leaders in technology. But simply having the latest and best technology isn't their goal. Instead, these great companies realize that technology is a powerful tool that enhances their business. They realize that it's not a replacement for understanding the economics of their business and creating a business model that allows them to be the best at what they do, but that it can help them perform better.

The increasing pace of technological change and the importance of continual innovation are quite evident. Within the context of managing strategically, technology and innovation do influence an organization's sustainable competitive advantage. The challenge is capturing and exploiting the unique advantages of technology by using the organizational innovation process to create valuable products and processes—and doing so globally. The challenges and opportunities of globalization are the final driving force we're going to look at.

Globalization

In Chapter 1, we discussed how globalization and the global economy are impacting strategic management. Globalization has been around for so long now (you undoubtedly hear about it in every business class you take) that it almost seems a cliché. However, globalization

---

FOR YOUR INFORMATION
Offshoring and Outsourcing: The Good, the Bad, and the Reality

This is a story about the global economy. It's about markets, politics, and public opinion. And as jobs—especially white-collar and professional jobs—continue to be outsourced and offshored, the story hits closer and closer to home. Although the terms *offshoring* and *outsourcing* are often used interchangeably, they do mean different things. **Offshoring** is relocating business processes (production and services) from one country to another. **Outsourcing** is moving noncore activities from being done internally to being done externally by an entity that specializes in that activity.

One of the realities of a global economy is that to be competitive, strategic decision makers must look for the best places to do business. If a car can be made more cheaply in Mexico, maybe it should be. If a telephone inquiry can be processed more cheaply in India or the Philippines, maybe it should be. And if programming code can be written more cheaply in China or Russia, maybe it should be. Almost any professional job that can be done outside the organization is up for grabs. There's nothing political or philosophical about the reason for shipping jobs elsewhere. The bottom line is that it can save companies money. But there's a price to be paid in terms of angry and anxious employees. So, are offshoring and outsourcing bad?

Critics say "yes." It's affecting jobs once considered "safe" across a wider range of professional work activities. And the offshoring and outsourcing have taken place at a breathtaking pace. What this means is that the careers college students are preparing for probably won't sustain them in the long run. This structural change in the U.S. economy also means that the workforce is likely to face frequent career changes and downward pressures on wages.

Proponents say "no." Their argument is based on viewing economic development as a ladder with every country trying to climb to the next rung. And it's foolish to think that in the United States, we've reached the top of the ladder and there's nowhere else to go. Although people fear that educated U.S. workers will face the same fate as blue-collar workers whose jobs shifted to lower-cost countries, the truth is that the United States currently still has a competitive advantage in innovation, although, as discussed earlier, that may be in jeopardy. The biggest danger to U.S. workers isn't overseas competition; it's worrying too much about other countries climbing up the economic ladder and not worrying enough about finding that next higher rung. Finally, economic forces at work in the latest global recession—which led to rapidly rising labor rates in those geographic areas where costs had been low, coupled with higher materials and shipping costs, and attractive tax incentives from various U.S. states—may combine to lure back U.S. firms.

Who's right? We probably can't answer that question just yet. Only time will tell. However, we do know that what we're seeing with offshoring and outsourcing is another example of why strategic decision makers need to be aware of the context within which their organizations are doing business.

TO DO

• Research this issue and come up with your own arguments for and against it.

Sources: J. Bussey, "Will Costs Drive Firms Home?" *Wall Street Journal,* May 5, 2011, pp. B1+; D. Wessel, "Big U.S. Firms Shift Hiring Abroad," *Wall Street Journal,* April 19, 2011, pp. B1+; P. Engardio, M. Arndt, and D. Foust, "The Future of Outsourcing," *BusinessWeek,* January 30, 2006, pp. 50–58; J. Thottam, "Is Your Job Going Abroad?" *Time,* March 1, 2004, pp. 26–36; L. D. Tyson, "Outsourcing: Who's Safe Anymore?" *BusinessWeek,* February 23, 2004, p. 26; A. Fisher, "Think Globally, Save Your Job Locally," *Fortune,* February 23, 2004, p. 60; "The New Job Migration," *The Economist,* February 21, 2004, p. 11; O. Thomas, "The Outsourcing Solution," *Business 2.0,* September 2003, pp. 159–160; and K. Madigan and M. J. Mandel, "Outsourcing Jobs: Is It Bad?" *BusinessWeek,* August 25, 2003, pp. 36–38.

has transformed and continues to transform the business environment.[13] We saw this ever more clearly as the global economic recession continued to drag on. Thus, more than ever, organizations—small and large—must strategically manage global issues. Globalization influences strategic management in two ways: (1) global markets and (2) global competitors.

Creating sustainable competitive advantage may entail looking globally for customers and resources. Although any location may be a potential market, strategic decision makers must recognize that the global economic climate and those of individual markets can—and do—have an impact. In addition, financial, material, human, and knowledge resources are available globally and should be acquired wherever it strategically makes sense to do so. In other words, globalization means that geographic boundaries don't constrain an organization's strategic decisions and actions.

As global markets open up, competitors can come from anywhere. They, too, are looking for a sustainable competitive advantage. Although doing business globally can be rewarding, competing in a global marketplace is challenging because now you're dealing with organizations that have their own unique set of experiences and resources, making it much more difficult to understand their strategic approach and intent. However, global competitors don't have to be a threat. Strategic decision makers might find that the most effective strategy for achieving a sustainable competitive advantage is to partner with a global competitor to create or market products. Because globalization is such an important factor, Chapter 7 is devoted to looking at global/international strategies that organizations use.

Each of these driving forces—information revolution, technology, and globalization—is affecting the context within which strategic decision makers manage strategically. What are the implications for strategic decision makers?

Implications of These Driving Forces

Look back at Figure 2.3, and you'll see that there are four major implications of these driving forces: continual change, the reduced need for physical assets, vanishing distance and compressed time, and increased vulnerability. Let's look at each.

Continual Change

Change is the order of business in today's context as *all* organizations deal with changing conditions. These changing conditions (externally or even internally) stimulate the need for **organizational change,** which is defined as a structured transition in what an organization does and how it does it. For example, greeting card companies had to change the way they did business as people began sending electronic greeting cards (a changing external condition). Or consider how other changing external conditions—such as increasing levels of obesity—have forced organizations to change the products they offer and how they're packaged and sold.

Reduced Need for Physical Assets

The business environment of a few years ago was one in which the more physical assets you had (manufacturing facilities, office buildings, equipment, inventory, etc.), the more economically powerful you were. However, success in today's economy isn't reliant simply on physical assets. Instead, value is found in intangible factors such as information, people, ideas, and knowledge. Companies such as Google, Amazon.com, Apple, and American Express find that they can achieve a sustainable competitive advantage with nonphysical assets such as customer databases, online ordering systems, continual product and process innovation, and employee knowledge sharing.

Vanishing Distance and Compressed Time

Physical distance and time constraints on an organization's strategic decisions have all but disappeared! Although geography traditionally played an important role in determining customers and competitors, that's no longer so. An organization's potential markets and competitors

STRATEGIC MANAGEMENT IN ACTION
The Global Perspective

Steve Chang, CEO and president of Trend Micro, Inc., a high-tech transnational company, believes that "borders are so twentieth century." As a provider of computer network antivirus and Internet security software, Trend Micro has spread its executives, engineers, and support staff around the world in order to improve its response time to new virus threats. It's routinely the first to go on the offensive when a new virus strikes, often 30 minutes before market leader Symantec (maker of the popular Norton Antivirus software) reacts. Although Trend Micro's corporate and financial headquarters are in Tokyo, its computer virus response center is based in Manila (where costs are low), product development is based in Taiwan (where there's a plentiful supply of Ph.D.s), and sales are centered in California's Silicon Valley (where there's easier access to the vast American market). No competitor has such an international reach. The company has succeeded because it's set up its business in a way that takes advantage of the realities of today's context.

TO DO

• Explain how Trend Micro has succeeded using Figure 2.3.

Sources: Company information from Hoover's Online [www.hoovers.com], December 9, 2011; D. Olenick, "Trend Micro Gets Social," *This Week in Consumer Electronics (TWICE)*, October 3, 2011, p. 40; J. Brandon, "Doing Battle with Online Threats," *Inc.*, October 2010, p. 46; B. Grow, "The Mind Games Cybercrooks Play," *BusinessWeek*, April 17, 2006, pp. 54–58; and S. Hamm, "Borders Are So Twentieth Century," *BusinessWeek*, September 22, 2003, pp. 68–73.

can be found anywhere. As the limitations of physical distance have disappeared, so too have the limitations of time. The ability to instantly interact (e-mail, text messaging, interactive Web sites, etc.) means staying on top of changes or finding your marketplace advantage temporary, at best. Although it isn't easy, it's important.

Vulnerability

Although their names are usually quite innocent and often very clever—Trojan Android, Backdoor Dorkbot, SoBig, The Love Bug, BugBear—global computer viruses can be destructive. They illustrate the final implication of the driving forces in today's context—the increased vulnerability that organizations face from interconnectedness and openness.[14] Threats from computer virus attacks, terrorist attacks, and biological attacks should be enough to make strategic decision makers realize that their information, facilities, and employees are vulnerable. Protecting valuable resources against such potential attacks is no longer a "maybe"—it's a strategic certainty and one that shouldn't be ignored.

Critical Success Factors

Three factors critical to success in this new business environment are (1) ability to embrace change, (2) creativity and innovation capabilities, and (3) being a world-class organization (see Figure 2.3). Let's look at each.

Ability to Embrace Change

If there's one word that captures the essence of this business environment, it's *change*—from technological advances, resource vulnerability, or information availability. Do you like change? Probably not. Few people enjoy or even seek out change. Most of us think change is annoying, scary, or both. We like the old and comfortable, not the new or unknown. But change is a given in today's business environment. Being successful in such an environment means not only being tolerant of change, but seeking it out and embracing it. Change brings opportunities to exploit and challenges in dealing with the changes. In any type of change efforts, the quality of strategic leadership can spell the difference between success and failure.

Strategic decision makers play an important role as change agents. Effective change doesn't just happen. Someone must initiate and oversee the change efforts. These individuals are called **change agents.** Whether the change is big or small, change agents are needed, and strategic decision makers can play this important role. Ideally, an organization's top managers provide a sense of long-term direction and offer support and rationale for needed changes.[15] But, strategic leaders at any organizational level play an important role in the change process.

Change is difficult. (Think about how you react if you have a substitute professor in class one day or if your professor changes the course assignment schedule to accommodate a change in plans. You may be anxious or even annoyed.) Although strong strategic leadership can't eliminate all the challenges associated with change, it can smooth the process and facilitate successful implementation of the change. Considering the number of dynamic forces facing today's organizations, strong strategic leadership can create an appropriate and supportive organizational environment in which employees are encouraged to take responsibility for problems and solutions.[16]

Creativity and Innovation Capabilities

Here's an abbreviated statement of how critical this factor is: "Create and innovate or fail!" It's that simple. In this context, strategic decision makers must be prepared to create new products and services and adopt state-of-the-art technology if their organizations are to compete successfully and survive. **Creativity,** the ability to combine ideas in a unique way or to make unusual associations between ideas, is an important capability.[17] A creative person or organization develops novel approaches to doing work or unique solutions to problems. But, creativity alone isn't enough. We know from our earlier discussion that innovation is the process of taking a creative idea and turning it into a product or process that can be used or sold. An innovative organization is characterized by its ability to channel creativity into useful outcomes. Both capabilities, creativity and innovation, are critical to strategic success in this business environment.

Being a World-Class Organization

Given the importance of creating a sustainable competitive advantage in today's business environment, you'd probably agree that ensuring an organization's long-run survival and success isn't easy. One concept with considerable potential for helping strategic decision

---

FOR YOUR INFORMATION
The DNA of Corporate Innovation

The members of the Innovation Network Inc. **[http://www.innovation network.biz/mission/dna/index.html]** put their heads together and developed The Innovation DNA Model. This model identifies seven dimensions that need to be in place for organizational innovation to take root. These dimensions include: (1) challenge—the bigger the challenge and the passion behind it, the more energy innovation efforts will need; (2) customer focus—all innovation should be focused on creating value for customers, external or internal; it requires understanding their needs; (3) creativity—everything starts from an idea, and the best way to get ideas is to generate a lot of possibilities; (4) communication—open communication of ideas, information, and feelings is the lifeblood of innovation; (5) collaboration—innovation is a group process; (6) completion—innovations require "doing"; that is,

decision making, delegating, scheduling, monitoring, and feedback skills; and completed projects should be celebrated; and (7) contemplation—learning from completed projects builds a knowledge base that creates an upward cycle of success. In addition, the organization's culture creates the playing field for all the other elements to happen.

TO DO

- Research a company (Starbucks, Apple, Microsoft, or pick your own) and assess it on these dimensions. Be sure to document your sources, and be prepared to share your findings in class.

Sources: Innovation Network Inc., January 8, 2009; and S. Caudron, "The Economics of Innovation," *Business Finance*, November 1999, pp. 23–27.

FIGURE 2.4

Characteristics of World-Class Organizations

Source: Based on Richard M. Hodgetts, Fred Luthans, and Sang M. Lee, "New Paradigm Organizations: From Total Quality to Learning to World Class," *Organizational Dynamics,* Winter 1994, pp. 4–19.

makers meet that challenge is that of a **world-class organization,** in which strategic decision makers take actions to help it be the best in the world at what it does.[18] Recall our earlier discussion of the business environment with respect to information and knowledge, technology, and increasing globalization, and you can begin to appreciate why being a world-class organization is important. Even if an organization operates in a single geographic location, it should still strive to be the best at what it does in its own little "world" or competitive arena. What characteristics does a world-class organization have? The major ones are shown in Figure 2.4.

LEARNING REVIEW   LEARNING OUTCOME 2.2

- Describe the three major driving forces of the business environment.
- Explain the four major implications of these driving forces.
- Discuss the three critical factors for succeeding in the business environment.

As strategic decision makers grapple with the challenges of guiding an organization in today's context, two organizational elements are a source of guidance: (1) organizational vision and mission and (2) corporate social responsibility (CSR) and ethics.

Organizational Vision and Mission

It's equally important for an organization to have both an organizational vision *and* a mission. These two concepts are often viewed as the same, but we think they're different. An **organizational vision** is a broad comprehensive picture of what a leader wants an organization to become. It's a statement of what the organization stands for, what it believes in, and why it exists. It presents a view beyond what the organization "is" to what the organization "could be."[19] Although it may

LEARNING OUTCOME 2.3

Discuss Two Organizational Elements That Guide Strategic Decision Makers in Managing Strategically in Today's Context seem that a vision is simply "fluff"—something that sounds good on paper but does nothing to improve the organization's performance—a clear vision articulated by leaders can motivate organizational members to contribute increased levels of effort.[20]

An effective organizational vision should include four components.[21] One is that the vision *be built on a foundation of the organization's core values and beliefs.* These values and beliefs address what's fundamentally important to the organization, whether it's conducting business ethically and responsibly, satisfying the customer, emphasizing quality in all aspects, or being a technology leader. The vision should stress whatever those core values might be. How important are values? A survey by the American Management Association found that almost 86 percent of the respondents said the values of their organization were specifically stated or written, and 64 percent said the values were linked to performance evaluations and compensation.[22] Although a statement of values doesn't guarantee success, it does provide employees behavioral expectations. For example, if employees know that outstanding customer service is valued by the organization, they can act in ways that champion customer service.

Second, the vision should *elaborate a purpose for the organization.* Every organization has a purpose, and that purpose should be specified in the organization's vision. That way, all organizational stakeholders are explicitly aware of why this organization exists.

The third component is that the vision should *include a brief summary of what the organization does.* While it doesn't provide explicit details (that's what the various mission statements do, which we'll discuss shortly), it should explain what's being done to fulfill the purpose. And, this is a good time to say that while they're related, there *is* a difference between an organization's purpose and what it does. For example, several organizations may have the purpose of ecological preservation, but the way they carry out that purpose (i.e., what they do) may be different.

The last component of the vision is that it should *specify broad goals.* Goals provide a target that all organizational members work toward meeting. Goals also serve to unify organizational members toward a common end. An organization's vision can and should be a guiding force in every decision.

Although an organizational vision provides an overall picture of where the organization would like to be in the future, a **mission statement** is a statement of what specific organizational units do and what they hope to accomplish. An organization will have a single vision and

STRATEGIC MANAGEMENT IN ACTION

Although many old-line manufacturers only dream of transforming themselves into nimble technology companies, Corning Inc. **[www.corning.com]** has actually pulled it off. Maybe you (or older family members or friends) still have Corning baking dishes in your kitchen. The Corning that manufactured those dishes and other glassware still works mostly in glass but in forms that most people would not recognize. The company has shifted its focus to products such as optical fiber and liquid crystal display screens. In fact, the company states that it has a proud history of "enriching people's lives through research and technological innovation."

TO DO

- Go to Corning's Web site, find the company's seven values, and describe them.
- How will these values affect the way organizational employees manage strategically?

Sources: J. A. Miller, Jr., "Out of Near-Death Experience Into a Chaotic Global Economy: How Corning Rediscovered Its Innovation Roots," *Research Technology Management,* November/ December 2011, pp. 26–31; R. A. O'Leary, G. Jusela, and H. N. Topper, "Corning Incorporated: Creating the Next Generation of Innovation Leaders," *Global Business & Organizational Excellence,* November/ December, 2011, pp. 71–89; S. Silver, "Corning's Biggest Bet Yet? Diesel-Filter Technologies," *Wall Street Journal,* March 7, 2008, pp. B1+; S. M. Mehta, "Bend It Like Corning," *Fortune,* August 6, 2007, pp. 69–70; S. Silver, "Corning May Offer Window of Opportunity," *Wall Street Journal,* August 24, 2006, p. C3; Associated Press, "Corning Chairman Houghton Steps Back from Active Duty," *Wall Street Journal,* May 2, 2006, p. B8; K. Maney, "Corning CEO Insists on Keeping His Eye on Long-Term Ball," *USA Today,* May 11, 2005, p. 3B; A. Carter, "Reigniting Corning," *Money,* May 2003 [www.cnnmoney.com]; J. Kimelman, "Corning May Be Turning a Corner," *New York Times,* May 4, 2003, Section 3, p. 6; and T. Aeppel, "Corning's Makeover: From Casseroles to Fiber Optics," *Wall Street Journal,* July 16, 1999, p. B4.

THE GREY ZONE

Are vision and mission statements just a bunch of empty words? A study of several securities firms and investment banks showed that many hours had been spent crafting elegant mission statements that extolled the virtues of teamwork, integrity, and respect for the individual. Yet, the partners at those firms treated their young analysts like second-class citizens. They gave them work that wasn't commensurate with their skills, were openly impolite to them, and, in many instances, were verbally abusive toward them. When these conditions were described to the top decision makers, they said that kind of behavior couldn't be happening—it went against their companies' mission statements. Yet, this type of situation doesn't occur just in securities firms.

THINK ABOUT

- Could this situation have been prevented? If so, how? If not, why not?
- How can strategic decision makers make sure that vision and mission statements are more than empty words?

potentially several mission statements (divisional, departmental, project work group, etc.) that contribute to the pursuit of the organization's vision. A mission statement provides a focus for employees as they make and implement strategic decisions. Although it's not as broad as the organizational vision, a mission statement provides an overview of each unit's purpose, what it does, and its goals. Each mission statement also aligns with the organizational vision.

CSR and Ethics

How much and what type of corporate social responsibility (CSR) business organizations should pursue has been a topic of heated debate for a number of years. **CSR** is the obligation of organizational decision makers to make decisions and act in ways that recognize the interrelatedness of business and society.[23] CSR recognizes the organization's various stakeholders and how they're dealt with. But, it's in the definition of "who" organizations are responsible to that we find a diversity of opinions.

The traditional view was that corporations existed solely to serve the interests of one stakeholder group—the stockholders.[24] The late Milton Friedman, the most outspoken advocate of this view, argued that corporate social programs and actions must be paid for in some way, which adds to the costs of doing business. Those costs must be either passed on to customers in the form of higher prices or absorbed by the organization. In either case, profitability suffers as customers might buy less at higher prices or organizational costs would increase. However, do understand that Friedman didn't say that organizations shouldn't be socially responsible. In fact, he felt they *should* be. But his argument was that the extent of the responsibility was to maximize shareholder returns.

However, the traditional—and purely economic—perspective of CSR has given way to a belief that organizations have a larger societal role to play and a broader constituency to serve than just stockholders alone. Yet, balancing various stakeholder demands is a complicated process as they typically have a wide range of needs and conflicting expectations.[25] What this means for managing strategically is making decisions in ways that will enhance the various stakeholder relationships. **Stakeholders** are individuals or groups who have a stake in or are influenced by an organization's decisions and actions and who, in turn, can influence the organization. Figure 2.5 identifies potential stakeholders with whom an organization may have to contend.

Many organizations believe that strong and socially responsible stakeholder relationships make them more competitive.[26] For instance, every day, General Mills ships three semitrailer trucks full of cereal and other packaged goods to food banks around the United States.[27] The message is loud and clear throughout the company that good corporate citizenship "doesn't

FIGURE 2.5

Potential Organizational
Stakeholders

end with the bottom line." In fact, performance reviews of top executives include an evaluation of community involvement. Although CSR emphasizes the broad picture of an organization's societal interactions, it's also important that these interactions take place in a context of "doing the right thing." That's where the concept of ethics comes in.

The financial scandals in 2001–2002 and 2008–2010 led many people to question how ethical corporate America really is. Thus, it was no wonder that 86 percent of consumers worldwide believe that a business needs to place at least as much weight on society's interests as it does on its own.[28] But it's not just corporate executives who deal with ethical issues. By this time in your life, you've undoubtedly faced numerous ethical dilemmas, both in school and, if you're employed, at your job. For instance, is it ethical to make a copy of inexpensive computer software for a friend who's short of money or to "donate" copies of completed case homework or other assignments to your sorority or fraternity? Or say that you work part-time as a telemarketing representative. Is it ethical for you to pressure customers to purchase a product just so you can win a prize? **Ethics** involves the principles that define right and wrong decisions and behavior. In other words, as we live our lives—attend school, work at a job, engage in hobbies, and so forth—certain decisions and behaviors are ethically "right" and certain decisions and behaviors are ethically "wrong." Ethical considerations should play a role in managing strategically. In fact, some individuals believe that ethics is both a personal and an organizational issue and should be part of the strategic management process.[29]

This means recognizing the ethical implications of the outcomes of strategic decisions and actions. It means considering more than just being in compliance with the law as organizational strategies are formulated and implemented. For example, Avon Products Inc. sells its cosmetics products mainly to women. When Avon asked women what their number one health concern

FOR YOUR INFORMATION
Ethics in Real Life

An ethics code should be more than great public relations. After all, Enron had a code of ethics, which is ironic considering the unethical behaviors exhibited by many of its top executives. The success—or failure—of corporate ethics programs has less to do with such things as written ethics codes and compliance hotlines and everything to do with why employees think the programs were established in the first place. For example, George David, former CEO of United Technologies Corporation (UTC), believed very deeply in the power of a code of ethics as does the current CEO Louis R. Chénevert, but the company's ethics program entails much more than that. Although the company has a detailed code of ethics, including 24 standards of conduct, it's not just having the written code that makes ethics work so well. (See the company's code at **http://utc.com/utc/Governance/Code_of_Ethics. html.**) It's the fact that employees know the behavioral expectations, especially when it comes to ethics. What can strategic decision makers do to make sure their companies' codes of ethics are effective? First, ethics codes should be developed and then communicated regularly and consistently to employees. Second, all levels of management should continually reaffirm the importance of the ethics code and the organization's commitment to it and consistently discipline those who break it. Finally, top management should set a good example. What they *do* is far more important than what they *say*.

THINK ABOUT

- What do you think of these suggestions? Do you agree? Why or why not?
- What are the implications of these ideas for managing strategically?
- What did you find at UTC's Web site that might be helpful to other strategic decision makers?

Sources: UTC Web site [http://utc.com/Governance/Ethics/Code+ of+Ethics], January 8, 2009; J. S. McClenahen, "UTC's Master of Principle," *Industry Week,* January 2003, pp. 30–36; and "Global Ethics Codes Gain Importance as a Tool to Avoid Litigation and Fines," *Wall Street Journal,* August 19, 1999.

---

was, breast cancer was the overwhelming answer. In response, Avon created its Worldwide Fund for Women's Health. This umbrella organization has spread around the globe. The company's biggest women's health program in this fund is the Breast Cancer Awareness Crusade in the United States. Through this program, the company's sales force educates women about breast cancer by distributing brochures about the disease on their sales visits. In this instance, Avon's strategic decision makers chose to develop and implement a sales strategy that addressed a significant customer concern. Was it the "right" thing to do? Well, Avon's decision makers think so. They were ethical in their dealings with customers, and those customers responded by boosting company sales. Although not every strategic decision will be this broad in scope, the ethical implications for managing strategically are clear: As you're managing strategically, ask yourself, what's the "right" thing to do in making this decision or taking this action? (The Grey Zone ethical dilemmas you'll see in each chapter emphasize the importance of understanding the role of ethics in strategic decision making.)

LEARNING REVIEW   LEARNING OUTCOME 2.3

- Discuss organizational vision and mission statements.
- Define corporate social responsibility.
- Explain who stakeholders are and why they're important to managing strategically.
- Discuss why ethics are important to strategic decision makers.

The Bottom Line

Learning Outcome 2.1: Describe the different perspectives on competitive advantage.

- *Managing strategically:* formulating and implementing strategies that allow an organization to develop and maintain a competitive advantage.
- *Competitive advantage:* what sets an organization apart; its competitive edge; necessary for long-term success and survival of an organization.
- *I/O view:* focuses on structural forces within an industry, the competitive environment of firms, and how these influence competitive advantage; developed by Mike Porter; involves understanding what makes an industry attractive, choosing an attractive industry in which to compete, and choosing an appropriate competitive position within that industry.
- *RBV:* a firm's unique resources are most important in getting and keeping competitive advantage; *resources* (all of the financial, physical, human, intangible, and structural/cultural assets used by an organization to develop, produce, and deliver products or services to its customers). To be unique, resources must add value (i.e., can be used to exploit positive or buffer against negative external changes), be rare (no other firms have it), be hard to imitate (duplicate) and substitute, and be exploitable.
- *Guerrilla view:* competitive advantage is temporary; successful organizations must be adept at rapidly and repeatedly disrupting current situations and radically surprising competitors to keep them off balance.

Learning Outcome 2.2: Explain the driving forces, implications, and critical success factors of the business environment.

- Three driving forces: (1) information revolution—information is the essential resource of production; (2) *technology* (using equipment, materials, knowledge, and experience to perform tasks), which impacts work in three ways: *innovation* (turning a creative idea into a product or process that can be used or sold), bottom-up or mass collaboration capability (customers and individuals have control), and performance (technology can be a powerful tool in helping organizations perform better); and (3) globalization (global marketplace and global competitors).
- Four major implications of these driving forces: (1) continual change stimulates need for *organizational change* (a structured transition in what organization does and how it does it); (2) reduced need for physical assets—value is found in intangible assets; (3) vanishing distance and compressed time—geography and time no longer play an important role in determining customers and competitors; (4) vulnerability—openness and interconnectedness can leave organization's information, facilities, and employees vulnerable.
- Three factors critical to success in this new context: (1) ability to embrace change—need *change agents* (someone who initiates and oversees change efforts); (2) *creativity* (ability to combine ideas in a unique way or to make unusual associations between ideas) and innovation capabilities; (3) being a *world-class organization* (an organization in which strategic decision makers are taking actions to help it be the best in the world at what it does).
- Characteristics include strong customer focus, continual learning and improvement, flexible organization structure, creative human resource management, egalitarian climate, and significant technological support.

Learning Outcome 2.3: Discuss two organizational elements that guide strategic decision makers in managing strategically in today's context.

- Need a single *organizational vision* (broad comprehensive picture of what a leader wants an organization to become), which should (1) be built on a foundation of the organization's core values and beliefs, (2) elaborate a purpose for the organization, (3) include a brief summary of what the organization does, and (4) specify broad goals.

- Also need a *mission statement* (statement of what specific organizational units do and what they hope to accomplish); likely will have several mission statements.

- Vision and mission reflect commitment to *CSR* (obligation of organizational decision makers to make decisions and act in ways that recognize the interrelatedness of business and society), to stakeholders (individuals or groups who have a stake in or are significantly influenced by the organization), and to *ethics* (principles that define right and wrong decisions and behavior).

YOU as strategic decision maker: building your skills

1. Organizational vision statements can take some interesting directions. Using the Web, find three examples of organizational vision statements and write them down.

   What do you think of these statements? Do they fit the four components of an organizational vision? How might these statements affect the strategic choices made by the company's strategic decision makers?

2. "Technology is fostering a free flow of information." Using a bulleted list format, write arguments supporting this statement. Then, write arguments against the statement. Be prepared to debate one or both sides in class.

3. To be useful, organizational "knowledge" has to be captured and used. Here are some suggestions for capturing and using it effectively: (a) keep it human; (b) focus on useful knowledge or "know-how"; (c) collect artifacts such as Post-it notes and other documents and make these public; (d) avoid an insular, isolated focus; and (e) keep your knowledge fresh. Explain what you think each of these suggestions means. As you write your explanations, discuss the implications for strategic decision makers.

4. For each of the following quotes, explain what you think they mean and the implications for understanding the context of managing strategically.
   - "To stay ahead, you must have your next idea waiting in the wings." (Rosabeth Moss Kanter, management professor/consultant/author)
   - "Time is a river of passing events, and strong is its current; no sooner is a thing brought to sight than it is swept by and another takes its place, and this too will be swept away." (Marcus Aurelius Antoninus)

5. Every year, *Fortune* publishes lists of America's most admired companies and the global most admired companies. Choose one list. Get the most recent one, and answer the following questions.
   - Define the key attributes used to evaluate companies.
   - What 10 companies are at the top of the list of most admired?
   - Why do you think these companies are at the top of the list? What are they doing differently—that is, how are they managing strategically?
   - What 10 companies are at the bottom of the list? How are they managing strategically?
   - What could strategic decision makers learn from both groups?

6. The total quality management (TQM) movement encouraged organizational managers to *Do it right the first time*. Make it right the first time, and you eliminate waste. Finish it right the first time, and you save money, time, and customer relationships. Makes sense, doesn't it? However, what if *doing it right the first time* stifles creativity and risk taking? Because breakthrough innovations are rarely well-planned, mistake-free processes, wouldn't an emphasis on *doing it right* suppress going out on a limb to try something different? Maybe *doing it right* isn't as important as *doing it best*. What do you think? Write a paper exploring these concepts.

STRATEGIC
MANAGEMENT
IN ACTION

CASES

CASE #1 Out of Focus

This Strategic Management in Action case can be found at the beginning of Chapter 2.

Discussion Questions

1. Using Figure 2.3, describe the context facing Kodak. Focus especially on describing the driving forces that are affecting the photographic film industry and the implications of these driving forces.

2. Again, using Figure 2.3, does Kodak have what it takes to succeed in light of this context? Explain.

3. What ethical and social responsibility issues do you think Kodak faces as it struggles? What can it do to ensure that it's meeting its responsibilities?

4. How would proponents of the I/O view analyze this case? How about proponents of the RBV? How about proponents of the guerrilla view?

CASE #2 Troubles in Toyland?

Move over, Ken—Barbie's got a brand new interest. Brought back out of obscurity in 2011 after being dumped on Valentine's Day 2004, Ken is once again about to booted to the backseat as Barbie ventures into the online world with Stardolls, the Web's largest online virtual paperdoll community. As the world's largest toymaker, Mattel plans to merge the offline and online worlds of doll play by offering an extensive line of "Stardoll by Barbie" fashion dolls. This is a significant strategic move for the company as Mattel "has been very hesitant to link its nearly $4 billion Barbie brand with other licensed brands." However, as one analyst said, "think of it as the marriage of the toy world's No. 1 fashion doll with the online world's No. 1 fashion doll." And it's a well-intentioned bid by Mattel to attract and keep a tough crowd: hard-to-please girls up to age 10. Although Barbie has been and continues to be a global best-seller for Mattel, the company's management team recognized that it had to look for ways to strategically move to where its market was moving. And that included the online world.

The company's CEO Robert Eckert, who came to Mattel from Kraft, Inc. in 2000, has said that running a toy company isn't much different from a food company since each is mainly a branded consumer goods company. However, a toy company has to appeal to moms on the entertainment value and increasingly, the educational value of its products. In doing this, competitors, such as Hasbro, have attempted to move into TV and movies. And Hasbro has had its share of problems. Toy experts say that Hasbro has been "slow to adapt to online gaming and has neglected its most profitable business, board games, as it pursues turning its toys into movie and television stars."

Under Eckert's leadership, however, Mattel has stuck with what fans say it does best—create and sell iconic toys. And recently, Mattel has had a string of hits, including a popular line of Monster High characters based on the teenage kids of the likes of Dracula and Werewolf, and a Hot Wheels Wall Tracks where a kid builds a track set on the wall instead of on the floor. Yet, Eckert says that the company has to walk a fine line between making toys too sophisticated. "If it does too much of the work and takes out too much of imagination and play value, it will fail."

Discussion Questions

1. Using Figure 2.3, describe the context facing Mattel. What driving forces are affecting the toy industry?

2. Think about toys you had as a child. How are today's toys different? What are the implications for the toy industry?

3. How is Mattel positioning itself to be successful in this context? What do you think of its approaches? Explain.

4. What issues might a company face when it replaces its top leader with someone who has no experience in that industry? Think both about the benefits and the drawbacks of doing so.

5. What can other companies learn from Mattel's approaches?

Sources: Based on A. Zimmerman, "Hasbro Falls Prey to 'Angry Birds,'" *Wall Street Journal*, December 15, 2011, pp. B1+; B. Horovitz, "Barbie Ventures Into Online World with Stardolls," *USA Today*, November 14, 2011, p. 1B; A. Zimmerman, "For Mattel's Chief: Toys and Cheese Aren't That Different," *Wall Street Journal*, November 7, 2011, p. B8; and J. Kell, "Mattel Has Holiday Hopes as Sales Keep Up Momentum," *Wall Street Journal*, October 15–16, 2011, p. B3.

CASE #3 Game Not Over, Not Yet

Although their expertise lies in creating games, it's definitely serious business for the video game industry. The computer and video game industry has struggled over the last couple of years as game makers looked for new sources of revenues and worked to hold down costs. And nipping at the industry's heels were companies like Zynga that saw the opportunities and jumped in on the burgeoning social gaming revolution. One company, Electronics Arts (EA), exemplifies the challenges of this industry, where customers are fickle and demanding and competition is intense. As one of the world's top three interactive entertainment software companies, EA lives and dies by its innovations. Its product lineup includes more than 100 titles such as *Battlefield*, *Madden NFL*, *FIFA Soccer*, *Rock Band*, *Need for Speed*, and *The Simpsons*. The company has created more than 50 best-sellers (each with more than 1 million copies sold) since 1998. In 2011, revenues were almost $3.6 billion—a decrease of almost 2 percent from the previous year—and the company had a net loss of $276 million. The last three years have been quite challenging as the company lowered its sales and profit projections because of changes in the behavior of consumers and retailers. In addition, EA missed the initial social gaming trend, but is now pushing hard to develop digital platforms for many of its popular games. As a result, its *Sims Social* is the number 2 game on Facebook, behind Zynga's CityVille.

EA continues to look for ways to prosper. Paranoia has been a critical part of EA's strategy for success. A top game title takes anywhere from 12 to 36 months to produce and costs between $5 million and $10 million. That's a significant investment risk riding on the company's ability to be innovative. John Riccitello (former president and chief operating officer who left the company in 2004 to start a private equity firm but then returned in 2007 as CEO) has guided much of the company's game design accomplishments. He said, "The forgotten aspect of creativity is discipline." The hard part, and the part that EA pursues relentlessly, "is identifying the right idea, assembling the best development team, solving the inevitable technical problems, creating a game that people want to play, getting all of the work done on schedule, getting it to market at the right time, and knowing how to generate buzz about it in an increasingly crowded market." How does EA do it?

It starts with the discipline of understanding ideas. Game designers try to identify the creative center of a game—what they call the "creative x"—so they understand what the game is about.

Then, it's the discipline of understanding the customers by using focus groups to pinpoint desires and likes and dislikes. And it's the discipline of sharing best practices and technologies through the company's intranet library. As one employee said, "If somebody develops a better blade of grass in one game, that grass will be in somebody else's game the next day." Then, there's the discipline of developing the next generation of creative leaders. The company's "emerging leaders" program gives participants firsthand experience in departments outside their own. *And* there's the discipline of studying the competition. Employees are encouraged to know the features of competitors' products. Then, it's disciplined project management. Riccitello, known for his strict discipline, said, "If you're working on a game and you miss your deadlines, you won't be working here very long." Although the discipline of creativity is important at EA, you can't overlook the passion of the company's game designers. Nearly everyone at EA grew up playing games. They love what they do and are inspired to look for new and creative challenges not only for the hard-core gamers, but for the casual gamers as well.

Discussion Questions

1. Describe EA's competitive advantage from each of the three perspectives on competitive advantage.
2. Does EA exhibit the critical success factors for the new business context? Explain.
3. Describe the types of resources EA appears to have. Do you think any of these resources might be unique? Explain.
4. What ethical and social responsibility issues might EA face as it develops new games? What would be the best approach for dealing with those issues?
5. What stakeholders might EA have to be concerned with, and how might those stakeholders affect EA's strategic decisions and actions?

Sources: Based on A. Konrad, "Electronic Arts' Digital Makeover," *Fortune*, December 12, 2011, p. 60; M. Snider, "EA Lets Slip the Dogs of War with 'Battlefield 3'," *USA Today*, October 24, 2011, pp. 1B+; D. Leonard, "Master of the Game," *Bloomberg BusinessWeek*, July 4–July 10, 2011, pp. 72–77; A. Vance, "EA's Plan to Get You To Play Everywhere," *Bloomberg BusinessWeek*, May 9–May 15, 2011, pp. 37–39; M. Snider, "Electronic Arts' Multiplatform Gaming Approach Pays Off," *USA Today*, May 6, 2011, p. 3B; T. Burke, "The Hitmakers," *CFO*, November 2008, pp. 43–47; and C. Salter, "Playing to Win," *Fast Company*, December 2002, pp. 80–91.

CASE #4 Bridging the Gap

It's a retailing puzzle Gap has been struggling to solve for almost a decade. The once-trendy brand "is stuck in American retail's hollowed-out midsection, which consumers have been abandoning for years as they split their dollars between cheap basics and must-have luxury items." CEO Glenn Murphy, "who has long preached the importance of speed to his executives," pushed to minimize the corporate bureaucratic processes and get clothes to stores faster, especially since foreign retailers like H&M and Zara

already do this and do it well. As Gap struggles, competitors are stealing customers with cheaper and fresher fashion. So what is Murphy facing as he attempts to turn around the company?

One problem facing Gap (but also other apparel retailers) is rising raw materials costs. Gap said that costs per item would increase 20 percent—an increase it wouldn't be able to pass on to customers. These costs, including increasing price for cotton and rising labor costs in manufacturing centers such as China, were going up faster than expected, putting strong pressure on profits. Although rising materials costs are serious for any business, the biggest problem Gap has struggled with is its clothing designs. After being the "must-have" brand during the 1980s and 1990s, Gap's fashions have stumbled. During the early years of the 21st century, Gap faltered when it completely misjudged fashion trends. As discount retailers like Target and Wal-Mart began to compete with Gap on its basic fashions, Gap began offering hip-huggers, sparkly t-shirts, and other pop fashions that failed to attract the Britney Spears' look-a-likes and drove away Gap's core target customers. Those customers—who always counted on Gap for fashion basics such as khaki pants, denim, t-shirts, polos, and other casual wear—fled to other competitors, and the company has suffered years of disappointing sales and earnings. How bad have things gotten at Gap? One crucial measure used by retailers—sales at stores open at least a year—showed that starting in 2005, Gap's North American stores have had annual decreases in sales; not the results that company executives want to see. And then there's Gap's marketing efforts. Gap's ad campaigns were once the talk of the fashion world. They were fun, quirky, and effective. However, as a leading ad agency executive said, "Gap has sort of lost its story and lost its focus on what made it different and special." Yet, the right marketing moves won't work without the right merchandise in Gap stores. As you can see, CEO Murphy and his executive team have their work cut out for them in tailoring a turnaround.

Discussion Questions

1. Using Figure 2.3, describe the context facing Gap. Focus especially on describing the driving forces that affect the fashion industry and the implications of these driving forces.
2. Again, using Figure 2.3, does Gap have what it takes to succeed in light of this context? Explain.
3. As the case stated, CEO Murphy has long preached the importance of speed to his executives. What does this mean as far as attempts to minimize the corporate bureaucratic processes and get clothes to stores faster? What would being "fast" or "speedy" involve? Be as specific as possible.
4. How would proponents of the I/O view analyze this case? How about proponents of the RBV? How about proponents of the guerrilla view?

Sources: Based on D. Mattioli and K. Hudson, "Gap to Slash Its Store Count," *Wall Street Journal,* October 14, 2011, pp. B1+; E. Holmes, "Gap Gets Squeezed by Costs," *Wall Street Journal,* May 20, 2011, p. B1; E. Holmes, "Gap CEO Tailors Urgent Revamp," *Wall Street Journal,* May 19, 2011, p. B8; S. Clifford, "Gap Dismisses Its Design Chief as Sales Falter," *New York Times Online,* May 5, 2011; S. Elliott, "Gap Seeks to Freshen Itself as a 'People's Brand'," *New York Times Online,* April 7, 2011; and J. Dickler, "Consumers: We Want Gucci or Target. Forget the Gap," *CNNMoney.com,* March 9, 2011.

Endnotes

1. M. Spector and D. Mattioli, "Kodak Teeters on the Brink," *Wall Street Journal,* January 5, 2012, pp. A1+; D. Mattioli and M. Spector, "Kodak's Rescue Plans Hit Hurdles," *Wall Street Journal,* December 19, 2011, pp. B1+; M. Daneman, "Kodak Is Determined to Survive," *USA Today,* December 13, 2011, pp. 1B+; M. Spector and D. Mattioli, "Kodak Shuffles Advisers as It Fights to Avoid Bankruptcy," *Wall Street Journal,* December 6, 2011, p. B7; D. Mattioli, "Kodak's Online Gallery Up for Sale," *Wall Street Journal,* November 18, 2011, p. B1+; D. Mattioli, "Squeeze Tightens on Kodak," *Wall Street Journal,* November 4, 2011, p. B2; M. Daneman, "Kodak's Future Rests on Loans, Patent Sale," *USA Today,* November 4, 2011, p. 2B; A. Martin, "Kodak Posts Wider Loss Than Expected," *New York Times Online,* November 3, 2011; D. Mattioli and M. Spector, "Kodak's Dwindling Cash Pile in Focus," *Wall Street Journal,* October 31, 2011, p. B2; M. Spector and D. Mattioli, "Kodak Seeks Rescue Funds," *Wall Street Journal,* October 25, 2011, p. B2; D. Mattioli and M. Spector, "Kodak Tensions Rise," *Wall Street Journal,* October 24, 2011, p. B7; A. Martin, "Negative Exposure for Kodak," *New York Times Online,* October 20, 2011; D. Mattioli, "Kodak Licenses Patents to Imax," *Wall Street Journal,* October 17, 2011, p. B3; B. Dobbin, "In Kodak's Troubles, A Snaphot of an Icon's Fall," Associated Press Business Writer, *Springfield, Missouri, News-Leader,* October 6, 2011, p. 4A; M. Spector and D. Mattioli, "Kodak Seeks Help As Fears Mount," *Wall Street Journal,* October 1–2, 2011, p. B1; A. Martin and M. J. De La Merced, "Kodak Hires Legal Adviser Amid Talk of Bankruptcy," *New York Times Online,* September 30, 2011; P. R. LaMonica, "Kodak: Death of an American Icon?" *CNNMoney.com,* September 28, 2011; D. Mattioli and M. Jarzemsky, "Clock Ticks as Kodak Burns Cash," *Wall Street Journal,* September 27, 2011, p. B1; A. Martin, "Kodak Stock Dives After Credit Line is Tapped," *New York Times Online,* September 26, 2011; D. Mattioli, J. S. Lublin, and E. Byron, "Kodak Struggles to Find Its Moment," *Wall Street Journal,* August 10, 2011, pp. A1+; and B. Dobbin, "A Decade-Long Nose-Dive in Photographic Film Sales Signals End of an Era," Associated Press, *Toledo Blade.com,* June 2, 2011.

2. This discussion of industrial/organization perspective is based on K. R. Conner, "A Historical Comparison of Resource-Based Theory and Five Schools of Thought within Industrial Organization Economics: Do We Have a New Theory of the Firm?" *Journal of Management,* vol. 17, no. 1, 1991, pp. 121–154; M. Porter, *Competitive Advantage: Creating and Sustaining Superior Performance* (New York: Free Press, 1985); and M. Porter, *Competitive Strategy: Techniques for Analyzing Industries and Competitors* (New York: Free Press, 1980).

3. This discussion of RBV is based on J. B. Barney, D. J. Ketchen, Jr., and M. Wright, "The Future of Resource-Based Theory: Revitalization or Decline?" *Journal of Management,* September 2011, pp. 1299–1315; R. Makadok, "The Four Theories of Profit and Their Joint Effects," *Journal of Management,* September 2011, pp. 1316–1334; B. Wernerfelt, "The Use of Resources of Resource Acquisition," *Journal of Management,* September 2011, pp. 1369–1373; J. C. Molloy, C. Chadwick, R. E. Ployhart, and S. J. Golden, "Making Intangibles 'Tangible' in Tests of Resource-Based Theory: A Multidisciplinary Construct Validation Approach," *Journal of Management,* September 2011, pp. 1496–1518; C. E. Armstrong and K. Shimizu, "A Review of Approaches to Empirical Research on the Resource-Based View of the Firm," *Journal of Management,* December 2007, pp. 959–986; S. L. Newbert, "Empirical Research on the Resource-Based View of the Firm: An Assessment and Suggestions for Future Research," *Strategic Management Journal,* February 2007, pp. 121–146; D. G. Simon, M. A. Hitt, and R. D. Ireland, "Managing Firm Resources in Dynamic Environments to Create Value: Looking Inside the Black Box," *Academy of Management Review,* January 2007, pp. 273–292; A. A. Lado, N. G. Boyd, P. Wright, and M. Kroll, "Paradox and Theorizing within the Resource-Based View," *Academy of Management Review,* January 2006, pp. 115–131; D. G. Hoopes, T. L. Madsen, and G. Walker, "Guest Editors' Introduction to the Special Issue: Why Is There a Resource-Based View? Toward a Theory of Competitive Heterogeneity," *Strategic Management Journal,* October 2003, pp. 889–902; A. M. Rugman and A. Verbeke, "Edith Penrose's Contribution to the Resource-Based View of Strategic Management," *Strategic Management Journal,* August 2002, pp. 769–780; J. B. Barney, "Looking Inside for Competitive Advantage," *Academy of Management Executive,* November 1995, pp. 49–61; J. B. Barney and E. J. Zajac, "Competitive Organizational Behavior: Toward an Organizationally Based Theory of Competitive Advantage," *Strategic Management Journal,* Winter 1995, pp. 5–9; R. Ashkenas,

"Capability: Strategic Tool for a Competitive Edge," *Journal of Business Strategy,* November/December 1995, pp. 13–15; J. B. Black and K. B. Boal, "Strategic Resources: Traits, Configurations, and Paths to Sustainable Competitive Advantage," *Strategic Management Journal,* Summer 1995, pp. 131–138; B. Wernerfelt, "The Resource-Based View of the Firm: Ten Years After," *Strategic Management Journal,* March 1995, pp. 171–174; D. J. Collis, "Research Notes: How Valuable Are Organizational Capabilities," *Strategic Management Journal,* Winter 1994, pp. 143–152; R. Hall, "A Framework Linking Intangible Resources and Capabilities to Sustainable Competitive Advantage," *Academy of Management Journal,* November 1993, pp. 607–618; M. A. Peteraf, "The Cornerstones of Competitive Advantage: A Resource-Based View," *Strategic Management Journal,* March 1993, pp. 179–191; R. Amit and P. J. H. Schoemaker, "Strategic Assets and Organizational Rent," *Strategic Management Journal,* January 1993, pp. 33–46; R. M. Grant, "The Resource-Based Theory of Competitive Advantage: Implications for Strategy Formulation," *California Management Review,* Spring 1991, pp. 114–135; J. B. Barney, "Firm Resources and Sustained Competitive Advantage," *Journal of Management,* vol. 17, no. 1, 1991, pp. 99–120; K. R. Conner, "A Historical-Based Comparison of Resource-Based Theory and Five Schools of Thought within Industrial Organization Economics: Do We Have a New Theory of the Firm?" vol. 35, 1991; J. B. Barney, "Asset Stocks and Sustained Competitive Advantage: A Comment," *Management Science,* December 1989, pp. 1511–1513; I. Dierickx and K. Cool, "Asset Stock Accumulation and Sustainability of Competitive Advantage," *Management Science,* December 1989, pp. 1504–1511; R. P. Rumelt, "Towards a Strategic Theory of the Firm," in R. B. Lamb (ed.), *Competitive Strategic Management* (Upper Saddle River, NJ: Prentice Hall, 1984), pp. 556–570; and B. Wernerfelt, "A Resource-Based View of the Firm," *Strategic Management Journal,* vol. 14, 1984, pp. 4–12.

4. This discussion of the guerrilla view is based on M.-J. Chen, H.-C. Lin, and J. G. Michel, "Navigating in a Hypercompetitive Environment: The Roles of Action Aggressiveness and TMT Integration," *Strategic Management Journal,* December 2010, pp. 1410-1430; R. R. Wiggins and T. W. Ruefli, "Schumpeter's Ghost: Is Hypercompetition Making the Best of Times Shorter?" *Strategic Management Journal,* October 2005, pp. 887–911; G. Hamel and L. Valikangas, "Zero Trauma—The Essence of Resilience," *Wall Street Journal,* September 16, 2003, p. B2; C. A. Lengnick-Hall and

J. A. Wolff, "Similarities and Contradictions in the Core Logic of Three Strategy Research Streams," *Strategic Management Journal,* December 1999, pp. 1109–1132; V. Rindova and C. J. Fombrun, "Constructing Competitive Advantage: The Role of Firm-Constituent Interactions," *Strategic Management Journal,* August 1999, pp. 691–710; K. M. Eisenhardt and S. L. Brown, "Patching: Restitching Business Portfolios in Dynamic Markets," *Harvard Business Review,* May–June 1999, pp. 72–81; B. Chakravarthy, "A New Strategy Framework for Coping With Turbulence," *Sloan Management Review,* Winter 1997, pp. 69–82; R. A. D'Aveni, *Hypercompetition: Managing the Dynamics of Strategic Maneuvering* (New York: Free Press, 1994); D. J. Collis, "Research Note: How Valuable Are Organizational Capabilities?" *Strategic Management Journal,* Winter Special Issue, 1994, pp. 143–152; and K. M. Eisenhardt, "Making Fast Strategic Decisions in High-Velocity Environments," *Academy of Management Journal,* December 1989, pp. 543–576.

5. J. B. Barney, "Looking Inside for Competitive Advantage," *Academy of Management Executive,* November 1995, pp. 49–61.

6. J. Collis and M. T. Hansen, "Collins on Chaos: Book Excerpt," *Fortune,* October 17, 2011, pp. 157-170; M. Conlin, "Ideas: The Concepts That Are Reshaping the Business World and All of Our Lives," *BusinessWeek,* December 18, 2006, pp. 96–107; M. Mandel, "Why the Economy Is a Lot Stronger than You Think," *BusinessWeek,* February 13, 2006, pp. 62–70; G. Hitt, "Can President's Plan Keep America Competitive," *Wall Street Journal,* February 2, 2006, pp. A1+; J. Robison, "Is the U.S. Losing Its Competitive Edge?" *Gallup Management Journal Online,* July 14, 2005; "10 Driving Principles of the New Economy," *Business 2.0,* March 2000, pp. 191–284; and M. Mandel, "The New Economy," *BusinessWeek,* January 31, 2000, pp. 73–77.

7. L. Mearian, "World's Data Will Grow by 50x in Next Decade," *Computerworld Online,* June 28, 2011; J. Gantz and D. Reinsel, "Extracting Value from Chaos," *idcdocserve.com,* June 2011; Pui-Wing Tam, "Cutting Files Down to Size," *Wall Street Journal,* May 8, 2007, p. B4; and B. Bergstein, "Study: More Data than Space to Hold It," *Springfield, Missouri, News-Leader,* March 11, 2007, p. 1E.

8. D. Sparks, "An Economy of Change," *Miller-McCune,* May–June 2009, pp. 18–19; A. Toffler and H. Toffler, *Revolutionary Wealth* (New York: Alfred A. Knopf, 2006); and P. F. Drucker, *Post-Capitalist Society* (New York: HarperBusiness, 1993).

9. J. McGregor, "The World's Most Innovative Companies," *BusinessWeek,* April 24, 2006, p. 64.

10. Enterprise Innovation Editors, "Innovation Key to Unlocking Business Success," *Enterprise Innovation. net,* April 15, 2011.

11. Ibid, p. 76.

12. G. Naik, "R& D Spending To Keep on Climbing," *Wall Street Journal,* December 16, 2011, p. A4; "Stability Returns to R&D Funding," *R&D Magazine,* December 2010, pp. 33–35; and M. D. Lemonick, "Are We Losing Our Edge?" *Time,* February 13, 2006, pp. 22–33.

13. C. Costea, A. Varga, and F. Cinnati, "How Transnational Companies Are Affected by Globalization," *International Journal of Management,* December 2011, pp. 286–290; S. A. Zahra, "The Changing Rules of Global Competitiveness in the 21st Century," *Academy of Management Executive,* February 1999, pp. 36–42; J. A. Petrick, R. F. Shcere, J. D. Brodzinski, J. F. Quinn, and M. F. Ainina, "Global Leadership Skills and Reputational Capital: Intangible Resources for Sustainable Competitive Advantage," *Academy of Management Executive,* February 1999, pp. 58–69; and H. Thomas, T. Pollock, and P. Gorman, "Global Strategic Analyses: Frameworks and Approaches," *Academy of Management Executive,* February 1999, pp. 70–82.

14. "Workplace Security," Special section of *Wall Street Journal,* September 29, 2003, pp. R1–R7; D. Kirkpatrick, "Taking Back the Net," *Fortune,* September 29, 2003, pp. 117–122; T. Purdum, "Preparing for the Worst," *Industry Week,* January 2003, pp. 53–55; and S. Leibs, "Lesson from 9/11: It's Not about Data," *CFO,* September 2002, pp. 31–32.

15. B. E. Perrott, "Strategic Issue Management as Change Catalyst," *Strategy & Leadership,* vol. 39, no. 5 (2011), pp. 20–29; and B. C. Reimann, "The New Strategic Leadership: Driving Change, Getting Results!" *Planning Review,* September–October 1994, pp. 6–8.

16. R. Rothermel and J. LaMarsh, "Managing Change Through Employee Empowerment," *Global Business & Organizational Excellence,* January/February 2012, pp. 17–23; and "People Power: Enlisting the Agents of Change," *Chief Executive,* May 1995, pp. 516+.

17. This definition is based on T. M. Amabile, "A Model of Creativity and Innovation in Organizations," in B. M. Staw and L. L. Cummings (eds.), *Research in Organizational Behavior,* vol. 10 (Greenwich, CT: JAI Press, 1988), p. 126.

18. J. B. Quinn, "The Intelligent Enterprise: A New Paradigm," *Academy of Management Executive,* November 2005, pp. 109–121; and R. M. Hodgetts, F. Luthans, and S. M. Lee, "New Paradigm Organizations: From Total Quality to Learning to World Class," *Organizational Dynamics,* Winter 1994, pp. 4–19.

19. P. Levy, "Mission vs. Vision," *Marketing News,* February 28, 2011, p. 19; S. F. Marino, "Where There Is No Visionary, Companies Falter," *Industry Week,* March 15, 1999, p. 20; D. I. Silvers, "Vision— Not Just for CEOs," *Management Quarterly,* Winter 1994–95, pp. 10–14.

20. J. Lord, "How to Define and Implement a Vision For Your Company," *Manager,* Summer 2011, p. 24; L. Larwood, C. M. Falbe, M. P. Kriger, and P. Miesing, "Structure and Meaning of Organizational Vision," *Academy of Management Journal,* June 1995, pp. 740–769; and S. L. Oswald, K. W. Mossholder, and S. G. Harris, "Vision Salience and Strategic Involvement: Implications for Psychological Attachment to Organization and Job," *Strategic Management Journal,* July 1994, pp. 477–489.

21. S. H. Cady, J. V. Wheeler, J. DeWolf, and M. Brodke, "Mission, Vision, and Values: What Do They Say?" *Organization Development Journal,* Spring 2011, pp. 63–78; and D. I. Silvers, "Vision—Not Just for CEOs."

22. AMA 2002 Corporate Values Survey, American Management Association Web site [www.amanet. org], October 30, 2002.

23. D. J. Wood, "Corporate Social Performance Revisited," *Academy of Management Review,* October 1991, pp. 691–718.

24. M. Friedman, *Capitalism and Freedom* (Chicago: University of Chicago Press, 1962).

25. L. D. Lerner and G. E. Fryxell, "CEO Stakeholder Attitudes and Corporate Social Activity in the *Fortune 500,*" *Business and Society,* April 1994, pp. 58–81.

26. E. Laise, "A Few Good Companies," *Smart Money,* January 2004, pp. 25–27; and P. W. Roberts and G. R. Dowling, "Corporate Reputation and Sustained Superior Financial Performance," *Strategic Management Journal,* December 2002, pp. 1077–1093.

27. M. Conlin, J. Hempel, J. Tanzer, and D. Polek, "The Corporate Donors," *BusinessWeek,* December 1, 2003, pp. 92–96.

28. G. M. Maddock and R. L. Viton, "Co-Creating Planet-Friendly Profits," *Bloomberg Businessweek Online,* December 21, 2010.

29. L. T. Hosmer, "Strategic Planning as if Ethics Mattered," *Strategic Management Journal,* Summer 1994, pp. 17–34; L. S. Paine, "Managing for Organizational Integrity," *Harvard Business Review,* March–April 1994, pp. 106–117; and A. E. Singer, "Strategy as Moral Philosophy," *Strategic Management Journal,* March 1994, pp. 192–213.

LEARNING OUTCOMES

3.1 **Describe an external analysis.**

3.2 **Explain how to do an external analysis of an organization's specific and general environments.**

3.3 **Discuss the benefits and challenges of doing an external analysis.**

STRATEGIC MANAGEMENT IN ACTION

CASE #1 Not Sold Out

After a couple of years of slight attendance increases, competitors in the movie theater industry had hoped the threats they faced were behind them.[1] Then along came the economic downturn. Ticket sales revenue in 2011 fell 4 percent from the previous year and attendance was down 4.8 percent. The numbers of people going to see a movie were the smallest since 1995. The industry tried to pump up revenue with high-profile movies, higher ticket prices, and premium amenities. What should industry decision makers do now?

The number of movie screens in the United States totals a little more than 39,000. Together, the four largest movie theater chains in the United States have almost 19,000 screens—and a lot of seats to fill. The largest, Regal Entertainment Group (based in Knoxville, Tennessee), has more than 6,800 screens. AMC Entertainment (based in Kansas City, Missouri) has some 5,400 screens. The other two major competitors are Cinemark (based in Plano, Texas—about 3,800 screens) and Carmike Cinemas (based in Columbus, Georgia—about 2,300 screens). The challenge for the big four competitors (and others in the industry) is getting people to watch movies on all those screens, a decision that encompasses many factors.

Aaron Kohr/Fotolia.com

One important factor, according to industry analysts, is the uncertainty over how people want their movies delivered, which is largely a trade-off between convenience and quality (or what the experts call fidelity experience). Will consumers choose convenience over quality and use mobile devices such as iPads? Will they trade some quality for convenience and watch at home on surround-sound, flat-screen, high-definition home theater systems? Or will they go to a movie theater with wide screens, high-quality sound systems, and the social experience of being with other moviegoers and enjoy the highest fidelity experience—even with the inconveniences? Movie theater competitors believe that mobile devices aren't much of a threat, even though they may be convenient. On the other hand, home theater systems may be more of a threat as they've become more affordable and have "acceptable" quality. Although not likely to replace any of these higher-quality offerings, drive-in theaters, analysts note, are experiencing a resurgence, especially in geographic locations where they can be open year-round.

Another factor strategic decision makers need to wrestle with is the impression consumers have of the movie-going experience. A consumer lifestyle poll showed that the major dislike about going to the movies was the cost, a drawback cited by 36 percent of the respondents. Other factors noted included the noise, uncomfortable seats, the inconvenience, the crowds, and too many previews/commercials before the movie.

A final question facing the movie theater industry *and* the major film studios is how to be proactive in avoiding the problems that the recorded music industry faced with the illegal downloading of songs. The amount of entertainment sold online (which includes both music and video) continues to experience double digit growth. The biggest threat so far has been YouTube, which has become a powerful force in the media world with owner Google's backing. To counter that threat, industry executives have asked for filtering mechanisms to keep unlawful material off the site and to develop some type of licensing arrangements whereby the industry has some protection over its copyrighted film content.

Given these factors, what are the movie theater chains doing? The president of the National Association of Theatre Owners says, "Every decade or so, some new technology is supposed to be the death of movies. Television, video cassettes, the Internet. But, we're still around." However, theater owners aren't just kicking back with a bucket of popcorn. Instead, they're finding ways to make the movie-going experience something special, using such strategies as variable pricing (extending matinee discounts to weeknights or even pricing certain films higher); an all-digital approach with digitized film, satellite delivery of film to theaters, digital keys that "unlock" the film and limit the number of times it can be played, and digital projection (visual and sound); and more and better amenities such as online ticket sales, babysitting, valet parking, alcoholic beverages, and freshly cooked meals. Some movie theaters are even broadcasting live simulcasts of baseball games and rock concerts. As one theater executive said, "We're a little like the drug business. We are the pushers and our customers are the users. Even if business is good, you have to keep giving people more of what they want."

This chapter-opening case illustrates why strategic decision makers must pay attention to changes in the external environment and continue to monitor those changes. As the case points out, external factors can significantly affect companies' strategic decisions and actions. Being alert to changing trends such as customer tastes and habits, what competitors are doing, and even technology is an important step in formulating effective strategies. In this chapter, we'll first describe an external analysis. Then, we'll look at how to do one and identify positive and negative aspects of the environment. Finally, we'll discuss why doing an external analysis is important in managing strategically and why managers at all levels of the organization need to analyze and understand what's happening in the external environment.

LEARNING OUTCOME 3.1

Describe an External Analysis

Over the last five years, annual spending on pet services (grooming, birthday parties, spa services, pet sitting, dog walking, etc.) has more than doubled to almost $3.79 billion.[2] That amount is only a small portion of the almost $51 billion spent annually in the United States by pet owners. Several factors contributing to this increase include the number of households that own a pet (62 percent), passionate pet owners who want to pamper their pets, increasing levels of disposable income, and time pressures. Managers at pet products companies must continue to monitor these trends, especially in light of today's economic climate, with consumers cutting back on nonessential expenditures. However, that's what an external analysis is all about!

An **external analysis** is the process of scanning and evaluating an organization's external environment. It's how strategic managers determine the opportunities and threats facing their organizations. **Opportunities** are positive external trends or changes that may help an

FIGURE 3.1

Strategic Management
in Action

organization improve its performance. **Threats** are negative external trends or changes that may hinder an organization's performance. In assessing the current situation, it's important to know what's happening in the external environment so new strategies can be formulated or current strategies changed in response to the opportunities or threats. Figure 3.1 shows how external analysis fits into the overall strategic management process.

Organizations as Open Systems

Organizations are **open systems,** which means they interact with and respond to their environment. As systems, organizations take inputs and process those inputs into outputs. Inputs have to come from somewhere and outputs must be distributed somewhere. That "somewhere" is the external environment. (See Figure 3.2.) In addition, as systems, organizations have interrelated and interdependent parts (departments, units, divisions, etc.) that function as a whole. Any change in any part (or subsystem) can affect the other parts. For instance, if a change is made in marketing, it's likely to affect what happens in manufacturing, accounting, human resources, and so forth. Chester Barnard, an early management theorist, first suggested in 1938 that organizations functioned as systems.[3] However, it took several years for his ideas about organizations as systems to be accepted in mainstream management theory.[4]

Perspectives on Organizational Environments

Because organizations interact with their environment, organizational researchers have looked for ways to describe and understand those environments and their potential impact on organizational performance. These studies can be summarized from two different perspectives: (1) the environment as a source of information and (2) the environment as a source of resources. Let's look at each more closely.

Environment as Information Perspective

In this approach, the environment is viewed as a source of information for decision making.[5] A key element is the idea of **environmental uncertainty,** which is defined as the amount of

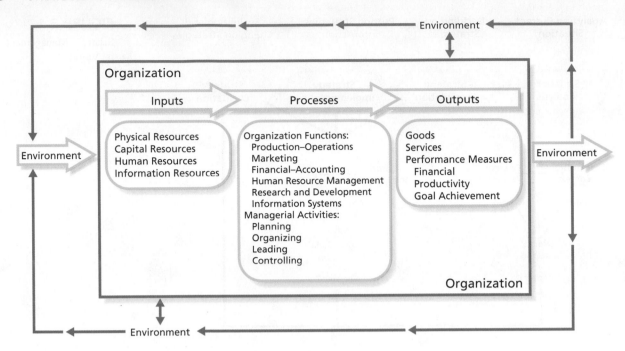

FIGURE 3.2

Organization as an
Open System

change and complexity in an organization's environment. The amount of change occurring in
an organization's environment can be either dynamic or stable. A more dynamic environment
is one that's changing rapidly. If changes are minimal or slow in occurring, the environment
is more stable. For instance, the environmental changes taking place in the oil-refining industry are not as rapid as those, say, in the cell phone industry. Therefore, the cell phone industry
would be considered more dynamic than the oil-refining industry. Similarly, if decision makers
must monitor a number of components in the environment, that environment is complex. If the
number of environmental components is few, it's a simple environment. The more complex and
dynamic the environment, the more uncertain it is and the more information decision makers
need about the environment to make appropriate decisions. According to this perspective, then,
the perceived uncertainty of the environment (amount of change and complexity) dictates the
amount and types of information that managers need about that environment. Where do strategic decision makers get that information? They get it from doing an external analysis—in other
words, the environment is a source of information.

Environment as Source of Resources Perspective

In this approach, the environment is viewed as a source of scarce and necessary resources
sought by competing organizations.[6] As the environment becomes more "hostile" (i.e., resources
become harder to obtain and control), organizations are subjected to greater uncertainty. Given
these uncertain conditions, managers look for ways to acquire and control those critical resources. They do so by monitoring the environment and making appropriate decisions based
on what they see happening, keeping in mind that the environment is the source of those scarce
resources. For example, when Toyota wanted to secure its supply of key components for its line
of popular hybrid vehicles, it did so by expanding its ownership in a maker of batteries for gasoline–electric hybrid engines.[7]

The main points of each approach are summarized in Table 3.1. Although these two perspectives provide us with a basic understanding of what's involved with an external analysis, how *can*
managers determine what's happening in the external environment? That's where environmental
scanning comes in.

TABLE 3.1 Summary of Two Perspectives on the Environment

Environment as Source of Information

- Environment viewed as source of information
- Environments differ in amount of uncertainty
- Uncertainty is determined by complexity and rate of change
- Reducing uncertainty means obtaining information
- Amount of uncertainty determines amount and types of information needed
- Information obtained by analyzing external environment

Environment as Source of Resources

- Environment viewed as source of scarce and valued resources
- Organizations depend on the environment for these resources
- Resources are sought by competing organizations
- Dependency is determined by the difficulty of obtaining and controlling resources
- Reducing dependency means controlling environmental resources
- Controlling environmental resources means knowing about the environment and attempting to change or influence it

Source: Based on Richard A. Bettis and Michael A. Hitt, "The New Competitive Landscape," *Strategic Management Journal,* Summer 1995, pp. 7–19.

Environmental Scanning and External Analysis

One impression we get from the previous discussion is that it's important for strategic decision makers to engage in environmental scanning—that is, to know and to evaluate what's happening in the external environment, whether the environment is seen as a source of information, a source of scarce resources, or both. In other words, you need to do an external analysis *and* identify the opportunities and threats facing the organization. For example, look back at the chapter-opening case. Based on their analysis of customer and competitor trends, strategic decision makers at the movie theater chains have chosen strategies they hope will exploit the opportunities and neutralize or avoid the threats in their environment.

STRATEGIC MANAGEMENT IN ACTION

Indra Nooyi, CEO of PepsiCo, is steering her company through the volatile economic climate by paying close attention to information. For instance, through information analysis, it became clear that the company's beverages division was being hit harder than its snack food division (Frito-Lay). One reason was that consumers who used to not finish an entire soda or water bottle before purchasing a new one are now finishing the beverage. In addition, according to information gathered from convenience-store operators, the housing downturn has led to fewer construction workers coming in and buying their sodas and snacks. A slowdown like this hadn't been seen in 25 years.

THINK ABOUT

- Put yourself in Nooyi's shoes. What other types of external information might you want to look at?
- How would you classify PepsiCo's environmental uncertainty (i.e., its amount of change and complexity)?

Source: Based on M. Esterl, "PepsiCo Board Stands by Nooyi," *Wall Street Journal,* January 13, 2012, p. B1; K. Evans, "Considering a Spinoff Is a Pepsi Challenge," *Wall Street Journal,* October 12, 2011, p. C1; V. Bauerlein, "CEO Indra Nooyi Stands by Strategy to Promote 'Good for You' Foods," *Wall Street Journal,* June 28, 2011, p. B1; M. Esterl and V. Bauerlein, "PepsiCo Wakes Up and Smells the Cola," *Wall Street Journal,* June 28, 2011, p. B1; and B. McKay, "PepsiCo CEO Adapts to Tough Climate," *Wall Street Journal,* September 11, 2008, pp. B1+.

LEARNING REVIEW   LEARNING OUTCOME 3.1

- What is an external analysis, and what does it show managers?
- How does the concept of an organization as an open system relate to external analysis?
- What does each perspective on organizational environments say?
- What role does environmental uncertainty play in external analysis?
- Why do managers need to do more than just scan the environment?

LEARNING OUTCOME 3.2

Explain How to Do an External Analysis of an Organization's Specific and General Environments

Now that we know *what* an external analysis is, we need to look at *how* you do one. What do managers look at in an external analysis? Where can they find information on the external environment, and how do they evaluate this information? How do managers at different organizational levels do an external analysis? We explore these topics in this section. When you've finished reading this material, you'll know how to do an external analysis and how to determine an organization's opportunities and threats.

External Environmental Sectors

The external environmental sectors comprise the specific environment and the general environment. The **specific environment** includes customers, competitors, suppliers, and other industry-competitive variables whereas the **general environment** includes economic, demographic, sociocultural, political-legal, and technological sectors. (See Figure 3.3.) Let's look at each.

Specific Environment

Analyzing the specific environment involves looking at industry and competitive variables. An **industry** is a group or groups of organizations producing similar or identical products. These organizations compete for customers to purchase their products and also must secure the necessary resources that are converted into products. To assess an organization's specific environment, we'll base our approach on Michael Porter's model and look at five competitive forces.[8] (See Figure 3.4 on page 62.)

One assumption Porter makes is that some industries are inherently more attractive than others; that is, the profit potential for companies in those industries is higher. For instance, airplane makers Airbus and Boeing have had higher profits than the airlines that buy their planes.[9] The strength and interaction of the five competitive forces are what influence profit potential. A strategic decision maker can determine the opportunities and threats in the specific environment by evaluating these five forces.

Existing Competitors (Porter's Term: Current Rivalry)   The existing competitors in your industry are your organization's current competitors that produce and market products similar to yours. For instance, in the soft drink industry, Coca Cola, PepsiCo, Cott, Dr. Pepper Snapple Group, and Wal-Mart (Sam's Choice house brand) would be existing competitors. In this part of the analysis, we determine how intense the rivalry is among these existing competitors. Is it intensely competitive or not? Is it "cutthroat" or "polite"? Are competitors constantly trying to take customers away from each other, or do competitors seem to get along with each other? The more intense the rivalry among existing competitors, the more the industry's profitability—and thus your company's profitability—is likely to suffer.

What affects the level of rivalry? Porter listed eight conditions that contribute to intense rivalry among existing competitors.[10]

1. *Numerous or equally balanced competitors:* If an industry has a number of competitors, there's a greater likelihood that some firms will think they can take competitive actions and

FIGURE 3.3

An Organization's
External Environment

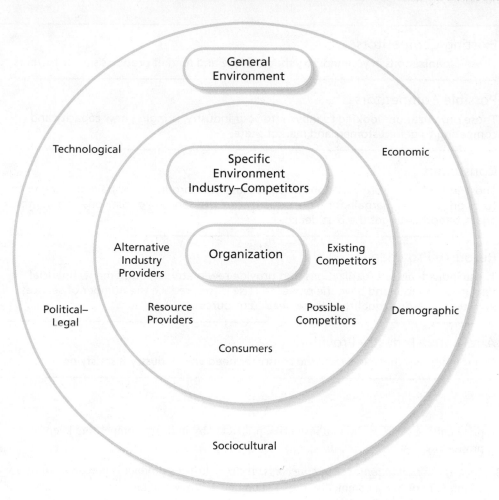

no one will notice, thus keeping the industry in constant competitive turmoil. Or, if competitors are equal in terms of size or resources, they'll constantly be jockeying for position, also creating intense competitive action.

2. *Slow industry growth:* When industry growth has slowed—in other words, consumer demand for the industry's products has leveled off—the "market pie" isn't getting any bigger. For your company to keep growing, you'll have to steal market share away from your competitors. Conditions will be ripe for competitors to battle with each other to maintain or increase market share, making the level of rivalry intense. For example, how many people read a daily newspaper? Not many. Statistics on daily newspaper readership have shown drastically declining numbers over the last 10 years. Newspaper publishers have struggled to find strategies to halt that trend and in the process upped the intensity of competition.[11]

3. *High fixed or storage costs:* If organizations have high fixed costs, they'll do whatever it takes to operate at capacity and thus spread out those fixed costs over a larger volume. This situation often leads to back-and-forth price cutting by competitors in order to attract customers, which increases competitive rivalry. Also, if the industry's products are difficult or costly to store, companies will want to sell their products as quickly as possible (keeping inventory at the lowest possible levels) and often resort to

FIGURE 3.4

Assessing Industry/ Competitive Factors

Source: Based on Michael E. Porter, *Competitive Strategy: Techniques for Analyzing Industries and Competitors* (The Free Press, 1980.)

Existing Competitors

Those organizations in your industry that produce and market products similar to yours.

Possible Competitors

Those organizations looking to move into your industry, bringing new capacity and competing to gain customers and market share.

Consumers

Those individuals or organizations who purchase your products and have the power to force prices down, bargain for higher quality or more services, or play one competitor against another to get the best deal.

Resource Providers

Those individuals or organizations that provide raw materials, equipment, financial resources, or labor and have the power to raise prices, reduce the number of services provided, or reduce quality of these needed resources.

Alternative Industry Providers

Other industries that can satisfy the consumer need your industry is satisfying.

price cutting to do so. In both instances, price cuts by industry competitors keep profits low.

4. *Lack of differentiation or switching costs:* If the industry's product is perceived to be a commodity or like a commodity (i.e., not unique in any way), then customers make their purchase decisions largely because of price and service. Both forms of competition lead to intense rivalry. For instance, you might not think the casual dining industry would face problems of differentiation. After all, industry competitors such as P. F. Chang's, Romano's Macaroni Grill, Olive Garden, and Chili's have spent significant dollars creating a theme and re-creating it in numerous locations. However, that's exactly what led to this lack of differentiation. Every format—American, Italian, Chinese, or Mexican—that's proved successful has been endlessly copied until it's practically impossible to tell these casual dining "theme" restaurants apart. This has created intense competitive rivalry as each chain attempts to capture consumers' dining-out dollars. Also, if there's no cost (either actual dollars or even the amount of time you'd have to invest to learn about a new product) associated with switching from one competitor's product to another's, then competitive intensity will be high because competitors will be trying to steal customers away from one another.

5. *Addition of capacity in large increments:* In industries where capacity must be added in large increments in order to be economically feasible, these additions by competitors can create competitive disruptions, because the industry will suffer from overcapacity, leading to price cutting and intense competitive rivalry. For instance, in the cruise line industry, a 1,200-passenger boat used to be considered large. Now, cruise ships can carry well over 5,000 passengers and capacity is still being added. For example, in 2011, Royal Caribbean put into service the world's largest (6,318 passengers) and most expensive cruise ship ($1.5 billion) named the *Allure of the Seas.* Longer by 5 millimeters, this new ship is a sister ship to Royal Caribbean's *Oasis of the Seas,* previously the world's largest cruise

ship, which can carry 5,400 passengers.[12] If the number of cruise customers decreases, there's intense competitive pressure to keep these boats filled.

6. *Diverse competitors:* When competitors differ in their strategic approaches, philosophies, or circumstances, it's hard to judge how they are going to act and react as they compete. This diversity increases the level of rivalry.

7. *High strategic stakes:* Industry competitors have strong reasons to want to succeed (such as CEO's reputation, large dollar investments, etc.) and will do whatever it takes to do so, even going so far as sacrificing short-run profitability. If industry competitors have this perspective, then rivalry will be high.

8. *High exit barriers:* Porter defines **exit barriers** as "economic, strategic, and emotional factors that keep companies competing in businesses even though they may be earning low or even negative returns on investment."[13] Examples of exit barriers include highly specialized assets that can't be used in other ways or that have low liquidation value; labor agreements that must be honored; or management's unwillingness to leave a business because of pride, fear, or other psychological reasons. If there are high exit barriers, the company is, in a sense, "stuck" in that industry and may use extreme tactics to compete.

One aspect of existing competitors that needs to be clarified is, "*Who* are our current competitors?" Obviously, if an industry includes several firms, you may find that not all those firms are your actual direct competitors or competitors that you'd be concerned with. One answer is to look at only the competitors currently in your **strategic group,** which is a group of firms competing within an industry that have similar strategies, resources, and customers. Strategy

---

STRATEGIC MANAGEMENT IN ACTION

Digital technology has disrupted all types of industries—from financial services to recorded music. One industry that's seen a significant impact is the publishing industry. E-book sales have skyrocketed, and one publisher went so far as to predict that e-books could account for as much as 40 percent of total revenue by the end of 2012. Reading those e-books requires a device and the competition in the e-book device industry is fierce. Amazon fired the first volley when it introduced the Kindle in November 2007. As with any new product, customers had to get used to the new technology, but once they did, the Kindles were on fire! Two years later, retailer Barnes & Noble introduced the Nook, a cheaper e-book device. Amazon responded by cutting the price of its cheapest Kindle. Three months later in January 2010, Apple introduced its iPad. Although it was a more expensive tablet, its functionality and options attracted a lot of attention and sales. In response, Barnes & Noble cut the price of its Nook, and Amazon again cut the price of the Kindle. By September 2011, Amazon dropped Kindle's starting price to $79 and launched Kindle Fire. Then in November 2011, Barnes & Noble joined the tablet battle with its $249 Nook Tablet. And these are just the top three competitors. Other industry competitors include the Sony Reader and Endless Ideas' Be Book Neo. As the popularity of e-books continues to grow, the "reader wars" are likely to continue.

TO DO

- Using the eight conditions, assess the level of current rivalry in this industry.
- Which of these eight conditions do you think are the most important to the level of current rivalry in this industry? Why?
- As the industry matures, do you think the intensity of rivalry will change? Explain.

Sources: Based on J. A. Trachtenberg and M. Peers, "Barnes & Noble Seeks Next Chapter," *Wall Street Journal*, January 6, 2012, pp. A1+; J. Bosman and M. J. De La Merced, "Barnes & Noble Considers Spinning Off Its Nook Unit," *IPO Offerings.com*, January 5, 2012; M. Maxwell, "Barnes & Noble's Digital Strategy Gaining Traction," *Wall Street Journal*, August 31, 2011, p. B3; J. A. Trachtenberg, S. Schechner, and G. Chon, "B&N Vulnerable to Rivals: Amazon, Apple Loom as Bookseller's Takeover Offer Dies," *Wall Street Journal Online*, August 20, 2011; A. Flood, "Hardback Sales Plummeting in Age of the ebook," *The Guardian*, [guardian.co.uk], August 12, 2011; and J. Bosman, "Publishing Gives Hints of Revival, Data Show," *New York Times Online*, August 9, 2011.

researchers have proposed that organizations within a strategic group compete more directly than other organizations that also may be in the industry.[14] For instance, even though Mercedes-Benz and General Motors are both in the automobile manufacturing industry, they're not considered direct competitors because they don't have the same customer base, don't have similar resources, and don't use similar strategies. In analyzing existing competitors, it makes sense to look at those organizations whose strategic actions have the most potential to affect your profitability; that means looking at those competitors in the relevant strategic group.

Possible Competitors (Porter's term: Potential Entrants) The market for tickets to any type of entertainment, sporting, or other live events has been dominated by Ticketmaster. However, concert promotion company AEG is starting a new service, Axs Ticketing. AEG's CEO said he "anticipates healthy competition with Ticketmaster." [15]

Not only do organizations have to be concerned with the opportunities and threats presented by their current competitors, they also need to be on the lookout for others moving into their industry. Why? Because these organizations bring new capacity to the industry, want to gain customers (market share), and perhaps even possess substantial resources that can be used to launch attacks against current competitors. The threat of possible competitors depends on the barriers to entry and the reaction by existing competitors to these entrants. **Barriers to entry** are obstacles to entering an industry. When barriers are high or existing competitors can be expected to take significant actions to keep newcomers out, then the threat of entry is low. A low threat of potential entrants is positive for an industry because profitability won't be divided up among more competitors. Porter described seven major entry barriers.[16]

1. *Economies of scale:* Economies of scale refer to the cost savings realized from volume increases. Producing more or doing more can lead to cost savings because fixed costs are spread out over a larger volume, driving the cost per unit down. Possible competitors might think twice because they'd have to come into the industry operating either at a large scale and risk retaliation by existing competitors or at a smaller scale and have a cost disadvantage compared to the others.

2. *Cost disadvantages from other than scale:* Established competitors may enjoy cost advantages that possible competitors can't duplicate even if they can operate at a large volume. Such factors include exclusive or protected product technology; favorable access to raw materials; favorable locations; government subsidies; or human resource advantages

---

FOR YOUR INFORMATION
The Benefits of Competition

Although we've highlighted the strategic challenges that come from intense competition, are there any benefits? The answer is, of course there are. An important one is that competitive rivalry forces organizations to be more innovative. Companies want to hold on to their customers and as they look for ways to do that, they must continually innovate their products as well as their work processes. Another benefit is that competition compels companies to be on their toes: to be effective and efficient at what they do. If they're not, they'll find it difficult to stay competitive and might find any competitive advantage they've been able to develop eroded by more efficient and effective competitors. So, although intense competitive rivalry is a threat, it *can* have some benefits.

THINK ABOUT

- Can you think of some industries in which competition has "forced" competitors to be better?
- What about benefits for customers? Is competition beneficial for them? Explain.

Sources: Based on D. Moyer, "Don't Fence It In," *Harvard Business Review,* December 2005, p. 156; L. Kiesling, "Articulating the Benefits of Competition," *Knowledge Problem* [www.knowledgeproblem.com], June 8, 2005; and S. Davies, H. Coles, M. Olkczak, C. Pike, and C. Wilson, "The Benefits from Competition: Some Illustrative UK Cases," *Department of Trade and Industry Economics Paper,* no. 8 [www.dti.gov.uk], July 2004.

because of employees' cumulative level of knowledge, learning, and experience. For example, looking back at our chapter-opening case, the top Hollywood studios agreed to a set of technical specifications defining how sharp digital films must be and creating mechanisms to fight illegal piracy.[17] Not only do such technical standards make the industry's products more appealing to customers, they serve as a barrier to others looking to come into the industry because potential entrants would have to adhere to the standards.

3. *Product differentiation:* Existing competitors usually have worked hard and spent large sums to establish unique product identification with customers. If it's strong enough, brand identity differentiates an organization and leads to loyal customers. To overcome this brand loyalty, possible competitors have to spend heavily on customer research, advertising, packaging, and other marketing activities, resulting in a significant barrier.

4. *Capital requirements:* If an organization has to invest significant financial resources in order to compete, this makes possible competitors think twice about coming into an industry. Take the ski industry, for example. As customers demanded better amenities at ski sites—good, consistent snow base; groomed trails; comfortable but luxurious accommodations—the capital investment required to satisfy these customer demands rose significantly. Unless possible competitors have that kind of capital, they're shut out of the industry.

5. *Switching costs:* Are you familiar with and do you consistently use one word-processing package? Maybe it's Word or iWork or Lotus WordPro. What keeps you from using another one? For most of us, it's the time and effort we'd have to invest in learning a new set of commands and keyboard shortcuts. That's an example of **switching costs**—the one-time costs facing the buyer who switches from one supplier's product to another's. These costs don't even necessarily have to be monetary costs. They also can be psychological costs associated with change.

6. *Access to distribution channels:* You have a product to sell, and you need an outlet or distribution channel for that product. If current competitors have already secured the logical distribution sources, you have to persuade these sources to accept your product. This may mean you have to give the distributor a price break or set up cooperative advertising arrangements, both of which reduce potential profits.

7. *Government policy:* If the government imposes laws and regulations (such as licensing requirements, controlling access to raw materials, air/water pollution standards, product safety standards, product testing time requirements, etc.), it creates a barrier to entry. Possible competitors would have to meet these requirements, which may cost a significant amount. For instance, in the real-estate industry, real-estate agents lobbied state governments to keep discount brokers from coming into their market.[18] If such regulatory or legal protections aren't there, barriers to entry will be lower.

Consumers (Porter's term: Bargaining Power of Buyers)   Your consumers are those individuals or organizations who purchase your products. How do consumers affect industry profitability? If they have a lot of bargaining power, they can force prices down, bargain for higher quality or more services, or even play competitors against each other trying to see who will give them the best deal. What makes a consumer powerful?[19] One factor is whether the *consumer purchases large volumes of the seller's product.* The implication is that the customer is more important to the seller than the seller is to the customer. This gives that customer a lot of bargaining power. For instance, Wal-Mart can account for a significant part of a manufacturer's revenues. With this much buying power, Wal-Mart can pretty much dictate selling terms. Another factor that influences consumers' bargaining power is whether the *products they purchase represent a significant portion of their costs or purchases.* In this situation, customers are going to look for the best price and shop around. Consumers will also have significant bargaining power if *the products they purchase are standard or undifferentiated.* Here again, a consumer likely will play one supplier against another in an attempt to find the best deal. One more factor that gives

STRATEGIC MANAGEMENT IN ACTION

The beverage giants (Coke and Pepsi) are at it again. The bottled water business, once an industry made up of numerous small regional players, continues to be a battleground for the major beverage companies. With a consumption decline in the carbonated soft drink market and with bottled water consumption increasing, it's not surprising that Coke and Pepsi want to continue making a big splash in the water market. However, they have to cope with getting their water on the shelves without sacrificing too much of the shelf space of their soft drink products. In addition, regional water bottlers are vulnerable to the giants' marketing tactics. It's an interesting battle. The economy has also affected competition as consumers cut back on spending.

TO DO

- Analyze this situation using the seven barriers to entry from the perspective of the existing competitors *and* from the perspective of the possible competitors.

Sources: Based on Press Release [www.beveragemarketing.com], "Bottled Water Recovers Somewhat from Recessionary Years, New Report from Beverage Marketing Corporation Shows," September 2011; and "Feature Analysis: Soft Drinks Losing Their Fizz," *Datamonitor,* March 2008.

greater bargaining power is if they *face little switching costs.* If there are few switching costs or if switching costs are low, then the customer doesn't feel obligated to stay with the original supplier and can shop around. The consumer may also exert bargaining power if *it has low profits or low income levels.* If that's the case, the customer will look for ways to reduce costs, which often means reducing purchasing costs. Another factor that gives consumers bargaining power is when *they have the ability and resources themselves to manufacture the products they're purchasing from the industry.* If the customer can make the product it's buying, then it's in a powerful position to ask for concessions from the supplier. For example, some businesses that purchase large quantities of electric power from local utilities have threatened to take their business elsewhere unless they get lower rates. Many of these businesses can do just that by either building their own power-generating plants or persuading a local government to form a municipal system to buy electric power at bulk rates. As consumers, these businesses are exerting power. Consumers also have bargaining power if *the industry's product isn't important to the quality of the buyers' products or services.* What this means is that if the consumers don't need the industry's products to get desired quality levels in their products or services, then they have the power to bargain with the industry over prices and services offered. On the other hand, if the industry's product *is* important to the quality of the consumers' products, then the consumers won't have much bargaining power. Lastly, consumers have bargaining power if *they have full information* about product demand, actual market prices, and supplier costs. This information gives the customer good ammunition to get the best possible prices from suppliers. The Internet has played a significant role in customers' access to information. For example, in the car industry, consumers can compare prices and features and bargain for the best deal.

Resource Providers (Porter's Term: Bargaining Power of Suppliers) Terex Corporation, a heavy-equipment maker, can't get enough big tires for its mining and other big earth-moving equipment. A shortage of workers at low-cost factories in China is leading to production and shipping delays. Indium—element 49 on the periodic table—plays a small but crucial role in manufacturing LCD screens, and it's in short supply. A shortage of a critical chemical used in de-icing runways threatens flight volume at major airports.[20]

If your industry's resource providers have bargaining power, they can raise prices or reduce the number of services provided or the quality of products your industry purchases. An industry's resource providers include raw materials sources, equipment manufacturers, financial institutions, and even labor sources. How can you tell whether an industry's resource providers are powerful?[21] One thing to look for is *domination by a few companies and more concentration than the industry.* If resource providers are few in number and are selling to an industry that's fragmented (i.e., the

THE GREY ZONE

Choose healthy groceries. Create fabulous Web sites. Destroy green pigs with angry birds. There are phone apps to do just about everything. Even knowing how to avoid sobriety checkpoints—locations where law enforcement officials stop some drivers and perform breath tests on those suspected of being drunk. In March 2011, U.S. Senators Harry Reid, Charles E. Schumer, Frank R. Lautenberg, and Tom Udall sent a letter to Apple, Google, and Research in Motion (BlackBerry's parent company) requesting that these companies remove those apps from their online stores. The senators believed the apps were "harmful to public safety" because it made it too easy for intoxicated drivers to avoid the checkpoints. BlackBerry agreed to pull its apps not longer after receiving the letter and thanked the group for bringing these apps to their attention. Apple and Google did not respond initially. However, three months later, Apple decided to restrict future apps with the checkpoint capability but not current ones. One point to make is that these apps do nothing illegal in supplying the precise locations of sobriety checkpoints. However, the vice president for policy at Mothers Against Drunk Driving said, "There's a difference between a broad announcement that there will be sobriety checkpoints in a general location versus a specific location that can be downloaded to your smartphone with the intent of allowing a drunk driver to evade a checkpoint."

THINK ABOUT

- What do you think? Are these apps ethical? Why or why not?
- When crafting strategy, should managers ever consider whether the strategy being implemented is offensive, objectionable, questionable, or unacceptable? Is it more acceptable or less acceptable when your company is considered an industry icon to continue with such strategies? Or does it matter?
- What stakeholders are most important in this situation, and what concerns might those stakeholders have?
- Do businesses have a responsibility to protect their consumers? Why or why not?

Sources: Based on L. Copeland, "Apple To Stop Accepting DUI Checkpoint Apps," *USA Today,* June 10, 2011, p. 3A; L. Copeland, "Sales of DUI Checkpoint App Rise Amid Scrutiny," *USA Today,* May 18, 2011; R. Stross, "Helping Drunken Drivers Avoid Tickets, But Not Wrecks," *New York Times Online,* April 16, 2011; "Senators Ask App Stores to End DUI Evasion Aids," *Telecommunications Reports,* April 1, 2011, p. 24; J. R. Quain, "DUI Checkpoint Apps Draw Ire and Fire," *Fox News.com,* March 29, 2011; M. Esteban and KOMO Staff, "App Designed to Sniff Out DUI Checkpoints Snuffed Out by Senators," *KOMO News.com,* March 25, 2011; and Associated Press, "Group Urges Sobriety Checkpoints," *Wall Street Journal,* January 13, 2005, p. A1.

buyers are small and not very powerful), then these providers will usually be able to exert considerable influence over prices, quality, and sales terms. Another characteristic to look for is *whether there are any substitute products.* If there aren't any good substitutes, then the resource provider can exert more power over the industry. But, if the resource provider has to compete with possible substitutes, then it doesn't have a lot of bargaining power over the industry. Resource providers can also exert power when *the industry is not an important customer.* If your industry is just one of many that the resource provider sells to, then it couldn't care less whether it keeps you as a customer and is more likely to exert bargaining power. On the other hand, if your industry is an important customer, the resource provider will want to protect that relationship and won't try to exert bargaining power. Another characteristic to evaluate is whether *the resource provider's product is an important input to your industry.* If it is, then the resource provider will have more bargaining power. For example, resource providers of silicon wafers have significant power over the semiconductor industry. Even though silicon is one of the most abundant elements on earth, shortfalls in the availability of silicon wafers affect the ability of chipmakers to satisfy demand for their product. This situation gives resource providers a lot of power over computer chip manufacturers. Also, it's important to know whether *the resource provider's products are differentiated or whether there are customer switching costs.* If the resource provider's products are differentiated or if your industry would experience switching costs, then the resource provider is able to exert more power.

The final characteristic for determining resource provider power is *the resource provider's ability to provide the products that your industry is currently providing.* If the resource provider can do what your industry does (i.e., produce or market your industry's products) and do it better or cheaper, then this gives the resource provider more bargaining power. In other words, if you don't agree to the resource provider's terms and conditions, they could start doing what you do. For instance, apparel conglomerates such as Liz Claiborne, Jones Apparel Group, and Kellwood have "grudgingly tolerated life under the thumb of department stores, tailoring clothing designs to the chains' seasonal whims and paying out markdown money to stores when fashions fail to sell." One supplier, Liz Claiborne, took a radical approach. Rather than rely on department stores, the company built its own retail stores. However, the downturn in the economy forced the company to sell its Liz Claiborne family of brands in order to focus on its more upscale kate spade, Juicy Couture, and Lucky brands. The company changed its name to Fifth & Pacific Companies in May 2012.[22]

Alternative Industry Providers (Porter's Term: Substitute Products)   The last industry force we need to discuss is the threat of alternative industry providers. The best way to evaluate this threat is to see whether other industries can satisfy the consumer need that our industry is satisfying. For instance, take a customer's need for something to drink. If your company is in the soft drink industry, alternative industry providers could come from other industries such as fruit drinks, energy drinks, alcoholic beverages, milk or milk-based products, and even bottled water. Any of these industries could fulfill the customer's need for something to drink. (Other soft drink manufacturers would be your competitors and would be evaluated as existing competitors.) If there are no or few alternative industry providers for your industry's product, then this threat isn't very high. However, if there are a few good alternative industry providers or even several not-so-good alternative industry providers for your product, then this isn't favorable for your industry's profitability.

By now, you should have a good grasp of what you examine in an organization's specific environment. Using a framework of five competitive factors provides a way to determine the opportunities and threats of the industry and competitive environment. A summary of these five competitive factors and what you need to look at as you determine whether they're favorable or unfavorable is shown in Table 3.2.

General Environment

The general environment includes the economic, demographic, sociocultural, political-legal, and technological sectors. The trends in these sectors could have a positive impact (opportunity) or a negative impact (threat) on the organization. However, not everything that happens externally

---

STRATEGIC MANAGEMENT IN ACTION

Apple's iPad is changing the way that magazine and newspaper publishers do business. Since Apple introduced the iPad, publishers have spent millions of dollars developing apps in the hopes that the device will change the way magazines are read and sold to customers. However, they're also discovering that while "Apple may offer new opportunities with its devices, it exacts a heavy toll." The fact that magazine sales on the iPad are limited to single issues (except for a limited number) has made it difficult for the publishers to fully capitalize on this potentially lucrative business model. Customers want a subscription option and don't want to have to pay per month. And many of those magazine apps cost as much as a printed copy of a magazine…"a difficult concept for consumers to get their heads around considering that a paper product is more expensive to assemble and distribute than an electronic version of a magazine."

TO DO

• Analyze this situation using the five competitive factors approach. Where do the opportunities and threats appear to be for publishers?

Source: Based on J. W. Peters, "For Magazines, A Bitter Pill in iPad," *New York Times Online,* January 16, 2011; and S. Ovide, Y. I. Kane, and R. Adams, "Apple Coaxes Publishers to Join It on iPad Subscription," *Wall Street Journal,* September 20, 2010, p. B8.

TABLE 3.2 **Evaluating the Five Competitive Factors**

Industry-Competitive Factors	Threat	Opportunity
Existing Competitors		
Numerous competitors	✓	
Few competitors		✓
Equally balanced competitors	✓	
One or a few strong competitors		✓
Industry sales growth slowing	✓	
Industry sales growth strong		✓
High fixed or inventory storage costs	✓	
Low fixed or inventory storage costs		✓
No differentiation or no switching costs	✓	
Significant differentiation or significant switching costs		✓
Large capacity increments required	✓	
Minimal capacity increments required		✓
Diverse competitors	✓	
Similar competitors		✓
High strategic stakes	✓	
Low strategic stakes		✓
High exit barriers	✓	
Minimal exit barriers		✓
Possible Competitors		
Significant economies of scale		✓
No or low economies of scale	✓	
Cost disadvantages from other aspects		✓
No other potential cost disadvantages	✓	
Strong product differentiation		✓
Weak product differentiation	✓	
Huge capital requirements		✓
Minimal capital requirements	✓	
Significant switching costs		✓
Minimal switching costs	✓	
Controlled access to distribution channels		✓
Open access to distribution channels	✓	
Government policy protection		✓
No government policy protection	✓	
Consumers		
Consumer purchases large volumes	✓	
Consumer purchases small volumes		✓
Products purchased are significant part of consumer's costs	✓	
Products purchased aren't significant part of consumer's costs		✓
Products purchased are standard or undifferentiated	✓	
Products purchased are highly differentiated and unique		✓
Consumer faces few switching costs	✓	
Consumer faces significant switching costs		✓
Consumer's profits are low	✓	
Consumer's profits are strong		✓
Consumer has ability to manufacture products being purchased	✓	
Consumer doesn't have ability to manufacture products		✓
Industry's products aren't important to quality of consumer's products	✓	
Industry's products are important to quality of consumer's products		✓
Consumers have full information	✓	
Consumers have limited information		✓

(Continued)

TABLE 3.2 **(Continued)**

Industry-Competitive Factors	Threat	Opportunity
Resource Providers		
Resource provider industry has few companies and is more concentrated	✓	
Resource provider industry has many companies and is fragmented		✓
There are no substitute products for resource provider's products	✓	
There are substitute products for resource provider's products		✓
Industry being supplied is not an important customer	✓	
Industry being supplied is an important customer		✓
Resource provider's product is an important input to industry	✓	
Resource provider's product is not an important input to industry		✓
Resource provider's products are differentiated	✓	
Resource provider's products aren't differentiated		✓
There are significant switching costs in resource provider's products	✓	
There are minimal switching costs in resource provider's products		✓
Resource provider has ability to do what buying industry does	✓	
Resource provider doesn't have ability to do what buying industry does		✓
Alternative Industry Providers		
There are few good alternative industry providers	✓	
There are several not-so-good alternative industry providers	✓	
There are no good alternative industry providers		✓

will be an opportunity or threat. Many changes may not even affect an organization. In addition, different industries will be affected differently by external changes. For example, rising interest rates will benefit some industries (i.e., be an opportunity) whereas for other industries, this trend is a threat.

Economic   In today's environment, the opportunities and threats of the economic sector are painfully obvious to many industries. For instance, managers in industries ranging from transportation to banking to retailing recognize the impact that energy and fuel costs have on supplies of raw materials, general business activity, new orders, and order backlogs. Retailers are facing consumers who have lost their appetite for spending, leading strategic decision makers to find strategies to try to get buyers back in the stores. For some retailers—including Circuit City, Linens 'N Things, Sharper Image, and Steve and Barry's, among others—the economic threats proved too strong. But for one retailer, Wal-Mart, the economic challenges provided opportunities to grow revenues as consumers spent more cautiously and looked for ways to stretch their dollars.

The economic sector includes macroeconomic data—current statistics and forecasted trends and changes—that reflect what's happening with the overall economy. The major economic data that might be important to scan and evaluate include interest rates; exchange rates and the value of the dollar; budget deficit or surplus; trade deficit or surplus; inflation rates; gross national product (GNP) or gross domestic product (GDP) levels and the resulting stage of the economic cycle; consumer income, spending, and debt levels; employment-unemployment levels; consumer confidence levels; and workforce productivity rates. You want to look at current information as well as forecasted trends when evaluating these economic statistics. What impact, if any, do they have for your organization? For instance, are rising interest rates good or bad—in other words, are they opportunities or threats? If the economy is growing moderately, what does this mean? What if the dollar falls in value against the Chinese yuan or against the euro? Is this good or bad? What if workforce productivity has leveled off and is predicted to stay stagnant? What does this mean? Take consumer debt levels. What industries might be affected positively or negatively by increases in consumer debt levels? These are the types of questions you need to ask as you evaluate the economic sector for opportunities and threats. And keep in mind that industries will be affected differently by these economic trends. For instance, rising interest rates tend to have a favorable impact on the credit card industry but are less favorable for the housing industry. Also, keep in mind that every organization in an industry is faced with the same economic trends and changes. That is, the inflation rate doesn't change just because it's McDonald's, as opposed to Wendy's. So an organization's performance ultimately is determined by how it responds to the various economic opportunities and threats, which is also true for the rest of the general environmental sectors we'll look at.

If your organization does business globally, the economic analysis won't change much. The biggest challenge is likely to be finding available and reliable sources of statistics, although all industrialized and most semi-industrialized countries collect economic data. Also, information is available from the United Nations and other sources such as the CIA *World Factbook*. You can find information on GNP or GDP, which provides clues to the stage of the economic cycle and whether a country's economy is growing or contracting. You also can find information on exchange rates, trade figures, interest rates, and inflation rates. Of these, the most important economic information probably includes inflation rates, interest rates, currency exchange rates, and consumer income spending-debt levels. Why? These factors tend to be the most volatile and could significantly affect strategic decisions.

Demographics   In January 2011, the first of some 76 million baby boomers turned 65. The number of people worldwide 65 and older is expected to more than double to about 1.5 billion by 2050. That means people 65 and over will soon outnumber children under 5 for the first time ever. [23] What industries might benefit from or suffer from these trends?

STRATEGIC MANAGEMENT IN ACTION
The Global Perspective

Reversing a trend that started years ago, many manufacturers are bringing production back to North America and halting plans to send more work overseas. Why? Rising shipping costs. For instance, the retail heating division of DESA LLC (the company best known for making the heaters you see along the sidelines of football fields) saw its cost for shipping one container from China jump from $4,600 to $5,600 over a six-month period. The president of the company said, "My cost of getting a shipping container here from China just keeps going up—and I don't see any end in sight." Economic experts concur, saying that the cost of shipping a container from Asia to the East Coast has tripled since 2000. These experts estimate that transportation costs are now the equivalent of a 9 percent tariff on goods coming into the United States. The higher transportation costs are particularly challenging for lower-value goods and for companies that manufacture heavier and bulkier products.

These circumstances are forcing many manufacturers to reevaluate their production strategies. However, there are some limits to what they can do. For instance, one problem with bringing production back home is that the basic infrastructure needed to support many industries (suppliers who produce parts or repair machines) has declined or disappeared altogether. In addition, many domestic shippers have added a transportation surcharge.

TO DO

- Find and graph the cost of a barrel of oil over the last three years.

- Why are higher transportation costs particularly challenging for manufacturers of lower-value goods and for heavier and bulkier products?

- What industries, in addition to the oil industry, might benefit from higher transportation costs?

Source: Based on B. Saporito, "Made (Again) in the U.S.A. Why Firms Like Jarden are Bringing Work Back from China," *Time*, October 10, 2011, p. 20; J. Bussey, "Will Costs Drive Firms Home?" *Wall Street Journal*, May 5, 2011, p. B1+; A. Goel, N. Moussavi, and V. N. Srivatsan, "Time to Rethink Offshoring?" *The McKinsey Quarterly* [www.mckinseyquarterly.com], September 2008; J. Lahart and C. Dougherty, "U.S. Retools Economy, Curbing Thirst for Oil," *Wall Street Journal*, August 12, 2008, pp. A1+; D. J. Lynch, "Transport Costs Could Alter World Trade," *USA Today*, August 12, 2008, pp. 1B+; and T. Aeppel, "Stung by Soaring Transport Costs, Factories Bring Jobs Home Again," *Wall Street Journal*, June 13, 2008, pp. A1+.

In the demographics sector, you'll evaluate current statistical data and trends in population characteristics. It includes the kinds of information that the U.S. Census Bureau gathers such as gender, age, income levels, ethnic makeup, education, family composition, geographic location, birth rates, employment status, and so forth. Many different organizations—government as well as business—use these data in making strategic decisions. As you look at population statistics, what positive or negative trends do you see that might affect your organization? For instance, census data show that the total U.S. population is almost 313 million; that there are more Americans over age 30 than under; that there are 96.7 males for every 100 females; that 32.8 percent of households are 2-person; and that Hispanics increased their standing as the largest minority group at 16 percent.[24] What strategic implications might such population changes have for different organizations?

You might find it's also important to examine the interaction of these variables. For instance, which age group has the fastest-growing incomes? Or, in what geographic locations is there a greater concentration of senior citizens? Or, what is the average level of education of Asian Americans? In fact, one particular population group (another term for this is *population cohort*) that you've probably heard a lot about is the baby boomers. This group typically includes individuals who were born between the years 1946 and 1964. A lot is written about the baby boomers because there are so many of them. Through every life stage (going to elementary school, teenage years, climbing the career ladder, and now retirement), they've had an enormous impact simply because of their sheer numbers. Although some experts believe that segmenting markets by age is inappropriate, others say it's a good clue to consumer attitudes and behavior. Other common age cohorts include: the Depression group (born 1912–1921); the World War II group (born 1922–1927); the Postwar group (born 1928–1945); the Generation X or "zoomers" group (born 1965–1977); and Generation Y or echo boomers/millenials (born 1978–1994). This last group also is predicted to be a source of significant demographic opportunities and threats simply because of its size.

As you can probably guess, demographic information is useful for understanding your current customers as well as targeting potential customers. By examining current and forecasted demographic shifts, positive and negative trends can be identified.

FOR YOUR INFORMATION
The Hourglass Phenomenon

"You can't understand the future without demographics. The composition of a society... shapes every aspect of civic life, from politics, economics, and culture to the kinds of products, services, and businesses that are likely to succeed or fail. Demographics isn't destiny, but it's close." This quote should make it obvious why it's important to examine demographics when identifying opportunities and threats.

A simple demographic tool, the population pyramid (in which all the people in a given population are stacked by age) shows some interesting changes about to occur in the United States. For "most stable, peace-time societies, the resulting figure would look like a pyramid, with the youngest people at the base and the oldest people up at the tip." That's what the United States used to look like and what countries such as India now look like. Currently, the U.S. pyramid has a giant midsection because of the baby boomers. However, starting in the next decade, the U.S. population pyramid will take on the shape of an hourglass, with a large number of now-older baby boomers at the top, and the largest generation of young people since the boomers—Generation Y—at the bottom. In the middle... the small number of Generation-Xers. This "hourglass" society will bring an increasing number of "new social challenges, cultural norms, and business opportunities."

THINK ABOUT

- What's your reaction to this description?
- How do you think strategic decision makers might be able to use this information?

Source: Based on A. Zolli, "Demographics: The Population Hourglass," *Fast Company,* March 2006, pp. 56–63.

STRATEGIC MANAGEMENT IN ACTION

The nation's fast-growing Hispanic population is attracting the attention of businesses from banks to mobile-phone services to retailers. For instance, Wal-Mart has teamed up with Pollo Campero, a Latin American fried-chicken favorite. In a Supercenter in Rowlett, Texas, you'll find a restaurant with the Guatemalan chain's popular fried chicken. For Wal-Mart, Pollo Campero offers an additional opportunity to capture a diverse range of shoppers and to customize and sell more culturally attuned products in its massive stores.

THINK ABOUT

- What potential drawbacks, if any, might there be to these strategies?

Source: Based on M. Arndt, "At Pollo Campero, Growth Is on the Menu," [http://mobile.businessweek.com/magazine/content/], March 11, 2010; News Release, "Now Serving at Wal-Mart: Pollo Campero's Delicious Latin Chicken," [www.campero.com], May 12, 2008; and CNNMoney.com, "Wal-Mart to Serve Fried Chicken," [www.cnnmoney.com], May 12, 2008.

The need for demographic information doesn't change if an organization is operating in other countries or is looking to expand globally. It's important to have as much demographic information as possible about current and potential global markets. Most countries collect census information. In developing countries, data collection and statistical analysis might not be as thorough or reliable as that of other nations. However, the United Nations and other organizations do collect a considerable amount of demographic information that could be useful in analyzing this external sector.

Sociocultural   The popularity of iPads, iPods, and iPhones has many younger office workers demanding Macs instead of the standard-issue PCs that run Microsoft's Windows operating system. For instance, the chief information officer at Juniper Networks stated that, "If we opened it up today, I think 25 percent of our employees would choose Macs." For Apple, the workplace market isn't even one that it has pursued recently. Instead, its "core calling is creating the next cool thing for the world's consumer."[25]

There's more to understanding your current and potential customers than just their demographic characteristics. It's also important to know what's going on with them culturally. In other words, what's a country's culture like, and how is it changing? What are the traditions, lifestyles, values, attitudes, beliefs, tastes, patterns of behavior, and how are these changing? These are what the sociocultural sector encompasses. Such trends often aren't as obvious or as easy to determine as the demographic information. Measuring and interpreting people's opinions, values, attitudes, or likes and dislikes tends to be more challenging. However, it's important for strategic decision makers to recognize both the current status and the trends in the sociocultural sector.

How can you determine what's happening in the sociocultural sector? Look at values and attitudes. For instance, some basic cultural values of the United States include individual freedom, strong work ethic, and equality of opportunity. These values influence people's behavior in the way they shop, work, raise their families, and otherwise live their lives. People's attitudes also influence their behavior. Some attitudinal changes over the last few years include (and this list is, by no means, complete) different views of openness versus privacy by the Internet generation, which is more willing to share information online with friends and strangers; most people aged 30 and younger don't follow the news closely at all; middle America volunteers the most; customers, especially younger ones, are getting pickier; more and more people have to leave for work before dawn; eating in (that is, at home) is gaining ground over eating out; a new emphasis on frugality; being "cheap" is cool; willingness to do-it-yourself, especially in home repair, retail transactions, and so forth; more emphasis on religion and spiritual activities, particularly by baby boomers; and increasing use of technology in workplaces, schools, and homes.

In evaluating this sector, you'd also want to look at changes or trends in people's activities, behavior, and purchases. For example, look at how Kraft and other food makers have responded to customers' changing attitudes about food. As consumers demanded healthier

STRATEGIC MANAGEMENT IN ACTION

Hallmark Cards always has been quite successful at "reading" social trends and translating those trends into greeting cards. That's why when baby boomers started turning 50, company strategists created a line of cards (birthday, friendship, thinking-of-you, anniversary, etc.) designed to "subtly flatter the aging boomer's flagging middle-aged ego"—a line they called Time of Your Life. They decided to display the line in its own separate section of Hallmark stores and to use advertising displays showing middle-aged people looking youthful in active settings. A Hallmark spokesperson said, "We had done a lot of research showing that baby boomers don't want to get old, but that if it's going to happen, they want to emphasize the positive side of aging." However, what Hallmark failed to understand was that given a choice between shopping in the regular greeting cards section and shopping in a special 50-plus section, potential customers, of course, chose the regular cards. After two years of miserable sales, the company scrapped the line. There's a lesson here about understanding the sociocultural component.

TO DO

- Go to Hallmark's Web site **[www.hallmark.com]**. Click on About Hallmark and then the Newsroom. In the search box, type in the word "trends." This will bring you to a page describing emerging and evolving trends as perceived by Hallmark.
- Which ones are described there? How might these affect strategies at Hallmark? What could other companies learn about sociocultural opportunities and threats from these descriptions?

Source: Based on Hallmark Web site [www.hallmark.com], January 24, 2012; E. Byron, "Making Cards Cool Again," *Wall Street Journal,* June 20, 2011, p. B7; and P. Paul, "Sell It to the Psyche," *Inside Business, Time Bonus Section,* October 2003, p. A2.

versions of their favorite snack foods, companies scaled back calories, sodium, and saturated and trans fats in many products. (Go to any grocery store and check out the number and variety of 100-calorie snacks, products that weren't available eight years ago.) Many organizations also have changed their marketing strategies to take advantage of another sociocultural trend—diverse population groups.

The importance of this sector doesn't change if you're in different global locations. However, getting and interpreting this information for different global locations may not be as easy as getting economic and demographic information. That's because there's no standard governmental collection of this type of information. Keep in mind that each country does have its own distinctive culture—generally accepted traditions, lifestyles, values, attitudes, beliefs, tastes, and patterns of behavior. The challenge is to understand that culture. In addition to knowing the current culture, any trends or changes should be analyzed to determine potential opportunities and threats.

Political-Legal Because of laws restricting the use of leaf blowers, manufacturers started producing quieter, more fuel-efficient models. New regulations now require that grocery stores identify the country of origin for meats, produce, and certain nuts. Disabled Americans now have expanded workplace protections under the Americans with Disabilities Act after the passage of a bill by the U.S. Senate.[26]

In this general environmental sector, various laws, regulations, judicial decisions, and political forces currently in effect at the federal, state, and local levels of government are analyzed. (Some of the more significant federal laws and regulations for businesses are shown in Table 3.3.) For instance, new bankruptcy laws have made it harder for consumers to avoid paying their debt and have helped credit card companies, such as American Express Corporation, reduce the number of bankruptcy write-offs they've had to take.[27] This sector might also include analyzing regulations enacted by professional associations (such as the Financial Accounting Standards Board [FASB]). Any legal, regulatory, and political changes or pending judicial decisions also need to be examined. For instance, agreeing with those who complained that existing patent rules stifled innovation, the U.S. Supreme Court issued a ruling making it easier to challenge patents legally.[28] What impact might this ruling have on different industries? Which might find opportunities? Which might face threats? Also, a country's political-legal climate can affect

TABLE 3.3 Significant Legislation Affecting Businesses

Occupational Safety and Health Act of 1970
Requires employers to provide a working environment free from hazards to health

Consumer Product Safety Act of 1972
Sets standards on selected products, requires warning labels, and orders product recalls

Equal Employment Opportunity Act of 1972
Forbids discrimination in all areas of employer–employee relations

Worker Adjustment and Retraining Notification Act of 1988
Requires employers with 100 or more employees to provide 60 days' notice before a facility closing or mass layoff

Americans with Disabilities Act of 1990
Prohibits employers from discriminating against individuals with physical or mental disabilities or the chronically ill; also requires organizations to reasonably accommodate these individuals

Civil Rights Act of 1991
Reaffirms and tightens prohibition of discrimination; permits individuals to sue for punitive damages in cases of intentional discrimination

Family and Medical Leave Act of 1993
Grants 12 weeks of unpaid leave each year to employees for the birth or adoption of a child or the care of a spouse, child, or parent with a serious health condition; covers organizations with 50 or more employees

North American Free Trade Agreement of 1993
Creates a free-trade zone between the United States, Canada, and Mexico

U.S. Economic Espionage Act of 1996
Makes theft or misappropriation of trade secrets a federal crime

Sarbanes-Oxley Act of 2002
Holds businesses to higher standards of disclosure and corporate governance

---

attitudes toward business and how much regulation an industry faces. Other major political-legal concerns include taxation, minimum wage, and product labeling/product safety laws, all of which can have a significant impact on an organization's financial performance. Some areas where businesses might see future laws and regulations include immigration, global warming, and executive compensation.[29]

If an organization does business in other countries, obviously the relevant laws and regulations must be obeyed. In addition, it's important to be aware of political changes as far as who or what political party is in power and the likelihood that new laws and regulations might be enacted. Although political stability is a given in most countries, some do still face volatile and unstable situations.

Another aspect of the global political environment is the various trade alliances among countries. These alliances—such as the North American Free Trade Agreement (NAFTA), the European Union, the Central America Free Trade Agreement, the Association of Southeast Asian Nations (ASEAN), and the African Union—have eased many of the political and economic restrictions on trade and created numerous opportunities and threats.

Technological   Seventy percent of Internet users in China are under the age of 30 and like to play online games, download video and music onto their cell phones and MP3 players, and participate in online imaginary worlds. "Pony" Ma Huateng, the CEO of Chinese Internet company Tencent (with 480 million users), says he "simply wants to let people in China use the Web the way they want."[30] Obviously, he understands the opportunities and threats associated with technological trends and changes, which is the last general environmental sector we want to look at.

STRATEGIC MANAGEMENT IN ACTION
The Global Perspective

Electronic waste. It's a growing problem for many locales worldwide. In Australia, some 140,000 tons of e-waste are generated annually and only 4 percent of that is recycled. The country's environment minister, Peter Garrett, said, "Given that we're seeing significant growth in the volumes of e-waste, we know that this is an issue of increasing importance to the community." In looking at ways to deal with this pressing issue, a decision was made not to tax consumers for recycling electronic goods such as computers, TVs, and mobile phones. Instead, Garrett went on to say that the federal government would begin developing policy to encourage consumers to dispose of e-waste in a proper manner. "I want to develop a national waste policy which maximizes our opportunities to increase recycling, working closely with state and local jurisdictions to consider the best options for reducing the amount of waste going to landfill. I am not ruling anything in or out at this stage."

TO DO

- Do some research on the electronic waste problem and how various governments are dealing with it. Check out a CBS News *60 Minutes* investigation called "The Electronic Wasteland," which can be found at **http://www.cbsnews.com/video/watch/?id=4586903n%3fsource=search_video**.
- What do you think? How might laws/regulations impact strategies of organizations (not the e-waste recyclers)?

Source: Based on K. Dearne, "Garrett Rules Out Electronic Waste Tax," *Australian IT News*, November 19, 2008; and Scott Pelley, "The Electronic Wasteland," CBS News *60 Minutes*, November 10, 2008.

Within the technological sector, we look for scientific or technological innovations that create opportunities and threats. The two organizational areas most affected by technology are product research and development and organizational work processes. How will changing technology affect your organization's products? Likewise, how will these changes affect the way you produce and deliver your products (your work processes)?

Computerization is one of the most important technological innovations and continues to affect both organizational work processes and product development. For example, retailers directly link to suppliers to replenish inventory as needed. Manufacturers have flexible manufacturing systems that allow them to mass customize products. Airlines have Web pages where customers can arrange flight times, destinations, and fares. Many organizational employees collaborate and communicate online. In addition, innovations in fields such as lasers, robotics, biotechnology, food additives, medicine, consumer electronics, and telecommunications could be opportunities and threats for many different industries. However, keep in mind that the impact of such innovations will be different for different industries. For instance, how might innovations such as smart cards, 3-D printing, and satellite imaging affect different industries?

If your organization is operating globally, a country's level of technological advancement could influence strategies used. Some countries won't have the needed infrastructure to support available technology. For instance, the phone system or telecommunications system may be unreliable or dated. Or, the power (electricity) generation system may be insufficient to support technological requirements. Or a country's highway system may be in poor shape or not conveniently located. Many variables determine whether a given technology will prove to be an opportunity or a threat to your organization in another global location, and it's important to assess those variables.

Finding Information on the External Environment and Evaluating It

To find information, look for specific data, statistics, analyses, trends, predictions, forecasts, inferences, or statements made by experts or other types of evidence of what's happening or predicted to happen in the sectors. Then this information needs to be evaluated. Will it help your organization improve its performance currently or in the future, or will it hinder its performance? In other words, does the current external environment present opportunities or threats to your organization? How about the trends? This information about the external environment is used by decision makers to evaluate current strategies and to formulate future strategies.

External information can be found using informal and unscientific observations or by using a more formal, systematic search. For many decision makers, it's enough to talk to customers and suppliers' sales representatives or to read industry trade journals and general news magazines. Such informal, unscientific information-gathering activities often provide sufficient clues to the trends taking place in certain sectors of the external environment, giving strategic decision makers a basis to make effective strategic decisions, even with rather limited information. However, a thorough and comprehensive external analysis requires more of a systematic, deliberate search. In fact, having some type of formal approach is the key to identifying specific opportunities and threats. An **external information system** is an information system that provides managers with needed external information on a regular basis. Again, keep in mind that the whole purpose of the external analysis is to identify potential trends and changes that could positively or negatively impact your organization's performance. How often decision makers need information about external sectors depends on how complex and dynamic an organization's environment is. The more complex and dynamic the environment (i.e., the more environmental uncertainty there is), the more often you'd want information. For some organizations in complex and dynamic industries, this might be as often as once a month. For others, gathering

---

FOR YOUR INFORMATION
Spotting Trends

The skill of observing. Do you have it? Can you pick up on what people think is "hot" or popular? Faith Popcorn, an author and well-known trend spotter, actually says that you don't have to be a pro to be good at it. In fact, professionals may be constrained from recognizing emerging trends by rigid organizational structures and their past successes. So, how can *you* become more in tune with what's happening and hone your skills at trend spotting? Here are some suggestions:

1. Remember that valuable information can be found anywhere and everywhere. Read magazines you don't normally read. Watch television shows or movies that you personally might not be interested in. Go places. Do things. Talk to people. Information is the bread and butter of a good trend spotter.

2. File the information away. If your memory isn't as good as it should be, use note cards. What you write down doesn't have to be long and complex. It could be something as simple as "avocado seems to be a hot color," "teens seem to be flocking to organized fitness programs," or whatever.

3. Determine whether the fads seem to be part of deeper, wider trends. Do this by assessing whether the fad seems to have staying power, whether the fad is a reflection of a change in people's attitudes or behaviors, and whether you see the fad in more than a few places.

4. Don't expect trends to jump out at you. After all, if they were easy to spot, everyone would be doing it. You have to be alert, be open to new and unusual possibilities, and be willing to work at it.

Spotting trends can be a good skill for strategic decision makers. Such information can provide them with significant insights into potential opportunities and threats.

THINK ABOUT

- How could trend spotting be part of an external analysis?
- Are there any drawbacks to trend spotting? Explain.

Sources: Based on D. Sull, "10 Clues to Opportunity," *Strategy & Business Online,* August 23, 2011; E. Ofek and L. Wathieu, "Are You Ignoring Trends That Could Shake Up Your Business?" *Harvard Business Review,* July–August 2010, pp. 124–131; G. Moran, "Be Your Own Trend Spotter," *Entrepreneur,* December 2008, pp. 17–18; B. Snyder Bulik, "Cool Hunting Goes Corporate," *Advertising Age,* August 1, 2005, pp. 3–26; L. Grossman, "The Quest for Cool," *Time,* September 8, 2003, pp. 48–54; and R. Furchgott, "Trend-Spotting Anyone Can Play," *Business Week Enterprise,* March 2, 1998, pp. ENT12–ENT16.

and assessing external information twice or even once a year might be enough. No matter how uncertain the external environment, if current strategies aren't working (getting desired results), decision makers will do something. And that starts with doing an external analysis to determine opportunities and threats.

Doing an external analysis isn't as difficult as it may sound! You may feel that you're going to spend hours locating and interpreting information. Actually, the problem you'll find is not about having *enough* information; it's having *too much* information. To manage this, approach it systematically. For each external sector, ask yourself what information would be important for your organization and industry, keeping in mind that industries differ in terms of the potential impact of external trends. For instance, in the economic sector, you may decide that interest rates are likely to have a significant impact on your industry, so you'd want to find current and forecasted interest rates. If your target customers are teenage girls, you'd probably want to know the demographic and sociocultural trends for this particular group. Thus, you should concentrate on getting the information that's important.

Responsibilities for External Analysis at Different Managerial Levels

In smaller and medium-sized organizations, all employees should monitor changes in the specific (industry-competitive) environment. In fact, in many smaller organizations, frontline employees often have the most direct interactions with customers and supplier representatives and may have some contact with competitors' employees. These employees, who often hear comments or statements from outsiders, should be educated about the organization's external environment and how important this type of information is to strategic decision making. If they hear comments that possibly indicate changing circumstances, encourage them to share that information. The managers/owners can then determine whether the situation needs further analysis before changing strategies.

In large organizations, doing a single external analysis for the entire organization isn't likely to provide good enough information for making strategic decisions. There are too many and too varied units and levels. In larger organizations, it's the managers who are likely to be responsible for monitoring external trends or changes and identifying potential opportunities or threats. Their responsibilities for the external analysis process will vary somewhat depending on their organizational level.

Just as in smaller organizations, the role of lower-level supervisors in those areas where employees have direct contact with customers and suppliers' sales representatives is to encourage those employees to listen for comments that might indicate emerging trends. The role of mid-level managers is to coordinate any external information provided from the different functional departments or divisional units and to share this information with other organizational units that might benefit. Their role is more of an information gatherer and disseminator. Also, mid-level managers might monitor changes in the general environment that are particularly important to their specific areas of responsibility and to use this information to change strategies. That leaves top-level managers who, because of their broad perspective on situations, see the "whole" picture. These managers will use external information in formulating corporate strategies. In larger organizations where there may be a separate strategy group, an external analysis will be completed as part of a formalized strategic planning process. If there isn't such a group, the information that has been compiled by the various business units and divisions about possible opportunities and threats is what top-level managers will rely on.

No matter at what organizational level you find yourself, you'll be involved in some aspect of external analysis. That reinforces one of this text's premises—that everyone in the organization is involved in managing strategically.

FOR YOUR INFORMATION
Competitor Intelligence

One approach to environmental scanning—**competitor intelligence**—is an information-gathering activity that seeks to identify who competitors are, what they're doing, and how their actions will affect your organization. It's been suggested that 80 percent of what strategic decision makers need to know about competitors can be found out from their own employees, suppliers, and customers. So, competitor intelligence doesn't *have* to involve organizational spying. Advertisements, promotional materials, press releases, reports filed with governmental agencies, annual reports, want ads, newspaper reports, and industry studies are examples of accessible information. Attending trade shows and talking to your company's sales representatives can be other good sources of information on competitors. Many organizations even buy competitors' products and have their engineers break them down (using reverse engineering) to learn about new technical innovations. And the Internet has opened up new sources of competitor intelligence as many corporate Web pages include new product information and other information such as press releases. However, when we hear about companies using unscrupulous methods to get sensitive information, questions and concerns come up regarding ways in which competitor information is gathered. Competitor intelligence becomes illegal corporate spying when it involves the theft of proprietary materials or trade secrets by any means. Often, there's a fine line between what's considered *legal and ethical* and what's considered *legal but unethical*.

THINK ABOUT

- Check out the Intelligence Index and CI Tools at **[www.fuld.com]**. What do you think about the information that's discussed there?
- Do you think competitor intelligence has a place in external analysis? Why or why not?

Sources: Based on M. Orey, "Corporate Snoops," *BusinessWeek*, October 9, 2006, pp. 46–49; K. Girard, "Snooping on a Shoestring," *Business 2.0*, May 2003, pp. 64–66; and D. Kinard, "Raising Your Competitive IQ: The Payoff of Paying Attention to Potential Competitors," *Association Management*, February 2003, pp. 40–44.

LEARNING REVIEW   LEARNING OUTCOME 3.2

- What does the five-forces model look at, and how is it used?
- What is examined in each of the five components of the general environment?
- How is an external analysis done for a company that's doing business globally?
- How is information on the external environment found and evaluated?
- Describe the different responsibilities for doing an external analysis.

By now, you should have a pretty good feel for what an external analysis is and how one is done, but still may not be convinced why it's important to know what's happening in your organization's external environment. In this section, we're going to look at *why* you need to do an external analysis and at some of the challenges of doing one.

Benefits of Doing an External Analysis

We've already mentioned that the reason for doing an external analysis is to identify potential opportunities and threats facing an organization. By deliberately and systematically analyzing the external environment, a manager can be a **proactive manager**—that is, a manager who anticipates changes and plans for those changes, instead of just simply reacting to them. In fact, proactive managers may, at times, be able to influence various external environmental sectors to the organization's benefit (i.e., encourage changes that would have a positive effect on the organization's performance). For instance, lobbying is one way managers proactively manage their external environment. However, external analysis is important for other reasons as well.

LEARNING OUTCOME 3.3

Discuss the Benefits and Challenges of Doing an External Analysis

An external analysis provides the information that strategic managers use in planning, decision making, and strategy formulation.[31] Think back to our discussion of the "environment as information" perspective. One real value in studying the external environment is the information it provides. This information is useful to the extent that strategic decision makers can determine ways to take advantage of the positive changes and ways to buffer against, neutralize, or adapt to the negative changes. How? By changing the organization's strategies. These strategies *should be* based on information about markets, customers, technology, and so forth.[32] Because an organization's environment is changing continually, having information about the various external sectors is important in formulating strategies that "align" the organization with its environment.

The "environment as source of resources" perspective also provides another reason for doing an external analysis. An organization's ability to acquire and control needed resources depends on having strategies that take advantage of the environment's abundant resources and strategies that cope with the environment's limited resources.[33] Think back to our description of an organization as an open system. Because the organization depends on the environment as a source of inputs (resources) and as an outlet for outputs, it only makes sense that strategies should be formulated that help the organization get needed resources that then can be converted into desired outputs. Organizations can do that most effectively by understanding what the environment has to offer.

Another reason for doing an external analysis is the realization that today's external environment is increasingly dynamic. Turbulent market conditions, fragmented markets, less brand loyalty, more demanding customers, rapid changes in technology, and intense global competition are just a few of the realities of today's business environment. And these conditions aren't the exception—they're the norm. All sizes and all types of organizations are facing increasingly dynamic environments. In order to effectively cope with these changes, managers need to examine the external environment.[34]

Our final reason for doing an external analysis relates to whether doing so really makes a difference. In other words, does an external analysis really make a difference in an organization's performance? The answer is that it *does* appear to make a difference. Research studies generally have shown that in organizations in which strategic decision makers did external analyses, performance was higher.[35] Performance was typically evaluated using a financial measure such as return on assets or growth in profitability. The fact that doing an external analysis appears to make a difference in performance results is a pretty good reason for wanting to know how to do one and to actually doing it as part of the strategic management process.

Challenges of Doing an External Analysis

There are some challenges associated with doing an external analysis. For one thing, the environment might be changing more rapidly—technology, new competitors, new customers, laws—than realistically can be kept up with. Such rapid change is happening in many industries, not just in high-tech industries. Just keeping track of the current situation *and* changing trends can be a challenge.

Another challenge of doing an external analysis is the amount of time it can consume. Systematically scanning and evaluating the environment is important, yet it takes time, and most strategic decision makers are busy managing and don't feel they have the time. However, external analysis *is* important as part of managing strategically. The key is to make the process as efficient and effective as possible. This may mean doing things such as identifying particularly critical external sectors and monitoring those more frequently and other sectors not as frequently; relying on specialized database searches, news clipping services, or even personalized Internet searches to monitor changes in those significant sectors; or even sharing the responsibilities for analyzing the external sectors with others in the organization.

Finally, you need to understand that while forecasts and trend analyses are a significant part of the external analysis, they aren't perfect. Forecasts aren't facts: they're the best predictions experts have about what they believe is going to happen. For instance, you've probably had the experience of leaving your home without a coat and umbrella after listening to the weather forecast for a sunny, warm day only to be greeted by a cold, pouring rain. Forecasts of business, economic, or attitudinal trends aren't always accurate either. However, strategic decision makers need to be flexible, open, and alert to changing circumstances. Managing strategically is an ongoing process. Strategies don't always succeed, for whatever reason. Results may fall short because of some internal shortcoming or because the predictions we'd made about external opportunities and threats were inaccurate. Whatever the reason, strategies can be changed as needed to take advantage of new information. Even though forecasts, predictions, and trend analyses aren't always 100 percent accurate, they can provide us with a sense of the strategic direction we need to go. Even given the shortcomings, that's a pretty good reason to continue to look at them.

LEARNING REVIEW   LEARNING OUTCOME 3.3

- List some benefits of doing an external analysis.
- Discuss the challenges associated with doing an external analysis.

The Bottom Line

Learning Outcome 3.1: Describe an external analysis.

- *External analysis:* process of scanning and evaluating the external environment in order to identify opportunities and threats.
- *Opportunities:* positive external trends or changes that may help improve the organization's performance; *threats:* negative trends or changes that may hinder the organization's performance.
- Based on the idea that organizations are *open systems,* which means they interact with and respond to their environment.
- Two perspectives on organizational environments: (1) environment as information is based on the idea of *environmental uncertainty:* amount of change and complexity in organization's environment; the more dynamic and complex the environment, the more uncertainty there is and the greater the need for information; (2) environment as a source of resources is based on the idea that as environments become more hostile, the more difficult it is to obtain and control resources; managers monitor environment in order to acquire and control those needed resources.
- Important to scan *and* evaluate external environment.

Learning Outcome 3.2: Explain how to do an external analysis of an organization's specific and general environments.

- External sectors are classified as *specific* (customers, competitors, suppliers, and other industry-competitive variables) and *general* (economic, demographic, sociocultural, political-legal, and technological).
- Specific environment is analyzed using the five competitive factors approach: (1) **existing competitors** are evaluated by eight factors: number of competitors and how balanced their market shares are, rate of industry growth, level of fixed or storage costs, amount of differentiation and switching costs, capacity increments required, diversity of competitors, extent of strategic stakes, and extent of *exit barriers* (those factors that keep companies competing in an industry); current competitors may be determined by *strategic group* (a group of industry firms that have similar strategies, resources, and customers); (2) **possible competitors** are determined by seven factors: *barriers to entry* (obstacles to entering an industry) including economies of scale, cost disadvantages from other than scale, product differentiation, capital requirements, *switching costs* (one-time costs a buyer faces when switching from one competitor's product to another), access to distribution channels, and government policy protection; (3) **consumers** are evaluated by eight factors: how much the consumer purchases, whether those purchases represent a significant portion of consumer's costs, how much standardization or differentiation products have, whether consumer faces switching costs, level of consumer's profits or income, consumer's ability to manufacture products being purchased, how important products are to consumer, and how much information consumer has; (4) **resource providers** are evaluated by seven factors: how many resource providers there are, how concentrated they are, whether there are substitute products, how important industry is to resource providers, how important resource providers' products are to industry, level of differentiation and switching costs, and whether industry can supply what resource providers offer; and (5) **threat of alternative industry providers** is determined by whether there is another industry that can satisfy customers' needs.
- The general environment includes five sectors that are evaluated: (1) **economic,** which looks at all the macroeconomic data that reflect what's happening with the overall economy; (2) **demographics,** which looks at current data and trends in population characteristics—census-type information; (3) **sociocultural,** which looks at current data

and trends in society and culture—values, attitudes, behavior patterns, and so forth; (4) **political-legal,** which looks at laws, regulations, judicial decisions, and political forces; and (5) **technological,** which looks at scientific or technological innovations.

- When looking for external information, look for data, statistics, analyses, trends, predictions, forecasts, inferences, or statements made by experts.
- External analysis can be informal and unscientific or more formal using an *external information system,* an information system that provides managers with needed external information on a regular basis.
- In smaller and medium-sized organizations, external analysis needs to be done by all employees, especially those on the front line. In larger organizations, external analysis is usually the responsibility of managers.

Learning Outcome 3.3: Discuss the benefits and challenges of doing an external analysis.

- *Benefits:* (1) makes *managers proactive:* managers who anticipate changes and plan for those changes instead of simply reacting; (2) provides information used in planning, decision making, and formulating strategy; (3) helps organizations get needed resources—environment as source of resources; (4) helps organizations cope with uncertain environments—environment as source of information; and (5) makes a difference in organization's performance.
- *Challenges:* (1) rapidly changing environment can be hard to keep up with; (2) it's time consuming; and (3) forecasts and trend analyses aren't perfect.

YOU as strategic decision maker: building your skills

1. Go to the U.S. Census Bureau Web site [**www.census.gov**]. List the major categories and subcategories found there. Choose one of the subcategories, and do a more thorough description and analysis of the information in it. How might this information be valuable to strategic decision makers? Evaluate the availability and ease-of-finding information found on the Web site. What "lesson(s)" did you learn from your immersion in the Census Bureau Web site?

2. It has been suggested that one simple way to do an external analysis is by asking these six questions: (a) What is happening in the world today? (b) What does it mean for others? (c) What does it mean for us? (d) What would have to happen first for the results we want to occur? (e) What do we have to do to play a role? and (f) What do we do next? What do you think of this approach to external analysis? What's good about it? Bad?

3. Find three different online sources that report basic economic data. Describe what each of the sources provides. Which would you recommend as a source of economic data? Why?

4. A study for the U.S. Department of Labor completed by the Rand Corporation, a think tank based in Santa Monica, California, showed that the nation's workforce will be smaller and more diverse, more mobile, and more vulnerable to global competition. What implications (positive and negative) do these trends have for organizational strategies?

5. The demographic trend of an aging baby boom generation, combined with struggling financial markets, has forced many people to delay retirement. This has created some interesting strategic scenarios, not only in marketing opportunities and threats, but also in the area of human resources. What opportunities and threats do you see in this convergence of demographic factors? How might these opportunities and threats change for different industries?

6. Two of the major competitors in the fast-food industry—Wendy's and McDonald's—have positioned themselves differently. Wendy's has taken the adult approach, practically ignoring the children's market with its advertising tie-ins and toy giveaways. McDonald's has long pursued the kids' market. Think about demographic and sociocultural trends and changes. How would each organization's interpretation of these trends and changes affect its choice of strategy? Which organization do you think is positioned better? Explain your choice.

7. A survey listing the most important cultural values of the United States included the following (most important listed first): protecting the family, honesty, stable personal relationships, self-esteem, freedom, friendship, and respecting one's ancestors. What do you think are the strategic implications of such findings? Might these implications change for different industries? If so, how? If not, why not?

8. In a survey that asked corporate leaders whether they communicated with their employees about how the economy was impacting their company, 70 percent said no. What do you think of this? Why might they be reluctant to do so? How might more open communication with employees be a benefit?

CASES

CASE #1 Not Sold Out

Aaron Kohr/Fotolia.com

This Strategic Management in Action case can be found at the beginning of Chapter 3.

1. What external trends do the strategic managers at the movie theater chains have to evaluate? What external sectors are these trends part of? Are these external trends of equal importance to the movie theater chains? Explain why or why not.

2. What opportunities and threats do you see in this situation? Describe.

3. How do you think these external trends might affect the strategies used by the movie theater chains? Be specific.

4. If you were a strategic decision maker at the corporate headquarters of one of these movie theater chains, what types of external information would you want? What if you were a manager at a local movie theater: what types of external information would you want?

CASE #2 Being the Best

As the nation's leading consumer electronics retailer, Best Buy *is* trying to be the best. But that's not been easy in light of the challenges it's facing in the external environment. Like many other retailers, the economic climate has forced Best Buy to carefully consider its strategic options.

Best Buy was founded under the name Sound of Music in 1966 as a home- and car-stereo store by Dick Schulze (he still remains as board chair), who got tired of working for his father, who would never listen to his ideas on how to improve the family's electronics distribution business. However, while chairing a school board in the early 1980s, Schulze realized that his target customer group—15- to 18-year-old males—was declining sharply. He decided to broaden his product line and target older and more affluent customers by offering appliances and VCRs. In 1981, a tornado wiped out his entire store (but not the inventory). Schulze decided to spend his entire marketing budget on advertising a huge parking lot sale. The successful sale taught him the importance of strong advertising, wide selection, and low prices—lessons that would serve him well as he built his business. In 1983, Schulze changed the name to Best Buy and began to open larger superstores. The change in store format and the fast-rising popularity of VCRs led to rapid growth. The number of stores grew from 8 to 24 and revenues skyrocketed from $29 million to $240 million.

In 1989, Schulze introduced the warehouse-like store format. By setting up stores so customers could browse where they wanted, the company was able to reduce the number of employees, a real cost saver. Larger store formats were introduced in 1994 and the company kept opening new stores. By 1997, the company realized that it had overextended itself with its expansion efforts, the super-sized stores, and costly consumer financing promotions. In response, the company went through a massive makeover, scaling back expansion plans and doing away

with its "no money down, no monthly payments, no interest" program.

In 1999, Best Buy went through another evolutionary change as digital electronics began to flood the market. Store formats now highlighted digital products and featured stations for computer software and DVD demonstrations. They also decided to branch out into audio and video stores by acquiring the Magnolia Hi-Fi chain of stores and The Musicland Group (Sam Goody Stores, Suncoast, On Cue, and Media Play music stores). This strategy turned out to be a mistake and Best Buy sold off the entire Musicland subsidiary in June 2003.

In 2004, the company began focusing on bundling high-end electronics with service and installation, without giving up the low prices. Best Buy's former CEO, Brad Anderson, admitted this strategy was risky, stating, "Nobody has been able to do this before. If we can only figure out the puzzle." Why did they start messing with a successful formula? Because Anderson felt there was "trouble" ahead. The company's store base was maturing. Imports were flooding the market and shorter product life cycles were exerting severe price pressures on some of the company's most profitable products—digital TVs, cameras, and home entertainment systems. And then there were Wal-Mart and Costco. These mass merchants and even direct seller Dell had ramped up their consumer electronics offerings. At the time, Anderson reasoned that, "If we do nothing, Wal-Mart will surpass us by the simple fact they're adding more stores than we are each year." There was no way Best Buy could win by "trying to chase the customer out of Wal-Mart." However, even though Best Buy felt that it couldn't compete on merchandise, it could compete with add-on services. Best Buy's acquisition of Geek Squad, a Minneapolis start-up, was an important key to that strategy. In addition, Best Buy began to sell private-label goods. It opened an office in Shanghai in September 2003 that allowed it to source products directly.

Then the company turned to a massive effort to identify and serve its most profitable shoppers (a process called "customer centricity"), an idea based on the belief that not all customers are profitable ones. Some are lucrative, whereas others cost more to sell to than their business is worth. After researching massive amounts of sales and demographics data, Best Buy identified some lucrative consumer segments and gave them the following names: Barry, the affluent tech enthusiast; Jill, a busy suburban mom; Buzz, a young gadget freak; Ray, a price-conscious family guy; Carrie, a young single woman; and others. Each store was oriented toward the segments that most reflected its customer base. Continuing its commitment to this centricity strategy, Best Buy is "getting in touch with its feminine side." As a company vice president said, "We were a boy's toy store designed *for* boys *by* boys." No more. Best Buy has feminized its stores by doing things such as turning down the volume of store music, lowering the bright lights, training salespeople to talk to customers about their lifestyles, and eliminating the flashing lights—all in an attempt to create a softer, more personal atmosphere.

In early 2011, Best Buy joined other retail chains in going smaller. It announced it was slowing growth of new "big-box" stores and instead focusing on Best Buy Mobile locations where smartphones were the primary attraction. In an attempt to better utilize the space in its larger stores, Best Buy also began moving into health and exercise equipment in addition to electronics and musical instruments.

There are risks associated with Best Buy's strategic moves. Uncertain economic conditions, a shaky global economy, and low consumer confidence mean that Best Buy must continue to find ways to weather the challenges. Doing nothing isn't a feasible option. It is substantially reducing new store openings and may be forced to lay off employees. In response to critics who have questioned the speed with which Best Buy was adapting its business model to growing online competition, former CEO Brian Dunn said that it was a "fair criticism." However, he also said that the belief that "specialty-store chains were doomed by the rise of Internet merchants such as Amazon.com" was off-base.

Dunn "cited a recent study which found that roughly 80 percent of electronics were still bought in stores, and added that Best Buy saw store visits climb in the last quarter of 2011."

Discussion Questions

1. What examples of environmental scanning do you see in this case? What role do you think environmental scanning has played in the company's evolution? What role will it need to play in the company's future?
2. Using the five competitive factors approach and the information in the case, do a brief industry-competitive analysis.
3. What types of information do you think Dunn might want from each of the five general environmental sectors? (You don't need to look up this information. Just indicate what trends they would probably want to keep track of.)
4. What opportunities and threats do you think are facing this industry?
5. Best Buy has 2,600 stores in Europe and China (and has stores in Canada) and is looking to global markets for growth. As the company goes more international, what types of external information will it need?
6. Update the information on Best Buy: number of stores, revenues, profits, and employees. Are these numbers increasing or declining?

Sources: Based on M. Bustillo and M. Jarzemsky, "Best Buy CEO Defies Critics," *Wall Street Journal,* January 7 and 8, 2012, p. B3; J. Graham, "Talking Your Tech: Interview with Brian Dunn, Best Buy CEO," *USA Today,* November 28, 2011, p. 4B; M. Scott, "Best Buy Pays $1.3 Billion for Cellphone Business," *New York Times Online,* November 7, 2011; M. Bastillo and M. Jarzemsky, "Best Buy Gets Squeezed," *Wall Street Journal,* September 14, 2011, pp. B1+; The Associated Press, "Competition Takes a Bite Out of Best Buy's Profits," *USA Today,* September 14, 2011, p. 3B; M. Bustillo, "Best Buy to Shrink 'Big-Box' Store Strategy," *Wall Street Journal,* April 15, 2011, p. B7; M. Anderson, The Associated Press, "Best Buy Thinking Small as Sales Fall," *Springfield, Missouri News-Leader,* March 25, 2011, p. 4A; and M. Bustillo, "As Big Boxes Shrink, They Also Rethink," *Wall Street Journal,* March 3, 2011, p. B1+.

CASE #3 Dressing Up

Even in good times, the department store industry is one of the toughest industries to compete in. Like many of its competitors, Kohl's Corporation struggles to find a way to continue its successes even when faced with a drastically changed external environment. Based in Menomonee Falls, Wisconsin, Kohl's has more than 1,100 discount department stores in 49 states. The company has aggressively moved into the western and southern United States, although nearly a third of its stores are located in the Midwest. In 2011, the company had revenues of over $18 billion (up 7 percent over 2010) and profits of over $1 billion, an increase from the previous year of almost 12.5 percent. One analyst described Kohl's as "the best-positioned department store in this economy and one of the leading retailers with respect to inventory management, technological innovation, and merchandising and marketing execution." To

continue its successes, it's important that Kohl's understands the changing needs of its customers.

Over the last few years, customers had become disillusioned with the overall shopping experience at many retail establishments. Long checkout lines, missing or vague product information, out-of-stock products, incorrect price tags, and scarce and often unknowledgeable sales staff have made the shopping experience quite unpleasant. Local shopping malls with their anchor department stores lost much of their popularity with shoppers. Unlike other department stores, Kohl's followed a different path.

Kohl's strategic approach has been built around convenience and price. A typical Kohl's store is a box-like structure with one floor of merchandise under inexpensive lighting where shoppers use carts or bags as they browse through the simple racks and shelves of clothing, shoes, and home apparel merchandise. The company is especially selective about its locations. Everything about the way Kohl's does business—who it sells to and how those customers shop—hinges on where it puts its stores. Its expansion goal is designed to achieve profitable growth. In 1992, at the time of its initial public offering, it had 79 stores in the Midwest. Now, it's in 49 states from coast-to-coast. In 2011, it had 300 stores in the Midwest, 110 stores in the Mid-Atlantic region, 147 stores in the Northeast, 143 stores in the South Central region, 183 stores in the Southeast region, and 244 stores in the West. In deciding where to place its store, Kohl's typically avoids malls when looking at store sites, believing that its target customers—young mothers—typically don't have the time for a long drive to a mall location and certainly don't want the parking hassles when they do go shopping. Its approach has been free-standing buildings with smaller parking lots in retailing power centers (a retailing destination where several large, specialty brand retailers often locate together) and other kinds of strip malls. For instance, the Kohl's store in Springfield, Missouri, is located adjacent to a Wal-Mart Super Center, a Home Depot, a McDonald's, a Michael's hobby and crafts store, and other casual dining restaurants.

Kohl's merchandising strategy is oriented around three consumer lifestyles: the classic (traditional, timeless look), the modern classic (modern, classic look), and contemporary (fashion-forward, contemporary look with the latest trends). The merchandise mix is 52 percent national brands (such as Levi's, Dockers, Reebok, Jockey, and Carter's) and 48 percent private and exclusive brands (such as Tony Hawk, Urban Pipeline, LC Lauren Conrad, Simply Vera Vera Wang, Dana Buchman, Candie's, and Croft & Barrow). In September 2011, Kohl's launched its Jennifer Lopez and Marc Anthony brands. Such brands are an attempt to keep pace with "cheap chic" rival Target and with J. C. Penney. As one retail expert put it, "The chains have decided to design apparel on their own, ensuring that their lower-income customers can buy skinny jeans and satchel bags at the same time as shoppers at higher-end stores." Kohl's also has a significant home accessories and home furnishings selection. For instance, there's a home furnishings collection called Casa Cristina (named for Cristina Saralegui, the host of a Spanish-language television show on Univision). It even has its own Food Network brand of dinnerware and cooking tools.

Although Kohl's has done well in a difficult industry, it is facing some serious challenges. Competitors ranging from J. C. Penney and Sears to Macy's have copied Kohl's approach. And on the discount end, Wal-Mart Stores has added national brands and improved the quality of its apparel. However, none is as aggressive in competing with Kohl's as J. C. Penney is. Penney's new CEO, who was Apple's top retailing executive, is shaking things up. He's launching several new strategies including creating dozens of 'stores within a store,' cutting back on private labels, eliminating sales in favor of everyday low prices, and making the center of the store a 'town square' space for events and attractions. "The idea is to make stores more inviting, highlight brand names, and gain more control over pricing." Despite these changes at J. C. Penny, in the latest (early January 2012) Harris Poll, Kohl's edged out J.C. Penny as the top choice for customer relationships. An analyst said, "While neck and neck with J.C. Penny on several metrics, what really stands in Kohl's favor is the customer's perception of the unique benefits offered by the department store." Although Kohl's seems to be on a winning streak, competitor actions and other external trends will keep strategic decision makers on their toes for a while!

Discussion Questions

1. What external areas and trends do you think strategic managers at Kohl's have to deal with?

2. If you were a strategic decision maker at the *headquarters* of Kohl's, what types of external information would you want? What if you were a Kohl's *local* store manager? What types of external information would you want?

3. Go to Kohl's web site **[www.kohls.com]** and find the latest Kohl's Fact book. (Hint: Look at the Investor Relations section.) What strategic initiatives is the company pursuing? Take one of those strategic initiatives and discuss how it will help Kohl's exploit external trends.

4. What industry/competition opportunities and threats do you see in this case?

Sources: Based on "Kohl's Edges J.C. Penney as the People's Pick in the Harris Poll Customer Relationship Series," *Harris Interactive Online* [www.harrisinteractive.com], January 11, 2012; Kohl's Fact book, [www.kohls.com], 2011; S. Clifford, "Nordstrom and Kohl's Expect Profit to Rise More," *New York Times Online*, August 11, 2011; E. Holmes and A. Zimmerman," Dowdy Department Stores Start Looking Cool Again," *Wall Street Journal*, August 4, 2011, pp. B1+; and C. Timberlake and M. Townsend, "How Department Stores Came Back Into Fashion," *Bloomberg BusinessWeek,*" March 21–March 27, 2011, pp. 32–33.

Endnotes

1. "U.S. Movie Market Summary 1995 to 2012," www.the-numbers.com/market, January 15, 2012; D. Germain, "Hollywood's 2011: Lower Attendance and Revenue," *NorthJersey.com*, December 29, 2011; M. Rosenbaum, "Box Office Bust: Movie Attendance Hits 16-Year Low," *ABCNews.com*, December 28, 2011; M. Cieply, "Charging a Premium for Movies, At a Cost," *New York Times Online*, July 31, 2011; M. Healy and K. Gelles, "Number of Movie Screens in the USA," *USA Today*, May 26, 2011, p. 1D; B. Barnes and M. Cieply, "Graying Audience Returns to Movies," *New York Times Online*, February 25, 2011; L. A. E. Schuker, "Double Feature: Dinner and a Movie," *Wall Street Journal*, January 5, 2011, p. D1+; J. O'Donnell, "Going to the Movies - At Home," *USA Today*, January 5, 2011, p. 3B; M. DeCuir, "Some Food and Alcohol with Your Flick? Cinemas Hope So," *USA Today*, March 27, 2008, p. 3A; B. Barnes, "At Cineplexes, Sports, Opera, Maybe a Movie," *New York Times Online*, March 23, 2008; D. Stuckey and K. Gelles, "Entertainment Sold Online," *USA Today*, February 26, 2008; and J. Carroll, "Americans Dislike the Cost of Going to the Movies," *Gallup News Service*, December 22, 2006.

2. "Spending on Pets Reaches All-Time High," The Associated Press, *Springfield, Missouri, News-Leader*, March 3, 2012, pp. 8A+; Industry Statistics and Trends, report by American Pet Products Manufacturers Association [www.americanpetproducts.org], January 23, 2012; and A. Martin, "For the Dogs Has a Whole New Meaning," *New York Times Online*, June 4, 2011.

3. C. Barnard, *The Functions of the Executive* (Cambridge, MA: Harvard University Press, 1938).

4. W. R. Dill, "Environment as an Influence on Managerial Autonomy," *Administrative Science Quarterly*, vol. 2, 1958, pp. 409–443; and J. G. March and H. A. Simon, *Organizations* (New York: John Wiley & Sons, 1958).

5. S. F. Matusik and M. B. Heeley, "Absorptive Capacity in the Software Industry: Identifying Dimensions That Affect Knowledge and Knowledge Creation Activities," *Journal of Management*, August 2005, pp. 549–572; R. L. Tung, "Dimensions of Organizational Environments: An Exploratory Study of Their Impact on Organizational Structure," *Academy of Management Journal*, vol. 22, 1979, pp. 672–693; J. R. Galbraith, *Designing Complex Organizations* (Reading, MA: Addison-Wesley, 1973); R. B. Duncan, "Characteristics of Organizational Environments and Perceived Environment Uncertainty," *Administrative Science Quarterly*, vol. 17, 1972, pp. 313–327; and P. R. Lawrence and J. W. Lorsch, "Differentiation and Integration in Complex Organizations," *Administrative Science Quarterly*, vol. 12, 1967, pp. 1–47.

6. C. A. Lengnick-Hall and T. E. Beck, "Adaptive Fit versus Robust Transformation: How Organizations Respond to Environmental Change," *Journal of Management*, October 2005, pp. 738–757; R. Bettis and C. K. Prahalad, "The Visible and the Invisible Hand: Resource Allocation in the Industrial Sector," *Strategic Management Journal*, vol. 4, 1983, pp. 27–43; J. Freeman, "Organizational Life Cycles and Natural Selection Processes," in B. M. Staw and L. L. Cummings (eds.), *Research in Organizational Behavior* (Greenwich, CT: JAI Press, 1982); H. E. Aldrich, *Organizations and Environments* (Englewood Cliffs, NJ: Prentice Hall, 1979); J. Pfeffer and G. R. Salancik, *The External Control of Organizations: A Resource Dependence Perspective* (New York: Harper & Row, 1978); H. E. Aldrich and J. Pfeffer, "Environments of Organizations," *Annual Review of Sociology*, vol. 2, 1976, pp. 79–105; S. Mindlin, *Organizational Dependence on Environment and Organizational Structure: A Reexamination of the Aston Group*, unpublished master's thesis, Cornell University, Ithaca, NY, 1974; J. Hage and M. Aiken, "Program Change and Organizational Properties," *American Journal of Sociology*, vol. 72, 1973, pp. 503–579; and March & Simon, *Organizations*, 1958.

7. J. Sapsford, "Toyota Moves to Secure Hybrid Parts," *Wall Street Journal*, October 6, 2005, p. A11.

8. M. E. Porter, *Competitive Strategy* (New York: The Free Press, 1980).

9. F. Norris, "Airbus and Boeing Show That Making Planes Beats Flying Them," *New York Times Online*, June 24, 2006.

10. M. E. Porter, *Competitive Strategy*, pp. 17–21.

11. Newspaper Association of America, "Daily Newspaper Readership Trend 1998–2007," [www.naa.org], January 11, 2009; and R. Smolkin, "Uncertain Times," *American Journalism Review* [www.ajr.org], December/January 2005.

12. S. J. Young, "Back to Back Cruises," *Travel Agent*, December 12, 2011, pp. 22–24; G. Sloan, "Sizing Up Three Mega-Sized Cruise Ships," *USA Today*, October 14, 2011, p. 6D; and G. Barker, "Aboard the Allure of the Seas: This Ship is Giant Fun," *The Palm Beach Post Online*, December 3, 2010.

13. M.E. Porter, p. 20.

14. J. C. Short, D. J. Ketchen, Jr., T. B. Palmer, G. Hult, and M. Tomas, "Firm, Strategic Group, and Industry Influences on Performance," *Strategic Management Journal,* February 2007, pp. 147–167; G. Leask and D. Parker, "Strategic Group Theory: Review, Examination, and Application in the UK Pharmaceutical Industry," *Journal of Management Development,* vol. 25, no. 4, 2006, pp. 386–408; J. R. Gregg, "Strategic Groups Theory: Past Nuances, Future Frontiers," *Southwest Academy of Management Proceedings,* March 1996, San Antonio, TX, pp. 29–32; J. R. Barney and R. Hoskisson, "Strategic Groups: Untested Assertions and Research Proposals," *Managerial and Decision Economics,* 11, 1990, pp. 187–198; K. Cool and D. Schendel, "Strategic Group Formation and Performance: The Case of the U.S. Pharmaceutical Industry, 1963–1982," *Management Science,* vol. 33, no. 9, 1987, pp. 1101–1124; G. Dess and P. Davis, "Porter's [1980] Generic Strategies as Determinants of Strategic Group Membership and Organizational Performance," *Academy of Management Journal,* vol. 27, no. 3, 1984, pp. 467–488; and M. S. Hunt, *Competition in the Major Home Appliance Industry 1960–1970,* unpublished doctoral dissertation, Harvard University, 1972.

15. E. Smith, "Ticket Service Set for Debut," *Wall Street Journal,* August 23, 2011, p. B4; and B. Sisario, "Ticket Sales Start-Up Aims at Smaller Box Offices," *New York Times Online,* July 31, 2011.

16. M. E. Porter, *Competitive Strategy,* pp. 7–17.

17. D. Lieberman, "Top Hollywood Studios Agree on Standards for Digital Films," *New York Times Online,* July 28, 2005.

18. N. Knox, "Realtors Fight for Business Model," *USA Today,* July 13, 2006, p. 4B.

19. M. E. Porter, *Competitive Strategy,* pp. 24–27.

20. A. Levin, "De-Icer Shortage Threatens Flights," *USA Today,* December 5, 2008, p. 1A; B. Hindo, "My Kingdom for a Tire," *BusinessWeek,* April 21, 2008, pp. 46–48; T. Aeppel, "Tight Supply Chain Is Good News for Terex," *Wall Street Journal,* August 28, 2006, p. A8; P. B. Kavilanz, "China Labor Pains and Holiday Woes," *CNNMoney.com,* August 9, 2006; B. Hagenbaugh, "Supplies Fall Short for Tall Tires," *USA Today,* May 17, 2005, p. 4B; and E. Ramstad, "Ever Heard of Indium? Screen Makers Have, and Some Are Worried," *Wall Street Journal,* August 9, 2004, p. B1.

21. M. E. Porter, *Competitive Strategy,* pp. 27–28.

22. Company information from *Hoovers.com,* January 23, 2012; and M. Barbaro, "At Liz Claiborne, a Bold Fashion Statement," *New York Times Online,* July 31, 2007.

23. E. Byron, "How to Market to an Aging Boomer: Flattery, Subterfuge and Euphemism," *Wall Street Journal,* February 5 - 6, 2011, pp. A1+; and N. Singer, "In a Graying Population, Business Opportunity," *New York Times Online,* February 5, 2011.

24. "American FactFinder," U.S. Census Bureau, [http://factfinder2.census.gov/], January 24, 2012.

25. P. Burrows, "The Mac in the Gray Flannel Suit," *BusinessWeek,* May 12, 2008, pp. 36–42.

26. A. Athavaley, "Lowering the Volume on Leaf Blowers," *Wall Street Journal,* January 7, 2009, p. D8; "Many Foods will Soon Be Labeled by Country of Origin," *New York Times Online,* October 1, 2008; and "Senate Approves Legislation to Expand Workplace Disability Law," *Workforce Management Online,* September 16, 2008.

27. "New Bankruptcy Law Aids American Express," *New York Times Online* (The Associated Press), January 23, 2007.

28. "Businesses Battle Over Patent Laws," *Wall Street Journal,* June 9/10, 2007, p. A7; G. Hitt, "Industries Brace for Tough Battle Over Patent Law," *Wall Street Journal,* June 6, 2007, pp. A1+; J. Bravin and M. Chase, "High Court Eases Way for Patent Challenges," *Wall Street Journal,* January 10, 2007, p. A8; L. Greenhouse, "Supreme Court Weighs the Meaning of 'Obvious,' " *New York Times Online,* November 29, 2006; and J. Bravin, "As Patents Grow More Contentious, Battleground Shifts to High Court," *Wall Street Journal,* November 28, 2006, pp. A1+.

29. "CEOs Want Tough Global-Warming Laws," *CNNMoney.com,* January 22, 2007; and S. Armour, "Crackdown on Hiring of Illegal Workers Shifts to Employers," *USA Today,* May 5, 2006, pp. 1B+.

30. "40 Under 40: "Pony Ma Huateng," *Fortune.com,* March 26, 2010; and D. Barboza, "Internet Boom in China Is Built on Virtual Fun," *New York Times Online,* February 5, 2007.

31. V. K. Garg, B. A. Walters, and R. L. Priem, "Chief Executive Scanning Emphases, Environmental Dynamism, and Manufacturing Firm Performance," *Strategic Management Journal,* August 2003, pp. 725–744; B. K. Boyd and J. Fulk, "Executive Scanning and Perceived Uncertainty: A Multidimensional Model," *Journal of Management,* vol. 22, no. 1, 1996, pp. 1–21; and R. L. Daft, J. Sormunen, and D. Parks, "Chief Executive Scanning, Environmental Characteristics, and Company Performance: An Empirical Study," *Strategic Management Journal,* March/April 1988, pp. 123–139.

32. P. F. Drucker, "The Information Executives Truly Need," *Harvard Business Review,* January–February 1995, pp. 54–62.

33. C. S. Korberg and G. R. Ungson, "The Effects of Environmental Uncertainty and Dependence on Organizational Structure and Performance: A Comparative Study," *Journal of Management,* Winter 1987, pp. 725–737.

34. R. S. Achrol and L. W. Stern, "Environmental Determinants of Decision-Making Uncertainty in Marketing Channels," *Journal of Marketing,* February 1988, pp. 36–50.

35. Garg, Walters, and Priem, "Chief Executive Scanning Emphases, Environmental Dynamism, and Manufacturing Firm Performance"; S. Kotha and A. Nair, "Strategy and Environment as Determinants of Performance: Evidence from the Japanese Machine Tool Industry," *Strategic Management Journal,* 16, 1995, pp. 497–518; R. Subramanian et al., "An Empirical Examination of the Relationship between Strategy and Scanning," *The Mid-Atlantic Journal of Business,* December 1993, pp. 315–330; and Daft et al., 1988.

LEARNING OUTCOMES

4.1 **Describe an internal analysis.**

4.2 **Explain how to do an internal analysis.**

4.3 **Discuss why an internal analysis is important.**

STRATEGIC
MANAGEMENT
IN ACTION

CASE #1 Making Over Avon

As the world's top direct seller of cosmetics and beauty-related items, Avon Products is building a global brand and attempting to get younger consumers to buy its products.[1] The company sells and distributes its products in more than 100 countries and territories and has a sales force of 6.5 million representatives. During the recent global recession with persistently high unemployment rates around the world, Avon increased its number of independent representatives by more than 12 percent. "Avon further enhanced its image as 'The Company for Women' by promoting business opportunities for women in countries where fewer choices are available to them." It has focused particularly on building its ranks of sales representatives in countries such as Russia and China where it's hoped that a growing middle class will increase its spending on consumer goods and services.

Irochka/Fotolia.com

In 2010, Avon celebrated its 125th year—a remarkable achievement, for sure. The company manufactures and packages almost all of its beauty products. Raw materials, which include essential oils, chemicals, containers, and packaging materials, are purchased from various suppliers. Most fashion and home products are purchased from various suppliers. However, as raw materials prices climbed, it hit the company hard. In addition, operational inefficiencies and an inability to execute strategies have negatively impacted the company. The company's 2011 revenues were almost $11.3 billion—a gain of 3.95 percent. However, net income declined 15.29 percent to $513.6 million. Its market share price also fell by 45 percent in 2011.

Then, there's the issue of the company's CEO. When Andrea Jung was hired in 1999, she was the first woman to run the woman-oriented company. Her first six years in charge saw double-digit growth. However, with no re-investment in the business, the company began showing its blemishes. As sales declined in major markets, Avon's share price dropped. Ms. Jung's restructuring strategies included laying off 25 percent of the senior staff, streamlining global manufacturing, and cutting costs everywhere except for advertising and promotion. Despite these actions, Avon never fully recovered. During the global economic crisis, Jung saw an opportunity to overtake Avon's rivals, but it didn't work. Some of the problems were beyond Avon's control: Brazil's economy (a big market) slowed down, Europe was in crisis, and even shoppers in America were cutting back. However, other problems were self-inflicted. In addition to those mentioned previously, the company screwed up its new IT system in Brazil, and its inventory management is poor. All these factors led to Avon's board replacing Jung as CEO, although she's staying in her position until a new CEO is hired, at which point she will serve as full-time executive chairman. Two of Jung's predecessors have objected, saying that Jung needs to step aside as they fear "her continued presence would make it hard to attract a new leader." In an interesting twist to Avon's story, in early April 2012, the fragrance manufacturer Coty offered to buy Avon for $10 billion, a takeover bid that was immediately rejected by the company, "which called it uncertain, stingy and opportunistic." (As of May 2012, Coty had withdrawn its offer.)

Despite its strengths, Avon has struggled. In this chapter, we're going to study the final step in analyzing the current situation—an internal analysis. (See Figure 4.1.) Just as we've done in earlier chapters, we'll first look at *what* an internal analysis is, then at *how* you do one, and finally at *why* an internal analysis is an important part of managing strategically.

In order to formulate appropriate and effective strategies, it's important to know what an organization can and cannot do particularly well, and what assets it has or doesn't have. As part of managing strategically, an **internal analysis** is the process of evaluating an organization's resources and capabilities. It provides important information about an organization's assets, skills, and work activities—what's good and what's lacking or deficient? The most important part of this analysis involves evaluating the organization's resources, capabilities, and core competencies, all of which we're going to look at next.

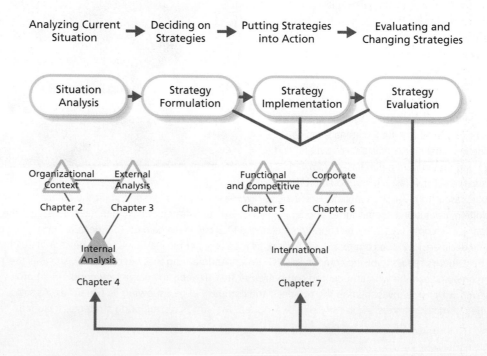

FIGURE 4.1

Strategic Management in Action

A Quick Review of Organizational Resources

We've already discussed resources in relation to the resource-based view of competitive advantage (see Chapter 2). As you'll recall, resources are simply the assets an organization has for doing whatever it's in business to do (making tacos, providing at-home healthcare, or creating and selling cosmetics). These resources (or assets) can be financial, physical, human, intangible, and structural-cultural. Financial resources include debt capacity, credit lines, available equity (stock), cash reserves, and other financial holdings. Physical resources include tangible assets such as buildings, equipment and fixtures, raw materials, office supplies, manufacturing facilities, machines, and so forth. Human resources include the experiences, knowledge, judgment, skills, accumulated wisdom, and competencies of the organization's employees. At Google, for example, employees' programming skills would be part of its human resources. Intangible resources include brand names, patents, trademarks, databases, copyrights, registered designs, and so forth. For instance, Nike's "swoosh" symbol is an intangible resource, as are the Avon and Crayola brand names. Finally, structural-cultural resources include such things as organizational history, culture, work systems, policies, relationships, and the organizational structure being used. For example, 3M Corporation's culture stresses employee innovation—an important resource because its competitive advantage is based on the ability to continually develop and market innovative products.

Although an organization's resources can be a source of competitive advantage (see Chapter 2), they're also important to the organization's capabilities and core competencies. Figure 4.2 illustrates this relationship.

From Resources to Organizational Capabilities

An organization's resources are the inputs needed to perform its work, whether that's making hamburgers, collecting blood plasma, or producing *Cats* at a local community theater. You can view them as the organization's "whats"—what it has, or owns. To illustrate, let's use the example

FIGURE 4.2

The Strategic Role of Organizational Resources and Organizational Capabilities

Source: Based on G. S. Day, "The Capabilities of Market-Driven Companies," *Journal of Marketing,* October 1994, pp. 37–52.

of someone who's considered an excellent chef. This person has resources such as pots and pans, spices, cooking skills, equipment, utensils, an efficiently designed kitchen, and other culinary supplies that are used in preparing delicious meals. Likewise, an organization has resources that are used by organizational members to do their work and are valuable in helping the organization reach its goals and hopefully contributing to a sustainable competitive advantage. However, by themselves, resources aren't productive—think of the chef who has to rely on his skills and experience to combine the spices and food ingredients using the best equipment to make those gourmet meals. Likewise, organizational resources must be combined and used in some way to get the value out of them. For instance, Travelocity's customer database isn't valuable unless someone uses her knowledge to "mine" the database and find the information needed to make good decisions. As such, resources are the inputs used in **organizational capabilities,** which are the various routines and processes that transform those inputs (resources) into outputs (products including physical goods and services).[2] These **organizational routines and processes** are the regular, predictable, and sequential work activities done by organizational members. An organization is a huge, complex network of these routines and processes encompassing such work activities as procuring raw materials to establishing various product pricing structures to generating end-of-quarter financial and other statistical reports. Think about Avon and the various capabilities needed in producing and marketing its products.

As organizational members do their work using organizational resources and routines and processes, they learn how best to capture the value of these resources and turn them into possible core competencies or distinctive organizational capabilities. After all, organizational capabilities don't result from just gathering resources. Instead, capabilities involve interactions between people and between people and other resources.[3] In fact, some organizations never get the hang of it. They're never quite able to develop efficient and effective capabilities, and they struggle exhaustively to survive in an increasingly dynamic and competitive marketplace. For instance, look at how Southwest Airlines and American Air Lines differ. Both have organizational resources (planes, logos, employees, customer information databases, etc.) and organizational routines and processes (loading and unloading planes, making reservations, doing safety inspections, customer service, etc.), yet Southwest has developed valuable capabilities and competitive advantages while American has struggled. However, organizational capabilities can change. Just because they were once the source of competitive advantage doesn't mean they will continue to be a source of

STRATEGIC MANAGEMENT IN ACTION

How might an organization's resources and capabilities have to change when its product continually changes? Hoover's Inc., a subsidiary of Dun & Bradstreet, is managing its resources and capabilities quite well under that scenario. It sells company, market, industry, and competitive data—covering basic information on more than 23 million public and private companies and in-depth information about some 44,000 of the world's top businesses. Maintaining this information's value to its customers means it must be constantly and continually updated. Its traditional information products, *Hoover's Handbooks,* available in libraries, have been surpassed by its online offerings. In fact, the majority of its revenues now come from Hoover's Online **[www.hoovers.com]**. In order to further support Hoover's Online, the company recently partnered with business network LinkedIn. Users (who are thought to be primarily sales professionals) will have more information available about contacts, which is a real value because "once users have found a key decision maker for the company they're targeting, it's helpful to find out as much as you can about that person so the salesperson can make a personal connection and get an 'in' at that business."

THINK ABOUT

• What resources and capabilities might be needed for a transition from a paper-based information company to an Internet-based information company? Describe and explain.

Sources: Based on B. N. Viveiros, "Hoover's Connects With IT," *ChiefMarketer.com,* October/November 2011, p. 14; B. Brynko, "Hoover's Links Up with LinkedIn," *Information Today,* February 2011, p. 32; and R. A. Oppel, Jr., "A Company Short on Buzz but Long on Results," *New York Times,* July 21, 1999, p. C1.

competitive advantage—that is, they don't always lead to a *sustainable* competitive advantage.[4] In today's dynamic and complex environment, capabilities that lead to a competitive advantage now may not do so in the future as conditions and competitors change. Some researchers have proposed that we need to think in terms of **dynamic capabilities**—an organization's ability to build, integrate, and reconfigure capabilities to address rapidly changing environments.[5]

From Capabilities to Core Competencies and Distinctive Capabilities

As we said earlier, every organization has capabilities that enable it to do what it's in business to do. Any major value-creating capabilities organizations have that are essential to their business are known as **core competencies.**[6] For example, executives at Nokia Corporation use their core competencies in product design and customer research to continually look for new applications and services.[7] At Nordstrom's, customer service is a core competency that results from capabilities in sales training and employee recruitment.[8] Although an organization's capabilities are the source of its core competencies, these core competencies also contribute to improving and enhancing other organizational capabilities. (Note the two-directional arrow in Figure 4.2.) So, which comes first? Organizational capabilities do. They're the fundamental building blocks for developing core competencies. Every organization has processes and routines to get work done. Any core competencies of an organization are created out of those routines and processes, accumulated knowledge, and actual work activities. If core competencies *are* established—and not every organization is able to do so—they can, in turn improve and enhance other organizational capabilities and contribute to developing distinctive capabilities, which as Figure 4.2 shows, is what leads to a competitive advantage.

Distinctive organizational capabilities are the special and unique capabilities that distinguish an organization from its competitors. For example, Southwest Airlines has developed distinctive organizational capabilities in organizational processes and routines such as gate turnaround, ticketing, and employee–customer interactions. Although every airline has these same organizational processes and routines, Southwest has developed them into distinctive capabilities, leading to a sustainable competitive advantage that has resulted in above-average performance. Even the company from our chapter-opening case, Avon, has developed its own set of distinctive capabilities. Distinctive capabilities have three characteristics (see Figure 4.3).[9] First, a distinctive capability contributes to superior customer value and offers real benefits to customers. You need to be good at—that is, have a distinctive capability in—whatever it is that your customers value. For instance, Aristocrat Leisure Limited, an Australian company, recognized that many gamblers at smaller, rural casinos wanted flashy, multiple-line penny, nickel, and dime slots that paid out more frequently

FIGURE 4.3

Characteristics of Distinctive Organizational Capabilities

than dollar slots. Aristocrat responded and turned these small-coin slots into the gaming industry's hottest product. One analyst said, "Aristocrat got ahead by figuring out what people want."[10] Why be good at something that your customers don't value? For example, Western Union, probably best known for its telegrams, sent the last one on Friday, January 27, 2006. Why? Because nobody sends telegrams anymore. That capability isn't valued by customers in today's world.[11]

The second characteristic of distinctive organizational capabilities is that they should be difficult for competitors to imitate. Think how we described organizational capabilities as the various organizational routines and processes that transform inputs into outputs. Making these capabilities difficult to imitate means balancing a complex array of employee skills and knowledge and harnessing the considerable learning that exists in the organization. It also means recognizing how capabilities span functional areas and how those areas interact with each other. If these complex interactions are strategically managed and exploited, it can be difficult for competitors to imitate even if they have similar resources and organizational processes and routines. For example, Anheuser Busch InBev (AB) has an incredibly accurate approach to finding out what beer drinkers are buying, as well as when, where, and why they're buying.[12] Its data-mining capability—known as BudNet—is AB's little-known "jewel" and the primary reason the company's share of the U.S. beer market edged up to over 50 percent from 48.9 percent, a huge gain in a market where a weak economy, lousy weather, and the threat of tougher drinking laws kept competitors' sales down. AB executives use the data from BudNet to constantly change marketing strategies, to design promotions for particular ethnic groups, and to get early warnings when rivals might have an edge. It's a capability that spans different functional areas, making it hard for competitors to imitate.

Finally, a distinctive organizational capability should be able to be used in a variety of ways. The organizational routines and processes developed in one area should be transferable to other areas of the organization. For example, Honda Corporation's capabilities at developing fuel-efficient, reliable, and responsive engines and drive trains has provided it with access to different markets including automobiles, motorcycles, lawn mowers, snowblowers, tillers, all-terrain vehicles, power generators, marine outboard engines, and now small passenger jets. As a company ad states, "We are first and foremost, an *engineering* company. But we're also the world's largest engine manufacturer."[13] Another example of using a capability in a variety of ways can be seen at United Technologies Corporation, which believes that its capabilities lie in developing technology that conserves energy. By transferring knowledge about the principles of energy conservation among its various business divisions, which include Pratt & Whitney (engines), Otis (elevators), Sikorsky Aviation (helicopters), Hamilton Sunstrand (aircraft systems and other flight controls), and Carrier (heaters and air conditioners), the company has been able to dominate most of its markets.[14] Another example can be seen at W. L. Gore, a company best known for its Gore-Tex fabrics, which are used in a variety of products, especially outdoors apparel. The fact that it's posted a profit every year since it was founded in 1958 confirms that the company has developed significant skills and capabilities in product innovation. More important, the company has shared those critical innovation skills and capabilities across multiple product lines in diverse industries ranging from guitar strings and dental floss to medical devices and filtration equipment. And for at least one of its products—guitar strings—the shared capabilities have led to the number two position in the market in a short span of time.[15]

Now for the two remaining boxes in Figure 4.2, which address competitive advantage and performance results. Competitive advantage, as we know, is what sets an organization apart—its competitive edge. As the figure shows, competitive advantage must come from an organization's unique resources or from its distinctive capabilities. Having a competitive advantage will affect an organization's performance results positively. Although it's possible for an organization to enjoy strong performance results in the short run without a significant competitive advantage, there are limits to how long such results can last. Without a sustainable competitive advantage, long-run success and survival are uncertain. It's important, therefore, that organizational decision makers know where the organization's strengths and weaknesses are in terms of its resources, capabilities, and competencies.

STRATEGIC MANAGEMENT IN ACTION

The clothing industry isn't an easy one to compete and be successful in. However, VF Corporation has become one of the world's largest, most profitable clothing conglomerates by doing many things well. One thing the CEO did was buy languishing fashion brands and turn them into winners. How? By using VF's capabilities: state-of-the-art distribution, global buying power, and keen merchandising instincts. For instance, VF bought the North Face brand for a bargain price of $135 million, revamped its sourcing, distribution, and financial operations, and was able to nearly double sales over a five-year period. As one analyst said, "The North Face is a great example of what VF can do. For VF it was easy, and it's not easy for everybody."

THINK ABOUT

- Which characteristics of distinctive capabilities does this illustrate? Explain.

Source: Based on, "VF Corporation: Company Profile," *Datamonitor,* December 30, 2011; A. J. Karr, "Global Growth Boosts VF Net," *Women's Wear Daily,* July 22, 2011, p. 2-1; R. Dodes, "VF Dresses Up Its Operations, Bucking Recession," *Wall Street Journal,* March 30, 2009, p. B3; and M. V. Copeland, "Stitching Together an Apparel Powerhouse," *Business 2.0,* April 2005, pp. 52–54.

The Role of Strengths and Weaknesses

The whole reason for doing an internal analysis is to assess what the organization has or doesn't have (resources) and what it can and can't do (capabilities)—in other words, its strengths and its weaknesses. **Strengths** are resources the organization possesses and capabilities it has developed, both of which can be exploited and developed into a sustainable competitive advantage. Not every strength will lead to a sustainable competitive advantage, but an organization's strengths should be nurtured and reinforced as its main competitive weapons. **Weaknesses,** on the other hand, are resources and capabilities that are lacking or deficient and prevent the organization from developing a sustainable competitive advantage. Organizational weaknesses need to be corrected if they're in critical areas that are preventing the organization from developing a sustainable competitive advantage. However, most organizations have limited resources to correct problems, so strategic decision makers often choose to simply minimize the impact of weaknesses as long as they aren't in areas crucial for developing a sustainable competitive advantage.

Organizational members at all levels of the organization struggle with these types of strategic decisions: What strengths and weaknesses are in my area(s) of responsibility, and how can I strategically manage these areas to high levels of performance? Now that we have a good understanding of *what* an internal analysis is, it's time to look at *how* you do one.

LEARNING REVIEW   LEARNING OUTCOME 4.1

- What is an internal analysis, and how is it different from an external analysis?
- Describe the relationship between resources, capabilities, and competitive advantage.
- What characteristics do distinctive organizational capabilities have?
- Define strengths and weaknesses.

In this section, we want to look at three different approaches for doing an internal analysis. The first views the organization's work—what it's in business to do—as a series of value-creating activities. The second is similar to a financial audit, but is used to examine and assess all internal areas of an organization instead of evaluating just financial information. The third focuses on developing a profile of the organization's capabilities. To conclude this section, we'll look at how to determine an organization's strengths and weaknesses.

LEARNING OUTCOME 4.2

Explain How to Do an Internal Analysis

Value Chain Analysis

Every organization needs customers if it's going to survive. Even not-for-profit organizations must have "customers" who use its services or purchase its products. The premise behind this approach is that customers want (demand) some type of value from the goods and services they purchase or obtain. This value can come from three broad categories: the product is unique and different, the product is low priced, or the product meets the needs of a specific group of customers quickly and efficiently. In order to assess an organization's ability to provide value, strategic decision makers can use an approach developed by Mike Porter called **value chain analysis,** a systematic way of examining all the organization's functional activities and how well they create customer value.[16]

As we said earlier, every organization has specific organizational routines and processes—work activities done by organizational members—that allow it to do whatever it's in business to do. Each of these activities creates varying levels of customer value and organizational costs. What strategic decision makers hope is that the customer value created—as evidenced by the products the organization distributes or the services it provides and what customers are willing to "pay" for that value—outweighs the costs of creating that value (the margin). In using the value chain, we're assessing the organization's ability to create customer value through its work activities. In other words, what are the organization's strengths and weaknesses in these areas? Porter believed there were nine activities—five primary and four support—that were important to assess.

The primary activities are those activities that create customer value. These include the organizational routines and processes involved with bringing resources into the business (inbound logistics), processing these resources into the organization's goods or services (operations), physically distributing them to customers (outbound logistics), marketing the goods and services to customers (marketing and sales), and servicing customers (customer service). However, it's not enough to know *what* these activities are; we must judge *how well* the organization is performing these activities. That's the information required to assess strengths and weaknesses. Table 4.1 lists some questions to ask when assessing the organizational activities that create value.

What about the support activities in the value chain? These activities support the primary activities as well as each other. Although it may seem that the primary activities are the most critical to the organization as they are the ones that create value, keep in mind that doing the primary activities wouldn't be possible without the support activities. For instance, if Hallmark didn't have effective human resources management processes and routines, it wouldn't have employees to design the cards, develop the marketing campaigns, or run the presses that imprint the latest holiday design on gift wrap. And if they can't do these things, they don't create value for the customer, the customer won't be willing to purchase the product, and organizational performance will suffer. How can you assess strengths and weaknesses in the support activities?

STRATEGIC MANAGEMENT IN ACTION

Harley-Davidson (H-D) is best known for its motorcycles and apparel. However, it started selling a "new source of fuel, one that goes into mouths instead of gas tanks and comes in such flavors as teriyaki and pepper." Yes, H-D is selling beef jerky. Joining forces with one of the largest U.S. packaged-foods companies, ConAgra Foods, H-D has put its familiar name and black-and-orange logo on a food product.

- Do you think this was a wise use of H-D's brand name? Why or why not?

Source: Based on K. Emmerson, "Product Review: Harley Davidson Motorcycles Road Food," January 4, 2008, http://voices.yahoo.com/product-review-harley-davidson-motorcycles-road-food-761193.html; and E. Fredrix, "Harley-Davidson Vrooms Way into Food Business with Jerky," *USA Today,* October 10, 2006, p. 3B.

THINK ABOUT

- Do you think H-D created customer value with this product? Explain.

TABLE 4.1 Assessing the Organizational Activities That Create Value

Acquiring and Handling Resources

- Are we able to get the resources (raw materials and other materials) we need when we need them and where we need them?
- Do we have a resource inventory control system that is efficient and effective?
- Do we have appropriate facilities and personnel for storing and managing our raw materials and other materials needed to do what we're in business to do?
- Is the way we store and manage our resources efficient and sufficient?

Processing Resources into Goods/Services

- Do we have the tools/equipment we need to do what we're in business to do? How do our tools/ equipment compare to others in our industry?
- Do we have appropriate facilities (type and amount) to do what we're in business to do? How do our facilities compare to others in our industry?
- How are our facilities and production/operations processes set up? Are our facilities set up in a way to be most efficient?
- Do we have operations controls in place that help us control quality and minimize costs? Are these controls efficient and effective?
- Are our facilities and business processes appropriate and automated as needed?

Getting Products to Customers

- Do we have the equipment/tools and personnel needed to get products to customers?
- Do customers have access to our products when, where, and how they are needed?
- Is our process for getting products to customers efficient?
- Are finished but unsold products stored appropriately?

Marketing Goods and Services to Customers

- Do we have efficient and effective market research that identifies potential customers and customer needs?
- Do we have creative and unique sales promotions and advertising?
- Do we have processes and procedures in place for pricing our products appropriately?
- Have we looked at ways to distribute our product through different channels?
- Do we have a trained and effective sales force? Are they energized and driven?
- What's our image with customers? Do they think our products have value?
- Does our firm have a good reputation? Is our firm on any "best" or "most" lists?
- Do we have a loyal customer base?
- Are we the market leader in the various markets we serve?

Servicing Customers

- Do we give customers the opportunity to provide input on our products/service?
- Do we take care of customer issues quickly and successfully?
- If customers want warranties and guarantees, do we have those guidelines in place?
- Are our employees well trained in educating and servicing customers?
- Are we able to provide replacement parts and repair services to customers if they want them?

Source: Based on Michael E. Porter, *Competitive Advantage: Creating and Sustaining Performance* (The Free Press, 1985).

Table 4.2 (see p. 100) lists some questions to ask in assessing the organizational activities that reinforce the others.

With both assessments, you get a good picture of the resources and capabilities that are strengths and those that are weaknesses. To the extent that the organization performs any of these activities more effectively or efficiently than its competitors, it should be able to achieve

TABLE 4.2 Assessing the Organizational Activities That Reinforce the Others

Purchasing
- Do we have alternative supply sources for resources we need in our business?
- Do we get needed resources when, where, and how we need them?
- Do we have efficient and effective procedures in place for doing large capital expenditures for items such as facilities and equipment?
- Are we able to determine whether leasing or purchasing is the most efficient and effective approach to facilities and equipment?
- Are our suppliers reliable? Do we have good, stable, and long-standing relationships with those suppliers?

Research & Development
- Are we able to take creative ideas and turn them into useful products or processes?
- Do we have procedures in place for getting employee input on ideas?
- What's our track record in product R&D? In process R&D?
- Does our R&D team collaborate well with other organizational departments or areas?
- Is our R&D team able to meet crucial goals (time, quality, amount, etc.)?
- Do we have excellent facilities for our R&D function?
- Are our R&D people well trained and qualified?
- Do our R&D people stay current in their areas of expertise?
- Does our organizational culture support and promote creativity and innovation?

Managing Human Resources
- Do we have appropriate organizational procedures and processes in place to get the employees we need in the right place at the right time?
- Do we have appropriate organizational procedures and processes in place in case we need to eliminate employee positions?
- Do we have appropriate employee performance appraisal and employee promotion policies?
- Do our organizational rewards/benefits motivate and engage employees?
- Do we have a work culture where employees want to come to work every day and stay with our organization?
- Do we have a good relationship with our employee unions?
- Do our managers and technical personnel stay on top of changes in their profession?
- Do we survey employees on their motivation, job commitment, and job satisfaction? What do those surveys tell us?

Other Organizational Activities, Processes, and Procedures
- Do we perform regular external analysis, identifying potential opportunities and threats?
- Do we have a strategic planning process in place? Is it used appropriately to help our organization achieve its goals?
- Are our employees aware of what our organization's mission and goals are?
- Do all our activities and functions work together efficiently and effectively in achieving our mission and goals?
- Are we able to secure appropriate financing when needed?
- Is our information system effective and efficient in getting information when, where, and how it's needed?
- Is our information system appropriate for being a strong competitor in our industry?
- Does our information system provide both internal and external information as needed?
- Do our stakeholders think we're doing a good job? Do we have a good relationship with those stakeholders?
- Do our customers, our community, and society believe that our firm is a responsible corporate citizen?

Source: Based on Michael E. Porter, *Competitive Advantage: Creating and Sustaining Performance* (The Free Press, 1985).

a competitive advantage. The advantage of looking at those organizational activities that create value and those that reinforce the others is that it emphasizes the importance of customer value and how well an organization performs those activities in creating customer value. However, this approach may not be easy to use because organizational work activities don't always fit nicely and neatly into the framework. Therefore, some strategic decision makers use another approach—an internal audit of organizational functions.

Using an Internal Audit

The internal audit approach starts with the premise that every organization has certain functions it must perform. In pursuing a sustainable competitive advantage, these functions may be performed well or performed poorly. We base our identification of strengths and weaknesses on how well these basic organizational functions are performed. You may be familiar with the concept of a financial audit, which is simply a thorough examination of an organization's financial records and procedures. An **internal audit** is a thorough assessment of an organization's internal areas. It's similar to a financial audit although it obviously focuses on much more than just the financial aspects. Strategic decision makers use the internal audit to assess the organization's resources and capabilities from the perspective of its different functions and organizational elements. Are the necessary resources available so that people can perform their assigned work activities and how well do they perform these work activities (i.e., what are their capabilities)?

An internal audit looks at six organizational functional areas: production–operations, marketing, research and development, financial–accounting, management (which typically includes human resources management and other general management activities), and information systems. Obviously, organizations may have unique functions that don't fit into these categories or they may not call their functions by these names, but these six are the most common. Table 4.3 (see p. 102) lists some key questions to use in assessing the strengths and

---

FOR YOUR INFORMATION
Organizations Need Physicals, Too

Have you ever had a physical exam? If you have, you know there's an intense scrutiny of past medical history, current health issues or complaints, and lifestyle factors. This physical exam may point to the need for additional scrutiny with test results compared to normal ranges. Doesn't this seem to be an appropriate analogy for assessing organizations? Could the concept of a "physical exam" be applied to organizations? Here's a guide to giving your organization a physical exam.

Brain function: This would be the organization's strategy and planning function. How well does your organization's "brain" function? Are the strategies and plans getting through to the rest of the organization? Is the "command center" functioning effectively and efficiently?

Nervous system: You need to check your company's reflexes. Are communication and information technology systems responsive as information is gathered and disseminated from the brain?

Eyes, ears, nose, and mouth: These sense organs respond to the outside world. Are the marketing and sales groups "sensing" customers' needs accurately?

Arms, hands, legs, feet, and associated muscle groups: These body parts convert energy into action. What kind of shape are your operations systems in? Do they acquire materials, make things, and deliver them efficiently and effectively?

Lungs and digestive system: In your body, the lungs and digestive system absorb nutrients and filter waste. Are resources being absorbed efficiently? Are you getting rid of waste efficiently?

The heart: You need to have a strong, highly conditioned heart to keep the rest of the body functioning properly. The organization's heart is its culture, its sense of meaning and purpose. How is the flow of culture throughout your organization? Has it cut off circulation, or is it sending out strength-giving nutrients?

Source: Based on J. Mariotti, "Give Your Company a Physical," *Industry Week,* October 5, 1998, p. 74.

TABLE 4.3 Internal Audit of Functional Areas

Production–Operations

- Does the organization have reliable and reasonably priced suppliers?
- Are facilities, offices, machinery, and equipment in good working condition?
- Are facilities strategically located close to resources and markets?
- Does the organization have effective inventory control policies and procedures?
- Does the organization utilize quality control procedures? Are these procedures effective?
- How does the organization do on quality assessments?
- Does the organization have an appropriate amount of capacity?
- What is the organization's safety record?
- Does the production-operations process work smoothly and with little disruption?
- Have production-operations goals been established, and are work activities aimed at achieving these goals?
- Do production-operations employees use appropriate operations planning and controlling tools and techniques?
- Has the organization developed any particular competencies in the areas of production-operations?

Marketing

- Does the organization segment markets effectively?
- What is the organization's market position or rank?
- Does the organization position itself well against its competitors?
- What is the organization's market share, and has it been increasing or decreasing?
- Does the organization conduct market research, and is this research effective?
- Is market research information used in making marketing decisions?
- Does the organization have an effective sales force?
- Has the organization priced its products and services appropriately?
- How is product quality, and how does it compare with that of competitors?
- Is customer service effective, and how does it compare with competitors?
- Is the advertising strategy effective?
- Are promotion and publicity strategies effective?
- Are customer complaints decreasing, increasing, or stable?
- Are customer complaints handled effectively and efficiently?
- Are present channels of distribution reliable and cost effective?
- Are marketing planning and budgeting effective?
- Do marketing employees use appropriate marketing planning and controlling tools and techniques?
- Has the organization developed any particular competencies in any of the marketing areas?

Research and Development

- Does the organization have adequate R&D facilities?
- Are the R&D employees well qualified?
- Does organizational culture encourage creativity and innovation?
- Is communication between R&D and other organizational units effective?
- Are the organization's products technologically competitive?
- If patents are appropriate, are patent applications increasing, decreasing, or stable?
- Is development time from concept to actual product appropriate?
- How many new products have been developed during the last year (or whatever time period is most appropriate)?
- Does the organization commit more, the same, or less to R&D than its competitors do?
- Do R&D employees use appropriate R&D tools and techniques?
- Has the organization developed any particular competencies in the R&D area?

TABLE 4.3 (Continued)

Financial and Accounting

- Is the organization financially strong or weak, according to the financial ratio analyses?
- What are the trends in the organization's financial ratios, and how do these compare with industry trends?
- Is the organization able to raise short-term capital?
- Is the organization able to raise long-term capital?
- What is the organization's working capital position? Is it sufficient?
- Are the organization's capital budgeting procedures effective?
- Has the organization established financial goals? Are they appropriate?
- Are dividend payout policies reasonable?
- What type of relationship does the organization have with its creditors and stockholders?
- Is there a match between the organization's sources and uses of funds?
- Do financial-accounting employees use appropriate financial-accounting tools and techniques?
- Has the organization developed any particular competencies in the financial-accounting area?

Management

- Do organization employees manage strategically?
- Are organizational goals clear and measurable? Are they communicated to organizational members?
- Is the organization's structure appropriate?
- What is the organization's culture? Does it support organizational goals and mission?
- Has the organization developed its vision? What about mission(s)?
- Does the organization attract appropriate job applicants?
- Are employee selection procedures effective?
- Does the organization provide employees with appropriate training?
- Are job descriptions and job specifications clear?
- Are jobs effectively designed?
- What is the level of employee morale?
- What is the level of employee turnover?
- Are organizational compensation and reward programs appropriate?
- Are organizational employee discipline and control mechanisms appropriate?
- How does the organization treat its employees?
- What kind of relationships does the organization have with employee groups?
- Does the organization effectively use work teams?
- Are legal guidelines followed in human resource management activities?
- Has the organization developed any competencies in its human resource management activities?
- Has the organization developed any competencies in the management area?

Information Systems–Information Technology

- How does the organization gather and disseminate information? Is it effective and efficient?
- Is the information system used by employees in making decisions?
- Is information updated regularly?
- Is information distributed effectively and efficiently?
- Do employees have access to contribute input to the information system?
- Has the organization made an investment in information technology that's greater than, equal to, or less than competitors?
- Is information technology used effectively and efficiently in all areas of the organization?
- Is the organization's information system secure?
- Is the organization's information system user friendly?
- Are training workshops or seminars provided for users of the information system?
- Are employees in the information systems–information technology area well qualified?
- Has the organization developed any competencies in the information systems–information technology area?

TABLE 4.4 Internal Audit of Other Organizational Elements

Assessing Strategic Managers (Board of Directors and Top Managers)
- Who are the members of the board of directors? The top management team?
- What background/skills do they appear to have?
- How many years of experience in this business and how many years of total experience do they have? Does this seem appropriate for the situation the organization is in now?
- What strengths do they appear to bring to the organization? What weaknesses do they have?
- Do they appear to be competent and effective?

Assessing the Organizational Structure
- What kind of structure does the organization appear to have?
- What can you tell from the organizational chart (if available)?
- Does the organization have any unusual/distinctive structural aspects?
- Does the structure support or inhibit the accomplishment of organizational goals?

Assessing the Organizational Culture
- What kind of culture does the organization have?
- What are the key characteristics of the culture?
- What does the organization seem to value?
- Does the culture appear to be strong or weak?
- Does the culture support or inhibit the accomplishment of organizational goals?

weaknesses of each functional area. This assessment concentrates on the availability or lack of critical resources and the level of capabilities (i.e., how efficiently and effectively work is being done) in each functional area.

In addition to the assessment of the functional areas, an internal audit should look at three other important organizational elements: the strategic managers, the organizational structure, and the organization's culture. Table 4.4 lists some key questions to use in assessing these areas.

Capabilities Assessment Profile

The last approach we're going to discuss is a **capabilities assessment profile,** an in-depth evaluation of an organization's capabilities. This approach was developed because strategic decision makers had few guidelines for identifying and evaluating their organization's distinctive capabilities.[17] Assessing capabilities can be rather complex since they arise from the ways that resources are combined in the organization's basic work processes and routines. They're not as easily determined as organizational functions or even the primary and support activities. However, the complex nature of capabilities also makes it harder for competitors to imitate, which makes them excellent sources of sustainable competitive advantage. That's why the capabilities assessment profile can be beneficial: It provides some guidelines for identifying the organization's distinctive capabilities.

A capabilities assessment consists of two phases: (1) identifying distinctive capabilities and (2) developing and leveraging these distinctive capabilities.[18] Because our main interest at this point is analyzing the internal aspects of the organization, we're going to concentrate on the first phase. Phase 2 addresses strategy development issues that are beyond the scope of our discussion of how to do an internal analysis. Figure 4.4 (see p. 105) illustrates the steps in phase 1.

Earlier in the chapter, we described what makes capabilities distinctive—they contribute to superior customer value, they are difficult for competitors to imitate, and they are usable in a variety of ways. These characteristics are important because they reflect the information that's gathered in a capabilities assessment. In fact, the first step in assessing organizational

FIGURE 4.4

Identifying Distinctive
Organizational
Capabilities

Source: Based on
Kenneth E. Marino,
"Developing Consensus
on Firm competencies and
Capabilities," *Academy of
Management Executive,*
August 1996, pp. 40–51.

capabilities—*preparing a current product–market profile*—emphasizes organization–customer interactions. In this step, we identify what we're selling, who we're selling to, and whether we're providing superior customer value and offering the customer desirable benefits. To do this, we need information about specific products and markets; principal competitors in each of these product-market segments; and performance measures, such as sales growth rates, market share, competitive position, contributions to sales and earnings—for each product-markct segment.

Once we have a current (and thorough) product-market profile, the next step in the capabilities assessment is *identifying sources of competitive advantage and disadvantage in the main product-market segments.* We want to know why customers choose our products instead of our competitors. This assessment would involve identifying specific cost, product, and service attributes. When customers purchase a product (a good or a service), what they're actually purchasing is a bundle of attributes they believe will satisfy their needs.[19] These attributes vary by product and market. For cxample, camera customers may be intcrested in product attributes such as picture clarity, camera speeds, camera size, or price. Airline customers might choose a particular airline based on attributes such as safety record, close adherence to arrival-departure schedules, customer service, meal availability, convenience of arrival-departure times, and price. Community arts customers might choose a live theater performance on the basis of attributes such as familiarity with the play, actors starring in the play, or ticket price. Again, in this step, we're attempting to identify those attributes that our customers value in our products and what competitive advantages or disadvantages these attributes provide us.

With this information, then, we're ready to pinpoint the organizational capabilities that lead to those sources of competitive advantage and disadvantage. Step 3 involves *describing organizational capabilities and competencies.* To identify those capabilities, you need to closely examine the resources, skills, and abilities of the organization's various divisions. Let's look at an example to help explain this. Suppose you're a strategic manager at one of the nation's airlines. Your analysis of sources of competitive advantage and disadvantage (step 2) showed that one reason customers choose your airline over competitors is because scheduled flights left on time consistently. In step 3, you need to uncover what resources and capabilities led to this competitive advantage. You might find, for example, that consistent departures were the result of a well-trained ground crew who loaded baggage efficiently and effectively; appropriate numbers of customer service representatives who processed passengers quickly; a system of paperless ticketing and boarding passes; and experienced pilots who knew the ins and outs of getting quick control tower clearance for takeoff. This intense analysis of the organizational resources and the routines and processes behind the capabilities is an important step. It forces strategic decision makers to really understand what has to happen in order to deliver superior customer value and benefits. Even strategic decision makers in not-for-profit organizations should assess what resources and routines and processes lead to customers' willingness to support, sponsor, and advocate their products and programs. This is probably the most difficult step in the capabilities profile. Yet, it's also the one that yields the most important information because it gets to the heart of the matter—the most basic aspects of organizational work and the important interactions that take place as this work is performed by organizational members.

What's next? Step 4 involves *sorting these core capabilities and competencies according to their strategic importance.* In other words, which capabilities are most important for building the organization's future? Judging which capabilities are strategically important is a matter of evaluating each according to three criteria: (1) Does the capability provide tangible customer benefits? (2) Is the capability difficult for competitors to imitate? (3) Can the capability provide wide access to a number of different markets? If these criteria sound familiar, it's because we described them earlier as the characteristics of a distinctive capability. This analysis will show you how organizational capabilities differ in their strategic importance. Those that are most important strategically should be placed at the top of the list and on down. By sorting organizational capabilities according to level of strategic importance, strategic decision makers gain an understanding of their organization's critical strengths and weaknesses. But, there's one more step in a capabilities assessment profile.

The final step involves *identifying and agreeing on the key competencies and capabilities.* Based on the ranking of strategic importance, decision makers can easily identify the organization's key competencies and capabilities. What's difficult is agreeing that these *are* the key ones. Obviously, when certain organizational capabilities are selected as more critical to competitive advantage than others, it's likely to affect future resource allocation and organizational support for various departments, units, or divisions. Therefore, even though organizational members may be impacted differently, getting agreement on the organization's key capabilities is an important step in capabilities assessment. Without agreement on these critical capabilities, managing strategically for a sustainable competitive advantage will be extremely difficult.

Although the capabilities assessment approach provides a thorough analysis of the organization's important strategic capabilities, it's a complicated process. It's an approach probably most useful to upper-level strategic managers because it requires assessing a vast number of underlying organizational capabilities that don't always fit nicely and neatly into narrowly defined specific functional areas.

STRATEGIC MANAGEMENT IN ACTION
The Global Perspective

Yves Guillemot has made his Ubisoft game studios some of the most efficient and creative in the videogame industry. (Note: The company's name is a combination of "ubiquity" and "software.") Although bigger competitors, like Electronic Arts, have spent millions building glitzy studios in southern California, Guillemot took a different approach. He chose to save costs by opening game studios in low-cost locations such as Morocco, China, Romania, and Canada. Today, the company has studios in more than 20 countries (including its newest ones opened in 2008 in China, Singapore, Ukraine, and India), and their average operating cost per employee is about a third less than the industry average. Recruiting and managing its young, talented, computer-savvy game designers is crucial to Ubisoft's strategy. The

company is also branching out with a new motion picture division. Guillemot says it was a logical step because "we create intellectual properties, universes and characters, that can exist in many formats, whether TV, movies, toys or video games."

THINK ABOUT

- What do you think of Ubisoft's approach?
- What are the implications for the resources and capabilities the company needs?

Sources: Based on "The Innovation Game," *Canadian Business,* Winter 2011/2012, pp. 60–62; "Case Study: Ubisoft," *Marketing Week,* July 21, 2011, p. 58; and G. Keighley, "Massively Multinational Player," *Business 2.0,* March 2005, pp. 64–66.

Determining Strengths and Weaknesses

Each internal analysis approach can be used to identify an organization's resources and capabilities. Whether it's from the perspective of analyzing customer value created by an organization's primary and support activities, from the perspective of auditing an organization's various functional areas, or from the perspective of identifying distinctive capabilities, we get a broad picture of an organization's resources and work routines and processes. However, that's only half the picture. We have to do more than just *identify* these factors. We also need to *determine* the organization's strengths and weaknesses in each of these areas. What are its strong points? What are its weak points? What resources and capabilities can be enhanced and exploited for a sustainable competitive advantage? What resources and capabilities are lacking or not used effectively? Strategic decision makers can determine this as they analyze the various internal organizational areas and measure them against some criteria.[20] Figure 4.5 identifies four such criteria.

One criterion that could be used to determine strengths or weaknesses is past performance trends. This criterion could include any performance measures such as financial ratios, operational efficiency statistics, employee productivity statistics, or quality control data. Any organizational area that's measurable could be assessed by looking at the trends. For instance, is market share increasing or decreasing? Are liquidity ratios going up or down? Is the number of product returns increasing or decreasing? Are employee-training expenditures reducing product reject rates? For example, think about what organizational performance trends Hallmark's CEO might assess when making strategic decisions. Such quantitative measures could be used as indicators of organizational strengths and weaknesses. Although performance trends show important information about the organization's use of resources and capabilities, it doesn't show us whether performance is up to standards.

Therefore, another criterion to use in assessing organizational strengths and weaknesses is how actual performance measures up against specific performance goals. **Organizational goals** are statements of desired outcomes. Every organization needs goals in all functional areas and at all levels that state *what* it hopes to accomplish by *when*. Such goals provide direction by specifying what and how organizational resources and capabilities are used in carrying out the organizational vision and missions. By comparing actual performance in the various functional areas against stated goals, strengths and weaknesses can be assessed. However, just looking at performance trends or how organizational performance measures up to the goals isn't enough to help us determine whether these strengths or weaknesses can be used to influence the development of potential sustainable competitive advantage. To do this, competitor comparisons are needed, which is another criterion we can use to measure strengths and weaknesses.

By comparing resources and capabilities against competitors, an organization can see how it stacks up. Remember from Chapter 3 that we looked at competitors as part of our external analysis. In an internal analysis, the focus needs to be on *how* competitors are doing. This information could include surveys and rankings published in external information sources. For instance,

Past Performance Trends

Comparison Against Competitors

Are organizational resources and capabilities strengths or weaknesses?

Specific Goals or Targets

Personal Opinions of Strategic Decision Makers or Consultants

FIGURE 4.5

Criteria to Judge Organizational Strengths and Weaknesses

FOR YOUR INFORMATION
Market Share Myth

One commonly used measure in comparing against competitors is market share. Is it an appropriate measure? Nearly every business is mesmerized by market share—keeping it or increasing it. Conventional wisdom about the importance of market share was that the biggest market share would give a company the biggest revenues and the lowest cost per unit. That approach may have worked in the past. However, the reality of today's environment is that increasing market share may not be the route to continued competitive advantage and profitability. Having the most customers doesn't automatically translate into having the most profits. In fact, one study found that 70 percent of the time, the company with the largest market share didn't have the highest rate of return. Strategic decision makers need to address how customers' needs are changing and how they can best meet those changing needs. Maybe *that's* how companies need to measure themselves against their competitors—by how well they're meeting customers' changing needs.

THINK ABOUT

- What do you think? Do you agree with the premises of this argument regarding the decreased importance of market share?
- What are the implications for doing an internal analysis?
- Are there customers an organization might not want? Explain.

Sources: Based on "The Myth of Market Share: Can Focusing Too Much on the Competition Harm Profitability?" *Knowledge@Wharton* [knowledge.wharton.upenn.edu], January 24, 2007; L. Selden and G. Colvin, "Will This Customer Sink Your Stock?" *Fortune,* September 30, 2002, pp. 127–130; and R. Brooks, "Alienating Customers Isn't Always a Bad Idea, Many Firms Discover," *Wall Street Journal,* January 7, 1999, pp. A1+.

Fortune publishes an annual corporate reputation survey that ranks industry competitors according to what companies are most admired. *BusinessWeek* publishes annual rankings of research and development expenditures. We also might find competitor information in articles in business or general news magazines, other types of public documents such as annual reports or Securities and Exchange Commission filings, industry association newsletters, networking at professional meetings, customer contacts, and even the competitor's Web home page. A key consideration for gathering this information is whether competitive-intelligence methods are legal and ethical. (See *The Grey Zone* ethical issue.) The legal aspect is fairly clear—competitor intelligence becomes illegal corporate spying when it involves stealing proprietary materials or trade secrets by any means.[21] However, deciding whether something is ethical may not be as easy. For example, there's nothing unethical about scouring published sources for competitor information, but ethical issues might arise if you decide to rummage through a competitor's trash bins for information or pretend to be a job applicant. These difficult decisions about competitive intelligence arise because often there's a fine line between what's considered *legal and ethical* and what's considered *legal but unethical.* For instance, at Procter & Gamble (P&G), executives hired competitive-intelligence firms to gather information on its competitors in the hair-care business. At least one of these firms misrepresented itself to competitor Unilever's employees, trespassed at Unilever's hair-care headquarters in Chicago, and went through trash dumpsters to gain information. In P&G's defense, when the CEO found out, he immediately fired the individuals responsible and apologized to Unilever.[22] Although there are no easy answers in these ethical dilemmas, be alert to the perceived "rightness" or "wrongness" of competitive intelligence-gathering methods.[23]

The last criterion for judging organizational strengths and weaknesses is personal or subjective opinions of strategic decision makers or consultants. Sometimes the best assessment is the personal opinion of those directly involved in the activity, as it may not be possible to quantitatively measure every resource or capability. And quantitative measures—such as trends or comparisons against standards—don't always capture what's really going on in a particular functional area, so qualitative opinions or assessments of organizational members can be useful in determining strengths or weaknesses. Also, if outside consultants are working with an organization's departments or divisions, what's their opinion? What do they see as strengths or

THE GREY ZONE

Some techniques that have been suggested for gathering competitor information include: (1) Pretend to be a journalist writing a story. Call up competitors' offices and interview them. (2) Dig through a competitor's trash. (3) Sit outside a competitor's place of business and count how many customers go in. (4) Get copies of your competitors' in-house newsletters and read them. (5) Call the Better Business Bureau and ask whether competitors have had any complaints filed against them and, if so, what kind of complaints. (6) Have friends call competitors for price lists, brochures, or other marketing information.

THINK ABOUT

- Do you think these methods are ethical or unethical? Why?
- What ethical guidelines might you propose for strategic decision makers when doing competitor intelligence?

weaknesses? Although this particular criterion can't be used to do case analysis for this class (unless you're studying a local organization), it's likely to be useful in assessing strengths and weaknesses when you're actually working in an organization.

By now, you should have a fairly good idea of what's involved in *doing* an internal analysis and identifying strengths and weaknesses. It's more than simply identifying an organization's internal resources and capabilities. It's also assessing whether those resources and capabilities are sufficient and can be sources of sustainable competitive advantage. Although we've discussed what internal analysis is and how to do one, we haven't yet addressed *why* it's an important part of managing strategically.

LEARNING REVIEW   LEARNING OUTCOME 4.2

- How would the value chain approach to internal analysis be used?
- What does an organizational internal audit evaluate?
- How do you judge which organizational capabilities are strategically important?
- Describe the criteria that can be used to judge organizational resources and capabilities as either strengths or weaknesses.

Doing an internal analysis is important for two reasons: (1) it's the only way to identify an organization's strengths and weaknesses, and (2) it's needed for making good strategic decisions. Let's explain.

As we stated at the beginning of the chapter, an internal analysis is a process of identifying and evaluating an organization's resources and capabilities. The outcome from an internal analysis is information about those resources, skills, and work routines and processes. What strengths do we have because of our specific resources and capabilities? What weaknesses do we have? If we didn't do this analysis, this critical strategic information wouldn't be available. But, this information in and of itself isn't useful. It's how strategic decision makers *use* this information that's important.

With the information from an internal analysis, strategic decision makers can make intelligent judgments about what competitive advantages the organization might currently have, what might potentially be developed into competitive advantages, and what might be preventing competitive advantages from being developed. This internal information, coupled with the information from the external analysis and information about the organizational context, provides the basis for deciding what strategic actions are necessary for sustainable competitive advantage.

LEARNING OUTCOME 4.3

Discuss Why an Internal Analysis Is Important

LEARNING REVIEW   LEARNING OUTCOME 4.3

- Why is an internal analysis an important part of managing strategically?

The Bottom Line

Learning Outcome 4.1: Describe an internal analysis.

- *Internal analysis:* process of evaluating an organization's resources and capabilities.
- *Resources (financial, physical, human, intangible, and structural-cultural):* can be a source of competitive advantage but are also important as the inputs needed for organization's capabilities and core competencies.
- *Organizational capabilities:* various routines and processes that transform inputs into outputs. This doesn't happen just by gathering together resources. Instead, the resources have to be used and combined. *Organizational routines and processes:* the regular, predictable, and sequential work activities done by organizational members.
- As organizational members do their work using resources and routines and processes, they learn how best to capture the value out of those resources and turn them into possible core competencies or distinctive capabilities. The capabilities that lead to a competitive advantage may change so organizations need to think in terms of *dynamic capabilities:* an organization's ability to build, integrate, and reconfigure capabilities to address changing environments.
- *Core competencies:* major value-creating capabilities essential to an organization's business. They are not sources of competitive advantage themselves, but can contribute to developing distinctive capabilities and improving other organizational capabilities.
- *Distinctive organizational capabilities:* the special and unique capabilities that distinguish an organization from its competitors. They have three characteristics: they (1) contribute to superior customer value, (2) are difficult for competitors to imitate, and (3) can be used in a variety of ways. Distinctive capabilities can lead to a competitive advantage.
- Main reason for doing internal analysis is to identify *strengths* (resources an organization possesses and capabilities an organization has developed, both of which can be developed into sustainable competitive advantage) and *weaknesses* (resources and capabilities that are lacking or deficient and prevent the organization from developing a sustainable competitive advantage).

Learning Outcome 4.2: Explain how to do an internal analysis.

- There are three different techniques to do an internal analysis: value chain, internal audit, and capabilities assessment profile.
- *Value chain:* a systematic way of examining all the organization's functional activities and how well they create customer value. The value chain was developed by Mike Porter and focuses on assessing primary and support work activities. The five primary activities discussed in this text include acquiring and handling resources; processing resources into goods/services; getting products to customers; marketing goods and services to customers; and servicing customers. The four support work activities described include purchasing; research & development; managing human resources; and other organizational activities, processes, and procedures.
- *Internal audit:* a thorough assessment of an organization's internal functional areas. It looks at six organizational functions: production–operations, marketing, research and development, financial–accounting, management, and information systems. In addition, the internal audit looks at three other organizational elements: the strategic managers, the organizational structure, and the organization's culture.
- The capabilities assessment profile is an in-depth evaluation of an organization's capabilities. It consists of two phases: (1) identifying distinctive capabilities and (2) developing and leveraging these distinctive capabilities. The five steps include (1) preparing

a current product-market profile, (2) identifying sources of competitive advantage and disadvantage in the main product-market segments, (3) describing organizational capabilities and competencies, (4) sorting these core capabilities and competencies according to their strategic importance, and (5) identifying and agreeing on the key competencies and capabilities.

- An organization's strengths and weaknesses can be assessed according to four criteria: (1) past performance trends, (2) *organizational goals:* statements of desired outcomes, (3) competitor comparisons, and (4) personal opinions of strategic decision makers or consultants.
- Competitor comparisons can introduce legal and ethical issues.

Learning Outcome 4.3: Discuss why an internal analysis is important.

- Important for two reasons: (1) only way to identify an organization's strengths and weaknesses and (2) needed for making good strategic decisions.

YOU as strategic decision maker: building your skills

1. The conventional view that leading brands maintain their market leadership for long periods of time may be inaccurate. Strategic decision makers can no longer assume they will be able to retain their companies' brand leadership over decades. In fact, studies of brands show that consumers are finding it harder to distinguish among competing products. With this in mind, answer the following questions: (a) What type of resources are brands? (b) What are the implications of these statements for internal analysis? (c) Could brands ever be the ultimate competitive weapon? Why or why not? (d) Could a brand ever be a weakness? Explain.

2. Customer loyalty can be a powerful competitive advantage. And customer loyalty is more than repeat purchasing. Customers who are loyal tend to buy more over time and, most important, tend to tell others about a company to their family, friends, and colleagues. Enterprise Rent-A-Car figured this out early on and, rather than having a complicated and sophisticated customer research program, they focused on two simple questions—one about the quality of the customer's rental experience and, the second, the likelihood that they would rent from the company again. What do you think about this view? What organizational capabilities would be necessary to develop customer loyalty? Check out Enterprise's Web site [**www.enterprise.com**]. Look at the statements of the company's mission, culture, and founding values. How do these relate to customer loyalty?

3. A study by Fuld & Company, a competitive-intelligence firm, found that companies fail to use as much as 70 percent of the online business data they buy.[24] Why do you think strategic decision makers might not look at business data? Why are such actions a problem? What recommendations might you have for strategic decision makers regarding business data?

4. Asking the right questions is an important skill for strategic decision makers. Here are some questions that might be useful:
   • How can we do that? (Don't ask "why can't we do that?")
   • How else can we do that? What else could we do?
   • Will you help me? Can you explain that to me again?
   • Who, what, why, where, when, how, and how much?
   • Who will do what and by when?
   Would these types of questions be useful in doing an internal analysis? Why or why not?

5. In the cosmetics industry, knowing what and how the various competitors are doing could be important strategic information in developing a sustainable competitive advantage. Suppose you're a manager at the Estée Lauder Companies. What types of competitive-intelligence information would you want, and where would you find it? Create a table showing what you've come up with. Be prepared to support your ideas in class. (You'll probably need to do some outside research—library, Internet, or otherwise—to complete this assignment.)

6. Find five different examples of companies' goals. List these goals on a sheet of paper. Then, do some reverse thinking, and list what organizational resources and capabilities would be needed to accomplish those goals.

7. Studies of companies that are leaders in achieving exceptional customer profitability show that there are six steps they have taken to do so: (1) figure out the needs of your most profitable customers; (2) get creative by imagining competitively superior ways to deliver value to customers; (3) test and verify your hypotheses; (4) tell customers how great your value propositions are; (5) apply the best approaches on a large scale; and (6) start over, as even the most successful initiatives need to be revised over time. What do you think of these suggestions? What are the implications for developing core competencies and distinctive capabilities? How could an internal analysis help an organization in this process?

STRATEGIC MANAGEMENT IN ACTION

CASES

CASE #1 Making Over Avon

Irochka/Fotolia.com

This Strategic Management in Action case can be found at the beginning of Chapter 4.

Discussion Questions

1. What resources and capabilities do you think it would take to become the top direct seller of cosmetics and beauty-related items? Does Avon Products seem to have any of those? What would it take to make its capabilities distinctive?

2. What strengths and weaknesses of Avon do you see from the limited information presented in this case?

3. Put yourself in the position of the new CEO at Avon. What approach to internal analysis would you suggest this person use? How would you go about learning the company's strengths and weaknesses?

4. What are some performance measures that Avon's strategic decision makers might use to evaluate the results of any restructuring initiatives it undertakes? (Hint: Think about how and where its products are sold.)

CASE #2 Fizz Factor

The Coca-Cola Company (Coke) is in a league by itself. It's the world's number one nonalcoholic beverage company. It has four of the top five soft drink brands (Coke, Diet Coke, Fanta, and Sprite). And it's huge—the company makes or licenses more than 3,500 drinks in more than 200 countries. As the world's largest manufacturer, distributor, and marketer of nonalcoholic beverages, Coke knows all about strengths and weaknesses. The company's flagship brand, Coca-Cola, competes directly with Pepsi Cola, the flagship brand of PepsiCo. However, Coke has something unique and valuable that Pepsi does not—an iconic global brand. Each year since 2001, global brand consulting firm Interbrand, in conjunction with *BusinessWeek,* has identified the best global brands. Every year so far, Coke has been number one on the list. Having the "best" global brand, at least according to this ranking, means the brand has value, just like any other asset. In another ranking of the Top 100 Brands done by consulting group Millward Brown, Coke was one of the top six companies for the last six years. Despite its market-leading brand, Coke cannot take anything for granted, especially in today's harsh economic climate. What's Coke serving up now?

CEO Muhtar Kent, who came onboard in July 2008, is focusing on ambitious, long-term growth for the company. His goals: Establish a long-term vision, and restore growth in North America. One of the first things he noticed about the company was its inward focus. "Most of the meetings we were holding were just with ourselves. We weren't going out to see how the world was changing." The organizational culture was insular, and some even described it as "arrogant."

Coke has had a rich heritage of marketing successes and one noteworthy marketing blunder. In 1985, the company introduced "new Coke," not realizing how passionately people felt about the original Coke. The company swiftly realized its error and reversed course. But other marketing has worked, and worked well—the company's polar bears, jingles, and advertisements are always popular. In the fall of 2011, the company unveiled a specially designed Coke can as part of a marketing campaign aimed at protecting polar bears and their habitat.

Finally, Coke's design strategy has always been important. Although it has a rich design heritage—from the shape of its bottle to the lettering and curves on that bottle—company executives felt it was time to step it up and do a total top-to-bottom redesign. When David Butler was hired as vice president of global design in 2003, he was told, "We need to do more with design. Go figure it out." In his review of design at Coke, he found that "Coke had 450 brands, more than 300 different models of vending machines, innumerable bottling and retail partners, and no consistent global design standards." Initial design changes have included the aluminum contour bottle, which has been called a "sexy update of the glass bottle" and which feels more modern but is less expensive to produce. In addition, Coke introduced a new sleeker, sculptural cooler, which uses 30 to 40 percent less energy. Realizing that its vendors might not want to invest in the new coolers when they had ones that were still working, Butler's team designed inexpensive modular panels that could be attached to those still-functional coolers. But both sides "won"—the retailer got a new fresh look, and Coke got consistency in its brand message. Butler's team continually reviews all the brands in the company's portfolio.

Discussion Questions

1. From this abbreviated description, what resources and capabilities do you think The Coca-Cola Company has? Does the fact that an organization is so heavily into global markets make it more difficult to develop unique resources and distinctive capabilities? Explain.

2. Do you think the company has any distinctive capability(ies)? Explain.

3. Go to Coke's Web site **[thecoca-colacompany.com],** and find five "fun" facts in the material about the company.

Write these down, and then discuss how each could be a strength, a weakness, or both.

4. What approach to internal analysis would you suggest that CEO Muhtar Kent use in assessing his organization's strengths and weaknesses? Why?

Sources: Adi Ignatious, "Shaking Things Up at Coca-Cola," *Harvard Business Review*, October 2011, pp. 94–99; S. Vranica, "Coke to Promote Polar Bear Campaign," *Wall Street Journal*, October 25, 2011, p. B4; "Best Global Brands Ranking," Interbrand [www.interbrand.com], October 4, 2011; P. Ziobro, "Coca-Cola Lifted by Overseas Sales," *Wall Street Journal*, July 20, 2011, p. B4; D. B. Stanford, "Can Coke Surpass Its Record High of $88 a Share?" *Bloomberg BusinessWeek*, June 6–June 12, 2011, pp. 49–50; "Top 100 Brand Ranking," Millward Brown [www.millwardbrown.com], May 9, 2011; and P. Ziobro and V. Bauerlein, "Coke Sales Rise Globally," *Wall Street Journal*, February 10, 2011, p. B4.

CASE #3 Shooting for Success

Using an exceptionally well-executed game plan, the National Basketball Association (NBA) has emerged as a truly global brand. The transformation of a once-faltering domestic sport into a global commercial success reflects a keen understanding of resources and capabilities. And much of the credit goes to NBA commissioner David Stern, who has been with the league since 1984, and has deliberately built the NBA into a global brand. He says, "Basketball is a universal language, and it's going to bloom on a global basis." In fact, some have suggested it be called the Global Basketball Association.

Professional basketball sparked the interest of fans and players around the globe in the mid-1990s, and the NBA cashed in on the game's universal appeal. At one time, if you had asked someone in China what the most popular basketball team was, the answer would have been the "Red Oxen" from Chicago (the Bulls). Today, NBA is the third most googled word in China, and China was the home of the now-retired Yao Ming, who was the 7'6" all-star centerpiece of the Houston Rockets. But he's not the only global player in the league. NBA team rosters feature 87 international players from 17 countries. Some of these players include the Dallas Mavericks' Dirk Nowitzki, a seven-footer from Germany; Pau Gasol of the Los Angeles Lakers, a native of Spain and also seven feet tall; San Antonio Spurs' guard Tony Parker from France; Denver Nuggets' forward Nenê from Brazil; Omer Asik from Turkey and now playing for the Chicago Bulls; and Darko Milicic, a seven-footer from Serbia, now playing for the Toronto Raptors. A trend that started as a trickle in the 1980s with occasional foreign stars like Hakeem Olajuwon (Nigeria) and the late Drazen Petrovic (Croatia) turned into a flood.

In addition to the global players now in the U.S. league, the NBA has taken its game global. The league holds several preseason games in Europe, Latin America, and Asia. And developers are building modern arenas in Europe to help promote expansion of the game. Attendance at Euroleague, the region's top professional basketball organization, has been steady. Even India is interested in growing its national game with the NBA's help. But today's global appeal hasn't come easily.

The brutal player contract negotiations during the 1998–1999 season and the lockout prior to the 2011–2012 season frustrated and angered fans. Then, there were the not one, not two, but three retirements of one of the NBA's most popular players ever, Michael Jordan (1993, 1999, and 2003), that took away one of the league's key draws, both as a player and as a global celebrity. However, even with these struggles, Stern didn't throw in the towel. To address the strategic challenges facing the NBA, he looked at what the league had to offer: consumer familiarity with basketball both domestically and globally, talented young players, and a recognized image and track record. He felt that if those things could be exploited, the NBA might be able to turn its game around.

One thing Stern did was expand the NBA's global network of offices. He explained, "The model is the rock concert. Sell lots of records. Tour occasionally." Another thing he did was enhance the league's global presence through its Web site and through its broadcasting deals. Today, more than 30 percent of the visitors to the NBA Web site are from China, although there are sites also in Spanish, Japanese, French, and German. This allows the NBA to push its games and merchandise to fans around the world via their computers. And coverage of the league from both the Internet and broadcasting now reaches 215 countries in 43 different languages. Ad revenues from NBA.com are estimated at almost $22 million, and the number of monthly unique visitors to the Web site ranged from 8 million to more than 12 million. To further improve the game and enrich the experiences of fans, on and off the court, the NBA teamed with Hewlett-Packard to provide real-time statistics. As Stern said, "It's the best reality programming that plays around the world." And further, says Stern, "This is globalization." Stern and his executive team at the NBA are continuing to take actions to enhance their resources and capabilities globally.

Discussion Questions

1. From this abbreviated description, what resources and capabilities do you think the NBA has? Does the fact that an organization is striving for global success make it more difficult to develop unique resources and distinctive capabilities? Explain.
2. Take each of the three approaches to internal analysis and describe how each could be used in analyzing the strengths and weaknesses of the NBA. Which one do you think is most appropriate for an organization like the NBA? Support your choice.
3. Look at each of the strategic initiatives implemented by Stern. Are they exploiting the NBA's strengths and minimizing its weaknesses? Explain.

Sources: Based on National Basketball Association [www.nba.com], January 31, 2012; L. A. E. Schuker, "NBA Removes Player Images," *Wall Street Journal*, July 11, 2011, p. B6; J. Adelman, "Bryant, China Form Partnership," Associated Press, *Springfield, Missouri News-Leader*, February 2, 2011, p. 5D; P. J. Sauer, "Give and Go," *Fast Company*, November 2010, pp. 64–66; S. Moore, "The Global Basketball Association," *Wall Street Journal*, October 23–24, 2010, p. A13; "Technology Tipoff," *Wall Street Journal*, October 30, 2008, p. A8; and D. Eisenberg, "The NBA's Global Game Plan," *Time*, March 17, 2003, pp. 59–63.

CASE #4 New Recipe

From the publication of her first book on entertaining back in 1982 to what is now the media empire called Martha Stewart Living Omnimedia (MSLO), Martha Stewart has capitalized on what she does best—helping people create a lifestyle in which the ultimate in cooking, decorating, entertaining, and other homemaking arts are emphasized and celebrated. What exactly does MSLO do? The company has two primary strategic goals: to provide original "how-to" content and information to as many consumers as possible and to turn customers into "doers" by offering them the information and products they need for do-it-yourself projects. The business is built around core subject areas including cooking, entertaining, weddings, crafts, gardening, home, holidays, babies and children, and keeping and preserving (clothes, mementos, decorative artifacts, etc.). From these different subject areas, content is developed for different media including magazines, books, network television, cable television, newspapers and radio, and digital. In addition, the core subject areas have evolved into merchandise lines (sheets, towels, table linens, paints, etc.) at Kmart, The Home Depot, and Macy's. Martha Stewart herself personified the Martha Stewart brand. It appeared that the company had positioned its resources and capabilities well to exploit sociocultural and demographic trends. However, when Stewart was convicted in March 2004 of obstructing justice and making false statements related to the timing of a sale of ImClone stock and sentenced to a five-month prison term, her namesake company braced for some serious challenges in maintaining its competitive advantage. And they did endure some serious challenges. While Stewart served out her sentence, her namesake TV show was put on hold and company executives tried to "carefully de-emphasize the 'Martha-ness' of its products." The company was not profitable from 2002 through 2006, but had a small profit of $10 million in 2007. Since that time revenues have continued to decline with no net profits. Despite all this, Stewart was not about to let go of the company that so personified her. She no longer serves as CEO or chairperson of the company (her title is chief editorial, media, and content officer), but Stewart's personal imprint is still strong.

Today, MSLO is organized into three business segments: publishing (magazines, books, and digital properties), broadcasting (*Martha Stewart Show*), and merchandising. In 2010, the publishing segment accounted for 63 percent of revenues. The flagship magazine, *Martha Stewart Living*, is the "significant generator of content for our asset library." Other publications include *Everyday Food, Martha Stewart Weddings,* and *Whole Living,* and numerous books on subjects ranging from housekeeping to baking to weddings. Digital properties include marthastewart.com, marthastewartweddings.com, wholeliving.com, and partial ownership of WeddingWire, pingg, and Ziplist. In addition, the company developed two digital apps. One was a digital magazine specifically designed for the Apple iPad and the other was a Cookie app for the iPad. The broadcasting division accounted for 18 percent of revenue in 2010 and includes company activities related to television programming, distribution of that programming domestically and internationally, and satellite radio. The cornerstone of this division is *The Martha Stewart Show,* a daily how-to series that's filmed in front of a studio audience. However, the company was dealt a blow when The Hallmark Channel announced in early 2012 that it was canceling the program because the costs of producing were not offset by the small audience of about 200,000 viewers. The *Martha Stewart Living* radio channel is still on Sirius XM radio. The merchandising division accounted for 19 percent of revenue in 2010 and is responsible for selling Martha Stewart–branded products at "multiple price points through several distribution channels." Important retail partnerships include the Martha Stewart Collection at Macy's, Martha Stewart Living at The Home Depot, Sandals® Weddings by Martha Stewart, Martha Stewart Everyday at Kmart, and Martha Stewart Flowers with 1-800-Flowers. In December 2011, Martha Stewart Living Omnimedia sold a 16.6 percent stake in the company (for $38.5 million) to J.C. Penney Co. Starting in 2013, consumers will be able to shop at a ministore in J.C. Penney stores that will be stocked with Martha Stewart products and will have trained employees who will provide advice and tips. However, Macy's sued MSLO to block this new agreement saying that it violated Macy's own exclusive arrangement with the Martha Stewart brand. The outcome of the suit is still pending. Another hit came in early 2012 when The Home Depot said it will end its line of Martha Stewart Living-branded paint products because of weaker-than-expected customer response. However, it will continue to offer Stewart's color palette mixed into its Glidden paint line.

The company's independent board is chaired by entertainment veteran Charles A. Koppelman, a man described as so "un-Martha-like that he refers to flowers as 'some pink things.'" The company continues to face challenges. One woman still defines the brand. What happens when Martha is no longer able to serve in all the capacities she currently does? And is Martha, the personality, overused and overexposed in the marketplace? In an attempt to extend the company's brands, negotiations with two prominent tastemakers—fashion designer Cynthia Rowley and home-decorating guru Jonathan Adler—were started but broken off before any deals were signed. And the company faces intense competition from new faces such as Rachel Ray (whose show averages 46 percent more viewers than Stewart's), Paula Deen, and Giada De Laurentiis. Finally, the economic climate has had an impact on advertising revenues and on consumer expenditures.

Discussion Questions

1. What resources and capabilities did MSLO appear to have? Do those resources and capabilities need to change? Why or why not?

2. Go to the company's Web site [**www.marthastewart.com**] and find the information on the company's business segments. (Hint: Start your search by looking at Investor Relations.) Pick one of the segments and describe and evaluate the strategies being implemented.

3. What are the benefits (strengths) and challenges (weaknesses) of a company whose products and brands are so tied up in one person's image? Can you think of any other companies that have this same issue? What are the implications for the company's strategic decision makers?

4. How could MSLO's strategic decision makers use value chain analysis in assessing the company's strengths and weaknesses? How about an internal audit? How about a capabilities assessment profile?

Sources: Based on "Martha Stewart Living Omnimedia, Inc.," *Hoover's* [www.hoovers.com], January 31, 2012; C. Bray and D. Mattioli, "Macy's File Suit Against Martha Stewart Living," *Wall Street Journal,* January 24, 2012, p. B3; D. Mattioli and R. Adams, "Martha's Deal Miffs Macy's," *Wall Street Journal,* December 8, 2011, p. B3; M. J. De La Merced, and S. Clifford, "J. C. Penney to Buy Stake in Martha Stewart Living," *New York Times Online,* December 7, 2011; "Martha Stewart Rejoins Her Board," The Associated Press, *New York Times Online,* September 26, 2011; 10K Filing, [www.marthastewart.com], March 15, 2011; and S. Ovide and S. Vranica, "Martha Stewart Shakes Up Ranks," *Wall Street Journal,* April 22, 2009, p. B6.

Endnotes

1. J. Cane, "Coty Withdraws $10.7 Billion Offer for Avon," *New York Times Online,* May 14, 2012; E. Glazer, G. Chon, and A. Das, "Scarred Avon Is Takeover Target," *Wall Street Journal,* April 3, 2012, pp. A1+; A. Dowell, "Avon Fires Vice Chairman," *Wall Street Journal,* January 31, 2012, p. B2; Hoover's, "Avon Products, Inc.," [www.hoovers.com], January 31, 2012; H. Karp and J. S. Lublin, "Avon Ex-Chiefs Slam Jung," *Wall Street Journal,* December 22, 2011, pp. B1+; "Andrea's Adieu," *Economist,* December 17, 2011, p. 115; J. S. Lublin and H. Karp, "Avon Replacing Jung as CEO," *Wall Street Journal,* December 14, 2011, pp. B1+; H. Karp and J. S. Lublin, "Avon's Jung Comes Under Fire," *Wall Street Journal,* October 28, 2011, pp. B1+; and Avon Annual Report 2010, [www.avoncompany.com].

2. S. K. Ethiraj, P. Kale, M. S. Krishnan, and J. V. Singh, "Where Do Capabilities Come From and How Do They Matter? A Study in the Software Services Industry," *Strategic Management Journal,* January 2005, pp. 25–45; and D. J. Collis, "Research Note: How Valuable Are Organizational Capabilities," *Strategic Management Journal,* Winter 1994, pp. 143–152.

3. R. M. Grant, "The Resource-Based Theory of Competitive Advantage: Implications for Strategy Formulation," *California Management Review,* Spring 1991, pp. 114–135.

4. Collis, *Strategic Management Journal,* pp. 143–152.

5. S. G. Winter, "Understanding Dynamic Capabilities," *Strategic Management Journal,* October 2003, pp. 991–995; C. E. Helfat and M. A. Peteraf, "The Dynamic Resource-Based View: Capability Lifecycles," *Strategic Management Journal,* October 2003, pp. 997–1010; S. A. Zahra and G. George, "Absorptive Capacity: A Review, Reconceptualization, and Extension," *Academy of Management Review,* April 2002, pp. 185–203; G. S. Day, "The Capabilities of Market-Driven Organizations," *Journal of Marketing,* October 1994, pp. 37–52; and C. K. Prahalad and G. Hamel, "The Core Competence of the Corporation," *Harvard Business Review,* May–June 1990, pp. 79–91.

6. Prahalad and Hamel, pp. 79–91.

7. C. Bryan-Low, "Nokia Maps Plan for GPS Handsets," *Wall Street Journal,* March 1, 2007, p. B4.

8. K. P. Coyne, S. J. D. Hall, and P. G. Clifford, "Is Your Core Competence a Mirage? *The McKinsey Quarterly,* no. 1, 1997 [www.mckinseyquarterly.com].

9. G. S. Day, *Journal of Marketing,* p. 39.

10. S. Hamner, "Heaven from Pennies," *Business 2.0,* August 2005, p. 54.

11. S. Freierman, "Telegram Falls Silent Stop Era Ends Stop," *New York Times Online,* February 6, 2006.

12. K. Kelleher, "66,207,897 Bottles of Beer on the Wall," *Business 2.0,* January–February 2004, pp. 47–49.

13. B. Vlasic, "Honda Stays True to Efficient Driving," *New York Times Online,* August 26, 2008; M. Maynard, "Honda Adding a Jet, a Six-Passenger Model, to its Lineup," *New York Times Online,* July 26, 2006; and Honda Ad, front inside cover of *Forbes,* July 7, 2003.

14. B. Nelson, "The Thinker," *Forbes,* March 3, 2003, pp. 62–64.

15. D. Sacks, "The Gore-Tex of Guitar Strings," *Fast Company,* December 2003, p. 46; and A. Harrington, "Who's Afraid of a New Product" *Fortune,* November 10, 2003, pp. 189–192.

16. See M. E. Porter, *Competitive Advantage: Creating and Sustaining Superior Performance,* chap. 2 (New York: The Free Press, 1985).

17. D. Ulrich and N. Smallwood, "Capitalizing on Capabilities," *Harvard Business Review,* June 2004, pp. 119–127; and K. E. Marino, "Developing Consensus on Firm Competencies and Capabilities," *Academy of Management Executive,* August 1996, pp. 40–51.

18. This discussion of the capabilities assessment profile is based on K. E. Marino, *Academy of Management Executive.*

19. P. Kotler, *Marketing Management,* 8th ed. (Upper Saddle River, NJ: Prentice Hall, 1996), p. 195.

20. H. H. Stevenson, "Defining Corporate Strengths and Weaknesses," *Sloan Management Review,* Spring 1967, pp. 51–68.

21. B. Rosner, "HR Should Get a Clue: Corporate Spying Is Real," *Workforce,* April 2001, pp. 72–75.

22. A. Serwer, "P&G's Covert Operation," *Fortune,* September 17, 2001, pp. 42–44.

23. K. Western, "Ethical Spying," *Business Ethics,* September–October 1995, pp. 22–23.

24. "Expensive Unused Data are Clogging up Budgets and Decision-Making," *Wall Street Journal,* July 1, 1999, p. A1.

FUNCTIONAL AND COMPETITIVE STRATEGIES

5

LEARNING OUTCOMES

5.1 **Describe the functional strategies an organization needs and explain how those strategies are implemented and evaluated.**

5.2 **Explain competitive advantage and what it implies.**

5.3 **Describe the different competitive strategies.**

5.4 **Discuss how competitive strategies are implemented and evaluated.**

STRATEGIC MANAGEMENT IN ACTION

CASE #1 Driving for Success

What a difference the passage of time makes. Toyota Motor Corporation's first U.S. import in the late 1950s flopped miserably.[1] That car—the Toyopet Crown—overheated, vibrated when it went over 60 miles per hour, and looked ridiculous. Despite that dreadful product launch in the all-important U.S. car market, Toyota has vastly improved its business over the years. Evaluations of Toyota's work methods and processes consistently conclude that the company's successes are due to a well-coordinated mix of functional strategies. The company leaves nothing to chance. Four management principles (the 4P model) guide employees: problem solving, people and partners, process, and philosophy. The idea behind these principles is that "Good Thinking Means Good Product." And that's where the scientific process—a significant part of Toyota's culture—plays a role. The scientific process is based on the idea that any change requires a rigorous problem-solving process with a detailed assessment of the current state of affairs and a plan for improvement. This approach is so ingrained at Toyota that the system actually inspires workers and managers to engage in the kinds of experimentation that are the hallmarks of an innovative organization.

Bagus Indahono/Newscom

For instance, at Toyota's new Miyagi factory, cars are positioned side-by-side on the assembly line, instead of the tip-to-tail approach used in most car factories. This made the assembly line 35 percent shorter, reducing installation costs and increasing productivity by not forcing workers to walk as far between cars. In addition, the Miyagi plant uses raised platforms instead of dangling car chassis from above as is the norm. These were 50 percent cheaper to install and allowed for lower ceilings in the factory, thus reducing heating and cooling costs. Then, the actual assembly line itself uses quiet friction rollers to move along pallets carrying cars rather than the

119

noisy chain-pulled conveyor belts found in most car plants. All of these ideas reflect Toyota's current philosophy of "retooling for production with simpler, slimmer and more compact equipment." While Toyota has always been strong in the production area, its other functional strategies also are solid. The company recognizes how important marketing research is. The company's human resource (HR) strategies emphasize education and training, especially as cars became more complex. In research and development (R&D), Toyota is a master. For instance, when Toyota wanted to find a way to make a custom car in five days (something unheard of in the car industry), it relied on R&D to help make that happen.

The last couple of years, however, have been challenges for Toyota. It struggled with quality recalls and with extreme natural disasters as the earthquake and tsunami led to critical parts shortages. Although it had been number one in worldwide sales (it surpassed General Motors in 2008), these challenges, as well as the global economic crisis, pushed Toyota out of that top spot. The U.S. car companies have made solid improvements, giving Toyota a run for its money. Yes, competition is alive and well!

Ahhhh.....the car industry. Now that's an industry in which the participants need to strategically manage their functional and competitive strategies. But that's also a reality for most industries. As our chapter-opening case illustrates, when an organization's functional strategies are managed strategically, it's able to exploit the resources, capabilities, and core competencies found in its various functions. As organizations develop strategies to exploit their current resources and capabilities, they find themselves in competition with other organizations doing the same thing. That's when a competitive advantage becomes crucial. In this chapter, we'll be discussing the role of the functional and competitive strategies in managing strategically.

LEARNING OUTCOME 5.1

Describe the Functional Strategies an Organization Needs, and Explain How Those Strategies Are Implemented and Evaluated

In this chapter, we begin to look at *how* strategic decision makers formulate and implement organizational strategies. We're approaching this step in strategic management by looking at functional and competitive strategies first.

Strategic Management in Action: Process

Although we've studied several aspects of strategic management in action, the process still may seem confusing. (See Figure 5.1.) The functional and competitive strategies help move the organization in the desired direction toward the established goals. That's why we want to look at these strategies first. But remember that these strategies are developed taking into account the organization's overall vision, mission(s), and corporate strategies. There is, however, one situation in which corporate strategies are addressed immediately, and that's when an organization is first founded. Here, the overall strategic goal(s) and direction are formulated by the CEO and the top management team, thus establishing what work activities organizational employees must do. Over time, as the organization does what it's in business to do and as employees in the various functional areas do their jobs, organizational resources are used, capabilities and core competencies are developed, and distinctive capabilities may begin to emerge that eventually become sources of sustainable competitive advantage. At that point, the specific functional strategies should support the business-level (competitive) and corporate-level strategies. Because you'll most likely encounter situations in which an organization or its divisions are *not* new, it makes sense to look at the functional and competitive strategies first as we look at the process of deciding the most appropriate strategies—that is, the ones that will lead to a sustainable competitive advantage. And what happens when the corporate strategies aren't working and need to be revised to accommodate changes in either the external or internal environments? Strategic decision makers would look at the organization's various functional units to see what is and isn't working and at the competitive strategies to assess the status of the organization's competitive advantage.

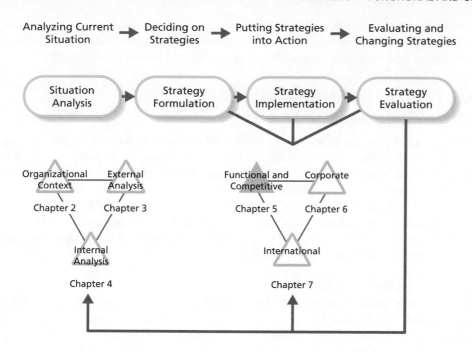

FIGURE 5.1

Strategic Management
in Action

What Happens After the SWOT Analysis?

After completing the SWOT analysis, decision makers have information about the positive and negative aspects of both the external and internal environments. If the organization's strengths in the various functional units can be exploited as competitive advantages, particularly in light of any relevant external opportunities, the organization may well be on its way to achieving high levels of performance. In addition, if the SWOT analysis points to threats in any of the organization's external areas or weaknesses in the internal areas, changes in functional strategies might be needed to counteract them.

The SWOT analysis points to strategic issues organizational decision makers must address in their pursuit of sustainable competitive advantage and high levels of performance. Many strategic issues concern good or bad performance in the various functional areas. Even if it's evident from

STRATEGIC MANAGEMENT IN ACTION

Super Bowl Sunday. It's the second highest food consumption day of the year, behind Thanksgiving. And a popular food of choice? Pizza. More pizza is sold on Super Bowl Sunday than any other day of the year. For the 2012 Super Bowl, Pizza Hut expected to sell more than 2 million pizzas, and Domino's expected to deliver more than 1.1 million pizzas. Why the increased demand on that one day? Pizza seems to meet game-day criteria: It's cheap. It's easy. And it's social. The challenge for the pizza companies is making sure they can meet customers' demands.

THINK ABOUT

- What are the implications of a "super" sales day for an organization's functional areas?
- Could a SWOT analysis help? Why or why not? If so, how? If not, why not?

Sources: Based on T. Kaufmann, "Pizza Hut Expects to Sell Over Two Million Pies Super Bowl Sunday," *Newsnet5.com,* February 3, 2012; "Pizza Fun Facts," *Pizza.com,* February 3, 2012; "Everything You Ever Wanted to Know About Pizza," *PizzaDelivery.com,* February 3, 2012; and S. Meehan, "Wings Fly High on Super Bowl Sunday," *USA Today.com,* February 3, 2012.

the SWOT analysis that the organization's corporate or competitive strategies need to be changed, strategists base their decisions on the resources, capabilities, and core competencies found in the functional areas—lending more support as to why we look at functional strategies first.

What Functional Strategies Does an Organization Need?

In Chapter 1, we defined an organization's **functional (or operational) strategies** as the goal-directed plans and actions of the organization's functional areas. We're going to look at these strategies with the assumption that all organizations must acquire and transform resources (inputs) into outputs (products), which then are made available to the organization's customers or clients. The functional strategies help ensure that the resources and capabilities found in the functional areas are used efficiently and effectively in doing the organization's business. In doing this, organizations have three functional concerns: the product, the people, and the support processes. Figure 5.2 illustrates this relationship.

Functional Strategies—The Product

It takes more than seven years to make the world's largest and most complicated warship—a nuclear-powered, Nimitz-class U.S. Navy aircraft carrier.[2] "Putting together an aircraft carrier is like no other manufacturing task in the world. It is the most technologically challenging and toughest product to manufacture." Each ship costs more than $4 billion and involves more than 47,000 tons of precision-welded steel, more than 1 million distinct parts, 900 miles of wire and cable, around 40 million skilled-worker hours, and massive numbers of engineers. Not many products are this complex, yet even organizations with a simple product must produce that product. Before this can happen, however, the product must be designed. And once the product is designed and produced, it must be marketed to appropriate customers. Design, production-operations, and marketing are the three main tasks associated with the product. And remember—products can refer to goods *or* services.

Product design strategies typically involve an organizations R&D functional area. Once products have been designed, they're ready to be produced, which involves an organization's production-operations strategies. The main strategic choices include how products will be

FIGURE 5.2

The Three Functional Concerns of Organizations

STRATEGIC MANAGEMENT IN ACTION

Loading passengers on a plane is part of the production-operations process for airlines. After all, "producing" the "service" that customers have paid for means the planes have to be back in the air as quickly as possible to get to the next destination. Also, airlines don't make money with their planes sitting on the ground. Even a few extra minutes to get a plane loaded can throw a day's schedule off. So, the airlines have tried a variety of techniques to find the best way to get people on and off planes. From a simple back-to-front approach that's still used by most airlines to more complicated approaches such as the reverse pyramid system, the outside-in technique, and the "nonsystem system" pioneered by Southwest Airlines in which passengers board in the order they arrive with no assigned seats. The variable that keeps airlines carefully planning their production-operations is the "unpredictability of human behavior." Because that behavior is so hard to predict, some experts believe that other tactics, such as limiting carry-on baggage, is likely to be more effective in faster gate turnaround than some complicated loading system.

THINK ABOUT

- What other production-operations strategies might be important to airlines?
- What are the implications of these production-operations strategies for the people strategies of airlines?

Source: Based on P. B. Finney, "Loading an Airliner Is Rocket Science," *New York Times Online*, November 14, 2006.

produced and where they will be produced. Once products are produced, the next step is to efficiently and effectively get those products to the customers when, where, and how they want them.[3] That's the role of marketing, in which the main strategic choices are aimed at effectively and efficiently managing the two "Cs"—customers and competitors. Those strategic choices involve decisions about target market, differentiation, positioning, marketing mix (commonly known as the 4Ps: product, pricing, promotion, and place), and gathering market insights.

Functional Strategies—The People

"At L'Oreal, success starts with people. Our people are our most precious asset. Respect for people, their ideas and differences, is the only path to our sustainable long-term growth."[4] How often have you heard a statement like "Our people are our most important asset"? More important, can an organization's people strategies (that is, the human resources or HR strategies) help it establish a sustainable competitive advantage? The answer seems to be "yes," as shown by various studies.[5] And if HR strategies can contribute to getting competitive advantage, can they affect performance? Other studies that have looked at the link between performance and HR policies and practices have shown that certain ones *can* have a positive impact on performance.[6] These **high-performance work practices** are ones that lead to both high individual and high organizational performance. Table 5.1 lists some of these practices. These types of HR practices can improve the knowledge, skills, and abilities of an organization's current and potential employees, increase their motivation, reduce loafing on the job, and help retain quality employees while encouraging nonperformers to leave the organization.

The strategic challenge facing many organizations in today's uncertain and daunting economic environment is how to maintain a balance of showing employees they are valued while trying to control costs. In such difficult times, painful decisions often have to be made in the HR area. Some companies, however, are bucking that trend as explained in the FYI box, "To Layoff or Not to Layoff."

An organization's HR strategies reflect its commitment to and treatment of its employees. Because an organization's people are the ones who do the work involved in implementing the other strategies, the HR strategies must closely align with those other strategies in order to assure that the right numbers of the appropriately skilled people are in the right place at the right time and that the organization's workforce is being used effectively and efficiently.[7] Strategic choices in the HR area involve getting people into the organization (HR planning, recruiting, and staffing); making sure they have the knowledge and skills necessary to do their jobs and helping

TABLE 5.1 Examples of High-Performance Work Practices

- Self-managed work teams
- Decentralized decision making
- Flexible job assignments
- Open communication
- Performance-based compensation
- Staffing based on person-job and person-organization fit
- Extensive employee involvement
- Giving employees more control over decision making

Source: Based on C. H. Chuang and H. Liao, "Strategic Human Resource Management In Service Context: Taking Care of Business by Taking Care of Employees and Customers," *Personnel Psychology,* Spring 2010, pp. 153–196; M. Subramony, "A Meta-Analytic Investigation of the Relationship Between HRM Bundles and Firm Performance," *Human Resource Management,* September–October 2009, pp. 745–768; M. M. Butts, et. al., "Individual Reactions to High Involvement Work Practices: Investigating the Role of Empowerment and Perceived Organizational Support," *Journal of Occupational Health Psychology,* April 2009, pp. 122–136; and W. R. Evans and W. D. Davis, "High-Performance Work Systems and Organizational Performance: The Mediating Role of Internal Social Structure," *Journal of Management,* October 2005, p. 760.

them do those jobs better (orientation and training); assessing how well they do those jobs and making needed corrections (performance appraisal and disciplinary actions); and motivating high levels of effort and compensating them fairly and appropriately (compensation and benefits). Other potential strategies may address HR issues such as employee relations, job design, diversity efforts, workplace safety and health, and workplace misbehavior.

We've discussed the first two of an organization's functional concerns: the product and the people. That leaves the third functional concern—the support processes.

Functional Strategies—The Support Processes

As organizations acquire and transform resources into products by doing what they're in business to do, they need information about the activities taking place and they need to account for the transactions and exchanges between the organization and its suppliers and customers. This is done through the organization's two main support processes—information systems and financial-accounting systems. Just like the other functional areas, these areas also involve certain strategies that help the organization efficiently and effectively do its work and, it is hoped, contribute to creating a sustainable competitive advantage.

How would you like to do your job as a student (study, write papers, take tests, etc.) without information? It would be pretty tough, wouldn't it? Information affects how effectively and efficiently organizational members can do their work. Without information, the payroll clerk doesn't know what deductions to make from paychecks; the sales representative doesn't know what prices to quote a potential customer; or the plant manager doesn't know how this month's product quality levels compared to last month's. It's essential to have information to make decisions and to carry out work duties.

What role do information and information systems play in managing strategically?[8] It depends on how important it is to have the right types of information when, where, and how organizational members need it. Two strategic decisions most associated with the organization's information system are the choice of system technology and the choice of types of information systems needed. These decisions will depend on how important information is to developing a sustainable competitive advantage. Also, it's unlikely that a single information system can provide all the information needed. Instead, an organization probably will have many different types of information systems serving different organizational levels and functions.

FOR YOUR INFORMATION
To Layoff or Not to Layoff

In February 2012, American Airlines declares bankruptcy and says it will cut 13,000 jobs. Danske Bank announces 2,000 job cuts. Alcatel-Lucent announces plans to cut up to 1,800 Europe jobs. Nokia plans to eliminate 4,000 jobs at 3 factories. PepsiCo announces 8,700 jobs to be cut. Are mass layoffs the answer to an unrelenting economic downturn? Some experts say no, and some companies are bucking the trend. The reason for layoffs is clear. Payrolls are one of the first places businesses look to cut expenses. However, layoffs may be a short-sighted fix. The increasing number of people looking for work means even more consumers are likely to spend less and foreclosures and credit card delinquencies might increase, leading to even weaker demand for products and more problems. And though some might think the surviving employees might be more motivated to work harder—I have a job and I want to be sure I keep it—that's not necessarily what happens. Employee morale and productivity often decline. "No one wins when people spend more time worrying about whether they're going to be the next to go than they do actually working." If employees aren't productive, customers will eventually notice, and a company could start losing business because of unsatisfactory customer service. In addition, deep HR cuts makes it that much tougher to meet consumer demand once it does bounce back.

Some companies have taken a different approach. They've vowed to not lay off any workers, even during times of financial hardships. Companies such as Lincoln Electric and Nucor had "no layoff" policies in place long before this economic downturn and have no plans to change them. Other companies, including Southwest Airlines, FedEx, Aflac, and Erie Insurance, don't have a formal policy barring layoffs but say that "there is no history of layoffs and no plans to lay off workers going forward." Although they're not using extensive layoffs to control labor costs, they often resort to other, less drastic measures such as four-day workweeks, unpaid vacations, unpaid furloughs of short duration, wage freezes, pension cuts, no bonuses paid, and flexible work schedules. The HR director at a Pennsylvania-based manufacturer said, "We have a very skilled and competent workforce, and the last thing we want to do is lose them when we're assuming this economy is going to come back." But there can be a downside to the sacrifices made by employees. Workers may grow frustrated, want their full compensation back, or may even prefer a layoff that at least provides a sense of permanence.

TO DO

- Do some research on employee layoffs. What are companies doing to make it easier for those being laid off? What about for the survivors?
- What do you think of a company asking employees to take a pay cut or work fewer hours so that no one has to be laid off? How willing would you be to do something like that?

Sources: Based on L. Petrecca, "More Companies Turn to Furloughs to Save Money, Jobs," *USA Today,* March 5, 2009, pp. 1B+; P. R. La Monica, "Layoffs Aren't the Answer," *CNNMoney.com,* January 27, 2009; "No Layoffs—Ever!" *CNNMoney.com,* January 23, 2009; W. J. McEwen, "Who's Caring for the Customers?" *Gallup Management Journal* [gmj.gallup.com], January 8, 2009; M. Richtel, "More Companies Cut Labor Costs without Layoffs," *New York Times Online,* December 22, 2008; and J. Dickler, "Employers: No Layoffs Here," *CNNMoney.com,* December 11, 2008.

THE GREY ZONE

Corporate blogs and other forms of social media are becoming popular in corporations. Because anyone can visit these sites and read the message, companies have become concerned about messages that may include sensitive data, criticize managers or competitors, use inflammatory language, or contain misrepresentations. Companies also worry about the reactions of stakeholders who may disagree with or be offended by blog postings. Many companies have developed blog policies for employees to follow.

THINK ABOUT

- What do you think of this? Should corporate blogs and other forms of social media be allowed? Why or why not?
- What ethical issues might arise?
- What guidelines might you suggest for the use of these?

STRATEGIC MANAGEMENT IN ACTION

Caesars Entertainment Corporation, the Las Vegas–based gaming company, is fanatical about customer service, and for good reason. Company research showed that customers who were satisfied with the service they received at a company casino increased their gaming expenditures by 10 percent and those who were extremely satisfied increased their gaming expenditures by 24 percent." The company was able to discover this important customer service–expenditures connection because of its incredibly sophisticated information system and because all employees were made aware of this information so they truly understood their vital role in providing outstanding customer service. Now, it's taking its knowledge management to a new level by developing a pilot project in which casino staff will forecast customer spending, which they hope will help boost revenue.

THINK ABOUT

- How does this illustrate a functional strategy?
- What could other companies learn from this example?

Sources: Based on "The Scientist," *McKinsey Quarterly,* Issue 3, 2011, pp. 42–45; J. Hagel and J. S. Brown, "Harrah's New Twist on Prediction Markets," *BusinessWeek Online,* December 23, 2008; J. Barsky, "Elite Rewards Programs Score High with Hotel Guests," *Hotel and Motel Management,* November 3, 2008, p. 27; D. Greenfield, "From Idea to Innovation: Companies Are Using Online Voting Tools and Prediction Markets to Conceive New Products," November 10, 2008, p. 26; M. Millstein, "Customer Relationships Make Playing the Odds Easy," *Chain Store Age,* December 2007, p. 22A; and G. Loveman, "Diamonds in the Data Mine," *Harvard Business Review,* May 2003, pp. 109–113.

The final organizational support process we're going to look at involves the organization's financial-accounting systems, which provide strategic decision makers with information about the organization's financial transactions, accounts, and standing. This information is critical in planning the organization's future strategies. In designing the financial-accounting systems, we must make sure we have the information we need, when we need it, and in the form needed. Strategic decisions in this functional area would involve choices about collecting and using financial and accounting data, evaluating financial performance (what types and how often), doing financial forecasting and budgeting (what types and how often), determining the optimum financing mix (equity or debt, short-term or long-term), and effectively and efficiently managing the financial-accounting functional area.

LEARNING REVIEW   LEARNING OUTCOME 5.1

- How does the work done in the functional areas support the creation of a competitive advantage?
- What happens after the SWOT analysis is completed?
- What are the three functional concerns of organizations?
- What strategies are important to each of those functional concerns?

LEARNING OUTCOME 5.2

Explain What Competitive Advantage Is and What It Implies

As we've said numerous times, competitive advantage is a key concept in strategic management. Getting it and keeping it is what managing strategically is all about. Remember that **competitive advantage** is what sets an organization apart. In other words, an organization does something that others can't or does it better than others do (distinctive capability). Or, an organization has something that other competitors don't (unique resource). An organization's competitive strategies are designed to exploit its competitive advantage. However, other organizations also are attempting to develop competitive advantage and their competitive actions can easily (and often quickly) erode your own competitive advantage. Because competitive advantage implies there are competitors, let's look at the competitive environment to better understand the conditions under which competitive advantage is sought.

Understanding the Competitive Environment

Competition is everywhere. Most industries and organizations have experienced some competition at some point. To understand the competitive environment, we first have to understand *what* competition is and then look at *who* our competitors are.

What Is Competition?

In the United States alone, there are 102 LCD television brands, 66 more than in 2002.[9] Do you think there's competition in that market? Absolutely! **Competition** is when organizations battle or vie for some desired object or outcome. For business organizations, that's typically customers, market share, survey ranking, or needed resources. Although individuals and teams also compete for desired objects or outcomes, our primary interest is competition as it relates to organizations. What competition might an organization face? We can answer this by looking at *who* competitors are.

Who Are Competitors?

There are three approaches to defining an organization's competitors. (See Figure 5.3.) Let's look at each.[10]

The industry perspective identifies competitors as organizations that are making and selling the same or very similar goods or services. Examples are the video rental industry, the supermarket industry, the automobile industry, the credit card industry, or the spa industry. As Figure 5.3 shows, these industries can be described according to the number of sellers and the degree of differentiation, both of which affect the intensity of competition.

The second approach, the market perspective, says competitors are organizations that satisfy the same customer need. So, for example, if the customer need is entertainment, competitors might range from video game companies to theme parks to movie theaters to the local community symphony orchestra to online video downloading. The intensity of competition in the market perspective depends on how well customers' needs are understood or defined and how well different organizations are able to meet those needs.

The third and final approach, the strategic groups concept introduced in Chapter 3, is based on the idea that there are groups of firms competing in an industry with similar strategies,

FIGURE 5.3

Three Approaches to Defining Competition

STRATEGIC MANAGEMENT IN ACTION

You can find competition in the most unlikely of situations and places. For instance, two of the nation's biggest nurses' unions are battling over workers. Each has tried to disrupt the other's organizing drives by using tactics such as ad campaigns, lawsuits, and breaking into Web job sites.

With fame and money at stake, rock 'n roll music acts lobby hard to be selected for induction into the Rock and Roll Hall of Fame in Cleveland. Getting that nod can lead to some big money and immortality for inductees. "Weekly record sales for a performer or band leap 40 to 60 percent, on average, in the weeks after selection. A nod from Cleveland can lift an entire back catalog."

Competition also has erupted among cities in emerging economies vying to be known as the world's next great financial center even as existing centers (London, New York, Berlin, and Zurich) fight to maintain their status as pillars of capitalism. For instance, the Shanghai World Financial Center is one of the world's tallest skyscrapers but also symbolizes Shanghai's bid to become a major financial center. In Taipei, the Financial Center Corp.'s Taipei 101 skyscraper is a symbol of Taiwan's financial aspirations.

THINK ABOUT

- Did you ever think of competition in situations like these?
- Can you think of other situations like this, outside business and athletics, where competition is taking place?

Sources: Based on J. Morrissey, "Battle of the Bands (and Egos) for the Rock Hall of Fame," *New York Times Online*, December 3, 2011; K. Maher, "Nurses Unions Square Off Over Workers," *Wall Street Journal*, May 19, 2008, p. A3; and A. Rappeport, "If You Build It, Will They Come?" *CFO*, October 2007, pp. 33–35.

resources, and customers.[11] In a single industry, you might find few or several strategic groups, depending on what strategic factors are important to customers. For instance, two factors that could be used to group competitors are price and quality. However, the dimensions used to group competitors can be different for every industry and even for different industry segments. Table 5.2 lists some dimensions that might be used to distinguish strategic groups. The strategic groups approach is a good way to define *who* competitors are because your most relevant competitors are those in your strategic group. Although competition might come from organizations in other strategic groups, your main competitive concern is those organizations in your own strategic group. How intense the competition is will depend on how effectively each competitor has developed its competitive advantage and on the competitive strategies each uses.

Although the strategic groups approach is frequently used to define an industry's competitors, there is some controversy about whether specific, identifiable strategic groups even exist.[12] These questions generally concern the factors used to define a strategic group and how those factors are chosen and used to establish specific and identifiable groups. Despite these questions, the strategic groups concept is useful in determining an organization's competitors and in explaining the components of organizational performance.[13]

No matter which approach is used to define competitors, it's clear that other organizations struggle to secure customers, resources, and other desired outcomes. Each of these competitors has resources and capabilities it's attempting to exploit. That's what we want to look at next—the role that resources and capabilities play in competitive advantage.

TABLE 5.2 Possible Dimensions for Identifying Strategic Groups

• Price	• R&D expenditures
• Quality	• Market share
• Level of vertical integration	• Profits
• Geographic scope	• Product characteristics
• Product line breadth-depth	• Any other relevant strategic factor
• Level of diversification	

STRATEGIC MANAGEMENT IN ACTION

Buffalo chicken wings made with cayenne pepper hot sauce have become one of the hottest (literally and figuratively) products around. This popularity has led to a hot sauce war. Long the veteran maker in this industry, McIlhenny Company has introduced a seventh flavor in its Tabasco line, Tabasco Buffalo Style hot sauce. This new flavor is celebrated in an ad campaign as "from the people who perfected hot sauce...offering classic Buffalo flavor with just the right amount of heat." Tabasco's principal rival, Frank's RedHot Sauce (made by Reckitt Benckiser, some of whose other products include French's mustard and Clearasil) is launching a "sassy TV campaign that carries the theme 'I put that—on everything.'" This blunt commercial features a bleeping sound over the word as it's said by a "mischievous older woman

named Ethel. On screen, her mouth is covered by a splat, as if a censor spilled sauce on the film."

THINK ABOUT

- Besides ads, in what other ways do organizations compete for customers?
- What other actions might Tabasco need to do to protect its competitive position? What other actions could Frank's use to enhance its competitive position?

Sources: Based on S. Elliott, "Rival Hot Sauce Makers in a Duel for Attention," *New York Times Online,* January 29, 2012; "Manufacturer Spotlight," *Restaurant Business,* May 2011, p. 58; and D. Kaplan, "At MVBMS, Roddy Finds His No 2s," *Adweek,* January 26, 2004, p. 9.

The Role of Resources and Distinctive Capabilities in Gaining Competitive Advantage

What makes some organizations more successful than others—however success is measured? Why do some professional basketball teams consistently win championships or draw large crowds? Why do some organizations have consistent and continuous growth in revenues and profits? Why do some colleges, universities, or departmental majors experience continually increasing enrollments? Why do some organizations appear consistently on lists ranking "the best," "most admired," or "most innovative?" Every organization has resources and capabilities to do whatever it's in business to do; however, not every organization effectively exploits the resources or capabilities it has or obtains the resources or capabilities it needs but doesn't have. Some organizations are able to put it all together and develop those distinctive organizational capabilities that provide them with a sustainable competitive advantage. Other organizations never get it done.

Organizations develop strategies to exploit their current resources and capabilities or to vie for needed resources and capabilities so they can get desired outcomes (customers, market share, resources, etc.). And other organizations are doing exactly the same thing. Competitive advantage, by its very nature, implies trying to gain the edge on others. As organizations fight for competitive advantage, the stage for competition—intense, moderate, or mild—is set.

From Competitive Advantage to Competitive Strategies

As organizations attempt to create a sustainable competitive advantage, they're looking for ways to set themselves apart and to compete. An organization or business unit does this using its **competitive strategy,** which is based on the competitive advantage(s) that the organization has been able to develop. For example, Netflix's competitive strategy was based on what it saw as its competitive advantage—its unique DVD rental and distribution service. (As you'll see in the case at the end of the chapter, that competitive advantage may be changing.) As an organization refines and sharpens its competitive advantage (whether found in unique resources or distinctive capabilities), the basis for its competitive strategy is established. What we're going to look at next, then, are the various competitive strategies.

STRATEGIC MANAGEMENT IN ACTION
The Global Perspective

When you think of Russian aircraft, you might picture Tom Cruise in *Top Gun* battling MiG fighter jets. Russia has a strong reputation in military aircraft. However, it's not as well known for commercial aviation. One Russian manufacturer, Ilyushin, couldn't keep pace with Boeing and Airbus and left the passenger aircraft business. Now, another manufacturer, the Sukhoi Holding Company, is staging a comeback with its Sukhoi Superjet 100, a regional jet designed to compete with the likes of Bombardier of Canada and Embraer of Brazil. Mikhail Pogosyan, chief executive of Sukhoi, says, "Our strategic goal is to be a world player in aviation. Our company is to be a winner. We are not to get a silver medal. We are to be first. By 2024, we hope to control 15 percent of the world's regional passenger plane market." The company is likely to find it tough going in this industry where the market is shrinking. "The world market for regional jets has contracted in recent years, and that trend is not expected to reverse, in part because so many regional jets have already been sold."

THINK ABOUT

- To compete, Sukhoi will have to find something (resources or capabilities) that will set it apart. What do you think that might be?
- What would be the implications for Sukhoi's functional strategies?

Source: Based on M. Pyadushkin, "Getting Going," *Aviation Week & Space Technology,* June 20, 2011, p. 102; M. Pyadushkin, "Just How Super?" *Aviation Week & Space Technology,* April 25, 2011, p. 41; News Release, "Sukhoi Aims to Control 15% of Regional Plane Market by 2024," [www.sukhoi.org/eng/news/company], June 7, 2008; A. Osborn, "Russia's $800 Million Airliner Bet Has High Stakes," *Wall Street Journal,* June 26, 2007, p. A6; and L. Wayne, "Russians Re-entering Passenger Jet Market," *New York Times Online,* July 20, 2006.

LEARNING REVIEW   LEARNING OUTCOME 5.2

- Is competition an issue for all organizations? Discuss.
- What is competitive advantage?
- Compare and contrast the three approaches to defining competitors.
- What role do resources and distinctive capabilities play in gaining competitive advantage?
- Define competitive strategy. What's the connection between competitive advantage and competitive strategy?

LEARNING OUTCOME 5.3

Describe the Different Competitive Strategies

Although it may seem there are numerous ways an organization competes, the number of competitive strategies is actually few. In this section, we look at some specific competitive strategies; first the traditional approaches and then some contemporary perspectives.

Traditional Approaches to Defining Competitive Strategy

Two popular approaches to defining competitive strategies include Miles and Snow's adaptive strategies and Porter's generic competitive strategies.[14]

Miles and Snow's Adaptive Strategies

Miles and Snow's approach is based on the strategies organizations use to adapt to their uncertain competitive environments. They identified four strategic postures: prospector, defender, analyzer, and reactor. Research using the Miles and Snow typology generally has supported the

TABLE 5.3 Miles and Snow's Adaptive Strategies

Strategy	Characteristics
Prospector	Organization seeks innovation
	Demonstrated ability to survey dynamic environment and develop new products-services to fit the changing environment
	Frequently and continually innovating, developing, and testing new products-services
	Competitors are uncertain about prospector's future strategic decisions and actions
Defender	Searches for market stability
	Produces only a limited product line
	Seeks to protect (defend) its well-established business
	Does whatever is necessary to aggressively prevent competitors from entering its turf
	Can carve out and maintain niches within its industry that competitors find difficult to penetrate
Analyzer	Strategy of analysis and imitation
	Thoroughly analyzes new business ideas (products, services, markets) before deciding to jump in
	Watches for and copies the promising and successful ideas of prospectors
Reactor	Lacks coherent strategic plan
	Simply reacts to environmental changes
	Makes strategic adjustments only when finally forced to do so
	Unable to respond quickly to environmental changes because resources-capabilities are lacking or are not developed or exploited properly

Source: Based on R. E. Miles and C. C. Snow, Organizational Strategy, Structure, and Process (New York: McGraw-Hill, 1978); S. A. Zahra, "Research on the Miles-Snow (1978) Typology of Strategic Orientation: Review, Critique and Future Directions," Academy of Management Best Papers Proceedings, *1987, pp. 56–60; S. M. Shortell and E. J. Zajac, "Research Notes, Perceptual and Archival Measures of Miles and Snow's Strategic Types: A Comprehensive Assessment of Reliability and Validity,"* Academy of Management Journal, *December 1990, pp. 817–832; and P. C. Fiss, "Building Better Causal Theories: A Fuzzy Set Approach to Typologies in Organization Research,"* Academy of Management Journal, *April 2011, pp. 393–420.*

appropriateness of these strategies' descriptions of how organizations are competing.[15] Table 5.3 summarizes the characteristics of each.

The **prospector strategy** is one in which an organization continually innovates by finding and exploiting new product and market opportunities. A prospector's competitive strength is its ability to survey a wide range of rapidly changing environmental conditions, trends, and situations and to create new products and services to fit this dynamic environment. The prospector's competitive strategy is to continually innovate, develop, and test new products. They're constantly prospecting—on the lookout—for new directions to pursue. This continual search for innovation creates uncertainties for the prospector's competitors; they never know what's going to happen next or what to expect from the prospector. If the prospector can develop new products that the market desires and is willing to pay for, it will have a competitive advantage. Examples of organizations using this strategy would be Fox Broadcasting Network and MTV in the broadcast television industry. Both are noted for their innovative television network programming and willingness to pursue new directions. They're able to tap into changing societal attitudes and interests (think *Jersey Shore* and *American Idol*) and develop TV programs that appeal to these new audiences. And they're willing to constantly push the envelope in developing new products. Their competitive advantage stems from their ability to assess environmental trends and continually create innovative programs.

The **defender strategy** is used by organizations to protect current market share by emphasizing existing products and producing only a limited product line. Defenders have well-established businesses that they're seeking to safeguard. They'll do whatever it takes to aggressively prevent competitors from coming into their turf.[16] Large companies with dominant market share, such as Anheuser-Busch InBev or IBM, may use a defender strategy to aggressively protect their crucial markets. Another example of a company using a defender strategy is Cleveland-based Lincoln Electric Holdings. As a leading manufacturer of welding products, it vigorously protects its product lines and market share against competitors by providing outstanding customer service and aggressively matching price cuts. It's also common to find small- or medium-sized companies using this strategy. A defender succeeds with this strategy as long as its primary technology and narrow product line remain competitive. Over time, defenders can carve out and maintain niches within their industries that competitors find difficult to penetrate.

Constantino de Oliveira Jr. has built a profitable airline—Brazil's Gol Linhas Aéreas Inteligentes (Gol Intelligent Airlines)—by "stealing ideas" from JetBlue and Southwest Airlines.[17] He's using the **analyzer strategy,** which is a strategy of analysis and imitation. Analyzers watch for and copy the successful ideas of prospectors. They compete by following the direction that prospectors pioneer. Organizations using this strategy also thoroughly analyze new business ideas before jumping in. They'll systematically assess and evaluate whether this move is appropriate for them. For example, consumer products company Unilever uses the analyzer strategy for its Suave shampoo and skin care product line. Suave markets its lines by matching the packaging, smell, and feel of rival's products. Another example is COSMI Corporation, which makes and mass markets inexpensive education, entertainment, and business software. Its chief corporate officer describes the company as an "imitator, not an innovator" and says that he'd rather leave being first in the market to the "Microsofts of the software world and come out with simpler versions of whatever proves successful."[18]

Finally, the **reactor strategy** is characterized by the lack of a coherent strategic plan or apparent means of competing. Reactors simply react to environmental changes and make adjustments only when finally forced to do so by environmental pressures. Oftentimes, reactors are unable to respond quickly to perceived environmental changes because either they lack the needed resources or capabilities or they're not able to exploit their current resources and capabilities. Obviously,

---

STRATEGIC MANAGEMENT IN ACTION
The Global Perspective

Francisco Deusmar de Queiros has built a successful chain of pharmacies—Pague Menos (which translates to Pay Less)—in Brazil. And he did it in an unconventional way, at least according to local standards. Rather than start his business in large metropolitan markets like Rio de Janeiro or São Paulo, Queiros used the "Wal-Mart" approach. He says, "Wal-Mart did not come from big cities. It grew from small cities." And that's exactly what he did. His Pague Menos chain now is in every one of Brazil's 26 states as well as the federal district of Brasilia. Sales are over $1.3 billion (USD). Deusmar further distinguishes his stores by carrying an inventory of about 12,000 products, versus the 8,000 items carried by traditional pharmacies. Nearly one-third of Pague Menos' sales come from non-drug items. And the company has been able to leverage the scale of its network of stores to offer customers competitive prices. Its name "Pay Less" reflects its competitive strategy.

- Which of the adaptive strategies best describes Pague Menos's approach? Why?

- Do some research on Brazil. Find the following: population, languages, age structure, urbanization, GDP composition by sector, and one other "fact" you find interesting. (Hint: Use the *CIA World Factbook*, **[https://www.cia.gov/library/publications/the-world-factbook/].**)

Sources: Based on Hoover's Online [www.hoovers.com], *February 8, 2012; T. Ogier, "Drugstore Pioneer," Latin Trade, March–April, 2011, pp. 16–17; and "Industry Trends & Developments,"* Latin America Monitor: Brazil Monitor, *January 2005, p. 7.*

this is *not* a recommended competitive strategy for developing a competitive advantage. In fact, the reactor strategy can be thought of as a "default" strategy, almost a nonstrategy position. Some examples of organizations that have used the reactor strategy—intentionally or not—include Sears, Sizzler International Inc. (the steakhouse chain), and Digital Equipment Corporation. In each of these instances, the organization lagged significantly behind its competitors in products offered and had no consistent strategic direction. Without significant strategic changes, a reactor will always be in a weak competitive position.

Porter's Generic Competitive Strategies

In addition to his five forces model (external analysis) and value chain (internal analysis), Porter also suggested that it's important for organizations to have an appropriate competitive strategy.

What is an "appropriate" competitive strategy? It's one based on an organization's competitive advantage, which Porter says can come from only one of two sources: having the lowest costs in the industry or possessing significant and desirable differences from competitors.[19] Another important strategic factor is the scope of the product market in which the organization wishes to compete—that is, broad (competing in all or most market segments) or narrow (competing in only one segment or a few segments). The mix of these factors provides the basis for his generic competitive strategies—cost leadership, differentiation, and focus.

You may be wondering why Porter called these strategies "generic." The term simply refers to the fact that they can be pursued by any type or size organization in any type or size industry. We're going to provide more detail on his strategies because they're so well known.

Cost Leadership Strategy   The **cost leadership strategy** (or low-cost strategy) is one in which an organization strives to have the lowest costs in its industry and produces products for a broad customer base. The main goal of the cost leader is to have *the* lowest costs in the industry. Notice that the emphasis here is on *costs,* not *prices.* In other words, the cost leader is striving to have the lowest total unit costs in the industry. Because the cost leader has the lowest costs in the industry, it can potentially charge the lowest prices and still earn profits. Although every

---

FOR YOUR INFORMATION
The Copycat Economy

Have you seen the Swiffer WetJet? How about ReadyMop? When Procter & Gamble brought out its Swiffer WetJet mop, they thought they had a breakthrough winner product and charged a premium price for it. But not long after Swiffer's debut, Clorox Company brought out its copycat product, ReadyMop, an action that forced P&G to cut its price in half. And this scenario has been repeated continuously in other industries with other products. The situation has been described as the "copycat economy." Whereas a hot new idea used to mean years of fat profits, rivals now move into markets almost instantaneously. The question for strategic decision makers is "How do you make money in such an environment, especially when demand is flat?" And, unfortunately, there are no easy answers. For some industries, product upgrades are the answer. In other industries, companies have to continuously pump out cutting-edge products that fetch premium prices, no matter for how short a time. Others find they have to continually fine-tune product formulas and designs. And finally, some companies have gone the opposite way by focusing research on fewer products, tenaciously defending patents, and vigorously promoting well-established brands with heavy marketing.

TO DO

- Find other examples of copycat products (goods or services).
- How has the initial player responded to the competitive challenge?
- What strategies is the copycat using?
- Can you think of other possible strategic responses that either player might use?

Source: Based on P. Engardio and F. Keenan, "The Copycat Economy," *BusinessWeek,* August 26, 2002, pp. 94–96.

organization should attempt to keep costs low—that's just smart business—the cost leader is choosing to *compete* on the basis of having the lowest costs. What are the advantages of having the lowest costs? Having the lowest costs means the cost leader can charge a lower price than its competitors and still earn significant profits. It also means that when competitive rivalry heats up and a price war breaks out, the cost leader is in a better position to withstand it and continue earning profits.

What does it take to successfully pursue the cost leadership strategy? Everything the cost leader does is aimed at keeping costs as low as possible. Efficiency in all areas is critical, and all resources, distinctive capabilities, and functional strategies are directed at that. The cost leader isn't going to have deep and wide product lines. That's too expensive, and the cost leader has chosen to compete on the basis of low costs, not on being different from competitors. The cost leader will market products aimed at the "average" customer. Little or no product frills or variations will be available. The cost leader organization isn't going to have fancy artwork on the walls or plush office furniture at corporate headquarters. It's unlikely that you'll see a cost leader with an elaborate high-tech, multimedia interactive Web site *unless* it was determined that this would be a cost-effective and efficient way to reach masses of potential customers. In fact, being a cost leader doesn't mean ignoring the latest advances in technology. Quite the opposite. If new and improved technology can pave the way to further lowering costs, the cost leader will jump on it. For instance, Collective Brands, Inc., a shoe retailer with more than $3.3 billion in annual sales, has a high-tech automated warehouse at corporate headquarters in Topeka, Kansas. Out of this warehouse, which spans 17 acres under one roof, the company's 4,900 stores can be restocked with styles and sizes with about a day's notice.[20] Another example of a company using the low-cost strategy is steel manufacturer Nucor Corporation. After three years of testing, it began using a "radical new process known as 'strip casting'...which should give the company a huge cost advantage over traditional steelmakers."[21] Then there's the ultimate low-cost leader—Wal-Mart. As the world's largest retailer, you'd expect business operations befitting such a corporate icon, but you'd be wrong. At Wal-Mart's headquarters, office furnishings are modern but plain. Employees take out their own trash. There's no free coffee or soda. And the bathrooms on corporate jets have curtains, not doors.[22] By focusing on efficient, cost-effective performance rather than on image, Wal-Mart has been able to prosper in a competitive industry. Other characteristics of cost leaders include strict attention to production controls; rigorous use of budgets; little product differentiation—just enough to satisfy what the mass market might demand; limited market segmentation; emphasis on productivity improvements; and resources, distinctive capabilities, and core competencies found in production-operations and materials management.

What are the drawbacks of this strategy? The main danger is that competitors might find ways of lowering costs even further, taking away the cost leader's cost advantage. The cost leader's competitive strategy is successful as long as it can maintain its cost advantage. Another drawback of this strategy is that competitors might be able to easily imitate what the cost leader is doing and erode the cost advantage. Finally, a drawback of the cost leadership strategy is that the cost leader, in its all-out pursuit of lowering costs, might lose sight of changing customer tastes and needs. In other words, it doesn't matter how cost efficiently you can produce or market a product or service if no one is willing to purchase it even at rock-bottom prices.

Differentiation Strategy The E. S. Kluft & Company ultraluxe handmade bed sells for more than $50,000. A 4-piece box of zChocolat chocolates costs $42. For that amount, you get 4 pieces of the world's most distinctive French artisan chocolates in a stylish mahogany box.[23] These companies are using a **differentiation strategy,** in which an organization competes by providing unique (different) products with features that customers value, perceive as different, and are willing to pay a premium price for. The main goal of the differentiator is competing by providing goods or services that are truly unique and different in the eyes of customers. If the differentiator can do this, it can charge a premium price because customers perceive that the product or service is different and that it uniquely meets their needs. This premium price provides the profit incentive to compete on the basis of differentiation.

What does it take to be a successful differentiator? All its capabilities, resources, and functional strategies are aimed at isolating and understanding specific market segments and developing product features that are valued by customers in those segments. The differentiator will have broad and wide product lines—that is, many different models, features, price ranges, and so forth. In fact, *how* the differentiator chooses to differentiate is practically endless. There are countless variations of market segments and product features that a differentiator might use. What's important to the differentiator is that the customer *perceives* the product or service as different and unique and worth the extra price. Because the differentiation strategy can be expensive, the differentiator also needs to control costs to protect profits, but not to the extent that it loses its source of differentiation. Remember: The differentiator is competing on the basis of being unique, not on the basis of having the lowest costs.

Other characteristics of differentiators often include differentiating themselves along as many dimensions as possible and segmenting the market into many niches. In addition, the differentiator works hard to establish **brand loyalty,** when customers consistently and repeatedly seek out, purchase, and use a particular brand. Brand loyalty can be a very powerful competitive weapon for the differentiator. Not surprisingly, the differentiator's unique resources and distinctive capabilities tend to be in marketing and research and development.

What are the drawbacks of the differentiation strategy? One is that the organization must remain unique in customers' eyes, which may be difficult depending on competitors' abilities to imitate and copy successful differentiation features. If the product loses its uniqueness in

FOR YOUR INFORMATION
Selling Luxury

Although the uncertain economic climate had an impact on shopping habits of many consumers, the wealthy are once again spending. Some experts have described it as the "hourglass economy." Stores catering to the rich are seeing, for the most part, double-digit sales increases. However, as the middle class curtails its spending, sales at stores such as Target, Kohl's, and Gap are growing only by single digits. That same middle class is trading down and shopping at stores such as Dollar Tree, Dollar General, and Costco, where sales increases are also in the double digits. Under such conditions, what's a differentiator to do? A recent study of affluence in America by Digitas sheds some light. One interesting insight was that millennials (those consumers between age 18 and 35) with incomes over $100,000 will define the next wave of luxury spenders. What sets this group apart from all others is "their intensely digital media behavior." They use mobile devices for communicating, consuming content, enjoying music, and gaming. Not surprisingly, the research also showed heavy use of social networks and blogs by this age group.

Other studies of luxury consumption have focused on the rising numbers of affluent consumers in China and India. The main point of these studies has been to identify clusters and segments. For instance, one study of affluent Chinese identified four clusters: luxury lovers, luxury followers, luxury intellectuals, and luxury laggards.

THINK ABOUT

- How does this research help organizations in defining a differentiation strategy?
- Is the differentiation strategy only appropriate for luxury goods? Explain.

Sources: Based on Y. Truong and R. McColl, "Intrinsic Motivations, Self-Esteem, and Luxury Goods Consumption," *Journal of Retailing & Consumer Services,* November 2011, pp. 555–561; K-P. Hung, A. H. Chen, N. Peng, C. Hackley, R. A. Tiwsakul, and C-L. Chou, "Antecedents of Luxury Brand Purchase Intention," *Journal of Product & Brand Management,* vol. 20, issue 6, 2011, pp. 457–467; S. Gandel, "Shopping: The Rich and the Rest," *Time,* October 10, 2011, p. 39; P. X. Lu, and B. Pras, "Profiling Mass Affluent Luxury Goods Consumers in China: A Psychographic Approach, *Thunderbird International Business Review,* July/August 2011, pp. 435–455; V. M. Young, "The Next Luxury Consumer," *WWD: Women's Wear Daily,* July 6, 2011, p. 9-1; and "Digitas' Proprietary Study 'Affluence in America: The New Consumer Landscape' Reveals the New Wave of Affluence in America," *PR Newswire Online,* May 25, 2011.

customers' eyes, they won't be willing to pay the premium price just to have the differentiated product. For example, Pottery Barn used to be one-of-a-kind in a fragmented home-furnishings industry. Its products were unique and had a style all their own. However, Pottery Barn lost some of that uniqueness as competitors such as Restoration Hardware, Target, and even Wal-Mart started offering similar but cheaper products.[24] Another drawback is that customers might become more price sensitive, and the product differences might become less important. In this instance, the organization might also find that its competitive advantage based on being different and unique no longer works.

Focus Strategy   The **focus strategy** is when an organization pursues either a cost or differentiation advantage but within a limited (narrow) customer group or segment. A focuser concentrates on serving a specific market niche. There are three broad ways to segment specialized market niches: (1) geographical, (2) type of customer, or (3) product line segment. A geographical niche can be defined in terms of region or locality. A customer niche focuses on a specific group of customers. In this specialized niche, customers can find products tailored to their unique needs. Finally, a product line niche focuses on a specific and specialized product line.

What's involved with the focus strategy? As stated earlier, a focuser can pursue either a cost or differentiation advantage. A cost focuser competes by having lower costs than the overall industry cost leader in specific and narrow niches. For example, U.K.–based Megabus offers a "discount airline" approach to bus service in about 50 destinations. Passengers can ride for as little as $1.50. To keep prices low, Megabus cuts costs by using online booking and sidewalk stops, instead of bus stations.[25] The cost focus strategy also can be successful if an organization can produce complex or custom-built products that don't lend themselves easily to cost efficiencies by the industry's overall cost leaders.

The differentiation focuser can use whatever forms of differentiation the broad differentiator might use—product features, product innovations, product quality, customer responsiveness, or whatever. The only difference, however, is that the focuser is specializing in one or a few segments instead of all market segments. For example, a Chicago company called Intelligentsia Coffee doesn't intend to follow the buy-low, sell-high business model. Instead, "they buy high and sell high." They pay above Fair Trade rates (50 to 200 percent over) for coffee beans they say are so good that "customers will pay $20 and more a pound retail." The company's green coffee buyer says, "On the grower side and the consumer side, we're trying to create a culture of quality."[26]

What are the advantages of the focus strategy? One distinct advantage is that the focuser knows its market niche well. The focuser can stay close to customers and respond quickly to their changing needs—often much quicker than organizations pursuing a broad market. By effectively and efficiently responding to customers' needs, the focuser can, in turn, develop strong brand loyalty. This brand loyalty can be hard for other competitors to overcome. Also, if the focuser can provide products or services that the broad competitors can't or won't, then it will have the niche all to itself.

What are the drawbacks of the focus strategy? One drawback is that the focuser often operates at a small scale, making it difficult to lower costs significantly. However, with technological advancements such as flexible manufacturing systems, this drawback isn't as critical as it once was. In other words, as information and computer technology have become more affordable, focusers have discovered that economies (cost efficiencies) don't necessarily have to come from large-scale production runs. Many times, the focuser can be just as efficient running small batches as the large-scale competitor can be running large batches. Another drawback is that the niche customers might change their tastes or needs. As it's often difficult for a focuser to change niches easily and quickly, this could be a serious problem. In addition, any technological changes that might impact the niche can have a similar effect. Finally, there's always the threat of a broad-based differentiator taking notice of the focuser's market niche, especially if the focuser is enjoying a significant level of success and moving in to offer products to those customers. In other words, the focuser is subject to being "outfocused" by its competitors—large and small.

STRATEGIC MANAGEMENT IN ACTION
The Global Perspective

Arif Masood Naqvi, the group chief executive officer of private equity firm Abraaj Capital, wants to "create a one-stop financial services shop, serving up everything that companies and investors need, from lending to investment banking to brokerage." An ambitious plan indeed. However, Mr. Naqvi focuses on serving the Middle East and Southeast Asia and on beating the large global banks that are establishing business in those fast-growing markets. Mr. Naqvi says, "The only way we can compete is to add scale and mass." In 2010, Mr. Naqvi was named CEO of the year in the first *Global Investor* Middle East awards.

THINK ABOUT

- Do you think a cost focus or a differentiation focus strategy might be more appropriate? Explain.

- Go to the company's Web site and find its mission and values. How might these affect an appropriate strategy?

Sources: Based on Abraaj Capital Web site [www.abraaj.com], February 12, 2012; "Abraaj Invests $28m in Five Companies," *MEED: Middle East Economic Digest,* November 12, 2010, p. 20; "Arif Naqvi," *Global Investor: Middle East Awards Supplement,* September 2010, p. 2; and H. Timmons, "A Middle East Equity Giant with a Small Global Footprint," *New York Times Online,* December 8, 2006.

The final aspect of Porter's generic competitive strategies we need to discuss is the concept of being **stuck in the middle,** which happens when an organization hasn't developed a low cost or a differentiation competitive advantage. An organization becomes stuck in the middle when its costs are too high to compete with the low-cost leader or when its products and services aren't differentiated enough to compete with the differentiator. As you can imagine, stuck in the middle isn't a good place to be. Getting unstuck means choosing which competitive advantage to pursue and then doing so by aligning resources, distinctive capabilities, and core competencies.

Contemporary Views on Competitive Strategy

Although the traditional approaches to describing an organization's competitive strategies are widely used, the contemporary views provide an expanded and more realistic description of the competitive strategies organizations are using. In this section, we want to look at two of these.

Integrated Low Cost–Differentiation Strategy

Porter's original work on competitive advantage and competitive strategies maintained that an organization could not simultaneously pursue a low cost and a differentiation advantage. To do so meant the risk of being stuck in the middle and not successfully developing or exploiting either competitive advantage. You had to do one or the other.[27] Despite strong empirical support for Porter's strategy framework,[28] several strategy researchers began to question this "mutual exclusivity" of the low cost and differentiation strategies.[29] Instead of having to pursue *either* low cost *or* differentiation, was it possible that organizations could pursue both strategies simultaneously and successfully? Strategy research evidence has shown that organizations *can* successfully pursue an **integrated low cost–differentiation strategy,** a strategy that involves simultaneously achieving low costs and high levels of differentiation.[30]

This strategy is not an easy one to pursue because an organization pretty much has to be good at everything it does. What are some examples of organizations that have successfully implemented such a strategy? One is McDonald's, which has succeeded in an intensely competitive market by continually innovating new products and by emphasizing efficiency and standardization to keep its costs low. Other organizations such as Southwest Airlines, Google, and Toyota also have been able to successfully pursue this hybrid competitive strategy. What makes an integrated low cost–differentiation strategy possible?

The answer is technology. Successfully establishing sources of differentiation can be expensive. When creating, manufacturing, and marketing a wide range of quality products or services, it's often difficult to keep costs as low as possible. Yet, the widespread availability and increasing affordability of information technology has made it easier for organizations to pursue product and service differentiation and still keep their costs low. Technological advancements such as flexible manufacturing systems, just-in-time inventory systems, and integrated information systems have opened the door for competing on the basis of having low costs *and* being unique. However, keep in mind that just because technology is available, it doesn't mean every organization that uses it will be able to successfully pursue an integrated low cost–differentiation strategy. It still takes strict attention to keeping costs as low as possible and providing products with enough desirable features for the marketplace.

Mintzberg's Generic Competitive Strategies

Henry Mintzberg has developed an alternative typology of competitive strategies he felt better reflected the increasing complexity of the competitive environment.[31] He proposed six possible competitive strategies as shown in Figure 5.4.

Differentiation by price is a modification of Porter's cost leadership strategy. Mintzberg argued that having the lowest costs didn't provide a competitive advantage by itself, but that the advantage came because it allowed the organization to charge below-average market prices. Therefore, an organization pursuing this strategy was instead differentiating on the basis of price. Differentiation by marketing image describes a strategy in which an organization attempts to create a certain image in customers' minds and uses that marketing image as a potent competitive weapon. The competitive strategy of differentiation by product design can be used to describe organizations that compete on the basis of providing desirable product features and design configurations. An organization that followed this strategy would attempt to give customers a wide selection of product features and different designs. Differentiation by quality described a strategy in which organizations compete by delivering higher reliability and performance at a comparable price. In this strategy, superior product quality was pursued as the organization's competitive advantage. The competitive strategy of differentiation by product support emphasized the customer support services provided by the organization. In this strategy, competitive advantage would be sought through providing an all-encompassing bundle of desired customer support services. Finally, the undifferentiated strategy described situations in which an organization had no basis for differentiation or when it deliberately followed a copycat strategy.

FIGURE 5.4

Mintzberg's Generic Competitive Strategies

STRATEGIC MANAGEMENT IN ACTION

Dell once was a shining example of the integrated low cost–differentiation strategy. It had succeeded in an intensely competitive market by providing high-quality products and services while holding down costs so it could undercut Gateway, Hewlett-Packard, IBM, and other PC makers in price. The secret? Dell was able to keep its costs low and its level of differentiation high by developing and exploiting a competitive advantage based on a disciplined, extremely low-cost corporate culture while still providing high-quality products and services. However, as they discovered, maintaining the resources and distinctive capabilities so necessary to being successful at this strategy isn't easy. The company has continued to struggle.

THINK ABOUT

- Why is an integrated low-cost differentiation strategy so difficult to pursue?
- What advice would you give to Dell's executive team?

Sources: A. VanderMey, "Dell Gets in Touch With Its Inner Entrepreneur," *Fortune,* December 12, 2011, p. 58; B. Worthen, "Dell Outlook Cloudy," *Wall Street Journal,* November 16, 2011, p. B4; R. Winkler, "Dell Gets Flooded With More Challenges," *Wall Street Journal,* November 15, 2011, p. C1; A. Ricadela, "An Erstwhile PC King Aims for the Middle," *Bloomberg BusinessWeek,* September 12–September 18, 2011, pp. 39–40; J. Scheck and B. Worthen, "Dell Inc. Lowers Its Sights for Gadgets, Consumers," *Wall Street Journal,* May 23, 2011, p. B1+; and B. Worthen, "Michael Dell Looks Beyond PC Business," April 25, 2011, p. B1+.

What's the verdict on Mintzberg's alternative generic competitive strategies typology? It appears that his approach may have merit.[32] Research shows it has strong conceptual clarity and descriptive power. Although it will probably never replace the popularity of Porter's competitive strategies or Miles and Snow's adaptive strategies, Mintzberg's typology does seem to capture the essence of competitive strategies used by organizations in today's complex and dynamic competitive climate. As such, it provides an alternative way to describe organizations' competitive strategies.

No matter how you describe competitive strategies, the main thing to remember about them is that they should exploit the competitive advantage(s) the organization has developed. Without a competitive advantage that's been developed from its unique resources or distinctive capabilities, it will be extremely difficult for an organization to compete successfully in any given situation, no matter what competitive strategy it might be using.

LEARNING REVIEW   LEARNING OUTCOME 5.3

- Describe each of Miles and Snow's four adaptive strategies.
- According to Porter, what are the two types of competitive advantage?
- Describe each of Porter's generic competitive strategies.
- What does it mean to be "stuck in the middle"?
- What is the integrated low cost–differentiation strategy, and how does it contradict the concept behind Porter's generic competitive strategies?
- Describe each of the competitive strategies in Mintzberg's generic strategy typology.

Look back at our chapter-opening case. What type of competitive strategy does Toyota appear to be pursuing? How can you tell? You'll probably note such things as its efficiency initiatives, its innovation, and its expertise in many functional areas. The competitive strategy an organization is using can be seen by what's actually being done or implemented. Strategy implementation is critical. If a strategy is not implemented, then it's nothing more than an idea. And, if you remember the entire strategic management process model, once a strategy is implemented, it must be assessed or evaluated, and modified if needed. In this section, we look at how organizations' competitive strategies are implemented, evaluated, and changed.

LEARNING OUTCOME 5.4

Discuss How Competitive Strategies Are Implemented and Evaluated

THE GREY ZONE

As you've probably experienced, college students are an attractive market for businesses. While the class of 2010 was into "labels, branding and bling," the class of 2015 is more value conscious. "They lived through the recession. They watched their parents coming home every day, worrying about their paychecks." Yet, studies show that students spend almost $500 a month on food, clothing, personal care, travel, and other categories not related to education expenses.

That's why companies like Chevrolet and Ford have a big on-campus presence. And why Bed Bath & Beyond created a college registry for students, much like a wedding or baby registry. And why Target created an interactive checklist meant to help students stay on budget. Hewlett-Packard, Zipcar, and Victoria's Secret Pink are a few of the brands that use student reps to promote its products on campus. The head of a company that runs campus marketing programs says, "The concept is a fast-growing phenomenon as marketers look to capitalize on word-of-mouth, and students jump at the chance to add a Fortune 500 company to their resumés."

THINK ABOUT

- What do you think of these approaches? Are they ethical? Discuss.
- What has been your experience with on-campus marketing efforts? Have you ever seen what you would call "ethically questionable" behavior?
- What benefits and drawbacks do you see for (a) students and (b) the marketers in these strategic approaches?

Source: Based on N. Zmuda, "Marketers Hitting Campus Harder Than Ever," *Advertising Age,* October 17, 2011, pp. 26–28; N. Singer, "On Campus, It's One Big Commercial," *New York Times Online,* September 10, 2011; and "The Campus Connection," *Adweek,* February 15, 2010, p. C1.

Implementing Competitive Strategy

How does Abercrombie & Fitch keep current styles in its stores? How does Collective Brands Inc. restock its stores within a day's notice? Obviously, employees, facilities and equipment, work activities, and work systems have to be in place to facilitate such accomplishments. (Think in terms of resources, distinctive capabilities, and core competencies.) That's what implementation is all about. An organization's resources and capabilities are developed and used within its various functional areas, so it shouldn't come as a surprise that the organization's functional strategies play a significant role in implementing competitive strategy. That's what we're going to look at first. We'll then discuss the competitive actions an organization might take as it implements its overall competitive strategy.

The Role of Functional Strategies

The challenge in implementing competitive strategy is to create and exploit a sustainable competitive advantage. As we've said many times, competitive advantage comes from an organization's ability to use its resources to develop capabilities that, in turn, may become distinctive. All of this happens through the functional strategies being used.

The functional strategies play a dual role in implementing competitive strategy. First, the initial choice of an appropriate competitive strategy depends on the organizational resources and capabilities currently available or being acquired and developed through the functional strategies. Each competitive strategy requires certain skills, resources, and capabilities to successfully attain a sustainable competitive advantage. For instance, in the low cost leader strategy, tight cost controls are critical, which means strategic decision makers want to develop skills, resources, and capabilities (e.g., engineering skills, low-cost distribution systems,

TABLE 5.4 Skills, Resources, and Capabilities Needed for Competitive Strategies

Low Cost Leader

- Willingness to spend money on cost control and minimization activities
- Employees trained and skilled in "lean" work approaches
- Employees encouraged to find ways to do more with less
- Strict product design focused on ease of manufacturing and assembling
- Efficient distribution system
- Strict cost controls
- Detailed and frequent work reports to help managers and employees control costs
- Closely monitored work activities
- Structured organization with little or no flexibility
- Employee work incentives based on stringent quantitative goals
- Organizational culture that supports and encourages employees finding ways to be efficient and cost-effective
- Production-operations area is the primary focus of cost-efficiencies, although efficiency is encouraged throughout all functional areas

Differentiator

- Effective and successful marketing abilities
- Effective and successful R&D as evidenced by creative and innovative employees
- Knows what customers want and value
- Excel at customer service
- Strong R&D process capabilities
- Good reputation in product quality and brand leadership
- Skilled at using technology to support marketing and R&D activities
- Good relationships developed with various marketing channel participants
- Strong collaboration between R&D, marketing, and product development
- Employee work incentives based more on qualitative, subjective measures
- Organizational culture that supports and encourages employee collaboration and creativity
- Marketing and R&D are the two most important functional areas

Focuser

- Combination of the above, depending on choice of low-cost or differentiation focus strategy

Source: Based on Michael E. Porter, *Competitive Strategy: Techniques for Analyzing Industries and Competitors,* The Free Press, 1980.

products designed for efficient manufacturing) that do just that. In the differentiator strategy, it's critical to understand customers and what they value, which means developing skills, resources, and capabilities in marketing, product design, market research, and so forth. (See Table 5.4.)

The functional strategies also play another role. Once the organization's competitive strategy is determined, the resources, capabilities, and competencies found in the various functional areas are *how* the competitive strategy is implemented.

The functional strategies used should support whatever competitive advantage—and, of course, competitive strategy—is pursued. This means that, for instance, if we've chosen to compete on the basis of having the lowest costs, then the functional strategies should support

STRATEGIC MANAGEMENT IN ACTION
The Global Perspective

Singapore Airlines (SIA) has long been a favorite of business travelers because of its amazing customer service and special amenities. The company's executive team is well aware of new rivals, the most "threatening" probably being Emirates, an airline based out of Dubai, United Arab Emirates, which is positioning itself as offering premium service but low prices. However, Singapore Airlines continues to emphasize what has made it successful—its focus on the details. It's those details that help it keep its strong customer appeal and yet be able to withstand the extreme cost-pricing pressures in the airline industry. For instance, to improve its food, the company invested $1 million in a simulator that mimics the air pressure and humidity found inside a plane. One thing it discovered—use less spices.

THINK ABOUT

- How has SIA recognized the importance of functional strategies to its ability to compete?

Source: Based on "Singapore's So Solid Crew," *Travel Trade Gazette,* December 15, 2011, p. 53; "Top-Performing Airlines," *Aviation Week & Space Technology,* July 11, 2011, pp. 42–44; S. McCartney, "The Middle Seat: Cooking Up Ways to Improve Steaks on a Plane," *Wall Street Journal,* January 20, 2009, p. B9; and J. Doebele, "The Engineer," *Forbes,* January 9, 2006, pp. 122–123.

and reinforce that strategy. Cost efficiencies would be pursued in all operational areas but particularly in production-operations. Also, financial strategies could support operational efficiency by determining what technology investments would best contribute to lowering costs. In fact, all an organization's resources, distinctive capabilities, and core competencies would be directed at attaining the goal of having the lowest costs. Likewise, if an organization chose to compete on the basis of differentiation or even on both low costs and differentiation, then its functional strategies should support those choices, or it will never develop a competitive advantage. To summarize, the functional strategies—that is, how the organization develops and exploits its resources, core competencies, and distinctive capabilities—influence both *what* competitive strategy is most appropriate and *how* that strategy is implemented.

It should be fairly obvious by now that an organization's functional strategies play a critical role in the implementation of its competitive strategy. Without developing and exploiting the organization's resources, capabilities, and core competencies—which is done through the functional strategies being used—there will be no hope of developing a competitive advantage. If the organization doesn't have or can't develop a sustainable competitive advantage, it's going to have a tough time competing and staying in business. Let's now look at the types of competitive actions an organization might use in implementing its competitive strategy.

Competitive Actions

Once an organization's competitive strategy is implemented through specific functional decisions and actions, the real fun begins! The very notion of "competitive" strategy means that the organization is going to be competing "against" other organizations—vying for customers, market share, or other desired objects or outcomes. What happens in this competitive "dance" is that organizations use certain tactics in the ongoing battle to acquire or keep whatever object or outcome they're after.

The competitive actions taken by organizations typically are described using a military or sports analogy—offensive and defensive moves. Why? Because that's what organizations are doing when they compete: they're going after competitors' positions or they're defending their own position. **Offensive moves** are an organization's attempts to exploit and strengthen its competitive position through attacks on a competitor's position. What are some offensive moves an organization might use?[33] A frontal assault is when the attacking firm goes head-to-head with its competitor and matches the competitor in every possible category such as price, promotion, product features, and distribution channel. This competitive move can be an effective way to gain market share from weaker competitors. It's also a good way to slice away rivals' competitive advantages. Another offensive tactic is to attack competitors' weaknesses. How? An organization might concentrate on geographic areas where its competitor is weak. Or it might begin serving customer segments that a competitor is ignoring or in which the competitors' offerings are weak. The organization might introduce new product models or product features to fill gaps its competitors aren't serving. What this offensive tactic entails is attacking wherever the competitor has specific weaknesses. Another offensive tactic is to use an all-out attack on competitors by hitting them from both the product *and* the market segment side. Needless to say, this all-out competitive attack requires significant resources and capabilities. Another type of offensive move is to avoid direct, head-on competitive challenges by maneuvering around competitors and subtly changing the rules of the game. How? The most typical way is that the organization attempts to create new market segments that competitors aren't serving by introducing products with different features. This competitive action cuts the market out from under the competitor and forces the competitor to play catch-up. Finally, another possible offensive tactic is to use "guerrilla" attacks—small, intermittent, seemingly random assaults on competitors' markets. For instance, an organization might use special promotions, price incentives, or advertising campaigns to lure away competitors' customers.

Offensive moves are good ways to attack competitors and strengthen your own competitive position. What happens when *your* organization is attacked or threatened with attack? That's where the defensive competitive moves come in.

Defensive moves are an organization's attempts to protect its competitive advantage and turf. Defensive moves don't increase an organization's competitive advantage but can make that competitive advantage more sustainable.[34] Let's look at some defensive moves an organization might use. One is to prevent challengers from attacking by not giving them any areas to attack. For instance, an organization could offer a full line of products in every profitable market segment, keep prices low on products that most closely match competitors' offerings, use exclusive agreements with dealers to block competitors from using them, protect technologies through patents or licenses, or use any other number of possible preventive strategic actions. Again, the intent of this particular defensive move is to make sure competitors don't have any holes or weaknesses to attack. Another possible defensive move is to increase competitors' beliefs that significant retaliation can be expected if competitive attacks are initiated. How could an organization signal the market that it's serious about retaliating if attacked? Public announcements by managers to "protect" market share are important, as are strong responses to competitors' moves. Doing things such as matching price cuts or matching promotion incentives signals competitors that you aren't going to sit back and let them steal away your customers. Competitive counterattacks are particularly critical if the markets or segments being attacked are crucial to the organization. These types of retaliatory actions should be approached cautiously, however, particularly in instances in which the attacker is a new entrant to the market. Why? Research has shown that the typical *new* entrant doesn't pose a serious threat and aggressive retaliation can be expensive.[35] The final type of defensive move involves lowering the incentive for a competitor to attack. If a potential attacker is led to believe that the expectations of future profits are minimal, chances are it won't want to challenge the current leader. For instance, an organization might use media announcements to highlight problems in the industry, or it might deliberately keep prices low and continually invest in cost-lowering actions. All these moves make it less attractive for a competitor to launch an attack.

Evaluating and Changing Competitive Strategy

The organization's competitive actions and responses being implemented through the various functional strategies must be monitored and evaluated for performance effectiveness and efficiency. What are the results of the various strategies? Are they having the intended effect? Are we successfully exploiting our competitive advantage? Why or why not? These are the types of questions to be asked when evaluating the competitive strategy. Because most organizations' competitive strategies are targeted at increasing sales revenues, market share, or profitability, data on these particular performance areas would be needed in order to determine the impact of the competitive strategies. Likewise, not-for-profit organizations should assess the results of their competitive strategies even though they're not focused on revenues, market share, or profitability. For instance, strategy evaluation might address such areas as: Did the number of plasma and blood donors increase? Did the number of contributors to the church building fund go up, or did the average donation amount increase? Did governmental funding of the community drug outreach program increase? No matter what type of organization or type of competitive strategy is used, it's important to measure its impact.

It's not enough, however, to look at only the results of the competitive strategy. What if results aren't as high as expected, or what if they're better than expected? Then what? Part of the evaluation of the competitive strategy is also to determine what happened and why. We do this by trying to pinpoint areas of competitive weakness. Has the market changed and we haven't? Are the organization's numerous resources and capabilities used effectively and efficiently so that the needed and crucial competitive advantage is developed and exploited? Which ones are and which ones aren't? As you can see, evaluating competitive strategy turns out to be an assessment of the organization's various functional areas and the activities performed there. If the evaluation shows that the intended impact or desired levels of performance haven't been reached, changes may be necessary. However, changing an organization's competitive strategy isn't something it wants to do frequently. Why? Because each competitive strategy entails the development of specific resources, distinctive capabilities, and core competencies. To change the competitive strategy would mean modifying or redeveloping those strategic elements, which is both difficult and expensive. This doesn't, and shouldn't, mean that an organization would *never* change its basic competitive approach; what it does mean, though, is that this type of major strategic change should be approached cautiously, realistically, and intelligently.

Although changing an organization's basic competitive strategy may not be common, modifying its competitive actions *is*. The popular business press frequently reports on organizations changing their competitive actions. As competitors battle for desired outcomes or objects, they'll try one thing. If that doesn't work, they'll try something else. That's the reality of the competitive struggle that's taking place. As we stated at the beginning of the chapter, competition is a given for all sizes and types of organizations. It's a game that the players are trying to win. Organizations improve their chances of doing so if they choose a competitive strategy that supports and exploits their competitive advantage.

LEARNING REVIEW   LEARNING OUTCOME 5.4

- Why is strategy implementation critical?
- Describe the role(s) that functional strategies play in implementing the organization's competitive strategy.
- Describe the offensive and defensive competitive actions an organization might use.
- How should an organization's competitive strategy be evaluated?

The Bottom Line

Learning Outcome 5.1: Describe the functional strategies an organization needs and explain how those strategies are implemented and evaluated.

- *Functional strategies:* short-term, goal-directed decisions and actions of the organization's various functional areas.
- All organizations must acquire and transform resources (inputs) into outputs (products), which are then made available to the organization's customers or clients.
- Organizations have three functional concerns: the product, the people, and the support processes.
- The Product: product functional strategies include product design, production-operations, and marketing. Product design usually involves an organization's R&D functional area. Once products have been designed, they're ready to be produced, which involves an organization's production-operations strategies. These strategies include how products will be produced and where they will be produced. Once products are produced, the next step is to efficiently and effectively get those products to the customers when, where, and how they want them, which is marketing. The main strategic choices in marketing involve decisions about target market, differentiation, positioning, marketing mix (commonly known as the 4Ps), and gathering market insights.
- The People: people (HR) functional strategies reflect an organization's commitment to and its treatment of its employees. HR strategies can be a significant source of competitive advantage and can have a positive impact on performance (*high-performance work practices:* HR practices that lead to both high individual and high organizational performance). Strategic choices involve getting people into the organization, making sure they have the necessary knowledge and skills to do their jobs and helping them do those jobs better, assessing how well they do those jobs and making needed corrections, and motivating high levels of effort and compensating them fairly. May also address other HR issues such as employee relations, diversity efforts, and so on.
- The Support Processes: support processes support the organization as it does its work. The two main ones include information systems and financial-accounting systems.
- Information affects how effectively and efficiently organizational members can do their work. Strategic choices in this functional area involve the choice of system technology and the choice of types of information systems desired.
- Financial-accounting systems provide strategic decision makers with information about the organization's financial accounts and financial position. Strategic choices include collecting and using financial-accounting data, evaluating financial performance, doing financial forecasting and budgeting, determining the optimum financing mix, and effectively and efficiently managing the financial-accounting area.

Learning Outcome 5.2: Explain what competitive advantage is and what it implies.

- *Competitive advantage:* what sets an organization apart, which can come from distinctive capabilities or unique resources. It implies there are other competitors.
- *Competition:* when organizations battle or vie for some desired object or outcome. The types of competition an organization might face can be understood by looking at who competitors are.
- Three approaches to defining an organization's competitors include: (1) industry perspective, which identifies competitors as organizations that are making and selling the same or highly similar goods or services; (2) market perspective, which says competitors are organizations that satisfy the same customer need; and (3) strategic groups concept, which is based on the idea there are groups of firms competing within an industry that have similar strategies, resources, and customers.

- Organizations develop strategies that exploit resources and capabilities to get a competitive advantage, thus setting the stage for competition.
- *Competitive strategy:* strategy for how an organization or business unit is going to compete.

Learning Outcome 5.3: Describe the different competitive strategies.

- The traditional approaches to defining competitive strategies are Miles and Snow's adaptive strategies and Porter's generic competitive strategies.
- Miles and Snow's four adaptive strategies include: (1) *prospector:* a strategy in which an organization continually innovates by finding and exploiting new product and market opportunities; (2) *defender:* a strategy used by an organization to protect its current market share by emphasizing existing products and producing a limited product line; (3) *analyzer:* a strategy of analysis and imitation; and (4) *reactor:* a strategy characterized by the lack of a coherent strategic plan or apparent means of competing.
- Porter's generic competitive strategies are based on competitive advantage (either low costs or unique and desirable differences) and product-market scope (broad or narrow). He identifies three strategies: (1) *cost leadership:* a strategy in which an organization strives to have the lowest costs in its industry and produces or provides products for a broad customer base; (2) *differentiation:* a strategy in which an organization competes by providing unique (different) products in the broad market that customers value, perceive as different, and are willing to pay a premium price for; the differentiator works hard to establish *brand loyalty,* which is when customers consistently and repeatedly seek out, purchase, and use a particular brand; (3) *focus:* a strategy in which an organization pursues either a cost or differentiation advantage in a limited customer segment.
- Porter also identifies a strategy of *stuck in the middle,* which happens when an organization can't develop a low cost or a differentiation advantage.
- There are two contemporary views on competitive strategy. The first is the *integrated low cost–differentiation strategy,* which involves simultaneously achieving low costs and high differentiation. Some organizations have been able to do this because of technology.
- The second contemporary view is Mintzberg's generic competitive strategies. He proposes that an organization's strategy is either differentiation or being undifferentiated. If it chooses differentiation, it does so by price, marketing image, product design, product quality, or product support.

Learning Outcome 5.4: Discuss how competitive strategies are implemented and evaluated.

- Competitive strategies are implemented through the functional strategies; that is, the resources and distinctive capabilities found in the functional areas influence which competitive strategy is most feasible. In addition, the functional strategies support the organization's competitive advantage and strategy.
- Competitive strategies are also implemented through competitive actions, which include: (1) *offensive moves:* an organization's attempts to exploit and strengthen its competitive position through attacks on a competitor's position, and (2) *defensive moves:* an organization's attempts to protect its competitive advantage and turf.
- Competitive strategies are evaluated by the performance results obtained. What competitive weaknesses and strengths does the organization have?
- Changing the competitive strategy isn't something that organizations do frequently because it's based on specific resources, distinctive capabilities, and core competencies developed in the functional areas. Changing would mean modifying or redeveloping those. What is likely to be changed are the organization's competitive actions.

YOU as strategic decision maker: building your skills

1. Although the styles and details may have changed, the shirts, skirts, and jackets we wear today aren't a whole lot different than what was worn a decade ago. However, the ways they're produced have been transformed by a forced infusion of information technology. When American apparel makers learned to view their product not as pieces of fabric sewn together but as a process of harnessing information along a chain that runs from the factory floor to the retail counter, they were able to improve their performance. Strategic factors such as bar coding, computer systems and software, high-tech distribution centers, and uniformity standards have played a role in this reinvention of the clothing industry. How would each of these factors affect a clothing manufacturer's functional strategies in R&D, production-operations, marketing, HR management, information systems, and financial-accounting systems?

2. Jack Welch, former CEO of General Electric, was noted for his managerial skills and abilities. The secret to his success was described as not a series of brilliant insights or bold gambles but a fanatical attention to detail. What do you think this statement means? What are the implications for strategically managing an organization's functional strategies?

3. There's a federal law called the Economic Espionage Act of 1996 that protects businesses from having their highly confidential product information stolen. Theft of intellectual property by trusted insiders (employees or contractors) happens frequently. One study estimated that intellectual property loss worldwide amounted to between $500 and $600 billion annually. Many types of organizations in many types of industries are vulnerable. What are the implications for the way an organization's functional strategies are formulated and implemented? Think about each functional area that might be affected and how it would be affected.

4. Many organizations are putting customer service activities online and making them available 24/7. What would be the advantages of this strategic approach? What disadvantages might there be? How could strategic decision makers address the disadvantages?

5. Corporate sponsorships of special events and programs (sports programs, entertainment attractions, festivals and fairs, medical-education-social causes, and the arts) are a unique type of marketing strategy. The number of such sponsorships is slowing down. Do some research on corporate sponsorships. Find five examples of companies using corporate sponsorships. Describe these examples in a brief paper. What types of corporate sponsorships are these companies doing? Given the nature of the company's industry, why do you think they chose the sponsorship they did? Do you think these corporate sponsorships are an effective and efficient marketing strategy? Why or why not?

6. How important is a fun workplace to employees? Many experts say that being recognized as a fun place to work can be an important competitive edge when recruiting in a tight labor market. Fun-loving firms indicate that incorporating humor and fun in the workplace reduces stress, increases job satisfaction, stimulates creativity, and increases productivity. Research the topic of fun and humor in the workplace. What are the pros and cons of this strategic choice? Make a bulleted list of your findings. Be prepared to debate the topic (from either side) in class.

7. "Why do companies spend billions of dollars on information technology systems that fail to respond to the needs of those who run them?" This complaint isn't unique. What are the implications for designing effective information systems strategies? Be specific.

8. Customer service would appear to be an important strategic goal of any organization. Yet, surveys of customer satisfaction by the University of Michigan conclude that customer service could be improved. Research the topic of customer service. Then, in a short paper, describe which functional strategies might have to change and how they need to change to improve customer service.

9. Every year, *Fortune* magazine honors the 100 best companies to work for. Get the latest list. (The list is published in February.) What are the top 10 companies on the list? Select three of these companies to research. What types of functional strategies are these three companies using? What could other companies learn from the strategies being used by these companies?

10. A patent is a legal property that allows its holder to prevent others from employing this property for their own use for a specified period of time. A patent protects an invention and is valid for up to 20 years from the date of filing a patent application. Research patents and the patent application process. (You might want to access the U.S. Patent & Trademark Office Web site at [www.uspto.gov].) How many types of patents are there? What other interesting information about patents did you find? Would patents play any role in an organization's choice of competitive strategy? Explain.

11. Competition is a whole lot like war. What can strategic decision makers learn from military strategists? Sun-Tzu, the great Chinese military strategist, wrote *The Art of War* sometime between 480 and 221 B.C. Could his warfare strategies be used in battling competitors? Here's one interpretation of some of these strategies:
    - Don't start what you shouldn't begin.
    - The impossible is impossible.
    - Don't attack a tank with a peashooter.
    - Attack what isn't defended.
    - If you can't attack, defend.
    - Illusion creates confusion.
    - Do what they don't expect.
    - Rather than assuming they won't attack, position yourself so they can't attack.
    - The unprepared can be defeated.
    - The unknowing can be outsmarted.
    - Do not challenge unless you have the means to win.
    - Do not fight unless you're determined to win.

    What do you think of these "strategies?" What implications do you see for an organization's competitive strategy?

12. Select an industry you know about or that you're interested in. (You might want to select an industry where you're concentrating your postgraduation job search.) Do a strategic groups analysis, covering as many of the potential competitors as you can. Determine what strategic dimensions would be most appropriate for grouping competitors. Then, group competitors according to your strategic dimensions. Be sure to put your analysis on a chart showing the strategic dimensions and the various strategic groups. Write up a brief explanation (1 to 2 pages) of what you did, how you did it, and why you did what you did.

13. Interbrand Corporation is a global design and marketing consultant known for its brand surveys. Go to the company's Web site [www.interbrand.com] and check out the latest global brand survey. Pick three companies from the top ten global brands. Research those companies and describe their competitive strategies (using any of the approaches we've discussed). Do you think the value of those companies' brands contribute to their ability to create a sustainable competitive advantage? Explain.

CASES

CASE #1 Driving for Success

Bagus Indahono/Newscom

This Strategic Management in Action case can be found at the beginning of Chapter 5.

Discussion Questions

1. What do you think are the keys to Toyota's success?
2. Do you think production or marketing would be most important to Toyota? Support your choice.
3. Is strategy coordination important to Toyota? Explain.
4. Go to the company's Web site [**www.toyota-global.com**]. Identify and describe three examples of functional strategies you find there.

CASE #2 They've Got Game

With one of the world's most recognizable slogans (Just Do It) and brand logos (the swoosh), you wouldn't think that Nike would have to worry about the competition. However, in the athletic apparel industry where consumer tastes are fickle and the intensity of rivalry high, even Nike needs effective competitive strategies.

Nike, the company, reflects the brash confidence of its founder and board chairperson, Phil Knight. He still believes, as one of his company's most controversial Olympic ads once stated, "You don't win silver. You lose gold." With that type of attitude, it's no wonder that its shoes are consistently top sellers and that Nike is the innovator and industry leader as the world's number one athletic apparel company with 40 percent of the U.S. athletic footwear market. How does Nike play the game?

One thing Nike understands well is the power of a competitive spirit, which continues to be a guiding force in the way the company does business. This competitive spirit, instilled by the late Bill Bowerman, Knight's mentor and track coach at the University of Oregon, has characterized the company's culture from the early days. The company (then called Blue Ribbon Sports) began with a handshake between Knight and Bowerman as they decided to import cheap, high-tech Japanese "Tiger" shoes to challenge Adidas, the industry leader. Even then, Knight was not afraid to go after someone, even the industry leader. And this competitive spirit influences strategic actions in other areas. For instance, when Foot Locker (one of Nike's biggest retailers), upset by Nike's hard-nosed marketing tactics, trimmed orders and slashed prices, Nike struck back by cutting shipments to the company on some of its top sellers. The move had serious consequences (Nike's U.S. sales fell 5 percent and its stock price plummeted), but it also brought Foot Locker back to the bargaining table. Later, an analyst said, "Nike knew its actions were going to have a negative impact, but they did it anyway" because they knew they'd prevail at the end. Even the company's name reflects this competitive spirit: Nike is the name of the Greek goddess of victory.

Another thing Nike understands well is marketing. Knight has been called the "most powerful person in sports" even though he's never played pro sports or owned a pro sports team. What he's done, though, is rewrite the rules of sports marketing. When he signed a young basketball player by the name of Michael Jordan, an endorsement relationship began that even today remains the gold standard. And Nike continues to go after the new sports geniuses. For instance, Nike consistently beats rivals to sign top athletes to endorsement contracts. And you can't discuss Nike's marketing prowess without mentioning the company's legendary ads. Nike has always taken chances in its advertising by sounding off on social and political issues in sports. Knight says he knows that he risks offending people but believes "the publicity and notoriety are worth it." CEO Mark Parker says that the company is making major changes at the retail level. He says, "We're grabbing the opportunity to take Nike and our industry to someplace new, where consumers have experiences that are physical and digital and mobile." In addition, the company acquired Umbro, one of the world's great football brands.

Not only is the company on the cutting edge in its marketing, but it continues to take risks in its products. It's focusing on more action markets such as skateboarding, snowboarding, and surfing. And it's developed a new collection of casual and sporty street apparel. Whether the company can exploit its brand power in these new markets remains to be seen. But one thing is for sure...this company's got game!

Discussion Questions

1. Describe Nike's competitive strategy using Miles and Snow's framework and Porter's framework. Explain each choice.
2. What competitive advantage(s) do you think Nike has? Have its resources, capabilities, or core competencies contributed to its competitive advantage? Explain.
3. Do Nike's functional strategies support its competitive strategy? Explain.
4. What do you think Nike has to do to maintain its strong competitive position?

Sources: Based on Nike 2011 Annual Report, [www.nike.com], February 8, 2012; L. Burkitt, "In China, Nike Sets Out to Alter Sports Mindset," *Wall Street Journal,* October 12, 2011, p. B7; T. Vega, "Nike Tries to Enter the Niche Sports It Has Missed," *New York Time Online,* Jun 1, 2011; "World's Most Admired Companies: Top Performers," *Fortune,* February 7, 2011, p. 23; E. Levenson, "Citizen Nike," *Fortune,* November 24, 2008, pp. 165–170; J. Greene, "This Social Network is Up and Running," *BusinessWeek,* November 17, 2008, pp. 74–76; S. Skidmore, "Nike to Change Shopping Experience," *Centre Daily Times Online,* March 23, 2007; S. Holmes, "Changing the Game on Nike," *BusinessWeek,* January 22, 2007, p. 80; and S. Elliott, "Nike Reaches Deeper Into New Media to Find Young Buyers," *New York Times Online,* October 31, 2006.

CASE #3 Rewind and Replay

There's no doubt that people like to watch movies, but how they watch those movies has changed. Although many people still prefer going to an actual movie theater, more and more are settling back in their easy chairs in front of home entertainment systems, especially now that technology has improved to the point where those systems are affordable and offer many of the same features as those found in movie theaters. Along with the changes in *where* people watch movies, *how* people get those movies has changed. For many, the weekend used to start with a trip to the video rental store to search the racks for something good to watch, an approach Blockbuster built its business on. Today's consumers can choose a movie by going to their computer and visiting an online DVD subscription and delivery site where the movies come to the customers—a model invented by Netflix.

Launched in 1999, Netflix's subscriber base grew rapidly. It now has more than 24.4 million subscribers and more than 100,000 movie titles from which to choose. "The company's appeal and success are built on providing the most expansive selection of DVDs, an easy way to choose movies, and fast, free delivery." A company milestone was reached in late February 2007, when Netflix delivered its one billionth DVD, a goal that took about seven-and-a-half years to accomplish— "about seven months less than it took McDonald's Corporation to sell one billion hamburgers after opening its first restaurant."

Netflix founder and CEO Reed Hastings believed in the approach he pioneered and set some ambitious goals for his company: build the world's best Internet movie service and grow earnings per share (EPS) and subscribers every year. In 2011, though, Hastings made a decision that had customers complaining loudly. Netflix's troubles began when it announced it would charge separate prices for its DVDs-by-mail and streaming video plans. Then, it decided to rebrand its DVD service as Qwikster. Customers raged so much that Netflix reversed that decision and pulled the plug on the entire Qwikster plan. As Netflix regained its focus with customers, it was once again ready to refocus on its competitors.

Success ultimately attracts competition. Other businesses want a piece of the market. Trying to gain an edge in how customers get the movies they want, when and where they want them, has led to an all-out competitive war. Now, what Netflix did to Blockbuster, Blockbuster and other competitors are doing to Netflix. Hastings said he has learned never to underestimate the competition. He says, "We erroneously concluded that Blockbuster probably wasn't going to launch a competitive effort when they hadn't by 2003. Then, in 2004, they did. We thought…well they won't put much money behind it. Over the past four years, they've invested more than $500 million against us." Not wanting to suffer the same fate as Blockbuster (it filed for bankruptcy protection in 2010 and was sold to Satellite TV service provider DISH Network in 2011), Netflix is bracing for other onslaughts. In fact, CEO Hastings, defending his misguided decisions in 2011 said, "We did so many difficult things this year that we got overconfident. Our big obsession for the year was streaming, the idea that 'let's not die with DVDs.'"

The in-home filmed entertainment industry is intensely competitive and continually changing. Many customers have multiple providers (e.g., HBO, renting a DVD from Red Box, buying a DVD, streaming a movie from providers such as Hulu, Apple, and Amazon) and may use any or all of those services in the same month. Video-on-demand and streaming are becoming extremely competitive.

To counter such competitive challenges, Hastings is focusing the company's competitive strengths on a select number of initiatives. He says, "Streaming is the future; we're focused on it. DVD is going to do whatever it's going to do. We don't want to hurt it, but we're not putting much time or energy into it." Others include continually developing profitable partnerships with content providers, controlling the cost of streaming content, and even licensing its original series. In fact, it just licensed its first original series called "House of Cards" and starring Kevin Spacey. With other companies hoping to get established in the market, the competition is intense. Does Netflix have the script it needs to be a dominant player? CEO Hastings says, "If it's true that you should be judged by the quality of your competitors, we must be doing pretty well."

Discussion Questions

1. Describe what you think Netflix's competitive strategy is using Miles and Snow's and Porter's frameworks. Explain each of your choices.
2. What competitive advantage(s) do you think Netflix has? Have its resources, capabilities, or core competencies contributed to its competitive advantage(s)? Explain.
3. How will Netflix's functional strategies have to support its competitive strategy? Explain.
4. What do you think Netflix is going to have to do to maintain its competitive position, especially as its industry changes?

Sources: S. Woo and I. Sherr, "Netflix Recovers Subscribers," *Wall Street Journal*, January 26, 2012, pp. B1+; J. Pepitone, "Netflix CEO: We Got Overconfident," *CNNMoney.com*, December 6, 2011; D. McDonald, "Netflix: Down, But Not Out," *CNN.com*, November 23, 2011; H. W. Jenkins, Jr., "Netflix Isn't Doomed," *Wall Street Journal*, October 26, 2011, p. A13; C. Edwards, "Netflix Drops Most Since 2004 After Losing 800,000 Customers," *BusinessWeek.*

com, October 25, 2011; N. Wingfield and B. Stelter, "How Netflix Lost 800,000 Members and Good Will," *New York Times Online*, October 24, 2011; C. Edwards and R. Grover, "Can Netflix Regain Lost Ground," *BusinessWeek.com*, October 19, 2011; and R. Grover, C. Edwards, and A. Fixmer, "Can Netflix Find Its Future By Abandoning the Past?" *Bloomberg BusinessWeek*, September 26–October 2, 2011, pp. 29–30.

CASE #4 Casting a Wider Net

One of the most popular tourist destinations in Missouri isn't what you might expect. You'd find it in the southwest corner of the state in Springfield. It's Bass Pro Shops Outdoor World. Some 4 million people visit this one store annually. (More than 100 million people visit all its stores annually.) Although most visitors are hunting, fishing, and outdoors enthusiasts, many come just to see the sights and to experience the retail atmosphere of the store. There's a four-story cascading waterfall, rifle and archery ranges, a putting green, and an indoor driving range. Visitors can get their hair cut at the barbershop and then arrange to have a lure made from their hair clippings. They can grab a latté at the coffee shop or eat a full meal at Hemingway's Blue Water Café, whose showpiece is a 30,000-gallon saltwater aquarium. And then there are the incredible wildlife displays throughout—many of which have become popular photo spots for visitors. Despite all of these fascinating attractions, the heart (and soul) of the store is still the row after row of guns, decoys, tents, rods, reels, lures, campers, clothing, and other sports and outdoors equipment and apparel. There's even one enormous store wing that showcases boats—speedboats, houseboats, pontoon boats, fiberglass boats, and aluminum boats. There's something for everyone to experience and enjoy.

Johnny Morris, founder of Bass Pro, was born and raised in Springfield. In 1971, he opened a bait shop in a small corner of his father's liquor store. From that humble beginning, the company has grown to be a dominant player in the outdoors and sporting goods market. Morris's operating philosophy is to never allow the customer to have a dull moment. His retailing approach has been one of excitement and entertainment. The design of the flagship (the "granddaddy") store—and ultimately, all the other stores—was developed after trips to other popular retailing destinations to understand their appeal. One visit to L. L. Bean in Freeport, Maine, was particularly memorable. Morris felt that if that store could draw well over 3.5 million visitors a year to the middle of nowhere, then he could do that, and better, in Springfield. The retailing success that is Bass Pro Shops has been duplicated now in 56 different locations across the United States and Canada. The company has additional stores planned (including one in East Peoria, Illinois and one in Harlingen, Texas) and continues to look for new opportunities.

Although the stores are a vital part of Bass Pro's strategies, they aren't the only way that customers can purchase Bass Pro's goods. The company's catalogs and Internet sales are important parts of its operations, as well. Bass Pro's catalog, first launched in 1974, was the first step in the company's national recognition. It mails more than 125 million catalogs and sale circulars annually to outdoor activity enthusiasts. Furthermore, its online portal **[www.basspro.com]** has been visited by more than 2 million people per month since its launch in 1996. These two marketing tools have played a significant role in helping develop the fierce brand loyalty of Bass Pro's many customers. In addition to these retailing strategies, Bass Pro also sponsors several TV and radio programs and runs a luxurious resort in the Ozark Mountains. Despite its name, as you can see, Bass Pro does more than sell fishing products. The company values all outdoor activities and wants its customers to do the same.

Discussion Questions

1. What examples of functional strategies do you see in this case? Label your examples and be specific in describing them.
2. As a company grows, what challenges might it face in replicating in different locations what's made it successful? How might these challenges be addressed?
3. How might a company's mission statement affect how it does its business? Find Bass Pro's mission statement on its Web site **[www.basspro.com].** (Hint: Look at the Newsroom link.) How does Bass Pro Shop's mission statement affect the way it does its business?

Sources: Based on B. Pacyniak, "Sweet Catch," *Retail Confectioner*, November 2011, pp. 36–40; "Bass Pro Shops, Inc.," *Datamonitor*, June 17, 2011; T. Pardee, "Bass Pro," *Advertising Age*," November 15, 2010, p. 20; Seven (Man-Made) Wonders of Missouri," *Springfield, Missouri, News-Leader*, March 30, 2010, pp. 5B+; D. Tang, "Bass Pro Casts a Wider Net," *Springfield, Missouri, News-Leader*, October 22, 2006, pp. 1E+; E. McDowell, "Adventures in Retailing," *New York Times*, March 20, 1999, p. B1; and author's personal experiences visiting the "granddaddy" store in Springfield.

Endnotes

1. "Auto Sales: Overview Charts," Market Data Center, *Wall Street Journal,* February 1, 2012; H. Tabuchi, "Toyota Cuts Annual Profit Forecast by 54 Percent," *New York Times Online,* December 9, 2011; C. Dawson, "For Toyota, Patriotism and Profits May Not Mix," *Wall Street Journal,* November 29, 2011, pp. A1+; J. Muller, " The Best-Selling Cars of 2011," *Forbes.com,* November 2, 2011; C. Woodyard, "Panel: Toyota Didn't Listen," *USA Today,* May 24, 2011, p. 3B; H. Tabuchi, "Toyota Sees Slow Return to Normal," *New York Times Online,* April 22, 2011; D. Searcey, "Toyota Maneuvers to Protect 'Crown Jewels'," *Wall Street Journal,* March 22, 2011, pp. B1+; J. Murphy, "Toyota's Global Woes Start to Hit Home in Japan," *Wall Street Journal,* November 4, 2008, p. A10; book review of "Toyota Culture: The Heart and Soul of the Toyota Way," by J. Liker and Michael Hoseus, in *Industry Week,* October 2008, p. 18; and H. Takeuchi, E. Osono, and N. Shimizu, "The Contradictions That Drive Toyota's Success," *Harvard Business Review,* June 2008, pp. 96–103.

2. P. Siekman, "Build to Order: One Aircraft Carrier," *Fortune,* July 22, 2002, pp. 180[B]–180[J].

3. Information for this section on marketing is based on P. Kotler and G. Armstrong, *Principles of Marketing,* 12th ed. (Upper Saddle River, NJ: Prentice Hall, 2008); P. Kotler and K. L. Keller, *Marketing Management,* 12th ed. (Upper Saddle River, NJ: Prentice Hall, 2006); and P. Doyle and P. Stern, *Marketing Management and Strategy,* 4th ed. (Upper Saddle River, NJ: Prentice Hall, 2006).

4. L'Oreal advertisement, *Diversity Inc.,* November 2006, p. 9.

5. A. Carmeli and J. Schaubroeck, "How Leveraging Human Resource Capital With Its Competitive Distinctiveness Enhances the Performance of Commercial and Public Organizations," *Human Resource Management,* Winter 2005, pp. 391–412; R. Batt, "Managing Customer Services: Human Resource Practices, Quit Rates, and Sales Growth," *Academy of Management Journal,* June 2002, pp. 587–597; J. Pfeffer, *The Human Equation: Building Profits By Putting People First* (Boston: Harvard Business School Press, 1998); A. A. Lado and M. C. Wilson, "Human Resource Systems and Sustained Competitive Advantage: A Competency-Based Perspective," *Academy of Management Review,* October 1994, pp. 699–727; J. Pfeffer, *Competitive Advantage Through People* (Boston: Harvard Business School Press, 1994); and P. M. Wright and G. C. McMahan, "Theoretical Perspectives for Strategic Human Resource Management," *Journal of Management,* 1991, pp. 295–320.

6. "Human Capital: A Key to Higher Market Value," *Business Finance,* December 1999, p. 15; M. A. Huselid, "The Impact of Human Resource Management Practices on Turnover, Productivity, and Corporate Financial Performance," *Academy of Management Journal,* June 1995, pp. 635–672.

7. Information for this section was based primarily on L. R. Gomez-Mejia, D. B. Balkin, and R. Cardy, *Managing Human Resources,* 5th ed. (Upper Saddle River, NJ: Prentice Hall, 2007).

8. Information for this section was based primarily on J. Laudon and K. Laudon, *Management Information Systems: Managing the Digital Firm,* 10th ed. (Upper Saddle River, NJ: Prentice Hall, 2007).

9. P. Engardio, "Flat Panels, Thin Margins," *BusinessWeek,* February 26, 2007; and D. Darlin, "The No-Name Brand Behind the Latest Flat-Panel Price War," *New York Times Online,* February 12, 2007.

10. P. Kotler, *Marketing Management,* 5th ed. (Upper Saddle River, NJ: Prentice Hall, 2000), pp. 220–223.

11. See Michael E. Porter, *Competitive Strategy* (New York: Free Press, 1980), Chapter 7.

12. D. J. Ketchen, Jr., C. C. Snow, and V. L. Hoover, "Research on Competitive Dynamics: Recent Accomplishments and Future Challenges," *Journal of Management,* vol. 30, no. 6, 2004, pp. 779–804; and D. Dranove, M. Peteraf, and M. Shanley, "Do Strategic Groups Exist? An Economic Framework for Analysis," *Strategic Management Journal,* November 1998, pp. 1029–1044; and J. B. Barney and R. E. Hoskisson, "Strategic Groups: Untested Assertions and Research Proposals," *Managerial and Decision Economics,* vol. 11, 1990, pp. 187–198.

13. J. C. Short, D. Ketchen Jr., T. B. Palmer, and G. T. M. Hult, "Firm, Strategic Group, and Industry Influences on Performance," *Strategic Management Journal,* February 2007, pp. 147–167.

14. D. J. Ketchen, Jr., "An Interview with Raymond E. Miles and Charles C. Snow," *Academy of Management Executive,* November 2003, pp. 95–118; D. E. Abell, *Defining the Business: The Starting Point of Strategic Planning* (Englewood Cliffs, NJ: Prentice Hall, 1980); M. E. Porter, *Competitive Strategy: Techniques for Analyzing Industries and Competitors* (New York: Free Press, 1980); and R. E. Miles and C. C. Snow, *Organizational Strategy, Structure, and Process* (New York: McGraw-Hill Book Company, 1978).

15. B. Kabanoff and S. Brown, "Knowledge Structures of Prospectors, Analyzers, and Defenders: Content, Structure, Stability, and Performance," *Strategic Management Journal,* February 2008, pp. 149–171; W. S. Desarbo, C. A. Di Benedetto, M. Song, and I. Sinha, "Revisiting the Miles and Snow Strategic Framework: Uncovering Interrelationships between Strategic Types, Capabilities, Environmental Uncertainty, and Firm Performance," *Strategic Management Journal,* January 2005, pp. 47–74; D. F. Jennings and S. L. Seaman, "High and Low Levels of Organizational Adaptation: An Empirical Analysis of Strategy, Structure, and Performance," *Strategic Management Journal,* July 1995, pp. 459–475; J. Tan and R. J. Litschert, "Environment-Strategy Relationship and Its Performance Implications: An Empirical Study of the Chinese Electronics Industry," *Strategic Management Journal,* January 1994, pp. 1–20; D. H. Doty, W. H. Glick, and G. P. Huber, "Fit, Equifinality, and Organizational Effectiveness: A Test of Two Configurational Theories," *Academy of Management Journal,* December 1993, pp. 1196–1250; D. Dvir, E. Segev, and A. Shenhar, "Technology's Varying Impact on the Success of Strategic Business Units Within the Miles and Snow Typology," *Strategic Management Journal,* February 1993, pp. 155–162; S. M. Shortell and E. J. Zajac, "Perceptual and Archival Measures of Miles and Snow's Strategic Types: A Comprehensive Assessment of Reliability and Validity," *Academy of Management Journal,* December 1990, pp. 817–832; S. A. Zahra and J. A. Pearce II, "Research Evidence on the Miles-Snow Typology," *Journal of Management,* December 1990, pp. 751–768; and D. C. Hambrick, "Some Tests of the Effectiveness and Functional Attributes of Miles and Snow's Strategic Types," *Academy of Management Journal,* March 1983, pp. 5–26.

16. J. H. Roberts, "Defensive Marketing: How a Strong Incumbent Can Protect Its Position," *Harvard Business Review,* November 2005, pp. 150–157.

17. K. A. Dolan, "From Buses to Planes," *Forbes,* October 31, 2005, pp. 118–120.

18. D. Fenn, "Money Rules," *Inc.,* April 2001, p. 94.

19. M. E. Porter, *Competitive Advantage* (New York: Free Press, 1985); and M. E. Porter, *Competitive Strategy* (New York: Free Press, 1980).

20. Hoover's Online [www.hoovers.com], February 11, 2009; and M. B. Grover, "The Odd Couple," *Forbes,* November 18, 1996, pp. 178–181.

21. D. Foust, "Soaring on Wings of Steel," *BusinessWeek,* April 4, 2005, p. 70.

22. "The Frugal Life of the Wal-Mart Muckety-Muck," *Business 2.0,* May 2002, p. 22.

23. M. Shank, "Making $50,000 Mattresses, Selling in Buffet's Furniture Stores," *Bloomberg.com,* March 11, 2011; and zChocolate web site [www.zchocolate.com], February 8, 2012.

24. M. E. Lloyd, "That Pottery Barn Look Isn't So Unique Anymore," *Wall Street Journal,* March 21, 2007, pp. B1+.

25. B. Austen, "The Megabus Effect," *Bloomberg BusinessWeek,* April 11, 2011, pp. 62-67; J. F. Schwieterman and L. A. Fischer, "Journal of Transportation Law, Logistics & Policy," *First Quarter 2011,* pp. 65-78; H. Barovick, "Pimp My Bus Ride," *Time,* November 23, 2009, p. 102; T. Kim, The Indianapolis Star, "Company Takes Southwest Approach to Bus Service," *USA Today,* May 30, 2006, p. 7B; and T. W. Martin, "Where $1.50 Buys You a 300-Mile Journey," *Wall Street Journal,* July 6, 2006, pp. D1+.

26. K. McLaughlin, "The Hot Blonde in the Coffee Shop: A Lighter Roast," *Wall Street Journal Online,* February 1, 2012; T. Nguyen, "10 Best Coffee Shops in Los Angeles," *LA Weekly Online,* December 19, 2011; and M. Weissman, "A Coffee Connoisseur on a Mission: Buy High and Sell High," *New York Times Online,* June 22, 2006.

27. Porter, *Competitive Advantage,* p. 17.

28. C. Campbell-Hunt, "What Have We Learned About Generic Competitive Strategy? A Meta-Analysis," *Strategic Management Journal,* March 2000, pp. 127–154; R. B. Robinson and J. B. Pearce, "Planned Patterns of Strategic Behavior and Their Relationship to Business Unit Performance," *Strategic Management Journal,* vol. 9, no. 1, 1988, pp. 43–60; D. Miller and P. H. Friesen, "Porter's Generic Strategies and Performance: An Empirical Examination with American Data," *Organization Studies,* vol. 7, 1986, pp. 37–55; G. G. Dess and P. S. Davis, "Porter's Generic Strategies as Determinants of Strategic Group Membership and Organizational Performance," *Academy of Management Review,* vol. 21, 1984, pp. 467–488; and D. Hambrick, "An Empirical Typology of Mature Industrial Product Environments," *Academy of Management Journal,* vol. 26, 1983, pp. 213–230.

29. E. Kim, D. Nam, and J. L. Stimpert, "The Applicability of Porter's Generic Strategies in the Digital Age: Assumptions, Conjectures, and Suggestions," *Journal of Management,* vol. 30, no. 5, 2004, pp. 569–589; S. Kotha and B. L. Vadlamani, "Assessing Generic Strategies: An Empirical Investigation of Two Competing Typologies in Discrete Manufacturing Industries," *Strategic Management Journal,* January

1995, pp. 75–83; H. Mintzberg, "Generic Strategies: Toward a Comprehensive Framework," *Advances in Strategic Management,* vol. 5 (Greenwich, CT: JAI Press, 1988), pp. 1–67; C. W. L. Hill, "Differentiation versus Low Cost or Differentiation and Low Cost," *Academy of Management Review,* July 1988, pp. 401–412; J. J. Chrisman, C. W. Hofer, and W. R. Boulton, "Toward a System for Classifying Business Strategies," *Academy of Management Review,* July 1988, pp. 413–428; and P. Wright, "A Refinement of Porter's Generic Strategies," *Strategic Management Journal,* vol. 8, no. 1, 1987, pp. 93–101.

30. C. W. L. Hill and G. R. Jones, *Strategic Management Theory,* 3rd ed. (Boston: Houghton Mifflin Company, 1995), pp. 178–179; S. Cappel, P. Wright, M. Kroll, and D. Wyld, "Competitive Strategies and Business Performance: An Empirical Study of Select Service Businesses," *International Journal of Management,* March 1992, pp. 1–11; D. Miller, "The Generic Strategy Trap," *Journal of Business Strategy,* January–February 1991, pp. 37–41; and R. E. White, "Organizing to Make Business Unit Strategies Work," *Handbook of Business Strategy,* 2nd ed., edited by H. E. Glass (Boston: Warren, Gorham, and Lamont, 1991), pp. 24.1–24.14.

31. R. J. Allio, "Henry Mintzberg: Still the Zealous Skeptic and Scold," *Strategy & Leadership,* vol. 39, no. 2, 2011, pp. 4-8; and Mintzberg, 1988.

32. Kotha and Vadlamani, 1995.

33. The information in this section is based on various articles in L. Fahey, ed., *The Strategic Management Reader* (Englewood Cliffs, NJ: Prentice Hall, 1989), pp. 178–205.

34. The information on this section is based on Porter, *Competitive Advantage,* pp. 482–512.

35. W. T. Robinson, "Marketing Mix Reactions to New Business Ventures," The PIMSletter on Business Strategy, no. 42 (Cambridge, MA: Strategic Planning Institute), 1988, p. 9.

LEARNING OUTCOMES

6.1 **Define corporate strategy.**

6.2 **Discuss organizational growth strategies.**

6.3 **Describe the organizational stability strategy.**

6.4 **Describe organizational renewal strategies.**

6.5 **Discuss how corporate strategy is evaluated and changed.**

STRATEGIC MANAGEMENT IN ACTION

CASE #1 Growing Up

It all started with a simple plan to make a superior T-shirt. As special teams captain during the mid-1990s for the University of Maryland football team, Kevin Plank hated having to repeatedly change the cotton T-shirt he wore under his jersey as it became wet and heavy during the course of a game.[1] He knew there had to be a better alternative and set out to make it. After a year of fabric and product testing, Plank introduced the first Under Armour compression product—a synthetic shirt worn like a second skin under a uniform or jersey. And it was an immediate hit! The silky fabric was light and made athletes feel faster and fresher, giving them, according to Plank, an important psychological edge.

Today, Baltimore-based Under Armour (UA) is a $1.4 billion company. In 16 years, it has grown from a college start-up to a "formidable competitor of the Beaverton, Oregon behemoth" (better known as Nike). The company has nearly 3 percent of the fragmented U.S. sports apparel market and sells products from shirts, shorts, and cleats to underwear. In addition, more than 100 universities wear UA uniforms. The company's logo—an interlocking U and A—is becoming almost as recognizable as the Nike swoosh.

Starting out, Plank sold his shirts using the only advantage he had—his athletic connections. "Among his teams from high school, military school, and the University of Maryland, he knew at least 40 NFL players well enough to call and offer them the shirt." He was soon joined by another Maryland player, Kip Fulks, who played lacrosse. Fulks used the same "six-degrees strategy" in the lacrosse world. (Today, Fulks is the company's COO.) Believe it or not, the strategy worked. UA sales quickly gained momentum. However, selling products to teams and schools would take a business only so far. That's when Plank began to look at the mass market. In 2000, He made his first deal with a big-box store, Galyan's (which was eventually bought by Dick's Sporting Goods). Today, almost 30 percent of UA's sales come from Dick's and The Sports Authority. But they haven't forgotten where they started, either. The company has all-school deals with 10 Division 1 schools. "Although these deals don't bring in big bucks, they deliver brand visibility..."

So, what's next for Under Armour? At the end of 2011, revenues had increased 38 percent over the prior year. Sustaining those growth rates will be a challenge. Some potential growth areas include women's apparel, which only make up 25 percent of the company's apparel sales; footwear, which makes up only 12 percent of corporate sales, but only 1 percent of the $14 billion U.S. athletic foot-wear market; and global sales, which right now are only 6 percent of revenue. A telling sign of the company's philosophy is found over the doors of its product design studios: "We have not yet built our defining product."

Deciding the optimal mix of businesses and the overall direction of the organization are key parts of corporate strategy. Examples of corporate strategy in the chapter-opening case can be seen in the decisions that strategic managers at Under Armour made as they grew their company. They didn't, and couldn't, know how those strategic actions would turn out, but they *did* know that the convergence of certain environmental threats and opportunities coupled with their organization's strengths and weaknesses would play a role. All strategic decision makers must look at the broad and long-term strategic issues facing their organizations and decide what corporate strategies best address those issues.

In this chapter, we'll first look at how corporate strategy differs for single- and multiple-business orga-nizations. In addition, we'll explore how corporate strategy is related to the other organizational strategies we've discussed in previous chapters. Then, we'll discuss the various types of corporate strategies that organizations might choose to implement. Finally, we'll look at what's involved with evaluating and changing corporate strategies.

LEARNING OUTCOME 6.1 **Define Corporate Strategy**	The struggling U.S. economy challenged many companies in industries from retail and travel to banking and automobiles and have proved to be too much for some. For instance, Steve and Barry's LLC, once one of the country's fastest-growing store chains and billed as "the future of discount retailing," filed for Chapter 11 bankruptcy protection.[2] In a short span of six months, the company went from a national retail phenomenon to collapse. Such are the realities and challenges associated with corporate strategy, the last type of organizational strategy we need to study.

We defined **corporate strategy** in Chapter 1 as a strategy concerned with the choices of what business(es) to be in and what to do with those businesses. One thing we need to know in relation to an organization's corporate strategy is whether it's a single- or multiple-business organization.

Single- and Multiple-Business Organizations

A **single-business organization** is primarily in one industry. A **multiple-business organization** is in more than one industry. For instance, Coca-Cola can be considered a single-business organi-zation because it competes primarily in the beverage industry. Even though it's a large company with multiple products, multiple markets, and multiple outlets, it is still primarily a beverage company. On the other hand, Coke's biggest competitor, PepsiCo, is a multiple-business or-ganization because it's in different industries. Its business units include its Pepsico Americas Beverage (beverage business), Frito Lay North America (snack food business), Quaker Oats

North America (prepared foods business), and then its global businesses—Latin America Foods, Europe, Asia/Middle East/Africa. PepsiCo also spun off a business—its restaurant unit, which included Taco Bell, Pizza Hut, and KFC and which is now known as YUM! Brands. Why is this distinction between single- and multiple-business organizations important? Because it influences an organization's overall strategic direction, what corporate strategy is used, and how that strategy is implemented and managed.

Another aspect we need to consider is how corporate strategy relates to the other organizational strategies. What role does corporate strategy play, and how does it relate to the functional and competitive strategies?

Relating Corporate Strategy to Other Organizational Strategies

The corporate strategy establishes the overall direction that the organization hopes to go and the other organizational strategies—functional and competitive—provide the means for making sure the organization gets there. As discussed in earlier chapters, those "means" are the resources, distinctive capabilities, core competencies, and competitive advantage(s) found in the organization's functional and competitive strategies. For example, suppose an organization, such as Kraft Foods, has a goal of expanding into developing countries. It uses appropriate functional and competitive strategies to help realize that goal. Figure 6.1 shows how corporate strategy fits into the overall strategic management in action process.

Each type of strategy—corporate, competitive, and functional—is important to whether the organization does what it's in business to do and whether it achieves its strategic goals. Coordinating these strategies is critical to managing strategically. The corporate strategy can't be implemented effectively or efficiently without the resources, capabilities, and competencies being developed and used in the competitive and functional strategies. And, the competitive and functional strategies implemented must support the overall strategic direction and corporate strategy. Next, we're going to look at the overall direction an organization might go.

FIGURE 6.1

Strategic Management in Action

What Are the Corporate Strategic Directions?

Strategic decision makers can choose from three corporate strategic directions: (1) moving an organization forward, (2) keeping an organization as is, or (3) reversing an organization's decline. What does each mean?

Moving forward means an organization's strategic managers hope to expand the organization's activities or operations—that is, to grow. How? By choosing a growth strategy (or strategies) that is appropriate, given the situation. Keeping an organization as is means it's not growing, but also isn't falling behind. This is a stability strategy. Finally, reversing a decline describes situations in which an organization has problems and may be seeing declines in one or more performance areas. These situations are typically addressed with a renewal strategy.

Now you know the three main types of corporate strategies: growth, stability, and renewal. In the rest of this chapter, we're going to discuss these strategies—what they are and how they're implemented, evaluated, and changed.

LEARNING REVIEW   LEARNING OUTCOME 6.1

- What is corporate strategy?
- Contrast single-business and multiple-business organizations.
- How is corporate strategy related to the other organizational strategies?
- Describe each of the three corporate strategic directions.

LEARNING OUTCOME 6.2

Discuss Organizational Growth Strategies

Growth is an appealing goal to business and not-for-profit organizations alike. For instance, a university develops new degree programs or changes old ones in order to attract more customers (students) and resources (funding, alumni donations, books, buildings, equipment, etc.). Under Armour pursues new markets. Or, McDonald's opens additional outlets in various cities throughout Southeast Asia. All these strategic actions illustrate different ways for an organization to grow.

A **growth strategy** is one that expands the products offered or markets served by an organization or expands its activities or operations either through current business(es) or through new business(es). Organizations use growth strategies to meet performance goals they may have. Typical goals for business organizations include increasing revenues, profits, or other financial/performance measures. Not-for-profit organizations might have goals such as increasing the number of clients served or patrons attracted, broadening the geographic area of coverage, or even perhaps increasing the number of programs offered. What specific growth strategies might organizations use in pursuing such goals?

Types of Growth Strategies

If an organization's strategic managers decide that growth is the direction they want to go, they have different ways to do this as shown in Figure 6.2.

Concentration

Concentration is a growth strategy in which an organization concentrates on its primary line of business and looks for ways to meet its growth goals by expanding its core business. When an organization grows by adding products or opening new locations, it's using the concentration strategy. As long as growth goals can be achieved with this strategy, most organizations will continue it.

Three concentration options are shown in Figure 6.3 and reflect various combinations of current product(s) and market(s), and new product(s) and market(s).[3]

FIGURE 6.2

Possible Growth
Strategies

Product–market exploitation describes attempts by the organization to increase sales of its current product(s) in its current market(s). How? It might use incentives to get current customers to buy more of the current product. For example, anytime Kraft uses a "buy 2, get 1 free" coupon for any of its brands, that's a strategy to increase revenues by getting customers to buy more of the current product. Or an organization might advertise other uses for a product as Church and Dwight Company did to increase sales of its Arm & Hammer baking soda. Just think of the numerous ways, beyond its original use in baking, that consumers are encouraged to use baking soda—air freshener, cleaner, deodorant, and so forth. There are numerous other ways an organization can try to get customers to use more of its current products.

Using the *product development* option, organizations create new products to sell to its current market (customers). What is a "new" product? It might be new products with new features (options, sizes, and ingredients) that often are aimed at current customers. In addition, it can include improved or modified versions of existing products. For instance, toy company Hasbro is well known for making toys and games based on movies and TV shows. Now they're making movies and TV shows based on its toys and games.[4] Another example is World Wrestling Entertainment's introduction of a new lifestyle magazine aimed at the same young, male fans watching its cable TV programming. And here's a unique strategy: The White Castle burger chain, famed for its mini-burgers, is now offering wine (at selected test locations). The company's COO said, "Our customers wanted beer, so we thought, why not try wine, too?"[5] In each of these examples, product development was intended to encourage sales of new or improved products to current customers.

FIGURE 6.3

Concentration Strategy
Options

The *market development* option describes when an organization sells its current products in new markets. What are "new" markets? It might be additional geographic areas or it might be other market segments not currently served. For instance, Ocean Spray Cranberries Inc. was faced with the challenge of how to grow the market for its cranberry products.[6] CEO Randy Papadellis said, "We need to find ways to introduce the cranberry to a whole new generation of consumers." The company added recipes to its Web site for a cranberry Cosmotini and cranberry bruschetta. It also showed customers how to use Craisins (dried cranberries) in products such as trail mix and salsa. Here's another example. Many orthodontists, long associated only with adolescence, are now marketing to adults who want prettier smiles. These orthodontists are trying to emphasize how good the adults are going to look and how, with a winning smile, they can increase their self-confidence.[7] Finally, many skin care companies are going after an important untapped market—males. Although department stores have sold expensive men's skin care products for years, skin care companies are now going mainstream with these products by selling them at drugstores and discount retailers. These are examples of market development—current products aimed at a new market.

To summarize the concentration strategy, an organization looks for ways to grow its core business using different combinations of product(s) and market(s). The focus is on finding ways to meet growth goals by concentrating on its core business.

The remaining option shown in Figure 6.3—product–market diversification—isn't usually viewed as a concentration option as it involves expanding into new products and new markets. This strategic move usually involves diversifying, which we'll discuss in a later chapter section.

The advantage of the concentration strategy is that an organization becomes very good at what it does. Strategic managers know the industry and their competitors well. The organization's functional and competitive strategies can be fine-tuned to ensure that a sustainable competitive advantage is developed because strategic managers know what customers want and know how to provide it. Everyone in the organization can concentrate on the primary business and on developing and exploiting the unique resources, distinctive capabilities, and core competencies critical to success in this market.

The main drawback of the concentration strategy is that the organization is vulnerable to both industry and other external changes. This risk can be minimized by noticing significant trends, but strategic managers need to be willing to adjust the organization's direction, should

STRATEGIC MANAGEMENT IN ACTION
The Global Perspective

Kuka Robotics is Europe's largest manufacturer of automated industrial machines (robots). The century-old German manufacturing equipment supplier found its profits disappearing because it relied too much on the automobile industry. As that industry slumped, Kuka's CEO, Berndt Liepert, began looking for new markets. Company engineers began to wonder whether its robotic equipment could be used in different industries. One said, "We could attach a chair to the end of it and make a fun ride." And that's just what they did! Kuka found lucrative markets in a variety of new industries and turned Kuka's robots into "the stars of internationally renowned action movies and theme parks." Its Robocoaster is "capable of 1.4 million combinations of programmable twists, swirls, and loops." One key to Kuka's success with this market development strategy was making sure its robots didn't look like industrial equipment. And one of the company's newest products is used in the beverage industry to handle those thinner-walled PET water bottles. As one industry veteran said, "The bottled water products were like a big bag of water balloons." Traditional handling methods were ineffective, thus creating a market for robotic handling.

> **TO DO**

- Research the use of robotics in manufacturing. How are robots used?
- What's the most interesting use of robotics you found?

Source: Based on J. Zegler, "Robotic Equipment Forges a New Future," *Beverage Industry,* October 2011, pp. 62–65; and S. Schubert, "Taking Robots for a Ride," *Business 2.0,* August 2005, pp. 46–47.

STRATEGIC MANAGEMENT IN ACTION

Maybe you've never heard of Navteq Corporation, but it has been recognized as a "hot growth company." The Chicago-based tech company, which was acquired by mobile phone maker Nokia, is a digital mapmaker that made its reputation selling maps for navigation systems in luxury cars. However, problems in the luxury car market dragged down Navteq's sales as well. CEO Judson C. Green needed to point his company in a new direction. He didn't abandon the car-based navigation market but instead looked at the growing opportunities in handheld devices. He says, "I'm imagining [location services] for tomorrow's household on both cars, all their cell phones, and even on their digital cameras, iPods, and games." As its revenue from navigation-equipped vehicles slipped to about 50 percent, revenue from handhelds climbed. Now, the company is helping its parent with a new weapon in the fight for its survival—mobile advertising.

THINK ABOUT

- How often do you use navigation tools?
- What do you think are some additional potential uses for Navteq's navigation products? Would these be market development or product development?

Source: Based on C. Lawton, "Nokia Maps New Ad Focus," *Wall Street Journal,* June 23, 2011, p. B7; and R. O. Crockett, "Location, Location, Location," *BusinessWeek,* November 6, 2006, pp. 90–94.

---

that become necessary. For example, the Royal Typewriter Company unwisely chose to continue producing typewriters even as personal computers became standard office equipment and demand for typewriters plummeted. The result—it's no longer in business. If an organization implements its concentration strategy blindly without understanding the opportunities and threats facing the industry, *not* achieving its growth goals may be the least of its problems!

Although the concentration strategy may seem ideal for small organizations, it isn't used exclusively by them. In fact, most large businesses started off using the concentration strategy, and many continue to use it to pursue growth. For example, Beckman Coulter, Inc., a California-based organization with annual revenues of almost $4 billion, has successfully used the concentration strategy to become one of the world's largest medical diagnostics equipment companies.[8] (It was acquired by Danaher Corporation in 2011.) The company has grown by continually innovating new products and processes in this industry. Another example is Bose Corporation of Framingham, Massachusetts. The company's innovative audio products have helped make it one of the world's leading makers of speakers for the home entertainment, automotive, and pro audio markets with annual sales of more than $773 million.[9] Again, this organization has grown because of product innovations concentrated in its primary industry.

If an organization can't meet its growth goals by concentrating on its core business, it may begin to look at other growth strategies.

Vertical Integration

The **vertical integration strategy** is one in which an organization grows by gaining control of its inputs (backward), its outputs (forward), or both. In backward vertical integration, the organization gains controls of its inputs or resources by becoming its own supplier. For example, eBay owns an online payment business that helps it provide more secure transactions and helps it gain control over one of its most critical work processes. Another example is CVS Pharmacy, the U.S. drug chain with the most outlets, which acquired Caremark RX, the number two company in pharmacy-benefits management, creating "the nation's premier integrated pharmacy services provider."[10]

In forward vertical integration, the organization gains control of its outputs (products or services) by becoming its own distributor such as through an outlet store or maybe through franchising. For example, Apple Computer has more than 360 retail stores worldwide to distribute its products. De Beers, the South African diamond mining company, has a few select retail locations around the globe. Even Coach, which was the first fashion manufacturer to open its own retail store in 1981, now gets about 75 percent of its revenue from its own outlets.

The vertical integration strategy is a growth strategy because an organization expands its activities and operations by becoming a source of supply or a source of distribution. However, because it's expanding into industries connected to its primary business, it's still considered a single-business organization. It's simply taking another path to meeting growth goals by controlling different parts of the value chain.

Studies of vertical integration strategies have shown mixed results in terms of whether the strategy helped or hurt performance. Generally speaking, the benefits of vertical integration seem to slightly outweigh the costs.[11]

Horizontal Integration

Live Nation, the largest concert promoter in the United States, combined operations with competitor HOB Entertainment, the operator of the House of Blues Clubs. Some critics "warned the deal would provide Live Nation excessive power in determining how much performers are paid and where they play."[12] French cosmetics giant L'Oreal acquired London-based retailer The Body Shop for $1.1 billion. Colgate-Palmolive acquired the all-natural personal care products manufacturer Tom's of Maine for $100 million. Each of these is an example of the **horizontal integration strategy,** which is a strategy in which an organization grows by combining operations with its competitors.

This growth strategy keeps an organization in the same industry and provides a way to expand market share and strengthen competitive position, but the big question with horizontal integration is: Is it legal? The U.S. Federal Trade Commission and Department of Justice assess the impact of such combinations on the industry competition and evaluate whether antitrust laws might be violated. Even globally, the European Union has been quite active in approving or rejecting proposed horizontal growth strategies, especially those with a potential impact on its member countries. If government regulators perceive that competition is likely to decrease or that the end consumer would be unfairly impacted, the combined business probably will not be allowed. Despite this potential problem, however, many organizations have successfully used this strategy to grow.

Horizontal integration can be an appropriate corporate growth strategy as long as (1) it enables the company to meet its growth goals, (2) it can be strategically managed to attain a sustainable competitive advantage, *and* (3) it satisfies legal and regulatory guidelines.

Diversification

The **diversification strategy** is a strategy in which an organization grows by moving into a different industry. There are two major types of diversification—related and unrelated. **Related (concentric) diversification** is diversifying into a different industry but one that's related in some way to the organization's current business. **Unrelated (conglomerate) diversification** is diversifying into a completely different industry not related to the organization's current business. Either strategy results in a multiple-business organization because it's no longer in just one industry. Let's look more closely at these two types of diversification.

How can diversification—which means "different"—ever be related? In other words, how is a different industry "related" to the one an organization is currently in? An organization using related diversification to achieve its growth goals is looking for some type of strategic "fit" where it can transfer its resources, distinctive capabilities, and core competencies to the new industry and apply those in such a way that a sustainable competitive advantage results. This search for strategic "synergy" is the idea that the performance of combined operations will be much greater than the performance of each unit separately. How does synergy happen? Through the interactions that occur as operations are combined and resources, capabilities, and core competencies are shared. A statement made by Steve Perry (lead singer of the 1980s rock group Journey) when the band got back together in 1996, describes synergy perfectly: "Individually, none of us made the music as magically as we collectively make it together."[13] That's what synergy is all about—the combined operations are more "magical" than what each unit could do

STRATEGIC MANAGEMENT IN ACTION
The Global Perspective

Horizontal integration knows no borders! Following a four-month long battle, United Kingdom-based SABMiller purchased Australian-based Foster's for $10.5 billion. SAB's CEO said, "Foster's will become an important part of our business, and through the application of our commercial capabilities and global scale, we expect to build on the initiatives that Foster's management has put into place, further enhancing Foster's performance and creating value for our shareholders." (Here's an interesting fact not related to the acquisition: SABMiller is one of the world's top bottlers of Coca-Cola products.)

THINK ABOUT

• What challenges do you think might arise in cross-cultural horizontal integration?

• What does SAB's CEO say about how his company will exploit this combination?

Source: Based on D. Primack, "M&A Deals," *CNNMoney.com* [finance.fortune.cnn.com], September 26, 2011; J. Werdigier, "SABMiller to Buy Foster's for $10.15 Billion," *New York Times Online,* September 21, 2011; and R. Schultes, "SABMiller's Opening Shot for Foster's," *Wall Street Journal,* June 22, 2011, p. C14.

separately. Figure 6.4 illustrates ways an organization might transfer resources, capabilities, and core competencies in achieving synergy.

What businesses have used a related diversification strategy? One is Apple, which is in a variety of businesses from music (iTunes Store and iPod) and cell phones (iPhone) to its personal computers (Macs) and tablets (iPad). Another is eBay, which acquired Skype Technologies for $2.6 billion. Although each industry (Internet auction and Internet phone) is different, they obviously have common characteristics, thus allowing eBay to share resources, capabilities, and competencies. As with any strategy, there's no guarantee that related diversification will always help an organization reach its strategic goals. Here's one example that *didn't* work. When Anheuser-Busch (prior to being bought by InBev) entered the snack food industry with its Eagle Snacks business unit, it felt it could exploit certain marketing synergies (distribution channels, customer use, product similarities) developed as the market leader in the beer business and transfer those resources and capabilities to the snack food industry. However, it was never able to develop a competitive advantage against industry leader Frito-Lay (a business unit of PepsiCo) in this intensely competitive market. As a result, the company shut Eagle Snacks down.

What about unrelated diversification? This growth strategy involves an organization moving into industries in which there is no strategic fit. Why would an organization choose to be in industries with no possible strategic relationships or potential synergies? Most often, it

FIGURE 6.4

Related Diversification: Achieving Synergy

will use this approach when its core industry and related industries don't offer enough growth potential. For an organization to pursue and achieve its growth goals, it has to look elsewhere. Also, some organizations might choose unrelated diversification if their specialized resources, capabilities, and core competencies can't be easily applied to other industries outside its core business. This obviously would limit the options for growth.

Because of the challenges of strategically managing such different businesses, there aren't many companies that use this growth strategy. For instance, three of the biggest conglomerates in the United States (Tyco, ITT, and Fortune Brands) have all split themselves into separate companies, dismantling the conglomerate.[14] However, some companies still do. One example from the global arena is none other than Toyota, which, in addition to its automobiles, is into prefabricated houses, advertising, roof gardens, and consulting, among other businesses.[15] Another global example is the Tata Group, India's largest conglomerate comprising more than 90 companies in businesses from manufacturing and chemicals to consumer products and business services.

Is diversification an effective growth strategy? Research studies have shown that, for the most part, related diversification is superior to unrelated diversification.[16] If an organization can develop and exploit the potential synergies in the resources, capabilities, and core competencies of its diversified operations, then it's likely to create a sustainable competitive advantage. However, doing that isn't easy, by any means. The ability to strategically manage diverse businesses and develop a sustainable competitive advantage—no matter how related the different industries might be—is crucial. Also, although performance results from unrelated diversification haven't fared as well according to certain research, the strategy probably can be valuable at times. Once again, it depends on how effectively the diverse operations are managed as a sustainable competitive advantage is sought.[17]

International

According to Figure 6.2 on p. 161, another growth strategy is international. An organization's corporate strategies might involve looking for ways to grow by taking advantage of the potential opportunities offered by global markets or by protecting the organization's core operations from global competitors.[18] The international strategies are so important that Chapter 7 is devoted to discussing them. We need to point out, however, that it is possible for an organization to "go international" as it pursues growth using any of the other strategies. That is, if an organization chooses to vertically integrate, it could do so globally as well as domestically. If a related diversification strategy is implemented, it could involve combining the operations of organizations in different countries as well as those in the home market.

Implementing the Growth Strategies

As we've just seen, organizations have specific corporate strategy alternatives they can use to pursue growth goals. As we've discussed in previous chapters, however, choosing a strategy is only part of the picture. That strategy must be implemented. For the growth strategies, implementation options include (1) mergers–acquisitions, (2) internal development, and (3) strategic partnering.

Mergers–Acquisitions

One way an organization can implement its growth strategies is to "purchase" what it needs. Such purchases are done through mergers and acquisitions, both of which describe situations in which an organization combines its operations with another's, but is done differently. A **merger** is a legal transaction in which two or more organizations combine operations through an exchange of stock and create a third entity. Mergers usually take place between organizations similar in size and are usually "friendly"—that is, a merger is usually acceptable to all the concerned parties. On the other hand, an **acquisition** is an outright purchase of an

FOR YOUR INFORMATION
Thinking Small

Growth. It's the Holy Grail of strategy and what every leader wants for his or her organization. However, maybe it's time to reevaluate that thinking. Maybe there are some benefits to be gained from thinking small. For instance, that's what the venerable IBM discovered as it attempted to navigate the ever-changing technology market with its behemoth technology services unit and all the accompanying layers of decision making and costs. As companies outsourced their technology needs to lower-cost Indian companies, IBM wasn't able to compete. That's when former CEO Sam Palmisano (who is now the company's chairman) decided it was time to think small. Instead of being the "classic" multinational company with country-by-country operations working in isolation, Palmisano reorganized IBM into an integrated global enterprise with centers of expertise focused on industries and technical skills. Rather than continuing to do business using massive corporate divisions and units, he created a much more nimble global network for delivering services. In fact, that strategic readjustment has helped the company improve its performance, financially and operationally.

In addition to allowing companies to be more nimble and responsive to markets, a focus on thinking small can deliver innovation benefits as well. A major impediment to creativity and innovation tends to be the bureaucratic hierarchies that can smother new ideas. By decentralizing decision making and giving employees the freedom they need to make significant decisions without having to jump through a bunch of corporate hoops, strategic leaders can create an environment that's more conducive to creativity, collaboration, and innovation. In today's environment, that might be the golden ticket—the ability to turn creativity into something productive.

THINK ABOUT

- Is growth bad? Discuss.
- What challenges does a company that's growing face?
- How can it handle those challenges?

Sources: Based on J. Rae-Dupree, "Even the Giants Can Learn to Think Small," *New York Times Online*, August 3, 2008; and S. Lohr, "I.B.M. Showing That Giants Can Be Nimble," *New York Times Online*, July 18, 2007.

---

organization by another. The purchased organization is absorbed by the purchasing organization. Acquisitions usually are between organizations of unequal sizes and can be friendly or hostile. Friendly acquisitions are ones in which the combination is desired by the respective organizations. When an organization being acquired doesn't want to be acquired, it's often referred to as a **hostile takeover.** In fact, the target of a hostile takeover often will take steps to prevent the acquisition.

The popularity of mergers and acquisitions seems to go in cycles.[19] Keep in mind that a merger or acquisition could be used by an organization when implementing *any* of the growth strategies—concentration, vertical integration, horizontal integration, or diversification. The main feature of mergers–acquisitions as a way to implement growth strategies is that the

---

STRATEGIC MANAGEMENT IN ACTION

General Electric (GE) believes significant opportunities exist in the airport security market. Rather than developing its own expertise in this area, GE's strategic decision makers purchased security firms. It made its first acquisition in 2002 when it purchased Ion Track, a company that makes devices used to screen carry-on baggage for bombs. To further build on its expertise in this area, in 2004, GE purchased InVision Technologies, the leading manufacturer of bomb detectors for passengers' checked bags, for $900 million in cash. One analyst says, "These acquisitions are a win-win situation for both companies" as GE's brand, size, and credibility teamed with the acquired companies' technologies should make "an appealing mix to potential customers."

THINK ABOUT

- Why do you think GE chose acquisitions as its way to grow?

Source: Based on G. Stoller, "GE to pay $900M for Security Firm InVision," *USA Today*, March 16, 2004, p. 3B.

organization is "buying" its expanded product lines, markets, activities, or operations. We want to look next at another alternative for implementing the growth strategies.

Internal Development

In **internal development,** an organization grows by creating and developing new business activities itself. In this approach, strategic decision makers believe they have the necessary resources, distinctive capabilities, and core competencies to do it themselves. Using internal development, strategic managers choose to acquire needed resources and develop crucial capabilities to meet desired growth goals rather than deal with the risks, aggravations, and challenges of combining two or more different organizations. This doesn't mean, though, that internal development doesn't face the same types of challenges.

When would mergers or acquisitions be preferable and when would internal development be preferable? The choice depends on: (1) the new industry's barriers to entry, (2) the relatedness of the new business to the existing one, (3) the speed and development costs associated with each approach, (4) the risks associated with each approach, and (5) the stage of the industry life cycle.[20] These factors are summarized in Table 6.1.

Although both merger–acquisition and internal development continue to be popular, organizations are using other approaches, which fall under the category of strategic partnering.

Strategic Partnering

Is it possible for an organization to exploit the benefits of combining operations with other organization(s) in order to pursue growth while also minimizing the challenges and risks of buying a business or developing one from the ground up? Welcome to the world of **strategic partnering,** in which two or more organizations establish a legitimate relationship (partnership) by combining their resources, distinctive capabilities, and core competencies for some business purpose. It's an umbrella term that covers a variety of situations from loose relationships among partnering organizations to formal legal arrangements. These cooperative arrangements can be used to implement any of the growth strategies. For instance, an organization may decide to strategically partner with one of its suppliers or distributors (vertical integration), or it might develop a strategic partnership with a competitor (horizontal integration) or with an organization in a related industry (related diversification). Rather than growing by acquisition or internal development, an organization's strategic decision makers choose to develop a strategic partnership. The three main types of strategic partnerships are: (1) joint ventures, (2) long-term contracts, and (3) strategic alliances.

In a **joint venture,** two or more separate organizations form a separate independent organization for strategic purposes. In this cooperative arrangement, the strategic partners typically own equal shares of the new joint venture. A joint venture is often used when the partners do not want to or cannot legally join together permanently. Instead, the partners create this separate entity to do whatever business activity they're joining together to do. These business activities

TABLE 6.1 Mergers–Acquisitions or Internal Development

Use Merger–Acquisition When:	Use Internal Development When:
• Maturity stage of industry life cycle	• Embryonic or growth stage of industry life cycle
• High barriers to entry	• Low barriers to entry
• New industry not closely related to existing one	• New industry closely related to existing one
• Unwilling to accept time frame and development costs of starting new business	• Willing to accept time frame and development costs of starting new business
• Unwilling to accept risks of starting new business	• Willing to accept risks of starting new business

range from product development to manufacturing or marketing a product. Also, a joint venture is a popular partnering method in international growth because it minimizes the financial and political–legal constraints that accompany mergers–acquisitions and internal development. One example is the strategic partnership between French hair care and cosmetics group L'Oreal SA and Swiss food group Nestlé SA to develop cosmetic nutritional supplements. The new company, called Laboratoires Inneov, is headquartered in France and makes products aimed at improving the quality of skin, hair, and nails by supplying nutrients essential to their care.[21] Another is when Clorox Company and Procter & Gamble entered a joint venture to develop products such as garbage bags and plastic wraps. Both companies provided employees and manufacturing equipment to the venture.[22] Another type of strategic partnership is a **long-term contract,** a legal contract between organizations covering a specific business purpose. Long-term contracts typically have been used between an organization and its suppliers. They're often viewed as a variation of vertical integration without an organization having to buy the supplier or internally develop its own supply source. Instead, it locks a supplier into a long-term relationship in which both partners understand the importance of developing resources, capabilities, and core competencies for a sustainable competitive advantage. The organization benefits by having an assured supplier that meets its cost and quality expectations. The supplier benefits by having an assured outlet for its products. The partners in a long-term contract often find that it's in their best interests to share resources, capabilities, and core competencies so that both can capture potential benefits. Again, that's the attraction of the long-term contract as a strategic partnership. The partners recognize and accept that they must work together in order for both to profit.

The last type of strategic partnership we're going to discuss is the **strategic alliance,** in which two or more organizations share resources, capabilities, or competencies to pursue some business purpose. You might be thinking that this sounds very similar to a joint venture. In the case of a strategic alliance, however, there's no separate entity formed. Instead, the partnering organizations simply share whatever they need to in order to do whatever they want to do. Most often, strategic alliances are pursued in order to encourage product innovation, bring stability to cyclical businesses, expand product line offerings, or to cement relationships with suppliers, distributors, or competitors. For example, Yahoo and eBay joined together in an alliance to boost each other's strengths in online advertising, payments, and communications.[23] PepsiCo and Lipton joined together to sell canned iced tea beverages. PepsiCo brought its marketing

FOR YOUR INFORMATION
Why Alliances Make Sense

Companies worldwide are finding ways to build bridges to each other. Although these resulting alliances may not always work, they often make more sense than acquisitions. Here are some reasons why alliances make sense: flexibility and informality of arrangements promote efficiencies; provide access to new markets and technologies; entail less paperwork when creating and disbanding projects; risks and expenses are shared by multiple parties; independent brand identification is kept and can be exploited; working with partners possessing multiple skills can create major synergies; rivals can often work together harmoniously; alliances can take on varied forms from simple to complex; dozens of participants can be accommodated in alliance arrangements; and antitrust laws can protect R&D activities. One expert says, "The future of business is that fewer companies will succeed by going it alone."

> **THINK ABOUT**

- Do alliances make strategic sense? What do you think?

Sources: Based on D. Durfee, "Try Before You Buy," *CFO,* May 2006, pp. 48–54; B. McEvily and A. Marcus, "Embedded Ties and the Acquisition of Competitive Capabilities," *Strategic Management Journal,* November 2005, pp. 1033–1055; R. D. Ireland, M. A. Hitt, and D. Vaidyanath, "Alliance Management as a Source of Competitive Advantage," *Journal of Management,* 2002, Vol. 28, No. 3, pp. 413–446; E. Krell, "The Alliance Advantage," *Business Finance,* July 2002, pp. 16–23; D. Sparks, "Partners," *BusinessWeek,* October 25, 1999, pp. 106–112; and D. Brady, "When Is Cozy Too Cozy?" *BusinessWeek,* October 25, 1999, pp. 127–130.

strengths in canned beverages, and Lipton brought its recognized tea brand and customer base. Although each organization could have attempted this on its own, the hurdles to developing a sustainable competitive advantage would have been much higher. By combining their strengths, the two partners have dominated this product line. Another example of a strategic alliance would be the arrangement between industrial giants Honda Motor and GE. The two teamed up to produce an engine to power a new generation of smaller, lower-cost business jets.[24] As you can see, each partner in a strategic alliance can reap the benefits of growth by contributing to the alliance its unique resources, capabilities, or core competencies.

Strategic partnering arrangements are growing in popularity.[25] Keep in mind that the intent of all strategic partnerships is to gain the benefits of growth while minimizing the drawbacks of buying or internally developing. Strategic partnerships should be approached with the same careful preparation and diligence as an acquisition–merger or an internally developed business. There's no guarantee that the hoped-for strategic benefits will be achieved using these arrangements. Trust among all strategic partners is a critical component to making these arrangements successful.[26]

LEARNING REVIEW LEARNING OUTCOME 6.2

- Define growth strategy.
- Describe the various corporate growth strategies
- Discuss how the corporate growth strategies can be implemented.

LEARNING OUTCOME 6.3

Describe the Organizational Stability Strategy

Although it may seem odd that an organization might want to stay as it is, there are times when its resources, distinctive capabilities, and core competencies are stretched to their limits and growing might risk the organization's competitive advantage. It's times like these when strategic managers may decide it's best for the organization to stay as is. The **stability strategy** is one in which an organization maintains its current size and current activities.

When Is Stability an Appropriate Strategic Choice?

There are times when strategic managers might decide that the stability strategy is most appropriate. One might be when an industry is in a period of rapid upheaval with several key industry and general external forces drastically changing, making the future highly uncertain. At times like this, strategic managers might decide that the prudent course of action is to sit tight and wait to see what happens. This doesn't mean that organizational resources and capabilities are allowed to deteriorate. Quite the contrary! In order to stabilize and maintain the organization's current position, it's important to maintain investments in the various businesses or functions. The stability strategy doesn't mean slipping backward, but it also doesn't mean moving ahead. It's simply stabilizing at the current level of operations.

Another time when strategic managers might pursue the stability strategy is if an industry is facing slow or no growth opportunities. In this instance, strategic managers might decide to keep the organization operating at current levels before making any strategic moves into new industries. This period of stability allows them time to analyze their strategic options—diversification, vertical integration, or horizontal integration—to address the disadvantages of being in a low- or no-growth industry. Given the current economic conditions in the United States and around the globe, many companies have decided to pursue stability until conditions improve.

An organization's strategic managers also might choose a stability strategy if it has been growing rapidly and needs some "down" time to build up its resources and capabilities again. For instance, Staples Inc., the office-supply retailer, believed it was important to open as many stores as possible and proceeded to open 1,500 stores in the United States over a 15-year period.

However, it pulled back on store expansion plans to better manage activities and operations at the current level. Once managers felt they had made current stores as competitive as possible, they started adding stores once again and have reached a level with almost 1,900 in North America and 2,300 worldwide.

Stability also might be an appropriate strategy for large firms in an industry that's in the maturity stage of the industry life cycle. In this situation, if profits and other performance results are satisfactory *and* if strategic decision makers are relatively risk averse, they may choose to "stay as they are" rather than pursuing growth.

Finally, although most strategic managers in large organizations prefer pursuing growth (and often are rewarded for doing so), many small business owners may follow a stability strategy indefinitely. Why? Because they may feel that their business is successful enough just as it is and that it adequately meets their personal goals.

Although there may be other times when a stability strategy is appropriate, these are the most common examples. Keep in mind that the stability strategy is typically a short-run strategy. Because industry and competitive conditions continue to change while an organization stays as is, it's important for strategic managers to strengthen the organization's resources, capabilities, and core competencies, so it doesn't lose its competitive position or competitive advantage.

Implementing the Stability Strategy

There's not much to implementing the stability strategy. Primarily, it involves *not* growing, but also *not* allowing the organization to decline. In other words, during stability, the organization won't be doing such things as putting new products out on the market, developing new programs, or adding production capacity. This doesn't mean that organizational resources, capabilities, and core competencies don't change during periods of stability. In fact, organizations often use this time to assess operations and activities and strengthen and reinforce those that need it. The stability period essentially gives the organization an opportunity to "take a breather" and prepare itself for pursuing growth.

Although stability can be an appropriate corporate strategy for an organization, it's important to remember that, for most organizations, it should be a short-run strategy. If an organization becomes too complacent, it's susceptible to losing its competitive position. And, if an organization finds during the period of stability that significant organizational weaknesses exist or that performance is declining, then it may be necessary to look at a different strategic direction altogether—organizational renewal, and that's the final corporate strategy we need to discuss.

LEARNING REVIEW   LEARNING OUTCOME 6.3

- What is a stability strategy?
- Why might an organization choose a stability strategy?
- Describe how a stability strategy is implemented.

Business periodicals frequently report on organizations that aren't meeting their strategic objectives or whose performance is declining. It's obvious that strategic managers in these organizations have *not* done an effective job of managing strategically and have been *not* been able to develop or exploit a sustainable competitive advantage. The organization is in trouble and something needs to be done. It can't achieve financial success or, in the worst-case scenario, might not survive. Given these circumstances, the organization's situation can be described as declining, and it's important for strategic managers to implement strategies that reverse the decline and put the organization back on a more appropriate path to successfully achieving its strategic goals. The strategies used to do this are called **renewal strategies.** In this section, we'll discuss two organizational renewal

LEARNING OUTCOME 6.4

Describe Organizational Renewal Strategies

strategies—retrenchment and turnaround—and how these strategies are implemented. Before we get into a discussion of these specific strategies, we need to look at some possible causes and indicators of performance declines.

What Leads to Performance Declines?

We can say that, generally speaking, an organization's strategic managers don't deliberately make bad strategic decisions thus causing an organization's performance to decline. However, strategic decisions they do make or strategies they do implement may create conditions that keep the organization from developing or exploiting a sustainable competitive advantage. Without this competitive advantage, it's going to be difficult for an organization to meet its strategic goals and have desirable performance outcomes. What leads to this situation? Figure 6.5 shows the main causes of performance decline that researchers have identified.[27] As you can see, the primary cause of corporate decline is poor management as all other causes can be traced to it. If strategic managers are inept, incompetent, or incapable of strategically managing all aspects of the organization, then organizational performance is likely to suffer. Strategic decisions to overexpand or expand too rapidly indicate poor management judgment. In addition, if an organization has inadequate financial controls or if costs are out of control or too high to be competitive, then its strategic managers aren't doing their job. Likewise, there's no excuse for not anticipating new competitors or shifts in consumer demand. Although strategic managers don't have all the answers, they should—as we discussed in Chapter 3—systematically scan and evaluate the external environment for significant trends. There's simply no excuse for strategic managers not to be aware of what's happening in their external environment. That's poor management! Finally, managers who are slow to respond or who never respond to significant changes in their external and internal situations are doing a poor job of managing strategically. Inertia can be a kiss of death in today's environment!

Can strategic managers tell when performance declines might be imminent? Some of the signs are listed in Table 6.2.[28] Again, if everyone in the organization is managing strategically

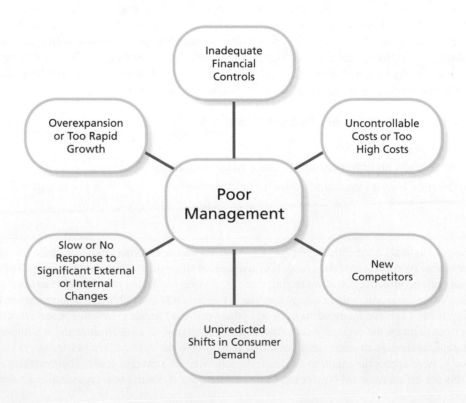

FIGURE 6.5

Possible Causes of
Corporate Decline

TABLE 6.2 Signs of Declining Performance

- Excess number of personnel
- Unnecessary and cumbersome administrative procedures
- Fear of conflict or taking risks
- Tolerating work incompetence at any level or in any area of the organization
- Lack of clear vision, mission, or goals
- Ineffective or poor communication within various units and between various units

and focused on developing and exploiting the organization's competitive advantage, then performance declines shouldn't happen. However, we know that doing a perfect job of managing strategically isn't likely or probably even realistic. Even the best-managed organizations sometimes find that performance results aren't what was expected and goals aren't being met. If an organization's overall performance is declining, then organizational renewal strategies may need to be implemented.

Renewal Strategies

The two main renewal strategies are retrenchment and turnaround. Both are designed to halt declining performance and to return an organization to more desirable performance levels.

Retrenchment

The **retrenchment strategy** is a short-run renewal strategy designed to address organizational weaknesses that are leading to performance declines. In a retrenchment situation, an organization doesn't necessarily have negative financial returns. Although it may have had some time periods when revenues didn't cover expenses, this isn't the typical sign that an organization needs to retrench. Instead, the usual situation in retrenchment is that the organization hasn't been able to meet its strategic goals. Revenues and profits aren't negative but may be declining, and the organization needs to do something to reverse the slide or it soon may face significant performance declines leading to severe financial problems.

Retrenchment is a military term that describes when a military unit "goes back to the trenches" to stabilize, revitalize, and prepare for entering battle again. That's pretty descriptive of what organizations must do, as well, in retrenching. Strategic managers must stabilize operations, replenish or revitalize organizational resources and capabilities, and prepare to compete once again. At a later point, we'll discuss how retrenchment strategies are implemented.

What happens if the organization's circumstances are more serious? What if the organization's profits aren't just declining, but instead there *aren't* any profits, only losses? And, what if other performance results are also significantly low or negative? Such a situation calls for a more drastic strategic response.

Turnaround

The **turnaround strategy** is a renewal strategy that's designed for situations in which the organization's performance problems are more serious. An organization has to be "turned around" or its very survival may be in jeopardy. Some well-known companies that have had to use a turnaround strategy include Sears, Delta Airlines, Kmart, Chrysler, General Motors, Ford Motor, Motorola, Mitsubishi, Newell Rubbermaid, The Home Depot, and Nokia, among many others. In each instance, the organization faced severe external and internal pressures and had to make strategic changes in order to remain a viable entity. There's no guarantee that a turnaround strategy will accomplish the desired results and make the organization a strong competitor once again, but without it, the organization is doomed to fail.

Implementing Renewal Strategies

Implementing the renewal strategies involves two actions: cutting costs and restructuring. A retrenchment strategy typically does not involve as extensive a use of these actions as a turn-around strategy does.

Cost Cutting

In Chapter 5, we discussed the concept of having low costs or even having the *lowest* costs in the industry as a source of competitive advantage. Cost cutting alone as a response to declining performance has little to do with developing a sustainable competitive advantage. Instead, the need to cut costs is approached as a way to bring an organization's performance results back in line with expectations. Strategic managers want to avoid severely cutting costs in those areas they feel are critical for the organization to retain or to exploit a competitive advantage, however weak that advantage may be. What strategic managers should try to do as they cut costs is revitalize the organization's performance (retrenchment) or save the organization (turnaround).

Cost cutting can be across-the-board (implemented in all areas of the organization) or selective (implemented in selected areas). Obviously, in a turnaround strategy, the cuts need to be more extensive and comprehensive.

How do organizations try to cut costs? Strategic decision makers evaluate whether there are any redundancies, inefficiencies, or waste in work activities (i.e., in the organization's capabilities) that could be eliminated. They'll also evaluate whether there are resources that could be eliminated or used more efficiently. For example, UPS found that it could cut costs by more than $200,000 annually by changing the light bulbs in the "Exit" signs in its buildings to a lower wattage. Although that might not seem like a significant amount to an organization whose revenues are in the billions of dollars, keep in mind that this is just one small cost cut with savings that could be redirected to other resources or capabilities that UPS needs for a sustainable competitive advantage or savings that could be applied directly to the bottom line. Either way, the company comes out ahead!

Generally, if additional cuts are needed to keep performance from declining further, strategic managers may have to look at reducing or eliminating certain work activities or even entire departments, units, or divisions. We'll discuss the more severe cost cutting when we get into the restructuring section and look at downsizing as an implementation option.

Restructuring

Other strategic actions an organization might take as it implements a retrenchment or turnaround strategy involve restructuring its operations. There are a number of ways that an organization can restructure. In many instances, it includes refocusing on the organization's primary business(es) as it sells off, spins off, liquidates, or downsizes. In fact, research has shown organizational refocusing to be the most beneficial form of restructuring an organization can do.[29] Let's look at the various ways an organization can restructure and refocus itself.

One possible strategic action an organization might take is to sell off one or more of its business units. Frequently, when an organization finds that a business unit isn't performing up to expectations or doesn't fit in with the organization's long-run direction, strategic managers will choose to sell it. The process of selling a business to another organization where it will continue as an ongoing business is called **divestment.** To whom might an organization sell a business unit? Possible buyers include independent investors, other companies, or the management of the business unit being divested. Remember our earlier discussion of ways to implement corporate growth strategies that one way for organizations to grow is through acquisition? Those acquisitions have to come from somewhere. When one company is acquiring, that means another company has to be selling.

Another possibility for restructuring is to remove a business unit through a **spin-off,** which typically involves setting up a business unit as a separate, independent business by distributing its shares of stock. Recent spin-offs include Marriott International unloading its timeshare business,

Kraft Foods splitting itself into separate companies specializing in snacks and groceries, Samsung spinning off its LCD operations into a separate business, and Marathon Oil spinning off its refining business to focus more on its core business of finding and producing energy.[30]

What happens if there's no buyer for a business unit or if there's no possibility of spinning off the business unit? The only strategic option at that point might be **liquidation,** which is shutting down a business completely. A business unit that's liquidated will not continue as an ongoing business. There may be ways to sell the business's assets, but that's the only revenue an organization could see from liquidating a business unit. As you can well imagine, liquidation is often a strategic action of last resort, but it may be the only option if a turnaround strategy hasn't worked.

Part of an organization's cost-cutting or restructuring efforts might involve **downsizing,** an organizational restructuring in which individuals are laid off from their jobs. Although downsizing can be a quick way to cut costs, simply cutting the number of employees without some type of strategic analysis of where employee cuts might be most beneficial is dangerous.[31] For the organization to be competitive when it eventually emerges from retrenchment or turnaround—if and when that happens—it's important that downsizing be done for the right reasons. In fact, research has shown that downsizing efforts can improve stockholder wealth when they're done for strategic purposes.[32] How can strategic managers make downsizing effective? Table 6.3 lists some recommendations.

Harry & David. Sbarro pizza chain. Hostess Brands snacks. Chevys Real Mex restaurants. Eastman Kodak. These are just a few of the companies that filed for bankruptcy recently.[33] The final option for restructuring the organization is one of last resort. **Bankruptcy** is the failure of a business, a process in which it's dissolved or reorganized under the protection of bankruptcy legislation. It's often the outcome of years of significant performance declines after other restructuring or cost-cutting actions have had little effect or have not been implemented effectively. What happens when an organization "goes bankrupt?"

The act of going bankrupt by a business dramatically changed with the Bankruptcy Reform Act of 1979.[34] This legislation encouraged firms to reorganize (Chapter 11 bankruptcy) rather than liquidate their assets (Chapter 7 bankruptcy). Thus, the aftermath of bankruptcy depends on which type of bankruptcy filing is used. An organization in Chapter 7 bankruptcy will have its assets liquidated by the court with the proceeds used to pay off as many outstanding debts as possible. An organization in Chapter 11 bankruptcy reorganizes its debts and is protected from creditors collecting on debts until such time as it can emerge from bankruptcy. Although bankruptcy may not be a preferred strategic action, when an organization's turnaround strategy hasn't been effective, it may be the *only* option open to the organization.

We need to clarify a couple of things regarding the alternatives for implementing organizational renewal strategies. One is that these strategic actions typically aren't used only one at a time or by themselves. Instead, it's often necessary to use a combination of these alternatives as an organization struggles to regain or develop a sustainable competitive advantage. In fact, most organizations faced with the need to retrench or to do serious restructuring (needed for

TABLE 6.3 **Making Downsizing Effective**

- Communicate openly and honestly about needed actions.
- Clarify goals and expectations before, during, and after downsizing
- Eliminate unnecessary work *activities* rather than making across-the-board cuts in *people.*
- Outsource work if it can be done more inexpensively and more effectively elsewhere.
- Provide whatever assistance is appropriate to downsized individuals.
- Counsel, communicate with, and seek input from those employees not downsized.
- Ensure that those individuals remaining after downsizing know they are a valuable and much-needed organizational resource.

STRATEGIC MANAGEMENT IN ACTION
The Global Perspective

Siemens AG is one of the world's largest electronics and industrial engineering companies. With some 750 subsidiaries and associated companies, Siemens is focused on three things: Industry, Energy, and Healthcare. In addition to its three main segments, Siemens has a financial services division and an enterprise communications business. Although it's on a roll these days, that wasn't the case back in 2008, when the company was embroiled in Germany's largest corruption scandal since World War II. A new CEO, a former General Electric executive, named Peter Löscher (who is Austrian) was brought on board to "clean house." Löscher wasted little time in showing that things wouldn't be "business as usual." He sold off Siemen's mobile phone business (once the company's most prized units) and its computer services unit. And, he replaced almost all of the company's executive team and some 50 percent of its middle managers. Löscher streamlined the portfolio of businesses, added managers with global experience, and held board meetings outside Germany to shake things up at the German conglomerate.

TO DO

- Go to the company's Web site **[www.siemens.com]**. Go to the About the Company information. First, choose one of its businesses, and describe what that business segment does.
- Next, check out the Siemens Worldwide tab. Pick one of the countries, and describe what Siemens does there.
- Finally, check out the Values→Vision→Strategy tab. Describe each of these.

Sources: Based on J. Burton, "Ways to Bet on a Rebound in Europe," *Wall Street Journal,* February 6, 2012, p. R7; E. Dwoskin and D. Voreacos, "The U.S. Goes After Bribery, On a Budget," *Bloomberg BusinessWeek,* January 23, 2012, pp. 31–32; V. Fuhrmans, "Shrugging Off Bribery Case, Siemens Gains Gavor in U.S.," *Wall Street Journal,* December 15, 2011, p. B1; N. Vardi, "Feds Charge Former Siemens Executives With Bribery," *Forbes.com,* December 13, 2011, p. 9; H. Struck, "Siemens Reports Profit Growth, Cites Euro Worries," *Forbes.com,* November 10, 2011, p. 26; and R. Weiss and B. Kammel, "How Siemens Got Its *Geist* Back," *Bloomberg BusinessWeek,* January 31–February 6, 2011, pp. 18–20.

a turnaround) will look at a coordinated long-run program of strategic actions. Another is that while we discuss restructuring and cost-cutting actions in relation to retrenchment and turnaround strategies, the fact is that organizations don't have to be pursuing *only* these strategies to implement these actions. Strategic managers may use selected cost-cutting or restructuring actions (such as divesting selected business units) even during periods of organizational growth if these strategic actions are viewed as contributing to the organization's development or exploitation of a competitive advantage. That's the important key—is the organization's competitive advantage(s) enhanced and strengthened by these actions?

LEARNING REVIEW	LEARNING OUTCOME 6.4

- Discuss the causes of corporate decline.
- Describe the two organizational renewal strategies.
- What two strategic actions are used in implementing the renewal strategies?
- Describe organizational restructuring actions.
- Why are most organizational renewal strategies used in combination?

LEARNING OUTCOME 6.5

Discuss How Corporate Strategy Is Evaluated and Changed

An organization's corporate strategy has been implemented. The competitive strategy and various functional strategies are aligned with the overall direction that strategic managers have chosen for the organization and are being implemented. How do you know it's all working as it should? How do you know whether the corporate strategy has been successful? How could the corporate strategy be evaluated? That's what we need to discuss in this section.

Evaluating Corporate Strategies

Evaluation is an important part of the entire strategic management process. Without evaluation, strategic managers wouldn't have a clue as to whether the implemented strategies—at any level of the organization—were working. We've discussed the specifics of evaluating the functional and competitive strategies in earlier chapters. Now we need to look at how the corporate strategy is evaluated. It shouldn't come as a surprise that the tools used in evaluating corporate strategy tend to be broad and encompass the overall performance of the organization rather than just focusing on narrow functional areas. We will look at four main evaluation techniques: (1) corporate goals; (2) efficiency, effectiveness, and productivity measures; (3) benchmarking; and (4) portfolio analysis.

Corporate Goals

The corporate goals indicate the desired end results or targets that strategic managers have established. Although each functional area and each business unit also have goals that are being pursued, corporate goals tend to be broader, more comprehensive, and longer-term than these others. However, remember that success in meeting the goals at the functional and competitive (business) levels determines whether corporate goals are met. In other words, attaining functional and competitive goals is how an organization achieves its corporate goals. If the functional and competitive goals aren't reached, an organization can't meet its corporate goals. Again, this simply reflects the interactions and interdependence among the various types or strategies.

What types of corporate goals might an organization have? Figure 6.6 lists some of common ones. For a publicly held corporation, maximizing stockholder wealth is an important goal. Why? As the organization's legal owners, stockholders expect an appropriate return on their investment in exchange for providing capital. However, even not-for-profit, government, and privately held organizations need corporate goals to guide decision making. Remember

FIGURE 6.6

Types of Corporate Goals

that the goals should reflect the organization's vision, missions, and the overall direction it intends to go.

In evaluating corporate strategy, goals become the standards against which actual performance is measured. Say, for instance, that a corporate goal is to increase the organization's market share by 1 percent. Strategic managers would evaluate to see whether this happened. It's helpful for corporate goals to be quantified but that may not always be possible. Nonquantifiable areas shouldn't be ignored, however; sometimes a qualitative (subjective) assessment can be just as useful in evaluating corporate performance as can a quantitative one. Also, remember that not every organization is pursuing growth. Organizations using the stability strategy or renewal strategies will have goals that reflect those organizational directions. In these situations, the attainment of those goals should be evaluated.

Efficiency, Effectiveness, and Productivity Measures

Three specific organizational measures that can be used in evaluating an organization's corporate strategy are efficiency, effectiveness, and productivity. These measures represent its ability to use its limited resources strategically in achieving high levels of corporate performance.

Efficiency is an organization's ability to minimize resource use in achieving organizational goals. **Effectiveness** is an organization's ability to reach its goals. **Productivity** is a specific measure of how many inputs it took to produce outputs and is typically used in the production–operations area. It's measured by taking the overall output of goods and services produced, divided by the inputs used in generating that output.

Although these organizational measures may not be easy to calculate, strategic decision makers should attempt to gauge how efficient, effective, and productive the organization is. They should be concerned with getting activities completed so that goals are attained (effectiveness) efficiently and productively. Total organizational performance is a result of the interaction of a vast array of work activities at many different levels and in different areas of the organization; therefore, these three measures are appropriate assessments of how well the organization works *and* how well it's doing at moving in the desired corporate direction (growth, stability, or renewal).

THE GREY ZONE

An organization's goals often include being a good corporate citizen by emphasizing ethical and socially responsible decisions and actions. What happens when an organization's values are continually on public display? That's the situation executives at Wal-Mart, the world's largest retailer, face. Wal-Mart, by virtue of its enormous size and reach, often has played an unwanted role as national conscience enforcer. Don Soderquist, former senior vice chairman, said it best, "The watchword for all of our people is 'Do what is right.' That's what we really preach and teach and we want, but there's so much gray." For instance, when handguns were booted off its shelves, Wal-Mart continued to sell hunting rifles as part of its strategy to create a dominant sporting goods department. Alcohol may not be sold in some traditional Wal-Mart stores but is sold in its Superstores in locations where it's legal. Wal-Mart claims its role as an "agent" for the consumer. It views its job as finding out what customers want and getting those products into stores at the lowest possible cost.

THINK ABOUT

- What are the ethical implications of this "public display" phenomenon for an organization measuring its performance to see whether corporate strategies are effective?
- *Can* corporate morality be "practical"? *Should* it be practical? Explain your position.

Source: Based on S. Sher, "A Framework for Assessing Immorally Manipulative Marketing Tactics," *Journal of Business Ethics,* August 2011, pp. 97–118; "Wal-Mart Chief Preaches the Value of Ethics in Business," *People Management,* July 15, 2010, p. 14; and B. Saporito, "Wrestling with Your Conscience," *Time,* November 15, 1999, pp. 72–73.

Benchmarking

Benchmarking is the search for best practices inside or outside an organization. The actual process of benchmarking may be useful for implementing strategy, whereas the specific "benchmarks" or best practices can be a standard against which to measure corporate strategy performance. In Chapter 2, we observed that a world-class organization strives to be the best in the world at what it does. Using the benchmarks, strategic managers can evaluate whether the organization is being strategically managed as a world-class organization and where improvements are needed. Is overall organizational performance up to the standards of the best in the world? For example, Southwest Airlines studied Indy 500 pit crews, who can change a race car's tire in under 15 seconds, to see how their gate crews could make their gate turnaround times even faster. Why benchmark against Indy pit crews? Southwest felt they were the best in the world at incredibly fast turnaround and, as Southwest's strategic managers reasoned, you don't make money sitting on the ground. You've got to have quick ground turnaround time and get the planes back in the air flying passengers to the next location. The benchmark or best practice was a standard against which to measure one aspect of corporate performance.

Portfolio Analysis

The last approach to evaluating corporate performance we're going to discuss is portfolio analysis. What's in an organization's "portfolio"? The answer would be an organization's various business units. If it has only one business unit, then portfolio analysis would be useless because there's no evaluation or comparison of specific businesses. (We should mention that single-business organizations with multiple brands may use portfolio analysis to evaluate those brands but that's not our focus here.) However, if the organization has multiple business units—in the same or different industries—then portfolio analysis can be used to evaluate corporate performance.

Portfolio analysis is done with two-dimensional matrices that summarize internal and external factors. We're going to focus on three main portfolio analysis approaches: (1) the BCG matrix, (2) the McKinsey–GE stoplight matrix, and (3) the product–market evolution matrix.

The *BCG matrix* (also known as the growth-share matrix) was created by the Boston Consulting Group as a way to determine whether a business unit was a cash producer or a cash user. It's a simple, four-cell matrix. The *X* axis is a measure of a business unit's relative market share. In a very general sense, market share is a proxy for its internal strengths and weaknesses. Relative market share is defined as the ratio of a business unit's market share compared to the market share held by the largest rival in the industry. If the ratio is greater than 1.0, then the business unit is said to have high relative market share. If it's less than 1.0, then the business unit has low relative market share. (Note that only if a business unit is the market leader in its industry will it have a relative market share greater than 1.0.) Some analysts have concluded that this 1.0 figure is too restrictive and have recommended using lower figures such as 0.75 or even 0.50.

The *Y* axis is a measure of the industry growth rate. Likewise, in a very general sense, industry growth rate is a proxy for the external opportunities and threats facing the business unit. We want to know whether this industry is growing faster than the overall economy as a whole. If it is, then industry growth rate is evaluated as high. If it's not growing faster, the industry growth rate is low.

Each of the organization's business units would be assessed according to these guidelines and placed as a circle in the appropriate cell on the matrix. The size of the circle would correspond to the size of the business unit, using some measure such as business unit proportion of total corporate revenues. Thus, the matrix will show the relative size of the organization's various business units—that is, some are bigger and some are smaller. A business unit's placement on the matrix provides strategic decision makers with information to determine appropriate strategic actions to take.

A business unit with low relative market share and low industry growth rate is classified as a *dog*. According to the BCG analysis, a dog offers few growth prospects and, in fact, may require significant investments of cash just to maintain its position. The strategic recommendation for a business unit evaluated as a dog often is to exit that industry by either divesting or liquidating. However, a strategy of harvesting—that is, gradually letting the business unit decline in a controlled and calculated fashion and using any excess cash flows to support other, more desirable business units—may be an option *if* the business unit is profitable. A business unit with low relative market share and high industry growth rate is classified as a *question mark*. The question marks are low in competitive strengths, but they're in an industry where there's a lot of potential. The recommendation for a business unit evaluated as a question mark is that those with the weakest or most uncertain long-term potential should be divested. Why? Meeting the cash needs of too many business units may spread organizational resources too thin and result in none being able to achieve star status. Question marks are easy to sell, however, because of the attractiveness of the industries. Those question marks with more potential should be infused with cash to attempt to turn them into market leaders. A business unit with high relative market share and high industry growth rate is classified as a *star*. Stars are the leading business units in an organization's portfolio. Depending on how competitive the industry is, stars may take significant cash resources to maintain their market leadership position or they may take little cash if they're in an industry where competitive rivalry isn't high. The recommendation for a business unit evaluated as a star is to maintain its strong position while taking advantage of the significant growth opportunities in the industry. Finally, a business unit with high relative market share but low industry growth rate is a *cash cow*. Cash cows are strong cash providers. The positive cash flows from cash cows should be used to support those question marks with potential and to support the stars.

Although the BCG matrix is relatively simple to use, its simplicity is both its biggest advantage and its biggest drawback. The reliance on relative market share and industry growth rate to evaluate a business unit's performance and future potential is an extremely limited view. The fact that the BCG matrix is easy to use and understand is the main reason for its continued popularity as a portfolio assessment tool.

The *McKinsey–GE Stoplight Matrix* was developed by McKinsey and Company for GE. This nine-cell matrix (shown in Figure 6.7) provides a more comprehensive analysis of a business unit's internal and external factors. In this matrix, the *X* axis is defined as business strength–competitive position. What's included in this analysis? It's more than just relative market share! It includes an analysis of the internal resources and capabilities that are believed by strategic managers to be important for success in this business. For instance, it might include an analysis of economies of scale, manufacturing flexibility, workforce morale, product quality, company image, and so forth—whatever strategic managers think the business needs to be good at in order to be competitive. The evaluation scale used in this analysis typically ranges from 1 (very weak) to 5 (very strong). The *Y* axis is defined as industry attractiveness, which again provides a much broader analysis than the BCG's industry growth rate. Industry attractiveness might include such factors as average industry profitability, number of competitors, ethical standards, technological stability of the market, market growth rate, and so forth. Again, strategic managers would use a measurement scale from 1 (very unattractive) to 5 (very attractive) to evaluate the industry a business unit is in. An organization's business units would be plotted on the matrix using these two measures.

As with the BCG matrix, the number of circles on the McKinsey matrix corresponds to the number of business units. In this instance, however, the size of the circle corresponds to the relative size of the industry and the shaded wedge corresponds to the market share held by the organization's business unit. With this matrix, we have a little more information to judge a business unit's position. How should strategic managers evaluate the placement of the business units on the matrix?

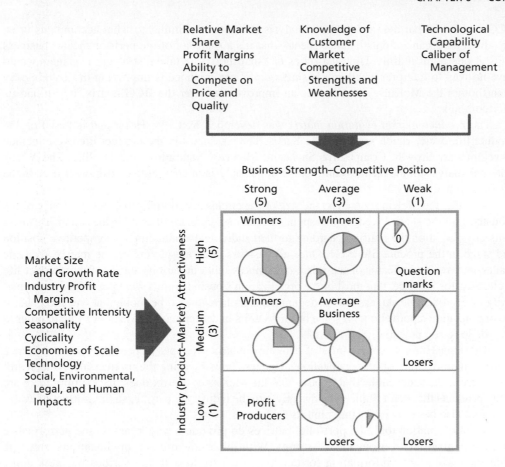

FIGURE 6.7

McKinsey–GE Stoplight Matrix

Source: Adapted from Strategic Management in GE, Corporate Planning and Development, General Electric Corporation.

The three cells in the lower right-hand corner of the matrix are evaluated as *losers.* These business units have weak competitive position–low industry attractiveness; weak competitive position–medium industry attractiveness; and average competitive position–low industry attractiveness. In the original GE stoplight matrix, these cells were colored red, indicating "stop investing in these business units." The three cells in the upper left-hand corner of the matrix are described as *winners.* These business units are evaluated as strong competitive position–high industry attractiveness; strong competitive position–medium industry attractiveness; and average competitive position–high industry attractiveness. As you can probably guess, these cells were colored green, indicating "go ahead, invest in, and grow these business units." Finally, the three cells along the diagonal in the matrix are evaluated as question marks (weak competitive position–high industry attractiveness), average businesses (average competitive position–medium industry attractiveness), and profit producers (strong competitive position–low industry attractiveness). These cells were colored yellow, indicating caution in strategic decisions about these business units. Obviously, the profit producers would be milked for their cash flows with the cash going to support the winners and those question marks with potential to turn into winners.

Although the McKinsey matrix overcame the problem of simplistic analysis that plagued the BCG matrix, its main drawback is the subjectivity of the analysis. Because the factors used to measure competitive position and industry attractiveness were created by an organization's decision makers (and because these individuals then rated business units on these factors), there was a risk that the analysis might be too subjective. Another drawback (also shared by the

BCG matrix) is that the performance analysis is static. It's similar to what accountants often say about an organization's balance sheet—that it's a snapshot of the performance of business units at one point in time. Unless a series of "snapshots" are taken, strategic managers would have no way to interpret whether a business unit's performance is improving or declining. So even though the McKinsey matrix was an improvement over the BCG matrix, it still had its shortcomings.

The *product–market evolution matrix* was developed by C. W. Hofer and is based on the product life cycle, which serves as the *Y* axis. The six stages in the product life cycle include Development, Growth, Competitive Shakeout, Maturity, Saturation, and Decline. The *X* axis (internal analysis of the business unit) is the same analysis of competitive position as used in the McKinsey matrix.

Also like the McKinsey matrix, the size of the circles corresponds to the relative size of the industry, and the shaded wedge corresponds to the market share of that business unit. Business units are placed on the matrix according to their individual evaluation on competitive position and stage in the product life cycle. Once all business units are plotted on the matrix, strategic managers have an indicator of the range of business units in various stages of the product life cycle. Say, for instance, that most of the organization's business units were positioned in the maturity or even decline stages. The strategic managers here should be looking at ways to balance the organization's portfolio with some business units in earlier stages of the life cycle in order to provide long-run potential.

Although Hofer's product–market evolution matrix attempts to provide some semblance of the dynamic nature of an organization's business units by using the product life cycle, it still suffers from the same subjectivity biases that the McKinsey matrix does. In addition, there are many products that don't fit nicely and neatly into the industry life cycle, so this particular evaluation tool also has drawbacks that limit its usefulness.

As an evaluation tool, the portfolio matrices do provide a way to assess the performance of the organization's various business units. With this evaluation, an organization's strategic decision makers have information for deciding what to do with the various business units: Should they be supported and strengthened? Should they be sold? Do we need to start looking for businesses to acquire? Because every portfolio analysis technique suffers from drawbacks, each should be used with caution or at least in conjunction with other strategy evaluation measures.

What happens after evaluating the corporate strategy? If the evaluation indicates that performance results aren't as strategic managers had hoped, then strategic changes are in order.

Changing Corporate Strategies

If the evaluation of corporate strategies shows that they aren't having the intended results—growth objectives aren't being attained, organizational stability is causing the organization to fall behind, or organizational renewal efforts aren't working—then some changes are obviously needed. Then, strategic managers have to decide whether to act and what actions to take.

If it's determined that changes are needed, they might look at changing the functional and competitive strategies that have been implemented. Perhaps some modifications to those will be enough to bring about the desired results. On the other hand, strategic managers might decide that more drastic action is needed and the corporate direction itself should be changed. If so, changes might also be necessary in the way the corporate strategy is being implemented. For example, when Microsoft's strategic decision makers realized that the Internet had dramatically altered the world of computing, they did a complete about-face and changed the corporate direction with an all-out focus on this area. What did this corporate strategic change involve? Several actions: Microsoft acquired various Internet and Web startup companies, reshuffled administrative duties, redesigned software already under development, and basically did what it had to in order to build up its commitment to this new corporate direction.[35] Notice how, in this example, the corporate strategy change affected the organization's functional and competitive strategies as well.

An organization's corporate strategy is important to establishing the overall direction the organization wants to go. As the chapter-opening case illustrated, strategic managers have to understand both the opportunities–threats and the strengths–weaknesses facing the organization in order to design appropriate strategies—ones that will develop or exploit the resources, distinctive capabilities, and core competencies the organization has in its various business units in order to realize a sustainable competitive advantage. Each level of the organization's strategies is linked through this all-encompassing effort to develop a sustainable competitive strategy. Each plays a different, but important, role in this process.

LEARNING REVIEW   LEARNING OUTCOME 6.5

- Why is it important to evaluate corporate strategies?
- What are the four ways to evaluate corporate strategies?
- Describe each of the portfolio analysis matrices including how it's used, the cells in the matrix, and its advantages and drawbacks.
- Why might an organization's corporate strategy need to be changed?
- How might an organization's corporate strategy be changed?

The Bottom Line

Learning Outcome 6.1: Explain corporate strategy.

- *Corporate strategy* is a strategy that's concerned with the choices of what business(es) to be in and what to do with those businesses. One thing we need to know is whether the organization is a *single-business organization* (in primarily one industry) or a *multiple-business organization* (in more than one industry).
- The corporate strategy establishes the overall direction the organization hopes to go while the other organizational strategies (functional and competitive) provide the means for getting there. Each type of strategy is important to whether the organization does what it's in business to do and whether it achieves its goals.
- The three corporate strategic directions include moving an organization forward (growth strategy), keeping an organization where it is (stability strategy), and reversing an organization's decline (renewal strategy).

Learning Outcome 6.2: Discuss organizational growth strategies.

- A *growth strategy* is one that expands the products offered or markets served by an organization or expands its activities or operations either through current business(es) or through new business(es). There are five different ways for an organization to grow.
- *Concentration* is a growth strategy in which an organization concentrates on its primary line of business and looks for ways to meet its growth goals by expanding its core business. Three concentration options include: (1) product–market exploitation, which is selling more current products to current markets; (2) product development, which is selling new products to current markets; and (3) market development, which is selling current products to new markets. The advantage of concentration is that this is the organization's primary business and it knows it well. The main drawback is the vulnerability to industry and other external changes.
- The *vertical integration strategy* is one in which an organization grows by gaining control of its inputs (backward), its outputs (forward), or both. The benefits of vertical integration seem to slightly outweigh the costs.
- *Horizontal integration* is a strategy in which an organization grows by combining operations with competitors. It can be a good growth strategy as long as it enables the company to meet its growth goals, it can be strategically managed, and it satisfies legal and regulatory guidelines.
- The *diversification strategy* is a strategy in which an organization grows by moving into a different industry. *Related (concentric) diversification* is diversifying into a different industry that's related in some way to the organization's current business. *Unrelated (conglomerate) diversification* is diversifying into a completely different industry not related to the organization's current business.
- The final type of growth strategy is international in which an organization grows by taking advantage of potential opportunities in global markets or protecting its core operations from global competitors.
- The growth strategies can be implemented in three ways: (1) *merger* (legal transaction in which two or more organizations combine operations through an exchange of stock and create a third entity) or *acquisition* (outright purchase of an organization by another; if the organization being acquired doesn't want to be acquired, it's referred to as a *hostile takeover*); (2) *internal development* (organization grows by creating and developing new business activities itself); and (3) *strategic partnering* (two or more organizations establish a legitimate relationship [partnership] by combining their resources, distinctive capabilities, and core competencies for some business purpose). Types of strategic partnerships include: *joint venture* (two or more organizations form

a separate independent organization for business purposes), *long-term contract* (a legal contract between organizations covering a specific business purpose), or *strategic alliance* (two or more organizations share resources, capabilities, or competencies to pursue some business purpose but no separate entity is formed).

Learning Outcome 6.3: Describe the organizational stability strategy.

- A *stability strategy* is one in which an organization maintains its current size and activities. In most instances, it should be a short-run strategy.
- Times when the stability strategy is appropriate include: industry is in period of rapid change, industry is facing slow or no growth opportunities, organization has just experienced rapid growth, organization is large and in an industry that's in the maturity stage of industry life cycle, or organization is a small business whose owners are satisfied with staying as is.
- Stability strategy is implemented by not growing but also by not allowing organization to decline.

Learning Outcome 6.4: Describe organizational renewal strategies.

- *Renewal strategies* are used when an organization's situation is declining and strategic managers want to reverse the decline and put the organization back on a more appropriate path to achieving its goals.
- The main cause of performance declines can be traced to poor management although factors such as inadequate financial controls, uncontrollable or too high costs, new competitors, unpredicted shifts in consumer demand, slow or no response to significant external or internal changes, and overexpansion or too rapid growth also contribute.
- There are two main renewal strategies: (1) *retrenchment* (a short run strategy designed to address organizational weaknesses that are leading to performance declines) and (2) *turnaround* (a strategy that's designed for situations in which organization's performance problems are more serious).
- These renewal strategies are implemented by cutting costs and restructuring. The amount and extent of these are determined by whether it's a retrenchment or turnaround.
- Restructuring actions include: (1) *divestment* (selling a business to another organization where it will continue as an ongoing business), (2) *spin-off* (setting up a business unit as a separate business by distributing its shares of stock), (3) *liquidation* (shutting down a business completely), (4) *downsizing* (individuals are laid off from their jobs), and (5) *bankruptcy* (failure of a business in which it's dissolved or reorganized under the protection of bankruptcy legislation).

Learning Outcome 6.5: Discuss how corporate strategy is evaluated and changed.

- There are four main techniques for evaluating corporate strategy: (1) corporate goals (were organization's goals achieved); (2) measuring *efficiency* (organization's ability to minimize resource use in achieving goals), *effectiveness* (organization's ability to reach its goals), and *productivity* (specific measure of how many inputs it took to produce outputs); (3) *benchmarking* (search for best practices inside or outside an organization); and (4) portfolio analysis, which is used to assess an organization's portfolio of businesses.
- Three main portfolio analysis techniques include the BCG matrix, the McKinsey–GE stoplight matrix, and the product–market evolution matrix.
- If the evaluation of corporate strategy shows it's not working, strategic managers might first change the functional and competitive strategies or they might take more drastic action and change the corporate direction.

YOU as strategic decision maker: building your skills

1. Do some research on mergers and acquisitions. What were the five largest mergers–acquisitions last year? Make a list of the partners in each. What reasons were given for the merger–acquisition? Do you think these mergers–acquisitions made strategic sense? Explain.

2. Using the Internet (company's Web site, Hoover's, or other Web sites), choose two of the companies listed below to research and answer the following questions:
   a. What corporate strategy(ies) does the company appear to be following? Explain your choice.
   b. Evaluate the company's performance using financial and other measures you choose.
   c. What changes might you recommend in the company's strategic direction? Explain why you did or did not recommend changes.
   Companies
   Cemex [**www.cemex.com**]
   Google [**www.google.com**]
   Unilever [**www.unilever.com**]
   Toshiba [**www.toshiba.com**]
   Smith Corona [**www.smithcorona.com**]

3. A company growing at an annual rate of 35 percent will double in size in just two years. A company growing at an 18 percent rate will double in size in four years. A company growing by 12 percent will double in size in six years. Persistent long-term growth is most achievable in moderate rates. Do you agree? Why or why not? What are the challenges of rapid growth?

4. Find examples in current business publications (*Wall Street Journal, BusinessWeek, Fortune,* etc.) of each of the types of corporate strategy (i.e., each of the types of growth strategies, stability strategy, and each of the types of renewal strategies). Describe your examples. Be sure to provide your citation information.

5. "The acid test for any corporate strategy is that the company's businesses must not be worth more to another owner." What do you think this statement means? Do you agree with this statement? Explain.

6. Can corporate growth have a downside? Explain. How might drawbacks be addressed?

7. Research into corporate "bloopers" by Professor Sidney Finkelstein pinpointed some reasons why smart executives made bad decisions.[36] Some of these reasons included: CEO identifies too closely with his or her company; CEO is too distracted by involvement in personal and social causes; CEO and executive team are so overconfident and aggressive that it's hard to trust them; CEO believes all problems are public relations-related and can be handled by putting a "good spin on it"; and CEO missed clear market signals. Find three examples of bad decisions made by executives. Do any of your examples fit under the reasons listed above? What could other organizations learn from these mistakes? What are the implications for an organization's corporate strategy?

CASES

CASE #1 Growing Up

Dash/Shutterstock.com

This Strategic Management in Action case can be found at the beginning of Chapter 6.

Discussion Questions

1. What examples of corporate strategies do you see in this mini-case?
2. What strategic challenges do you think Kevin Plank must deal with?
3. Using the Internet, find Under Armour's mission statement. How do you think its mission statement influences its corporate strategic choices?
4. What corporate strategy evaluation measures might you suggest that the company use? Explain your choices.
5. Update the information on Under Armour: revenues, profits, and strategic initiatives.

CASE #2 Time for Bread

From the heartland of America comes bread baked with heart. As a leader in the fast-casual dining business, St. Louis–based Panera Bread Company operates and franchises more than 1,540 bakery-cafés in 40 states and Canada under the Panera Bread, St. Louis Bread Company, and Paradise Bakery & Café trademark names. Its mission statement—A loaf of bread in every arm®—reflects the company's purpose and its passion.

Panera's beginnings can be traced to 1981 when CEO Ron Shaich cofounded Au Bon Pain Company, which operated bakery-cafés on the East Coast and internationally. Shaich and his management team were looking for a concept that combined Au Bon Pain's quality food with the potential for a broader appeal. In late 1993, Shaich met the owners of St. Louis Bread Company, which had 19 bake shops doing about $1 million in lunch business a year. St. Louis Bread had targeted suburban areas where real estate was less expensive, the competition was less intense, and the target customers lived. Shaich sensed an opportunity, seeing it as "our gateway into the suburban marketplace and backward into a manufacturing business." After studying the business inside and out, they decided to sell Au Bon Pain Company and purchase the St. Louis Bread Company. Their goal—turn the concept into a national brand under the Panera Bread name.

The management team at Panera (Latin for "time for bread") spent considerable time trying to figure out what this business should look like. They looked at restaurants, coffeehouses, and even retailers in an attempt to understand what it would take to be successful. One thing they discovered was that consumers were tired of the boring sameness of dining-out choices. Shaich said, "Customers are rejecting fast food. They want something better, something special." The new owners knew they would have to achieve that perception by paying careful attention to the details. They also used what they had learned in running Au Bon Pain—quality makes a real difference. In Panera's case, that means, among other things, making fresh dough every single day in 26 locations and trucking it to the cafés for baking.

During 2011, Panera opened 68 new stores. Compare that to 2007 when the company had opened 169 new stores.

The uncertain economic environment over the last couple of years led the executive team to pursue a more moderate rate of growth. Panera's locations, of which about 62 percent are owned by franchisees, sell custom sandwiches made with artisan breads as well as soups and salads. Customers also can buy bread, bagels, pastries, and gourmet coffees to go. Panera has attracted customers and built significant loyalty by concentrating on the quality of their fresh-baked breads and other ingredients. Although the average customer check at a typical Panera store is $8.51, company executives recently implemented a "category management" strategy to redefine its menu structure and utilize store associates to change customer behavior. The goal was to increase gross profit per sales transaction. An important component of this strategy was a systemwide rollout of breakfast items that utilized many of the ingredients already in the stores and that were easy to make, meaning no increase in fixed labor costs. Another important component was the rollout of the MyPanera™ Loyalty Program. Guests who register can earn a combination of rewards and enjoy unique experiences allowing Panera to deepen relationships with its most loyal customers. This program has resulted in increased purchase frequency with MyPanera™ members.

Even in today's worrisome economy, the company appears to have tapped into a consumer phenomenon of affordable indulgences. Consumers want to "reward" themselves with small but good-quality products in a few categories that are important to them. Panera's premium sandwiches, bread, and pastries fit into this category. Maybe it really is Panera's "time for bread!"

Discussion Questions

1. What corporate, competitive, and functional strategies is Panera using to realize its goal of turning the concept into a national brand under the Panera Bread name? Be as specific as possible.
2. How would you recommend Shaich and his management team evaluate whether the company is accomplishing its corporate strategy?

3. Panera Bread was on *Fortune* magazine's 2010 list of 100 Fastest-Growing Companies, was awarded #1 ranking for Best Salads and Top Rated Facilities (for chain restaurants with less than 5,000 outlets) by Zagat in its annual consumer-generated 2011 Fast-Food Survey, and was named Casual Dining Brand of the Year in the 2011 Harris Poll EquiTrend®. What does being on such lists tell you about the company's strategic management? Although the company continues to grow, what problems might arise if the company grows too fast? How might they know whether they were growing too fast?

4. The company depends heavily on franchising to fuel its growth. Do some research on franchising. What advantages and drawbacks might it present?

5. What other examples of affordable indulgences can you think of? What strategic risks are there to such a trend? How can Shaich ensure that Panera doesn't fall victim to those risks?

Sources: Based on Company News Release, "4th Quarter and Full-Year Data," [www.panera.com], February 7, 2012; "Panera Bread Company," *Datamonitor,* October 14, 2011, pp. 1–9; "2011 MUFSO Award Winners," *Nation's Restaurant News,* September 26, 2011, p. 36; L. Patton, "The Great Casual-Dining Upheaval," *Bloomberg BusinessWeek,* August 29, 2011, pp. 23–24; 2010 Annual Report, [www.panera.com], D. Brady, "Ronald M. Shaich," *Bloomberg BusinessWeek,* February 7, 2011, p. 92; C. DeBaise, "How I Built It: Panera Serves Up Business," *Wall Street Journal,* January 20, 2011, p. B6; and "How Panera Bread Kept Rising Through the Recession," *BusinessWeek.com,* November 9, 2010.

CASE #3 Speed Bump

"After a few bumpy years marked by declining TV ratings and weakened traction in the vital 18- to 34-year-old male demographic, Nascar regained some footing in 2011." TV viewership increased in all three Nascar series, both overall (up 10 percent) and in the target group of young men (up 17 percent). And several key sponsors—including Sprint, UPS and Kraft—renewed their sponsorships. However, Nascar is still battling the professional team sports (think . . . . football, baseball, and basketball) that are continually on the air season after season. Nascar needs to reach new audiences, and it's doing so with a 5-year plan with 5 key goals: "build the star power of individual drivers, increase engagement among children and college-age consumers, attract a multicultural fan base, craft more cohesive digital- and social-media strategies, and improve the racetrack experience for fans.

What comes to mind when you think of Nascar (National Association for Stock Car Auto Racing)? Fast cars, roaring engines, the smell of gasoline, beer-guzzling spectators? After the death of well-known driver, Dale Earnhardt, Sr. in 2001, Nascar attempted to make the sport "safer" but some questioned whether those attempts made it less appealing to the fans who watch races so they can experience vicariously in the stands or on television the speed, danger, and excitement of going really, really fast in a crowd of cars. France says, "Our traditional Nascar fan likes it when close competition happens. They care about how is my driver doing or how is my team doing." However, those approaches and images need to change to appeal to new market segments as identified in its goals.

In order to find out how a Nascar race "stacked up against other sports," Nascar did some interesting research. They sent (anonymously) families of four or four college buddies to a Nascar race, an NFL game, and the circus or a concert. Afterwards, each group was asked by a third-party researcher what they liked about each one. The results were eye-opening. For instance, a new fan, especially if they're not with someone who has been to a race before, "doesn't know how to be a fan." They didn't know where to park or how to find their seat. And guys were coming in button-down shirts and khakis, not realizing it's a big party.

So, some of the things Nascar has planned to go after the new and "casual" fan include streamlining the points system so it's easier to follow and understand. Nascar also created a wild card, like most other sports have for getting into the playoffs, making end-of-season outcomes that much more interesting. And then, there's the monumental shift to a digital and social strategy. France realizes that it's going to be an important part of the future Nascar "story." The organization is hiring someone to oversee that aspect and "a big part of the job will be training an entire industry—from driver reps to driver teams to our own internal teams—on social media." Finally, Nascar is using specific strategies to attract a new, multicultural audience, especially Hispanics. For instance, it's using heavy ad/media spending in specific markets. It created a virtual garage tour in Spanish. And the Web site has also been translated into Spanish. However, Nascar is also looking to create specialized digital content in Spanish.

Discussion Questions

1. What strategic challenges do you think Brian France faces as he guides his company? Using what you know about managing strategically, how might he respond to these challenges?

2. Look at the goals the top management team had for the company. What are the implications for corporate strategy? How about for the other organizational strategies (functional and competitive)?

3. The success of NASCAR depends on its ability to satisfy the race teams, the drivers, advertisers–sponsors, the drivers, and the customers. What are the implications for the company as it formulates appropriate strategies?

4. What corporate strategy evaluation tools might you recommend for NASCAR? Explain your choices.

Sources: Based on B. Grossman, "Is NASCAR Back on Track?" *Broadcasting & Cable,* January 16, 2012, pp. 14–16; J. Del Rey and N. Zmuda, "Nascar Targets New Audience, Revs Up Social-Media Strategy," *Advertising Age,* January 2, 2012, p. 19; V. Bauerlein, "Nascar Revs Up Rough Side to Win Back Fans," *Wall Street Journal,* February 14, 2011, pp. B1+; and S. Gregory, "NASCAR Needs Another Gear," *Time,* April 26, 2010, pp. 54–57.

CASE #4 Changing The Menu

"How do you spell cheese? K-R-A-F-T." Although that slogan may say what many people think Kraft Foods is about, that impression would be wrong. As the world's second-largest food company in revenues behind Switzerland-based Nestlé (it is the number one food company in the United States), Kraft is so much more than cheese. And Kraft's history is a fascinating digest of a company that's used many different aspects of corporate strategy.

From its beginning in 1903 to today, Kraft has looked for ways to grow its business. It has continually developed new products—Miracle Whip, macaroni and cheese dinners, Parkay margarine, Tang powdered beverages, Velveeta, Oscar Mayer Deli Creations flatbread sandwiches, and most recently its Velveeta Cheesy Skillets. In 1980, Kraft diversified its businesses by merging with Dart Industries, although each business continued to operate separately. This combination lasted six years. In 1988, Kraft was acquired by Philip Morris Companies (the tobacco company), which merged it with another of its units, General Foods, in 1989. This combination created the largest U.S. food maker, Kraft General Foods, although both businesses continued to run independently. During the 1990s, other global competitors became more powerful and Kraft General Foods struggled. To cut costs, the two businesses discontinued almost 300 food items. In 1995, corporate parent Philip Morris integrated both businesses into Kraft Foods. It immediately sold some businesses (Lender's bagels, Log Cabin, the bakery unit, and others) and bought others (Del Monte's pudding business, Taco Bell's grocery line, Boca Burger, and Balance Bar). In 2000, parent company Philip Morris purchased Nabisco Holdings and folded it into Kraft Foods. In 2001, Kraft Foods went public and sold several business divisions. In 2002, a corporate restructuring eliminated several thousand jobs. The company also sold some brands—primarily its candy brands—that didn't fit its portfolio. In 2003, the company announced it was reducing the fat and sugar content and portion sizes of its products, a strategy abandoned a year later after research showed that consumers didn't like it. Also, in 2004, the chairman of corporate parent Altria (Philip Morris Company's new name) announced a complete spin-off of Kraft Foods, which officially happened on March 30, 2007. With Altria's 88.6 percent stake in Kraft distributed to its shareholders, Kraft Foods was now independent, with all the performance expectations associated with being a publicly traded company. As one analyst said, "Altria may have been okay with an underachiever, but outside stockholders generally want to see quick results." At that point, CEO Irene Rosenfeld "crafted" a corporate direction for the company that exploited its competitive advantage in light of the changes taking place in the food industry. After assuming the CEO job at Kraft in June 2006, Rosenfeld "spent months talking to employees and peeking inside consumers' kitchens—from suburban Chicago to the capital of China." Her conclusion? Kraft Foods "had lost sight of how its offerings fit into consumers' lives. Deep cost cutting had affected product quality, eroding the strength of some brands and causing the company to lose market share. Workers were afraid to speak up when they saw problems." Her solution: a strategy to reignite growth by expanding into developing countries, cutting costs without hurting quality, and empowering local managers to make decisions. She took the company's great portfolio in a direction that was more consistent with the reality of consumers' lives today. The challenge was leveraging those assets to accelerate growth. Despite these actions, company revenues dropped from 2008 to 2009. However, revenues bounced back strongly in 2010 and again in 2011. Now, Kraft Foods's corporate menu is about to change again.

In mid-2011, the company said it was spinning off its North American business from its global snacks group. The snacks business, to be headed by Rosenfeld, will focus on "fast-growing developing markets and in instant consumption channels." The North American grocery business, to be headed by Anthony Vernon (Kraft's executive VP and president of Kraft North America), will focus on "continuing to develop the brands distributed through more traditional grocers." The two executives are "sorting out the fates of several brands, structuring their sales forces, and making a number of personnel decisions" so the breakup plan can be filed with the Securities and Exchange Commission sometime in the second quarter of 2012.

Discussion Questions

1. What examples of corporate strategies do you see in this situation? Explain.
2. What strategic challenges is the company likely to face now?
3. When an organization frequently changes its strategic direction, what problems can arise? (Think in terms of its functional and competitive strategies.)
4. What corporate strategy evaluation measures might you suggest that the split companies use? Explain your choices.
5. Update the information on the two companies—Kraft Foods (North American grocery) and the global snacks company (not yet named): revenues, profits, and strategic initiatives.

Sources: J. Jargon, "Velveeta Shows Its Sizzle Against Hamburger Helper," *Wall Street Journal,* December 29, 2011, pp. B1+; J. Jargon and P. Ziobro, "Kraft Picks Leaders for Split," *Wall Street Journal,* December 6, 2011, p. B3; P. Ziobro, "Kraft Defends Split," *Wall Street Journal,* September 8, 2011, p. B6; S. Ovide, "Kraft's Twisted Family Tree," *Wall Street Journal,* August 5, 2011, p. B2; G. Chon, A.Das, P. Ziobro, D. Kesmodel, S. Ovide, and S. Ng, "Activists Pressed for Kraft Spinoff," *Wall Street Journal,* August 5, 2011, pp. B1-B2; M. J. De La Merced, "Kraft Foods in Split, Is Keeping Oreos but Not Velveeta," *New York Times Online,* August 4, 2011; A. R. Sorkin and C. V. Nicholson, "Kraft to Split Its Snacks and Grocery Businesses," *New York Times Online,* August 4, 2011; and J. Jargon, "Kraft Spiffs Up Its Old Brands," *Wall Street Journal,* June 30, 2011, p. B10.

Endnotes

1. Press Release, "Under Armour Reports Fourth Quarter Net Revenues Growth of 34% and Fourth Quarter EPS Growth of 40%," [investor.underarmour.com], January 26, 2012; D. Roberts, "Under Armour Gets Serious," *Fortune*, November 7, 2011, pp. 153–162; E. Olson, "Under Armour Applies Its Muscle to Shoes," *New York Times Online*, August 8, 2011; M. Townsend, "Under Armour's Daring Half-Court Shot," *Bloomberg BusinessWeek*, November 1–November 7, 2010, pp. 24–25; and E. Olson, "Under Armour Wants to Dress Athletic Young Women," *New York Times Online*, August 31, 2010.

2. J. McCracken and P. Lattman, "Apparel Chain Faces Closure Three Months After Rescue," *Wall Street Journal*, November 18, 2008, p. B1; E. Wilson, "Steve & Barry's, a Retailer, Files for Bankruptcy Protection," *New York Times Online*, July 10, 2008; J. McCracken and P. Lattman, "Steve & Barry's, Short of Cash, May Shut Stores," *Wall Street Journal*, July 1, 2008, p. B3; and P. Lattman and J. McCracken, "Steve & Barry's Faces Cash Crunch," *Wall Street Journal*, June 21/22, 2008, p. A4.

3. The discussion of these concentration strategy options has been slightly modified from information found in P. Kotler, *Marketing Management* (Upper Saddle River, NJ: Prentice Hall, 2000), pp. 74–75.

4. G. Schmidt, "Hasbro, Intent on Expanding Its Toy Brands, Is Playing All the Angles," *New York Times Online*, February 12, 2012.

5. B. Newman, "An Unconventional Pairing: Wine and 'Sliders' at the Castle," *Wall Street Journal*, February 22, 2012, pp. A1+.

6. A. Pressman, "Ocean Spray's Creative Juices," *BusinessWeek*, May 15, 2006, pp. 88–90.

7. A. A. Newman, "Orthodontists Market to Adults Seeking Prettier Smiles," *New York Times Online*, February 1, 2012.

8. Beckman Coulter Inc., [www.beckmancoulter.com], February 21, 2012; and B. Upbin, "What Have You Invented for Me Lately?" *Forbes*, December 16, 1996, pp. 330–334.

9. Bose Corporation [www.bose.com], February 21, 2012; and W. M. Bulkeley, "How an MIT Professor Came to Dominate Stereo Speaker Sales," *Wall Street Journal*, December 31, 1996, pp. A1+.

10. G. C. Marcial, "Hail to CVS/Caremark," *BusinessWeek Online*, April 9, 2007, p. 84.

11. R. D'Aveni and D. J. Ravenscraft, "Economies of Integration versus Bureaucracy Costs: Does Vertical Integration Improve Performance," *Academy of Management Journal*, October 1994, pp. 1167–1206.

12. J. Leeds, "Big Promoter of Concerts to Acquire House of Blues," *New York Times Online*, July 6, 2006.

13. The Associated Press, "Journey Back With New Album, Tour Plans," *Springfield News-Leader*, January 21, 1997, p. 5B.

14. J. S. Lublin and B. Tita, "End of An Empire," *Wall Street Journal*, September 20, 2011, pp. B1+; J. R. Hagerty, G. Chon, and A. Das, "ITT Plans Breakup As Bigness Loses Favor," *Wall Street Journal*, January 13, 2011, pp. A1+; and M. Anderson and S. Skidmore, "Maker of Jim Beam, Titleist to Split into 3," The Associated Press, *Springfield, Missouri, News-Leader*, December 9, 2010, p. 8A.

15. I. Rowley, "Way, Way, Off-Road," *BusinessWeek*, July 17, 2006, pp. 36–37.

16. L. E. Palich, G. R. Carini and S. L. Seaman, "Internationalization as a Moderator in the Diversification-Performance Relationship: An Empirical Assessment," *Academy of Management Proceedings on CD-Rom*, August 1996; I. Goll and R. B. Sambharya, "Corporate Ideology, Diversification and Firm Performance," *Organization Studies*, Vol. 16, No. 5, 1995, pp. 823–846; C. C. Markides and P. J. Williamson, "Related Diversification, Core Competencies, and Corporate Performance," *Strategic Management Journal*, Vol. 15, 1994, pp. 149–165; H. Singh and C. A. Montgomery, "Corporate Acquisition Strategies and Economic Performance," *Strategic Management Journal*, Vol. 8, No. 4, 1987, pp. 377–386; K. Palepu, "Diversification Strategy, Profit Performance, and the Entropy Measure," *Strategic Management Journal*, Vol. 6, No. 3, 1985, pp. 239–255; D. J. Lecraw, "Diversification Strategy and Performance," *Journal of Industrial Economics*, Vol. 33, No. 2, 1984, pp. 179–198; R. A. Bettis, "Performance Differences in Related and Unrelated Diversified Firms," *Strategic Management Journal*, Vol. 2, No. 4, 1981, pp. 379–393; R. Rumelt, 1974; and H. I. Ansoff, *Corporate Strategy* (New York: McGraw-Hill, 1965).

17. L. Palich, G. R. Carini, and S. L. Seaman, 1996; R. B. Sambharya, "The Combined Effect of International Diversification and Product Diversification Strategies on the Performance of U.S.-based Multinational Corporations," *Management International Review*, Vol. 35, No. 3, 1995, pp. 197–218; V. L. Blackburn, J. R. Lang, and K. H. Johnson, "Mergers and Shareholder Returns: The Roles of Acquiring Firms'

Ownership and Diversification Strategy," *Journal of Management,* December 1990, pp. 769–782; B.W. Keats, "Diversification and Business Economic Performance Revisited: Issues of Measurement and Causality," *Journal of Management,* March 1990, pp. 61–72; and A. Seth, "Value Creation in Acquisitions: A Re-examination of Performance Issues," *Strategic Management Journal,* February 1990, pp. 99–115.

18. J. Birkinshaw, A. Morrison, and J. Hulland, "Structural and Competitive Determinants of a Global Integration Strategy," *Strategic Management Journal,* Vol. 15, 1995, pp. 637–655; "Competitors: Some Criteria for Success," *Business Horizons,* January–February 1988, pp. 34 41; and B. S. Chakravarthy and H. V. Perlmutter, "Strategic Planning for a Global Business," *Columbia Journal of World Business,* Spring 1985, pp. 3–10.

19. B. Villalonga and A. M. McGahan, "The Choice Among Acquisitions, Alliances, and Divestitures," *Strategic Management Journal,* December 2005, pp. 1183–1208; D. Henry, "Mergers: Why Most Big Deals Don't Pay Off," *BusinessWeek,* October 14, 2002, pp. 60–70; M. Arndt, "How Companies Can Marry Well," *BusinessWeek,* March 4, 2002, p. 28; L. Capron, "Historical Analyses of Three Waves of Mergers and Acquisitions in the United States: Triggering Factors, Motivations, and Performance," *Academy of Management Proceedings on CD-Rom,* August 1996; and M. H. Lubatkin and P. J. Lane, "Psst…the Merger Mavens Still Have It Wrong," *Academy of Management Executive,* February 1996, pp. 21–39.

20. P. Haspeslagh and D. Jemison, *Managing Acquisitions* (New York: Free Press 1991); E. R. Biggadike, *Corporate Diversification: Entry, Strategy, and Performance* (Cambridge, MA: Division of Research, Harvard Business School, 1983); G. S. Yip, "Diversification Entry: Internal Development versus Acquisition," *Strategic Management Journal,* Vol. 3, 1982, pp. 331–345; M. S. Salter and W. A. Weinhold, *Diversification Through Acquisition: Strategies for Creating Economic Value* (New York: Free Press, 1979); and H. L. Ansoff, *Corporate Strategy* (New York: McGraw-Hill, 1965).

21. "L'Oreal, Nestle Team Up on Product Line," *Springfield News-Leader,* June 26, 2002, p. 6B.

22. "Clorox, P&G to Form Joint Venture," *Wall Street Journal,* November 15, 2002, p. A10.

23. M. Liedtke, The Associated Press, "Yahoo, eBay Join Forces in Partnership," *ABC News Online,* Mary 25, 2006.

24. C. Woodyard, "Honda, GE Build New Jet Engine," *USA Today,* February 17, 2004, [www.usatoday.com].

25. D. Durfee, "Try Before You Buy," *CFO,* May 2006, pp. 48–54; B. McEvily and A. Marcus, "Embedded Ties and the Acquisition of Competitive Capabilities," *Strategic Management Journal,* November 2005, pp. 1033–1055; R. D. Ireland, M. A. Hitt, and D. Vaidyanath, "Alliance Management as a Source of Competitive Advantage," *Journal of Management,* 2002, Vol. 28, No. 3, pp. 413–446; E. Krell, "The Alliance Advantage," *Business Finance,* July 2002, pp. 16–23; C. Ellis, "Making Strategic Alliances Succeed," *Harvard Business Review,* July–August 1996, pp. 8–9; C. M. Brown, "Partnering for Profit," *Black Enterprise,* June 1995, p. 43; R. Maynard, "Striking the Right Match," *Nation's Business,* May 1995, pp. 18–28; Roundtable Discussion, "Strategic Partnering," *Chief Executive,* November 1995, pp. 52–62; D. E. Gumpert, "Business 2000: Partnerships for Success," *Inc.,* December 1995, pp. 133–146; N. Templin, "More and More Firms Enter Joint Ventures with Big Competitors," *Wall Street Journal,* November 1, 1995, pp. A1+; N. S. Levinson and M. Asahi, "Cross-National Alliances and Interorganizational Learning," *Organizational Dynamics,* Autumn 1995, pp. 50–63; and J. Bleeke and D. Ernst, "Is Your Strategic Alliance Really a Sale?" *Harvard Business Review,* January–February 1995, pp. 97–105.

26. S. Parise and A. Casher, "Alliance Portfolios: Designing and Managing Your Network of Business-Partner Relationships," *Academy of Management Executive,* November 2003, pp. 25–39; Ireland, Hitt, and Vaidyanath, *Journal of Management,* 2002; M. Kotabe and K. S. Swan, "The Role of Strategic Alliances in High Technology New Product Development," *Strategic Management Journal,* Vol. 16, 1995, pp. 621–636; J. B. Barney and M. H. Hansen, "Trustworthiness: Can It Be a Source of Competitive Advantage?" *Strategic Management Journal,* Vol. 15, Special Issue, 1994, pp. 175–203; and C. W. L. Hill, "Cooperation, Opportunism, and the Invisible Hand: Implications for Transaction Cost Theory," *Academy of Management Review,* Vol. 15, 1990, pp. 500–513.

27. See S. Minter, "The Four Reasons that Companies Fail," *Industry Week,* [www.industryweek.com], July 20, 2011; J. M. Ivancevich, T. N. Duening, and W. Lidwell, "Bridging the Manager–Organizational Scientist Collaboration Gap," *Organizational Dynamics,* May 2005, pp. 103–117; C. Siafter, *Corporate Recovery: Successful Turnaround Strategies and Their Implementation* (Hammondsworth, England: Penguin Books), 1984; R. C. Hoffman, "Strategies for Corporate Turnarounds: What Do We Know About

Them?" *Journal of General Management,* Vol. 14, 1984, pp. 46–66; D. Schendel, G. R. Patton, and J. Riggs, "Corporate Turnaround Strategies: A Study of Profit Decline and Recovery," *Journal of General Management,* Vol. 2, 1976, pp. 1–22; and J. Argenti, *Corporate Collapse: Causes and Symptoms* (New York: McGraw-Hill, 1976).

28. P. Lorange and R. T. Nelson, "How to Recognize—and Avoid—Organizational Decline," *Sloan Management Review,* Spring 1987, pp. 41–48.

29. C. C. Markides, "Diversification, Restructuring, and Economic Performance," *Strategic Management Journal,* February 1995, pp. 101–118; W. W. Lewis, "Strategic Restructuring: A Critical Requirement in the Search for Corporate Potential," in M. L. Rock and R. H. Rock, eds., *Corporate Restructuring* (New York: McGraw-Hill, 1990), pp. 43–55; and "Shifting Strategies: Surge in Restructuring is Profoundly Altering Much of U.S. Industry," *Wall Street Journal,* August 12, 1985, p. 1.

30. J-A. Lee and M-Lee, "Samsung Plans to Spin Off LCDs," *Wall Street Journal,* February 21, 2012, p. B2; V. Monga, "A Path to Value: Spinoffs," *Wall Street Journal,* December 21, 2011, p. B4; M. Krantz, "Firms Break Up to Buck Up," *USA Today,* September 20, 2011, p. 1B; G. Chon, A. Das, P. Ziobro, D. Kesmodel, S. Ovide, and S. Ng, "Activists Pressed for Kraft Spinoff," *Wall Street Journal,* August 5, 2011, pp. B1-B2; A. Berzon and K. Hudson, "Marriott Unloads Share Business," *Wall Street Journal,* February 15, 2011, pp. B1+; and M. Krantz, "Spinoffs Appear to be Back in Corporate Rotation," *USA Today,* January 14, 2011, p. 1B.

31. G. D. Bruton, J. K. Keels, and C. L. Shook, "Downsizing the Firm: Answering the Strategic Questions," *Academy of Management Executive,* May 1996, pp. 38–45; and W. McKinley, C. M. Sanchez, and A. G. Schick, "Organizational Downsizing: Constraining, Cloning, and Learning," *Academy of Management Executive,* August 1995, pp. 32–44.

32. D. L. Worrell, W. M. Davidson, and V. M. Sharma, "Layoff Announcements and Stockholder Wealth," *Academy of Management Journal,* Vol. 34, 1991, pp. 662–678.

33. D. Cauchon, "Bankruptcy A Reprieve for Some Companies," *USA Today,* January 23, 2012, p. 3B; J. Palank, "Chevys Owner to Restructure," *Wall Street Journal,* October 5, 2011, p. B3; R. Feintzeig and D. FitzGerald, "Pizza Chain Sbarro Files for Chapter 11," *Wall Street Journal,* April 5, 2011, p. B4; and A. Effinger, "Harry & David Kicks the Basket," *Bloomberg BusinessWeek,* April 4–April 10, 2011, pp. 51–52.

34. Y. Chen, J. F. Weston, and E. I. Altman, "Financial Distress and Restructuring Models," *Financial Management,* Summer 1995, pp. 57–75; J. P. Sheppard, "Strategy and Bankruptcy: An Exploration Into Organizational Death," *Journal of Management,* Vol. 20, No. 4, 1994, pp. 795–833; and C. M. Daily, "Bankruptcy in Strategic Studies: Past and Promise," *Journal of Management,* Vol. 20, No. 2, 1994, pp. 263–295.

35. J. Markoff, "Tomorrow, the World Wide Web," *New York Times,* January 16, 1996, pp. C1+; and K. Rebello, "Inside Microsoft," *BusinessWeek,* July 15, 1996, pp. 56–67.

36. S. Finkelstein, *Why Smart Executives Fail and What You Can Learn from Their Mistakes* (New York: Penguin Books), 2003; and J. Merritt, "The ABCs of Failure," *BusinessWeek,* June 9, 2003, p. 126.

LEARNING OUTCOMES

7.1 **Describe international strategy, and explain why it's important.**

7.2 **Explain the issues that arise as organizations go international.**

7.3 **Describe the important international strategy alternatives and explain how they're implemented and evaluated.**

STRATEGIC MANAGEMENT IN ACTION

CASE #1 Fast Fashion

When Amancio Ortega, a former Spanish bathrobe maker, opened his first Zara clothing store, his business model was simple: sell high-fashion look-alikes to price-conscious Europeans.[1] After succeeding in this, he decided to tackle the outdated clothing industry in which it took six months from a garment's design to consumers purchasing it in a store. What Ortega envisioned was "fast fashion"—getting designs to customers quickly. And that's exactly what Zara has done!

The company has been described as having more style than Gap, faster growth than Target, and logistical expertise rivaling Wal-Mart's. Zara, owned by the Spanish fashion retail group Inditex SA, recognizes that success in the fashion world is based on a simple rule—get products to market quickly. Accomplishing this, however, isn't so simple. It involves a clear and focused understanding of fashion, technology, and their market, *and* the ability to adapt quickly to trends.

Inditex, one of the largest fashion retail groups worldwide, has seven chains: Zara (including Zara Kids and Zara Home), Pull and Bear, Massimo Dutti, Stradivarius, Bershka, Oysho, and Uterqüe. The company has more than 5,400 stores in 75 countries although Zara pulls in more than 60 percent of the company's revenues. Despite its global presence, Zara is not yet a household name in the United States, with just over 50 stores open, including a flagship store in New York City.

Colin Sinclair © Dorling Kindersley

What is Zara's secret to excelling at fast fashion? It takes just two weeks to get a new design from drawing board to store floor. And stores are stocked with new designs twice a week as clothes are shipped directly to the stores from the factory. Thus, each aspect of Zara's business contributes to the fast turnaround. Sales managers at "the Cube"—what employees call their futuristic-looking headquarters—sit at a long row of computers and scrutinize sales at every store. They see the hits and the misses almost instantaneously. They ask the in-house designers—who work in teams, sketching out new styles and deciding which fabrics will provide the best combination of style and price—for new designs. Once a design is drawn, it's sent electronically to Zara's factory across the street, where a clothing sample is made. To minimize waste, computer programs arrange and rearrange clothing patterns on the massive fabric rolls before a laser-guided machine does the cutting. Zara produces most of its designs close to home—in Morocco, Portugal, Spain, and Turkey. Finished garments are returned to the factory within a week. Finishing touches (buttons, trim, detailing, etc.) are added, and each garment goes through a quality check. Garments that don't pass are discarded while those that do pass are individually pressed. Then, garment labels (indicating to which country garments will be shipped) and security tags are added. The bundled garments proceed along a moving carousel of hanging rails via a maze of tunnels to the warehouse—a four-story, 5-million-square-foot building (about the size of 90 football fields). As the merchandise bundles move along the rails, electronic bar code tags are read by equipment that send them to the right "staging area," where specific merchandise is first sorted by country and then by individual store, ensuring that each store gets exactly the shipment it's supposed to. From there, merchandise for European stores is sent to a loading dock and packed on a truck with other shipments in order of delivery. Deliveries to other locations go by plane. Some 60,000 items each hour—more than 2.6 million items a week—move through this ultrasophisticated distribution center. And this takes place with only a handful of workers who monitor the entire process. The company's just-in-time production (an idea borrowed from the auto industry) gives it a competitive edge in terms of speed and flexibility.

Despite Zara's success at fast fashion, its competitors are working to be faster. But CEO Pablo Isla isn't standing still. To maintain Zara's leading advantage, he's introducing new methods that enable store managers to order and display merchandise faster and is adding new cargo routes for shipping goods. And the company has finally made the jump into online retailing. One analyst forecasts that the company could quadruple sales in the United States by 2014, with a majority of that coming from online sales.

Zara is a great success story! Its ability to strategically manage a global empire in the rough-and-tumble world of fashion is especially admirable. It's a good way to start our chapter on international strategies. We've already covered many international examples in previous chapters—all those Strategic Management in Action: Global Perspective boxes you've seen—as we discussed various strategy topics. In this chapter, we focus exclusively on the challenges associated with the international strategies.

LEARNING OUTCOME 7.1

Describe International Strategy, and Explain Why It's Important

When you think of wine, what countries would you say have the highest consumption? If you thought, well, of course, France and Italy, you'd be wrong! According to a wine industry consulting firm, Americans drank 3.96 billion bottles of wine in 2010, compared to 3.85 billion bottles of wine consumed by the French (latest figures available). Not only has wine consumption worldwide continued to rise, the value of the worldwide wine market has continued to increase as consumers (especially in the United States and other industrialized countries) drink better and more expensive wines. But the biggest surprise has to be China, which has risen to become one of the world's most important wine markets. Although it's only the seventh-largest consumer of wine, the wine market in China continues to grow by double digits.[2] What organizations might be most interested in this forecast, and what strategic implications (opportunities and threats) might it have for those organizations?

The International Environment

One way to see how international the world marketplace has become is to consider the country of ownership origin for some familiar products. You might be surprised to find that many products you thought were made by U.S. companies aren't! Take the following quiz[3] and then check your answers at the end of the chapter on page 213.

1. Tombstone and DiGiorno frozen pizzas are products of a company based in:

   a. Italy   b. United States   c. Canada   d. Switzerland

2. Lebedyansky juices are owned by a company based in:

   a. Japan   b. United Kingdom   c. United States   d. Russia

3. Rajah spices are products of a company based in:

   a. United States b. Brazil   c. India   d. Switzerland

4. Tetley Tea is owned by a company located in:

   a. Great Britain b. India   c. Japan   d. Spain

5. Volvo cars are products of a company based in:

   a. United States b. United Kingdom   c. Japan   d. China

6. Dos Equis, Tecate, and Sol beer products are owned by a company based in:

   a. The Netherlands b. Mexico   c. United States   d. Colombia

7. The company that produces Boboli pizza crust is based in:

   a. United States b. Mexico   c. Italy   d. Spain

8. The parent company of Braun electric shavers is located in:

   a. Switzerland   b. Germany   c. United States   d. Japan

9. The company that owns Sephora Cosmetics retail stores is located in:

   a. Germany   b. Canada   c. France   d. United States

10. The digital ad firm Barbarian Group is owned by a company based in:

    a. United Kingdom b. United States   c. Greece   d. South Korea

11. Lean Cuisine frozen meals are products of a company based in:

    a. Germany   b. United States   c. Switzerland   d. Brazil

12. The British newspaper, the *Independent,* is owned by a company based in:

    a. Russia   b. United Kingdom   c. South Africa   d. Canada

13. The company that makes French's mustard is based in:

    a. China   b. United Kingdom   c. Japan   d. United States

14. Eight O'Clock Coffee is owned by a company located in:

    a. India   b. Costa Rica   c. United States   d. Canada

15. Frédérick Fekkai & Co. hair care products are marketed by a company based in:

    a. Switzerland   b. United States   c. France   d. Italy

How well did you do? Were you aware of how many products used every day that are made by companies *not* based in the United States? Probably not! Most of us don't fully appreciate the truly international nature of today's marketplace.

FOR YOUR INFORMATION
What's Your Global Perspective?

Take a look at these statistics: • 90 percent of the world's people will never leave the country where they were born. • 95 percent of the news people get is from domestic sources. • It's not unusual for Germans, Italians, or Indonesians to speak three or four languages. "More than half of all primary school children in China now learn English and the number of English speakers in India and China—500 million—now exceeds the total number of mother-tongue English speakers elsewhere in the world." On the other hand, most U.S. children study only English in school—only 24,000 are studying Chinese. And only 22 percent of the population in the United States speaks a language other than English. Americans tend to think of English as the only international business language and don't see a need to study other languages. This could lead to future problems as a major research report commissioned by the British Council says that the "competitiveness of both Britain and the United States is being undermined" by only speaking English.

Monolingualism is one sign that a nation suffers from **parochialism**—viewing the world solely through one's own eyes and perspectives. People with a parochial attitude do not recognize that others have different ways of living and working. They ignore others' values and customs and rigidly apply an attitude of "ours is better than theirs" to foreign cultures. This type of narrow, restricted attitude is one approach that strategic decision makers might take, but isn't the only one.[4] In fact, there are three possible global attitudes. Let's look at each more closely.

First, an **ethnocentric attitude** is the parochialistic belief that the best work approaches and practices are those of the *home* country (the country in which the company's headquarters are located). Strategic decision makers with an ethnocentric attitude believe that people in foreign countries don't have the needed skills, expertise, knowledge, or experience to make the best business decisions as people in the home country. They don't trust foreign employees with key decisions or technology.

Next, a **polycentric attitude** is the view that employees in the *host* country (the foreign country in which the organization is doing business) know the best work approaches and practices for running their business. Strategic decision makers with this attitude view every foreign operation as different and hard to understand. Thus, they're likely to let employees there figure out how best to do things.

The final type of global attitude strategic decision makers might have is a **geocentric attitude,** a *world-oriented* view that focuses on using the best approaches and people from around the globe. Individuals with this type of attitude have a global view and look for the best approaches and people regardless of origin. For instance, Carlos Ghosn, CEO of Nissan and Renault, was born in Brazil to Lebanese parents, educated in France, and speaks four languages fluently. He could very well be the "model of the modern major corporate leader in a globalized world bestraddled by multinational companies." Ghosn's background and perspective have given him a much broader understanding of what it takes to manage in a global environment, something characteristic of the geocentric attitude. A geocentric attitude requires eliminating parochial attitudes and developing an understanding of cross-cultural differences. That's the type of approach successful strategic managers will need in today's global environment.

THINK ABOUT

- Do you speak another language? Have you ever traveled to another country? Why or why not? Would you consider yourself parochialistic?
- As a student, what information did you read here that "hit home" with you? Why?

Sources: Based on P. Ghemawat, "The Cosmopolitan Corporation," *Harvard Business Review,* May 2011, pp. 92–99; T. K. Grose, "When in Rome, Do as Roman CEOs Do," *U.S. News & World Report,* November 2009, pp. 38–41; Reuters Limited, *USA Today Online* [www.usatoday.com], February 21, 2006; and "Learning the Lingo," *USA Today,* January 26, 2006, p. 1A.

Doing business internationally isn't new. Countries and organizations have been trading with each other for centuries. DuPont started doing business in China in 1863. H. J. Heinz Company was manufacturing food products in the United Kingdom in 1905. Ford Motor Company set up its first overseas sales branch in France in 1908. By the 1920s, other companies, including Fiat, Unilever, and Royal Dutch/Shell, had gone international. But it wasn't until the mid-1960s that international companies became quite common. Today, smaller organizations, such as SOL Inc. (a Palm City, Florida, based manufacturer of solar-powered outdoor lighting), to larger organizations, such as heavy equipment maker Caterpillar (with 60 percent of total revenues from international sales), are finding ways to do business internationally.

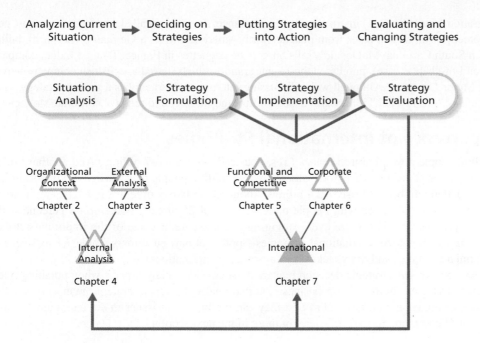

FIGURE 7.1

Strategic Management in Action

What exactly is an **international strategy**? It's a corporate strategy that describes companies that do business in multiple countries simultaneously. "Doing business" can involve the marketplace, people, or finances. Organizations are considered international if they exchange goods and services with consumers in other countries. They could also be considered international if they utilize managerial and technical employee talent from other countries. Finally, they can be considered international if they use resources and financial sources outside their own home country.

As noted in the last chapter, international strategy is a type of growth strategy and can be an important part of the strategic management in action process. (See Figure 7.1.) Businesses can pursue growth—that is, expand their activities or operations—in markets other than their domestic one. Or they can pursue any of the other growth strategies (concentration, vertical integration, horizontal

---

STRATEGIC MANAGEMENT IN ACTION

Mickey is headed to the Republic of India. The Walt Disney Company agreed to take a controlling interest in one of India's largest media and entertainment providers, UTV Software Communications Ltd. The chairman of Walt Disney International said, "UTV is the leading Indian movie studio and they have a very successful group of TV networks. This is about providing us with scale and a complementary set of brands and assets to help drive growth for the company." Disney already operated three TV channels in India and employed 200 people. That number of employees will now jump to more than 1,100.

- If you were on Disney's executive team, which of Disney's operations would you look to expand into India? (For instance: Disneyland, TV shows, movies, characters, etc.)

Sources: Based on E. Orden, "Disney Agrees to Acquire Indian Broadcaster, Film Studio," *Wall Street Journal*, February 1, 2012, p. B3; M. Garrahan, "Disney Completes Acquisition of India's UTV," *FT Online* [www.ft.com], January 31, 2012; and R. Golum, "Disney to Acquire Control of India's UTV Film and TV Producer," *Bloomberg Online* [www.bloomberg.com], January 31, 2012.

THINK ABOUT

- Why do you think Disney chose to invest in India?
- What challenges do you think Disney might encounter in doing business in India?

integration, diversification) internationally. For instance, Avon, a so-called American company, gets 79 percent of its annual sales from outside North America. BMW, a German-owned firm, builds cars in South Carolina. McDonald's sells burgers on baguettes in France. Tata, an Indian company (see end-of-chapter case), purchased the Jaguar brand—which started as a British company—from Ford Motor Company. Although we're discussing international strategy as a growth strategy, once a company "goes global," it may also have to utilize the stability and renewal corporate strategies.

Importance of International Strategies

7 billion people now inhabit the earth. (Yes, you read that right—7 billion.) And another billion people will be added by 2024. Today, there are 893 million people over the age of 60 worldwide. By 2050, that number will rise to 2.4 billion. About one in two people live in a city, and in about 35 years, two out of three will. People under the age of 25 already make up 43 percent of the world's population.[5] Those are eye-opening numbers and reflect one of the important reasons why companies pursue international strategies—potential new customers. Table 7.1 lists several potential advantages and drawbacks when a firm goes international.

As you can see, strategic decision makers must consider many aspects when pursuing international strategies. Before doing business internationally, however, strategic managers need to explore, examine, and understand as best they can the important issues in the international environment. We're going to look at several of these in the next section.

LEARNING REVIEW LEARNING OUTCOME 7.1

- Explain international strategy.
- Describe the possible advantages of being international.
- Describe the potential drawbacks of being international.

TABLE 7.1 **Potential Advantages and Drawbacks of Being International**

ADVANTAGES:
- Interdependencies among multiple countries can be exploited
- Way to learn more about a particular market or world region
- Strategically locate for tax benefits and regulations
- Potentially lower operational costs
- Way to supplement or strengthen domestic growth
- Can lead to achieving benefits of economies of scale
- Become a stronger competitor, both domestically and internationally

DRAWBACKS:
- Protectionism, especially in scenarios with continued high unemployment and economic malaise
- Disruptions in supply times/supply chains
- Quality issues
- Differences in language, culture, and value systems
- Ethnic, religious, and cultural tensions
- Disruptive changes such as terrorist attacks, natural disasters, disease outbreaks
- Financial and economic risks
- More complex and challenging process of managing strategically
- Difficulty in finding similarities in markets or operational capabilities
- Difficulty in capturing and exploiting advantages
- Increased global competition for jobs, markets, and talents
- Greater need for cross-cultural understanding and savvy

For five weeks in June and July of 2011, the entire senior leadership team at Starwood Hotels relocated to Shanghai, China. Why? Because clearly China is a huge growth market and "working closely with people from a different culture helps you to see pitfalls and opportunities in a very different way."[6] We can't forget that international strategy *is* part of the strategic management process. As such, there will be opportunities and threats to consider. And, just like we saw in our study of opportunities and threats back in Chapter 3, international Os and Ts arise in the external environment, especially in the legal-political, economic, and cultural areas. So let's look at each component.

LEARNING OUTCOME 7.2

Explain the Issues That Arise As Organizations Go International

The Legal-Political Environment

The legal-political environment in the United States is stable. Changes are slow, and legal and political procedures are well established. The laws governing the actions of individuals and institutions are fairly stable. The same can't be said for all countries. Various assessments of global political risk categorizes countries into different stability categories. Some countries on the maximum political stability list included Australia, Germany, Japan, and the United States. Some countries on the low political stability list included Pakistan, Nigeria, Iran, and Venezuela.[7] Organizations wanting to do business in countries with low stability levels face greater uncertainty and strategic threats as a result of that instability. But even in countries with fairly stable political-legal environments, the fact that those environments differ is reason enough to understand the constraints and opportunities that exist.

As we discussed in Chapter 3, if your organization is doing business in another country, you'll want to know the relevant laws and regulations. You'll also want to stay informed of any political changes as far as who or what political party is in power and the likelihood that new laws and regulations might be enacted.

The Economic Environment

Strange as it may sound, 17,000 tons of Parmesan cheese, with an estimated value of $187 million, are held in the vaults of Italian bank Credito Emiliano. The cheese is collateral from Italian cheese makers struggling through the recession.[8] Such an example of an economic factor of business may seem peculiar for those of us in the United States, but it's not all that unusual for Italian businesses.

STRATEGIC MANAGEMENT IN ACTION

BP could have warned Exxon about the challenges of doing business in Russia. During its long involvement in the country, BP has "had so many police run-ins that its stock price often nudges up or down in response to raids or the arrests of employees." However, almost a quarter of BP's output comes from Russian oil and natural gas, so the company has learned to live with the disruptions. Recently, not long after Exxon formed a strategic alliance with Russia's state-owned oil company, armed commandos raided BP's offices in "one of the ritual armed searches of white-collar premises that are common here." These incidents are so common that they've been "given a nickname: masky shows (so-called because of the balaclavas—ski masks—the agents often wear). The episode was sure to "send a signal that when it comes to dealing with the state-run business world of Prime Minister Vladimir V. Putin, Exxon wasn't in Texas anymore."

THINK ABOUT

• What's your reaction to this?
• If you were the person in charge of the Russian Exxon office, what would you tell your employees?

Sources: W. Mauldin, "Russians Search BP Office Second Day," *Wall Street Journal,* September 2, 2011, p. B6; and A. E. Kramer, "Memo to Exxon: Business With Russia Might Involve Guns and Balaclavas," *New York Times Online,* August 31, 2011.

FOR YOUR INFORMATION
Global Trade

One important feature of today's global environment is global trade, which today is being shaped by regional trading alliances. These trade alliances have developed because member countries believe it's in their best interests economically and globally to band together and strengthen their economic position. You should know about several important regional trade alliances.

First, the **European Union (EU)** is an economic and political partnership of 27 democratic European countries. Eight countries are currently seeking membership in the EU. The last couple of years have been difficult economically for the EU and its members, like it was for many global regions. "The traditional concept of 'solidarity' is being undermined by protectionist pressures in some member countries and the rigors of maintaining a common currency for a region that has diverse economic needs." Some analysts believe the EU is at a pivotal point. "They can spur growth across the region by following through on long-overdue pledges to trim benefits and free up labor markets. Or they can face a decade of economic stagnation."

Next is the **North American Free Trade Agreement (NAFTA),** an agreement on key economic and trade issues by the Mexican, Canadian, and U.S. governments. This trade bloc remains the largest in the world in terms of combined GDP of its members and is a powerful force in today's economy. Other Latin American trade alliances include the U.S.–Central America Free Trade Agreement, Southern Common Market (Mercosur), and other smaller ones.

The **Association of Southeast Asian Nations (ASEAN)** is a trading alliance of 10 Southeast Asian nations. Although Southeast Asian leaders agree that closer regional integration would help economic growth, the large differences in wealth among ASEAN members have made it "difficult to create common standards because national standards remain so far apart." However, the challenges brought on by the latest worldwide recession, which adversely affected many countries in this region, triggered greater interest in pushing for integration. In fact, on January 1, 2010, China and ASEAN launched an ambitious free trade agreement, making it the world's third largest trade bloc.

Finally, other trade alliances include the 53-nation African Union (AU), the East African Community (EAC), and the South Asian Association for Regional Cooperation (SAARC). Their goal, like all the other regional trade alliances, is to allow free flow of goods and services.

THINK ABOUT

- What benefits do these regional trade alliances have for businesses in these countries?
- What drawbacks might these regional trade alliances have for these businesses?
- How do regional trade alliances make businesses more globally competitive?

Sources: Based on "Times Topics: European Union," *New York Times Online,* January 23, 2012; J. Bhatti and N. Apostolou, "In Europe, Economic Meltdown Tears At Unity," *USA Today,* October 12, 2011, p. 1A+; M. Walker and A. Galloni, "Europe's Choice: Growth or Safety Net," *Wall Street Journal,* March 26, 2010, p. A1; "Asia's Never-Closer Union," *Economist,* February 6, 2010, p. 48; "East Asia Summit: Regional Unity Decades Away," *Business Monitor International* [www.asia-monitor.com], 2009/2010; "China-ASEAN FTA: Winners and Losers," *China & North East Asia,* February 2010, p. 2S; and Erlanger and S. Castle, "Growing Economic Crisis Threatens the Idea of One Europe," *New York Times Online,* March 2, 2009.

Strategic decision makers must be aware of economic issues when doing business in other countries. First, it's important to understand a country's type of economic system. The two major types are a free market economy and a planned economy. A **free market economy** is one in which resources are primarily owned and controlled by the private sector. A **planned economy** is one in which economic decisions are planned by a central government. Actually, no economy is purely free market or planned. For instance, the United States and United Kingdom are toward the free market end of the spectrum but do have governmental intervention and controls. The economies of Vietnam and North Korea are more planned. China is also a more planned economy, but until recently had been moving toward being more free market. Other economic issues that could affect strategic decisions include currency exchange rates, inflation rates, and diverse tax policies.

When an organization is doing business internationally, its profits can vary dramatically depending on the strength of its home currency and the currencies of the countries in which it operates. For instance, prior to the overall global economic slowdown, the rising value of the euro against both the dollar and the yen had contributed to strong profits for German companies.[9] Any currency exchange revaluations can affect managers' decisions and the level of a company's profits.

STRATEGIC MANAGEMENT IN ACTION

"China's economic growth and upwardly mobile population of 1.3 billion have been irresistible lures for Western companies." But as many have discovered, those opportunities also involve threats. For instance, Yum Brands Inc.'s KFC and Pizza Hut casual-dining chains are thriving in the country. However, the company is struggling to balance its strategy of low-price appeal with the reality of surging labor and food costs. Yum had to raise its menu prices by 2 percent, and the company said it would have to continue to raise prices until costs caught up with inflation or inflation slowed.

- Go to Yum Brands Web site [**www.yum.com**] to find information about its global strategies. Summarize what the company is doing.

Sources: Based on K. Chu, "Yum Brands CEO Takes Global View on Fast Food," *USA Today,* February 27, 2012, p. 2B;D. E. Bell and M. L. Shelman, "KFC's Radical Approach to China," *Harvard Business Review,* November 2011, pp. 137–142; A. Gasparro, "China's Lure Has Dark Side," *Wall Street Journal,* October 6, 2011, p. B1; and C. R. Schoenberger and D. McMahon, "The Corporate Shuffle," *Wall Street Journal,* June 2, 2011, p. C10.

THINK ABOUT AND TO DO

- What other industries in China might be affected by surging labor and food costs?

Inflation means that prices for products and services are increasing. But it also affects interest rates, exchange rates, the cost of living, and the general confidence in a country's political and economic system. Country inflation rates can, and do, vary widely. The *World Factbook* shows rates ranging from a negative 1.10 percent in the Faroe Islands to a positive 40.9 percent in Belarus.[10] Strategic decision makers need to monitor inflation trends so they can anticipate possible changes in a country's monetary policies and make good business decisions regarding purchasing and pricing.

Finally, tax policies can be a major economic worry. Some countries' tax laws are more restrictive than those in a business's home country. Others are more lenient. About the only certainty is that they differ from country to country. Decision makers need accurate information on tax rules in countries in which they operate to strategically manage their business's overall tax obligation.

The Cultural Environment

McDonald's, the king of fast foods, is offering couples in Hong Kong a unique experience—a wedding package with all the fixings: themed invitations and decorations, McDonaldland character party favors, and burgers and fries served tableside.[11] And then the happy couple can continue celebrating their McWedding with a wedding cake made out of apple pies. Yes, couples can celebrate their nuptials in traditional fashion with up to 100 people in a McDonald's. Now that definitely would be a unique cultural experience!

Although legal, political, and economic differences among countries are fairly obvious, cultural differences often aren't as easy to see. For instance, when a large global oil company found that employee productivity in one of its Mexican plants was down 20 percent, it sent a manager to find out why. After talking to several employees, the manager found out that the company used to have a monthly fiesta in the parking lot for all the employees and their families. Another manager had canceled the fiestas saying they were a waste of time and money. The message employees were getting was that the company didn't care about their families anymore. When the fiestas were reinstated, productivity and employee morale soared.[12] As this example points out, it's important that strategic decision makers understand **national culture,** which is the values and attitudes shared by individuals from a specific country that shape their behavior and their beliefs about what is important. The FYI box "Understanding National Culture" describes two frameworks for assessing a country's culture. When cultural differences exist between countries in which an organization does business, it could affect what strategies are used and how that organization is managed.

FOR YOUR INFORMATION
Understanding National Culture

One of the most widely used approaches for understanding national culture was developed by Geert Hofstede. His research focuses on five dimensions of a country's culture: individualism versus collectivism (degree to which people in a country prefer to act as individuals or as members of groups), power distance (measure of the extent to which a society accepts that power in institutions and organizations is distributed unequally), uncertainty avoidance (degree to which people tolerate risk and prefer structured over unstructured situations), achievement versus nurturing (degree to which a country values assertiveness and competitiveness versus relationships and concern for others), and long-term versus short-term orientation (measure of a country's orientation toward life and work). For instance, using these five dimensions, the national culture of the United States is characterized as individualistic, small power distance, low uncertainty avoidance, strong achievement, and short-term orientation. On the other hand, the national culture of Japan is characterized as collectivistic, large power distance, high uncertainty avoidance, strong achievement, and long-term orientation.

Another framework for understanding national culture comes from the Global Leadership and Organizational Behavior Effectiveness (GLOBE) research project, an ongoing investigation of cross-cultural leadership behaviors that focuses more on the managerial and leadership implications of cultural differences. It uses many of the same dimensions as identified by Hofstede but expands the cultural analysis to nine dimensions including assertiveness, future orientation, gender differentiation, uncertainty avoidance, power distance, individualism/collectivism, in-group collectivism, performance orientation, and humane orientation. Details from the GLOBE findings appear to be most useful to managers who want to be effective leaders. Why might these approaches to understanding national culture be important to strategic decision makers?

Sources: Based on J. S. Chhokar, Felix C. Brodbeck, and R. J. House (eds.), *Culture and Leadership Across the World: The GLOBE Book of In-Depth Studies of 25 Societies* (Mahwah, NJ: Lawrence Erlbaum Associates, 2007); R. T. Moran, P. R. Harris, and S. V. Moran, *Managing Cultural Differences: Global Leadership Strategies for the 21st Century,* 7th ed. (Oxford, UK: Elsevier, 2007); R. J. House, P. J. Hanges, M. Javidan, P. W. Dorfman, and V. Gupta, *Culture, Leadership, and Organizations: The GLOBE Study of 62 Societies* (Thousand Oaks, CA: Sage, 2004); and G. Hofstede, *Culture's Consequences: International Differences in Work-Related Values,* 2nd ed. (Thousand Oaks, CA: Sage, 2001).

Once strategic managers are familiar with the opportunities and threats found in the various components of the international environment, they can begin to look at strategies for doing business internationally.

LEARNING REVIEW   LEARNING OUTCOME 7.2

- What aspects of the legal-political environment do strategic decision makers need to examine?
- What economic issues might affect a company's international strategy?
- Discuss why it's important to understand national culture.

LEARNING OUTCOME 7.3

Describe the Important International Strategy Alternatives and Explain How They Are Implemented and Evaluated

McDonald's Corporation, the world's largest fast-food company, added rice burgers—fried beef slices served between two pressed rice cakes—to its menu in Singapore to appeal to local palates.[13] This example illustrates one of the first important strategic decisions that must be made: A multicountry approach or a global approach?[14] After we've discussed this, we'll look at different international strategy alternatives.

Multicountry Approach versus Global Approach

A multicountry approach is one in which an organization's strategies vary according to the countries in which it does business. This approach is based on developing a differentiation advantage. Products are tailored to fit consumer tastes and preferences. Marketing and distribution are

FOR YOUR INFORMATION
Globalization—Glocalization—Grobalization

Disney's theme park in Paris, initially called Euro Disney, was a financial disaster. "The mistake that Disney made was to use its traditional method to force-feed its U.S. products...to local cultures." Recognizing its mistakes, the park was changed to one in which local preferences were incorporated and renamed Disneyland Paris. Is this the appropriate strategy for all situations? Think about this: "Most companies' global strategies have been based on a vision of a world that's steadily, even rapidly, becoming more integrated, where the key challenge is keeping up with that integration. But given what we've witnessed recently, it makes more sense to adopt a vision in which national differences remain pronounced (and may become even more so), and managing those differences is the primary challenge."

As today's companies look for the best international strategy, decision makers are essentially choosing how to balance global scale and local adaptation. It's never an easy choice. To give you an elementary understanding of the tradeoffs, let's look at what international strategy researchers have called globalization, glocalization, and grobalization. Here's a quick summary description of each:

Globalization: Often described as a multidimensional phenomenon (economic, cultural, and political), globalization is seen as a way to eliminate borders of all kinds and to become more interconnected. Globalization offers organizations the opportunity to standardize, centralize, and integrate activities and functions.

Glocalization: Glocalization focuses on the uniqueness and differences in areas of the world and offers organizations the opportunity to specialize and tailor activities and functions to each market. Think: local responsiveness.

Grobalization: This concept, which came out of sociology, can best be understood as glocalization "to the extreme." It's when corporations "impose themselves on various

geographic areas" and has been described as "imperialistic." In this view, a business retains centralized control although the market experience is tailored to local cultural norms.

The challenge for all organizations wanting to do business internationally is the same: how to balance local adaptation and global scale, scope, and coordination. Tackling that challenge involves decisions about appropriate corporate, competitive, and functional strategies; and then decisions about fundamental structural and operating approaches.

THINK ABOUT

- What is the importance of these concepts for the strategic management process?
- What are some of the challenges that today's organizations have to think about in developing a successful international strategy?

Sources: R. Alcadipani and A. R. Rosa, "From Grobal Management to Glocal Management: Latin American Perspectives as a Counter-Dominant Management Epistemology," *Canadian Journal of Administrative Sciences,* December 2011, pp. 453–466; J. Matusitz, "Disney's Successful Adaptation in Hong Kong: A Glocalization Perspective," *Asia Pacific Journal of Management,* December 2011, pp. 667–681; N. Kumar and P. Puranam, "Have You Restructured for Global Success," *Harvard Business Review,* October 2011, pp. 123–128; M. Dewhurst, J. Harris, and S. Heywood, "Understanding Your 'Globalization' Penalty," *McKinsey Quarterly,* Issue 3, 2011, pp. 12–15; M. Voronov, D. DeClercq, and C. R. (Bob) Hinings, "Grobalization, Glocalization and Theorization in the Ontario Wine Industry," *Academy of Management Annual Meeting Proceedings,* 2011, pp. 1–6; M. Hoogenboom, D. Bannink, and W. Trommel, "From Local to Grobal, and Back," *Business History,* October 2010, pp. 932–954; J. Matusitz, "Disneyland Paris: A Case Analysis Demonstrating How Glocalization Works," *Journal of Strategic Marketing,* June 2010, pp. 223–237; and P. Ghemawat, "Finding Your Strategy in the New Landscape," *Harvard Business Review,* March 2010, pp. 54–60.

adapted to local customs and cultures. Competitive actions are chosen to fit the unique circumstances of the market. Such local responsiveness is important when significant country-to-country differences exist. Although there may be some sharing of organizational capabilities and competencies, that's not the goal of the multicountry approach. On the other hand, the global approach is one in which the strategies are basically the same in all countries in which the organization does business. This approach is designed to help develop a low-cost advantage. There's more of an emphasis on globally integrating operations rather than on local market responsiveness. Products may have minor variations, but this approach emphasizes coordination between functions and business units and more sharing of capabilities, competencies, and technologies across those functions and units.

International Strategy Alternatives

When organizations do go international, they often use different strategies. (See Figure 7.2.) Managers who want to get into a global market with minimal investment may start with **global sourcing** (also called global outsourcing), which is purchasing materials or labor from around the world wherever it is cheapest. The goal: Take advantage of lower costs in order to be more competitive. For instance, Massachusetts General Hospital uses radiologists in India to interpret CT scans.[15] Although global sourcing may be the first step to going international for many companies, they often continue to use this approach because of the competitive advantages it offers. Each successive stage of going international beyond global sourcing, however, requires more investment and thus entails more risk for the organization.

The next step in going international may involve **exporting** the organization's products to other countries—that is, making products domestically and selling them abroad. In addition, an organization might do **importing,** which involves acquiring products made abroad and selling them domestically. Both usually entail minimal investment and risk, which is why many small businesses often use these approaches to doing business globally.

Managers also might use **licensing** or **franchising,** which are similar approaches involving one organization giving another organization the right to use its brand name, technology, or product specifications in return for a lump sum payment or a fee usually based on sales. The only difference is that licensing is primarily used by manufacturing organizations that make or sell another company's products and franchising is primarily used by service organizations that want to use another company's name and operating methods. For example, Chicago consumers can enjoy Guatemalan Pollo Campero fried chicken, South Koreans can indulge in Dunkin' Brands' coffee, Hong Kong residents can dine on Shakey's Pizza, and Malaysians can consume Schlotzky's deli sandwiches—all because of *franchises* in these countries. On the other hand, Anheuser-Busch InBev has *licensed* the right to brew and market its Budweiser beer to brewers such as Kirin in Japan and Crown Beers in India.

When an organization has been doing business internationally for a while and has gained experience in international markets, managers may decide to make more of a direct foreign investment. One way to increase investment is through a strategic alliance, which we discussed in the previous chapter as a partnership between an organization and a company partner or partners—this time, a foreign company—in which both share resources and knowledge in developing new products or building production facilities. For example, Honda Motor and General Electric teamed up to produce a new jet engine. A specific type of strategic alliance in which the partners form a separate, independent organization for some business purpose is called a joint venture. For example, Hewlett-Packard has had numerous joint ventures with various suppliers around the globe to develop different components for its computer equipment. These partnerships provide a relatively easy way for companies to compete globally.

Finally, managers may choose to directly invest in a foreign country by setting up a **foreign subsidiary** as a separate and independent facility or office. This subsidiary can be managed as a

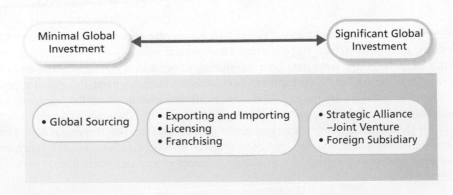

FIGURE 7.2

International Strategy
Alternatives

THE GREY ZONE

Workers' rights. It's not something we often think about when we're purchasing the latest tech gadget. However, look at this list of some issues that investigations have uncovered: work shifts lasting up to 60 hours; factory explosion killing numerous workers that resulted from a buildup of combustible dust; repetitive motion injuries that are so bad workers lose the use of their hands. "According to recent press reports, that's what work is like for assembly workers in China who build Apple's iPhones, iPads, and iPods." In other locations where workers are assembling products for other tech companies, factory workers have committed suicide because of the pressure and stress.

THINK ABOUT

- Whose responsibility is it to ensure that workplaces are safe, especially when work is outsourced? Discuss.

- "It's a tricky dance between first-world brands and third-world production." What do you think this statement means?

- Should ethical/corporate responsibility issues be part of the international strategy decision-making process? Why or why not?

Sources: S. Deffree, "Foxconn Explosion Ignites Conversation on Corporate Responsibility," *EDN,* June 23, 2011, p. 8; J. Bussey, "Measuring the Human Cost of an iPad Made in China," *Wall Street Journal,* June 3, 2011, pp. B1+; A. Satariano, "Apple Risks iPad Production Loss of 500,000 After Blast," *Bloomberg BusinessWeek,* May 26, 2011; and E. Savitz, "Apple: Analysts See Limited Risks From Hon Hai Plant Explosion," *Forbes.com,* May 23, 2011, p. 4.

multidomestic organization (local control) or as a global organization (centralized control). As you can probably guess, this arrangement involves the greatest commitment of resources and poses the greatest amount of risk. For instance, United Plastics Group of Westmont, Illinois, built two injection-molding facilities in Suzhou, China. The company's executive vice president for business development said that level of investment was necessary because "it fulfilled our mission of being a global supplier to our global accounts."[16]

Implementing and Evaluating International Strategies

Daimler, Nissan Motor, and Renault are part of a strategic partnership that is sharing small-car technology and power trains—an arrangement that all three automakers say will allow them to better compete in an environment where cutting costs is crucial. Until he moved to Japan, Arturo Vega, a Spanish-language teacher, had no idea that the Sofyl brand of yogurt he always bought in his native Mexico was actually made by a Japanese company called Yakult Honsha. Reckitt Benckiser, the U.K.-based maker of consumer products (Lysol, Woolite, and French's mustard are just a few of its products), has operations in more than 60 countries and its top 400 managers represent 53 different nationalities. The Missouri State Employees' Retirement System pays retirement benefits to recipients in 20 countries outside the United States.[17] As these examples show, organizations in different industries and from different countries do business globally. But *how* do they do so?

Structuring International Organizations

One major implementation decision by strategic decision makers is how to structure their international organization. There's not a generally accepted approach to describe the different types of international companies; different authors have called them different things. We use the terms *multinational, multidomestic, global,* and *transnational.*[18] A **multinational corporation (MNC)** is any type of international company that maintains operations in multiple countries.

One type of MNC is a **multidomestic corporation,** which decentralizes management and other decisions to the local country. A multidomestic corporation doesn't attempt to replicate its domestic successes by managing foreign operations from its home country. Instead, local employees typically are hired to manage the business and marketing strategies are tailored to that country's unique characteristics. For example, Switzerland-based Nestlé is a multidomestic corporation. With operations in almost every country on the globe, its managers match the company's products to its consumers. In parts of Europe, Nestlé sells products not available in the United States or Latin America. Another example is Frito-Lay, a division of PepsiCo, which markets a Dorito chip in the British market that differs in both taste and texture from the U.S. and Canadian version. Even the king of retailing, Walmart Stores, has learned that it must "think locally to act globally" as it tailors its inventories and store formats to local tastes.[19] Many consumer product companies organize their global businesses using this approach because they must adapt their products to meet the needs of local markets.

Another type of MNC is a **global company,** which centralizes its management and other decisions in the home country. Global companies treat the world market as an integrated whole and focus on the need for global efficiency and cost savings. Although these companies may have considerable global holdings, management decisions with company-wide implications are made from headquarters in the home country. Some examples of global companies include Sony, Deutsche Bank AG, Starwood Hotels, and Merrill Lynch.

Other companies use an arrangement that eliminates artificial geographical barriers. This type of MNC is often called a **transnational, or borderless, organization.**[20] For example, IBM dropped its organizational structure based on country and reorganized into industry groups. Ford Motor Company is pursuing what it calls the One Ford concept as it integrates its operations around the world. Another company, Thomson SA, which is legally based in France, has eight major locations around the globe. The CEO said, "We don't want people to think we're based anyplace."[21] Managers choose this approach to increase efficiency and effectiveness in a competitive global marketplace.[22]

Other International Strategy Implementation and Evaluation Decisions

In addition to the structural decision, international companies must address implementation issues that concern various aspects of its functional and competitive strategies. As we discussed in Chapter 5, for the functional strategies, this encompasses production/operations, marketing, human resources, information systems, and financial-accounting systems and determining what approaches will allow the company to effectively and efficiently do its business. An international

---

STRATEGIC MANAGEMENT IN ACTION

Ford Motor Company unveiled a new SUV that showcases the company's new "world car strategy." The 2012 Escape is made from a common set of parts and components that Ford will use to make its Focus compact car, two future minivans, and at least six other models. Those same components will be found in vehicles assembled and sold in North and South America, Europe, and Asia. By mid-2012, Ford hoped to be "producing more than two million vehicles a year around the globe that are all made from the same basic parts and assembled in plants that use the same type of tooling." Why was this strategy so important to CEO Alan Mulally? Because it allows the company to leverage design and manufacturing economies of scale and get huge savings from its $50 billion annual budget for auto parts.

TO DO

- Go to Ford's Web site **[corporate.ford.com]**.
  Summarize any information you can find about Ford's "global" strategy.

Sources: M. Ramsey, "Ford SUV Marks New World Car Strategy," *Wall Street Journal,* November 16, 2011, p. B1+; E. Hughes-Cromwick, "Ford Motor Company's Global Electrification Strategy," *Business Economics,* September 2011, pp. 167–170; B. Vlasic, "Ford Strategy Will Call for Stepping Up Expansion, Especially in Asia," *New York Times Online,* June 7, 2011; and B. Pope, "Ford Advances Global Purchasing Strategy," *Ward's Auto World,* July 2008, pp. 36–38.

business will also need to determine which competitive strategy is most appropriate given the realities of the competitive environment it faces. Most likely, this decision will consider the emphasis given to low costs, differentiation, or both.

Finally, like any of an organization's corporate strategies, if the international strategy(ies) aren't resulting in desired performance levels, something needs to be done. An evaluation of an organization's international strategy is best done using an approach that provides strategic decision makers with the best information. Whether it relies on an assessment of whether corporate goals have been met, benchmarking, efficiency/effectiveness/productivity analysis, or portfolio analysis, an organization's international strategy should be assessed and changed if, and as, needed.

LEARNING REVIEW   LEARNING OUTCOME 7.3

- Contrast the multicountry and the global approaches.
- What are the five international strategy alternatives?
- Explain how international organizations might be structured.
- Describe other international strategy implementation and evaluation decisions.

The Bottom Line

Learning Outcome 7.1: Describe international strategy and why it's important.

- An international strategy is a corporate strategy that describes companies that do business in multiple countries simultaneously.
- International strategy is important because of the potential advantages it offers. These include exploiting interdependencies among multiple countries, learning more about a particular market or world region, strategically locating for tax benefits and regulations, lowering operational costs, supplementing or strengthening domestic growth, achieving benefits of economies of scale, and becoming a stronger competitor. However, there are drawbacks to the international strategy. These include protectionism, disruptions in supply times and supply chains, quality issues, differences in language/culture/value systems, ethnic/religious/cultural tensions, disruptive changes, financial and economic risks, more complex and challenging process of managing strategically, difficulty in finding similarities in markets or operational capabilities, difficulty in capturing and exploiting advantages, increased global competition for jobs/markets/talents, and greater need for cross-cultural understanding and savvy.

Learning Outcome 7.2: Explain the issues that arise as organizations go international.

- Strategic decision makers should know about the legal-political environment (laws and regulations and political stability), the economic environment (currency exchange rates, inflation rates, and tax policies), and the cultural environment (the *national culture:* the values and attitudes shared by individuals from a specific country that shape their behavior and their beliefs).

Learning Outcome 7.3: Describe the important international strategic decisions and explain how they're implemented and evaluated.

- One strategic decision is whether to use a multicountry (strategies vary across the countries where an organization does business) or global approach (strategies are basically the same in all countries where an organization does business).
- Five international strategy alternatives include (1) global sourcing—purchasing materials or labor form around the world wherever it is cheapest, (2) exporting—making products in the home country and transporting them for sale to other countries and importing—selling products made in another country in the home country, (3) licensing—an arrangement in which a foreign licensee buys the right to manufacture and market a company's product in that country for a fee, (4) franchising—an arrangement in which a business sells franchisees in other countries limited rights to use its brand name in return for a lump-sum payment and share of profits, and (5) direct investment—when an organization owns or controls assets in another country usually through a strategic alliance, joint venture, or foreign subsidiary.

as strategic decision maker: building your skills

1. Using current business periodicals, find examples of the ethnocentric, polycentric, and geocentric attitudes toward global business.

2. The U.K.-based company, Kwintessential, has several cultural knowledge "quizzes" on its Web site [**http://www.kwintessential.co.uk/resources/culture-tests.html**]. Go to the Web site and try two or three of them. Were you surprised at your scores? What do your scores tell you about your cultural awareness?

3. On this Web site, you'll also find Country Etiquette Guides. Pick two countries to study (from different regions) and compare them. How are they the same? Different? How would this information help a strategic decision maker?

4. Interview two or three professors or students at your school who are from other countries. Ask them to describe what the business world is like in their country. Write a short paper summarizing what you found out.

5. Suppose you were being sent on an overseas assignment to another country (you decide which one). Research that country's economic, political/legal, and cultural environments. Write a report summarizing your findings.

CASES

CASE #1 Fast Fashion

Colin Sinclair © Dorling Kindersley

This Strategic Management in Action case can be found at the beginning of Chapter 7.

Discussion Questions

1. Look back to Chapter 2 at Figure 2.3. Describe the context facing Zara. Focus especially on describing the driving forces that are affecting the fashion industry and the implications of these driving forces. Does Zara have what it takes to succeed in this context? Explain. What are the implications for its international strategy?

2. What examples of managing strategically do you see in this case?

3. What strategic challenges might Zara face as the company continues to compete internationally?

4. Which part of the strategic management process do you think might be most important to an international business such as Zara? Explain your answer.

CASE #2 Missed Call

Do you remember your first or even second mobile phone? Chances are it might have been one made by Finnish company, Nokia Corporation. Mine was. It was a beautiful steel blue color and was, I thought, pretty slick. Nokia phones back then were quite popular with consumers and positioned the company as one of the leading mobile phone makers. In 1998, Nokia sold more than 40 million mobile phones to surpass Motorola as the world's #1 mobile phone company. During this time period, Nokia was light years ahead of its rivals with digital phones. However, "Nokia was caught sleeping in 2007 when Apple Inc.'s iPhone redefined the cellphone as a PC-like device with a touch screen and sleek software." Since that crucial time, Nokia has lost 75 percent of its market value and is struggling to catch up to Apple and Google Inc.'s Android.

Despite its failure to recognize the market-changing characteristics of Apple's iPhone, Nokia is still the world's largest handset manufacturer by volume. Europe is the company's largest combined market, with about a third of sales. Somewhat surprisingly, China is Nokia's largest single-country market, accounting for nearly 20 percent of sales. And the United States accounts for only 4 percent of sales, and India (another important target) accounts for only 7 percent of sales. The company has been crafting strategies it hopes will help position it as a dominant force once again in this industry. New CEO Stephen Elop, the first non-Finnish leader and a former top Microsoft executive, pledged to turn around the struggling company.

CEO Elop's initial plans were aimed at streamlining its smartphone operations costs and speeding delivery of new products. He said, "Nokia has been characterized as an organization where it is too hard to get things done." More than anything else, the changing market dynamics demand that we must improve our ability to aggressively lead through changes in our environment." Getting its products to market faster would be a key failing that would have to be improved. In addition to the first

round of 1,800 jobs cut, Elom eliminated several senior officials on the company's group executive board. He also sent a memo to Nokia employees that compared the company's predicament in catching up to Apple and Google in smartphones to "that of a man who was standing on a burning oil rig at sea. Standing there, he needed to make a choice and he decided to jump." He went on to say that "Nokia, too, had to jump metaphorically—to take bold action to make up for lost ground." And bold actions it has taken.

In February 2011, Jo Harlow, the head of smart devices at Nokia, "stood before a packed convention hall at the Mobile World Congress, the cellphone industry's most important trade show, to explain the Finnish company's new software alliance with Microsoft." That agreement had been announced in London only a few days earlier. But, "the need for the deal had been so urgent that Nokia and Microsoft, grasping for a foothold in a mobile computing industry that was quickly slipping away from them, had gone public without a definitive legal agreement, just a handshake and a promise to work together, somehow." She told the audience that Nokia and Microsoft would produce their first phone using the Windows operating system by the end of the year—a pace two to three times faster than Nokia's past product introductions. Getting that done would "require an accelerated, effective collaboration with a completely different corporate culture in a creative endeavor so intimate that both would have to discard mutual distrust to make it work."

By mid-2011, Nokia had unveiled a new smartphone and three lower-priced handsets as initial steps in its transition to Microsoft software. Although analysts described the products as well-designed with an intuitive user interface, they also said the products would be unlikely to help improve the company's difficulties as there was no carrier support or apps developers. In early fall 2011, the company sold 2,000 wireless patents and patent applications to Ottawa, Canada-based Mosaid Technologies. Many technology companies are using this strategy to "essentially outsource the sometimes expensive process of squeezing revenue out of their patent holdings." In addition, the company announced another 3,500 job cuts by closing a factory in Romania and transferring production to more efficient plants in Asia. Elop said, "We are seeing solid progress against our strategy, and with these planned changes we will emerge as a more dynamic, nimble and efficient challenger."

Now, it's do-or-die for Nokia. One year after the announcement of the Microsoft alliance, the company's Nokia Lumia 900 smartphone was introduced at the Consumer Electronics Show in Las Vegas in February 2012. "The high-end device marks perhaps the company's last chance to re-establish itself as a serious player in the U.S." Will the market once again hang up on Nokia or will it take the call?

Discussion Questions

1. What international strategy advantages and drawbacks can you see in this case? Discuss.
2. What do you think are the difficulties in being a market-leading competitor trying to compete in so many different geographic areas? What resources and capabilities would such an organization need? What impact would the fact that the competitor's industry is a continually changing one have on its strategies?
3. What steps has Nokia's CEO taken to turn around his struggling company? Be specific.

4. One of the most interesting things to me about this story is the alliance between Nokia and Microsoft. How did this get done? What do you think that process entailed?
5. Update the information on Nokia: revenues, profits, market shares, products, etc. Have its strategies worked? Why or why not?

Sources: K. J. O'Brien, "One Year Later, Nokia and Microsoft Deliver," *New York Times Online,* February 27, 2012; C. Huston, "Nokia Corporation," *Hoover's Online,* February 26, 2012; C. Lawton, "Nokia Takes Aim at High-End U.S. Market," *Wall Street Journal,* January 10, 2012, p. B5; C. Lawton, "It's Crunch Time for Nokia," *Wall Street Journal,* October 25, 2011, p. B6; K. J. O'Brien, "Nokia to Cut 3,500 More Jobs," *New York Times Online,* September 29, 2011; C. Lawton, "Nokia's Troubles Hit Suppliers," *Wall Street Journal,* September 27, 2011, p. B8; C. Lawton, "Nokia Aims Software At Low-End Phones," *Wall Street Journal,* September 29, 2011, p. B11; B. Dummett, "Nokia Sells 2,000 Patents," *Wall Street Journal,* September 2, 2011, p. B2; C. Lawton and C. H. Wong, "Nokia Shows Off New Phones," *Wall Street Journal,* June 22, 2011, p. B6;C. Lawton, "Missed Call: Nokia Reversal of Fortune Is Also Finland's," *Wall Street Journal,* June 3, 2011, p. A12; C. Lawton, "Investors Hang Up on Nokia," *Wall Street Journal,* June 1, 2011, pp. B1+; S. Lohr, "Playing Catch-Up, Nokia and H.P. Try to Innovate," *New York Times Online,* February 9, 2011; J. S. Lublin and C. Lawton, "New CEO of Nokia Readies Shake-Up," *Wall Street Journal,* February 7, 2011, pp. B1+; G. Sandstrom and C. Lawton, "Nokia CEO Makes His Mark," *Wall Street Journal,* October 22, 2010, p. B3; and J. Ewing and C. Kharif, "Nokia Takes Aim at Apple," *Bloomberg BusinessWeek Online,* August 27, 2009.

CASE #3 Tata's Time

It holds the number 6 spot on the list of the world's most admired companies in the steel industry. The Tata Group, based in Mumbai, India, is the largest conglomerate in that country. Its latest revenues are estimated at $67.4 billion, of which 61 percent is from business outside India. Tata has more than 100 operating companies in seven main business groups doing business in 80 countries: chemicals, information systems and communications, consumer products, energy, engineering, materials, and services. Its two largest businesses are Tata Steel and Tata Motors. Its Tata Tea, which owns the valued Tetley brand, also is one of the largest tea producers in the world. Ratan Tata, Tata Group's chairperson, has forged a strategy that encompasses the globe. In 1999, he issued a "clarion call to push outside India with acquisitions and exports." One of the company's executive directors recalled, "We didn't know what to expect, to be honest."

Today, Tata controls many businesses ranging from Eight O'Clock Coffee Co. in the United Sates to the Taj Group of hotels, which took over management of the landmark Pierre Hotel on Central Park in New York City. Tata made its boldest global strategic push, however, in October 2006 when Tata Steel formally proposed buying British steelmaker Corus Group PLC for about $8 billion USD. Corus, which was formed by a merger of British Steel and Hoogovens, was three times the size of Tata Steel. The buyout offer soon turned into a bidding war when Tata Group discovered another company, Companhia Siderúrgica

Nacional of Brazil (CSN), was also preparing a bid and therefore upped its opening offer to $9.2 billion; CSN then raised the stakes by offering to pay $9.6 billion. A Tata Group spokesman said that the company's attempt to acquire Corus was "based on a compelling strategic rationale." Ratan Tata explained further by saying, "The revised terms deliver substantial additional value to Corus shareholders." The increased takeover bid did not impress investors as the company's share price fell 6 percent after the news was announced. Analysts and investors both "expressed concern that Tata is overpricing Corus, whose operating costs are among the highest of any steel maker—something that would affect its profitability and its plans to expand in India." However, Ratan Tata knew that the acquisition could catapult Tata Steel from its mid-50s ranking in the global steel list to the sixth-largest industry competitor. He said, "Analysts were taking a short-term, harsh view of the deal. Hopefully, the market will look back and say it was the right move." By the end of January 2007, the U.K. Takeover Panel called an auction in order to end the bidding war and "presided over the contest that started on Tuesday, January 30." The "contest" continued for several hours until CSN pulled out. Tata Steel won its coveted prize for $12.2 billion—a 22 percent premium over what it had originally offered. That acquisition represented the latest consolidation in the global steel industry. The combined Tata-Corus can produce 25 million tons of steel a year. The deal also represented the largest foreign acquisition by an Indian company and made the diversified Tata Group the largest company in India.

In 2008, Tata made an even bigger global splash, at least in terms of recognized consumer brand names. It acquired the Land Rover and Jaguar brands from Ford for an estimated $2.3 billion.

Tata's leaders believe the group "can survive on the world stage only by being both too big to beat and too good to fail." In December 2012, when Chairman Ratan Tata steps down, Cyrus Mistry will take over as chairman of Tata Group and he "faces the daunting challenge of steering a giant, increasingly multinational conglomerate of more than 100 companies through economic headwinds at home and abroad."

Discussion Questions

1. Discuss the advantages and drawbacks of going international using Tata Group's experiences.
2. What strategic challenges do you think Cyrus Mistry might face as he guides his company? Using what you know about managing strategically, how might he respond to these challenges?
3. Do some research on India's economic and political-legal environments. What opportunities and threats do you see?

In light of these, do you think Ratan Tata's strategy of pushing outside India makes sense? Explain.
4. Do some research on the Tata Group **[www.tata.com].** What is its purpose? How would its core values influence strategic choices? Does its international strategy approach seem to be working?
5. Do you think an international conglomerate would be more difficult or less difficult to strategically manage than a more focused company? Discuss.
6. What implications does the statement about "surviving on the world stage" have for the future strategies pursued by the Tata Group?

Sources: Based on Tata Group [www.tata.com], February 26, 2012; A. Sharma, "Tata's New Boss Faces Headwinds," *Wall Street Journal,* November 25, 2011, p. B1; A. Taylor III, "Tata Takes on the World," *Fortune,* May 2, 2011, pp. 86–92; G. Colvin, "The World's Most Admired Companies," *Fortune,* March, 21, 2011, pp. 109+; A. Graham, "Too Good to Fail," *Strategy + Business Online,* Spring 2010; and P. Wonacott and J. Singer, "Ratan Tata Builds Indian Behemoth Into Global Player," *Wall Street Journal,* October 7–8, 2006, pp. B1+.

CASE #4 Global Stumble

It's not always easy to do business globally, as executives at Japanese brokerage firm Nomura Holdings Inc. are discovering. Nomura acquired Lehman's international operations in late 2008 after Lehman's parent company sought Chapter 11 bankruptcy protection, an action that added about 8,000 non-Japanese workers. For Nomura, the time seemed right to strengthen its global expansion strategy. However, since the acquisition, cultural and business differences between the two organizations have been a major stumbling block. Although blending two diverse cultures requires intentional efforts when different organizations merge or are acquired, it's particularly challenging when key assets in the cross-border acquisition are the people employed by the organization being acquired.

Workplace tensions arose over executive compensation, how quickly decisions were made, and how women were treated. For instance, during Nomura's initial training session for new hires, the men and women were separated. The women—many of whom had earned prestigious degrees from the likes of Harvard—were taught how to wear their hair, serve tea, and choose their clothing according to the season. The company's dress code was strictly interpreted for women, also. Women from Lehman were told to remove highlights from their hair, to wear sleeves no shorter than mid-bicep, and to avoid brightly colored clothing. Several women were sent home from the trading floor for dressing "inappropriately." One said, "I was sent home for wearing a short-sleeve dress, even though I was wearing a jacket." A Nomura spokesperson said, "The dress code is displayed on the company's intranet and is intended to ensure that clients and colleagues don't feel uncomfortable."

Lehman bankers also said they found the process for getting approval on deals was "slower and more difficult than it was at Lehman." Also, at Lehman, clients were categorized, in large part, by the fees they paid. At Nomura, more emphasis was placed on other factors, such as the length of the relationship. The bankers at Nomura said that "their new colleagues were too willing to dump loyal clients for a quick profit."

In its defense, Nomura has tried to blend the two cultures. In offices in Europe and in Asia outside of Japan, there's a mix of nationalities. Also, the company has promoted a handful of non-Japanese employees to high-ranking positions. "To reduce the Tokyo-centric nature of the company, Hiromi Yamaji, head of global investment banking, moved to London, and Naoki Matsuba, global head of equities, moved to New York." Until March 2010, Nomura's executive committee was all Japanese men. However, in an attempt to make the company more globally oriented, an ex-Lehman executive and foreigner, Jasjit "Jesse" Bhattal, a native of India, was promoted to the committee. Nomura's deputy president and chief operating officer, Takumi Shibata, said, "When your business is global, management needs to be global." Two years later, unable to garner support from Tokyo for an overhaul of the global wholesale-banking operations, however, Bhattal recently resigned as Nomura's highest-ranking foreign executive.

Discussion Questions

1. What obvious cultural differences between Nomura and Lehman do you see in this situation?
2. What global attitude do you think characterizes Nomura? Be specific in your description. Do you see any evidence of that changing?

3. Do some cultural research on Japan and the United States. Compare those cultural characteristics. What similarities and differences exist? How might these cultural differences be affecting the situation at Nomura?
4. What could Nomura executives do to support, promote, and encourage cultural awareness among employees? Explain.
5. What do you think the statement, "When your business is global, management needs to be global," is saying? In your opinion, is Nomura doing this? Explain.
6. What do you think the resignation of Jesse Bhattal says about the international "strategy" of the company?

Sources: A. Tudor, "Global Finance: Nomura Banker Resigns Over Cuts," *Wall Street Journal,* January 2012, p. C3; "Nomura Hits Bumps in Road Less Travelled," *Euroweek,* November 18, 2011, p. 82; A. Tudor, "Bhattal's Goal; Keep Lehman Talent," *Wall Street Journal,* April 19, 2010, p. C5; A. Tudor, "Lehman Defections Continue at Nomura," *Wall Street Journal,* March 23, 2010, p. C5; A. Tudor, "Nomura Turns to a Foreigner from Lehman," *Wall Street Journal,* March 18, 2010, p. C1; A. Or, "More Quit Nomura as Bonuses Lapse," *Wall Street Journal,* March 12, 2010, p. C2; A. Rozens, "The Return of Nomura," *Investment Dealers' Digest,* February 12, 2010, p. 1+; "Nomura Set for Fight on All Fronts," *Euroweek,* December 4, 2009, p. 49; L. Peacock, untitled, *Personnel Today,* November 10, 2009, p. 25; and A. Tudor, "Nomura Stumbles in New Global Push," *Wall Street Journal,* July 29, 2009, pp. A1.

Answers to "Who Owns What" Quiz

1. **d. Switzerland**
   Nestlé SA bought both the Tombstone and DiGiorno frozen-pizza brands from Kraft Foods in 2009.
2. **c. United States**
   The maker of Lebedyansky juices was acquired by PepsiCo Inc. and Pepsi Bottling Group Inc. in March 2008.
3. **a. United States**
   Rajah Spices are products of the Lea & Perrins sauce division, which the H.J. Heinz Company acquired in June of 2005.
4. **b. India**
   Tetley Tea is owned by the Tata Tea Group, a subsidiary of Indian conglomerate Tata Group.
5. **d. China**
   Ford Motor Company sold the Volvo brand to Chinese car maker Zhejiang Geely Holding Group Co. in March 2010.
6. **a. The Netherlands**
   Mexico's second-largest beer producer was acquired by Heineken N.V. in January 2010.
7. **b. Mexico**
   Grupo Bimbo, one of the world's largest bakeries, bought the rights to make and distribute Boboli pizza crusts in 2002.
8. **c. United States**
   Braun electric shavers are a part of Global Gillette, which was purchased by the Procter & Gamble Company in October 2005.
9. **c. France**
   LVMH Moët Hennessy Louis Vuitton SA, the world's largest luxury-goods group, owns Sephora.
10. **d. South Korea**
    The Boston-based Barbarian Group was acquired by South Korea's largest advertising agency, Cheil Worldwide, in December 2009.
11. **c. Switzerland**
    Nestlé SA purchased the maker of Lean Cuisine frozen meals in 2002.
12. **a. Russia**
    Russian tycoon Alexander Lebedev acquired the *Independent* in March 2010.
13. **b. United Kingdom**
    French's mustard is a product of Reckitt-Benckiser.
14. **a. India**
    Tata Coffee, a division of Indian conglomerate Tata Group, purchased Eight O'Clock Coffee in 2006.
15. **b. United States**
    Consumer products giant Procter & Gamble purchased the luxury hair-care brand from a private equity firm in 2008.

Endnotes

1. Press Releases, "Inditex Achieves Net Sales of 9,709 Million Euros, An Increase of 10 percent," [www.inditex.com], February 22, 2012; C. Bjork, "'Cheap Chic' Apparel Sellers Heat Up U.S. Rivalry on Web," *Wall Street Journal,* September 6, 2011, pp. B1+; A. Kenna, "Zara Plays Catch-up With Online Shoppers," *Bloomberg BusinessWeek,* August 29–September 4, 2011, pp. 24–25; K. Girotra and S. Netessine, "How to Build Risk Into Your Business Model," *Harvard Business Review,* May 2011, pp. 100–105; M. Dart and R. Lewis, "Break the Rules the Way Zappos and Amazon Do," *Bloomberg BusinessWeek Online,* April 29, 2011; K. Cappell, "Zara Thrives by Breaking All the Rules," *BusinessWeek,* October 20, 2008, p. 66; and C. Rohwedder and K. Johnson, "Pace-Setting Zara Seeks More Speed to Fight Its Rising Cheap-Chic Rivals," *Wall Street Journal,* February 20, 2008, pp. B1+.

2. U. Auger, J. Chen, C. Ho, and A. Rowe, "Uncorking China's Wine Market," *Knowledge@Wharton,* [knowledge.wharton.upenn.edu], January 3, 2012; M. Halverson, "U.S. Now the Largest Wine Market in the World," *Press Democrat.com,* March 15, 2011; and Reuters, "U.S. Set to be Largest Wine Market—Study," *CNNMoney.com,* January 30, 2007.

3. The idea for this quiz was adapted from R. M. Hodgetts and F. Luthans, *International Management,* 2d ed. (New York: McGraw-Hill, 1994).

4. M. R. F. Kets De Vries and E. Florent-Treacy, "Global Leadership From A to Z: Creating High Commitment Organizations," *Organizational Dynamics,* Spring 2002, pp. 295–309; P. R. Harris and R. T. Moran, *Managing Cultural Differences,* 4th ed. (Houston: Gulf Publishing Co., 1996); R. T. Moran, P. R. Harris, and W. G. Stripp, *Developing the Global Organization: Strategies for Human Resource Professionals,* (Houston: Gulf Publishing Co., 1993); Y. Wind, S. P. Douglas, and H. V. Perlmutter, "Guidelines for Developing International Marketing Strategies," *Journal of Marketing,* April 1973, pp. 14–23; and H. V. Perlmutter, "The Tortuous Evolution of the Multinational Corporation," *Columbia Journal of World Business,* January–February 1969, pp. 9–18.

5. "World Population Clock Projection," U.S. Census Bureau, [www.census.gov], February 24, 2012; "Population Seven Billion: UN Sets Out Challenges," *BBC News World Online,* [www.bbc.co.uk], October 26, 2011; and "State of World Population 2011," *United Nations Population Fund,* [www.unfpa.org], 2011.

6. D. M. Airoldi, "Starwood Studies Abroad," *CFO,* September 2011, pp. 29-30; A. Sheivachman, "Starwood Puts Priority on Chinese Development," *Hotel Management,* August 1, 2011, p. 15; and A. Berzon, "Frits Van Paasschen: Starwood CEO Moves to China to Grow Brand," *Wall Street Journal,* June 6, 2011, p. B6.

7. A. Mortimer, "Country Risk September 2011: Past Defaults Offer Little Comfort to Troubled Eurozone," *Euromoney Online,* [www.euromoney.com], September 12, 2011; and I. Bremmer, "Managing Risk in an Unstable World," *Harvard Business Review,* June 2005, pp. 51–60.

8. "Leading Indicator," *Newsweek,* September 14, 2009, p. 14.

9. M. Landler, "Germany's Export-Led Economy Finds Global Niche," *New York Times Online,* April 13, 2007.

10. *CIA World Factbook* [https://www.cia.gov/library/publications/the-world-factbook/rankorder/2092rank.html], 2011.

11. "Introducing McWeddings," *Rachael Ray Magazine,* May 2011, p. 33; and "Best of the Blogs," *Caterer & Hotelkeeper,* April 22, 2011, p. 20.

12. T. Raphael, "Savvy Companies Build Bonds with Hispanic Employees," *Workforce,* September 2001, p. 19.

13. Reuters, "McDonald's Goes Local in Asia," *CNNMoney.com,* January 3, 2006.

14. P. Ghemawat, "Regional Strategies for Global Leadership," *Harvard Business Review,* December 2005, pp. 98–108; and P. Ghemawat, "The Forgotten Strategy," *Harvard Business Review,* November 2003, pp. 76–84.

15. B. Davis, "Migration of Skilled Jobs Abroad Unsettles Global-Economy Fans," *Wall Street Journal,* January 26, 2004, p. A1.

16. J. Teresko, "United Plastics Picks China's Silicon Valley," *Industry Week,* January 2003, p. 58.

17. D. Jolly, "Daimler, Nissan, and Renault Unveil Partnership," *New York Times Online,* April 7, 2010; M. Tanikawa, "Japanese Food Companies Seek Growth Abroad," *New York Times Online,* April 2, 2010; B. Becht, "Building a Company Without Borders," *Harvard Business Review,* April 2010, pp. 103–106; and "Statistical Information" [www.mosers.org], March 15, 2010.

18. C. A. Bartlett and S. Ghoshal, *Managing Across Borders: The Transnational Solution,* 2d ed. (Boston: Harvard Business School Press), 2002; and N. J. Adler, *International Dimensions of Organizational Behavior,* 4th ed. (Cincinnati, OH: South-Western, 2002), pp. 9–11.

19. M. Bustillo, "After Early Errors, Wal-Mart Thinks Locally to Act Globally," *Wall Street Journal,* August 14, 2009, pp. A1+.

20. P. F. Drucker, "The Global Economy and the Nation-State," *Foreign Affairs,* September–October, 1997, pp. 159–171.

21. P. Dvorak, "Why Multiple Headquarters Multiply," *Wall Street Journal,* November 19, 2007, pp. B1+.

22. B. Becht, "Building a Company Without Borders"; D. A. Aaker, *Developing Business Strategies,* 5th ed. (New York: John Wiley & Sons, 1998); and J.A. Byrne et al., "Borderless Management," *BusinessWeek,* May 23, 1994, pp. 24–26.

STRATEGIES FOR ENTREPRENEURIAL VENTURES AND SMALL BUSINESSES

In this section, we look at strategic management in entrepreneurial ventures and small businesses. Before we can do that, however, we need to know what these organizations are.

What Is an Entrepreneurial Venture, and What Is a Small Business?

Many people think entrepreneurial ventures and small businesses are the same, but they're not. The key differences are summarized in Table 1. Entrepreneurs create **entreprencurial ventures**—organizations that pursue opportunities, are characterized by innovative practices, and have growth and profitability as their main goals. On the other hand, a **small business** is an independent business having fewer than 500 employees that doesn't necessarily engage in any new or innovative practices and that has relatively little impact on its industry.[1] A small business isn't necessarily entrepreneurial because it's small; to be entrepreneurial means that the business is innovative and seeking out new opportunities. Even though entrepreneurial ventures may start small, they pursue growth. Some new small firms may grow, but many remain small businesses, by choice or by default.

Why Are These Types of Organizations Important?

Using any number of sources, you can find statistics on how many small businesses there are, how many workers they employ, and how much of the national economic output they're responsible for. For example, small businesses represent more than 99 percent of all employers, employ over half of all private workers, and account for 50 percent of the private sector output.[2] The importance of these organizations can be shown in three areas: job creation, new start-ups, and innovation.

Job Creation

How important are these organizations to job creation? Accepted "wisdom" based on statistics has been that small companies create more jobs.[3] However, newly released figures covering a time period from April 1990 through March 2011 are challenging that assumption.[4] The work of several economists suggests that most small businesses are not particularly good at creating jobs, or at least not the best jobs. What this research is finding is that businesses just getting off the ground contribute most of the job growth. Older small businesses tend to cut as many employees

TABLE 1 Characteristics of an Entrepreneurial Venture versus a Small Business

Entrepreneurial Venture	Small Business
• Innovative strategic practices	• Independently owned, operated, and financed
• Strategic goals are profitability and growth	• Fewer than 500 employees
• Seeks out new opportunities	• Doesn't emphasize new or innovative practices
• Willingness to take risks	• Little impact on industry

as they add. But this new research is also showing that small-company employment seems to have more stability in good times and bad. As one economist said, "If you want jobs, you have to focus on the innovative firms trying to provide something new and different."[5]

Number of New Start-ups

Entrepreneurship is important to every industry sector in the United States and in other global economies. People continue to start businesses, probably for a couple of reasons. First, continual changes in the external environment—competition, technology, consumer wants, and so forth—provide a fertile climate for entrepreneurial ventures because these organizations often are better able to respond quickly to changing conditions than larger, more bureaucratic, and less flexible organizations. Also, many of the cost advantages that large organizations traditionally had because of their size (economies of scale) have been eroded by technological advances. This means that smaller organizations can compete against larger ones and aren't at a disadvantage because of their small size.

How many new start-ups are there? The latest U.S. figures show that some 644,000 businesses were started in 2005; 670,000 in 2006; 668,000 in 2007; 626,000 in 2008; and 552,000 in 2009.[6] Add these new start-ups to the large number of small businesses (estimated at more than 5 million employer firms) already operating, and you can begin to understand the economic importance of entrepreneurial ventures and small businesses.

What about entrepreneurial activity outside the United States? How extensive is it, and what kind of impact has it had? An annual assessment of global entrepreneurship called the Global Entrepreneurship Monitor (GEM) estimates the level of involvement in early-stage entrepreneurial activity by looking at nascent entrepreneurs (individuals who have taken some action toward creating a new business) and new business owners (individuals who are active as owners-managers of a new business that has paid wages or salaries for more than three months but less than 42 months).[7] The GEM 2011 Report covered 54 countries that were divided into three clusters—emerging economies, developing economies, and mature economies. Here are just a few of the study results:

- Entrepreneurs now number near 400 million in 54 countries.

- Total early-stage entrepreneurial activity increased significantly (double digits) across all levels of economic development.

- Intent to start businesses is highest in emerging economies. People in these economies are most likely to see opportunities and believe in their ability to start a business. They also hold entrepreneurship in high regard. These measures tend to fall as countries in economic development. Russia and the United Arab Emirates have the lowest entrepreneurial intention rates of all countries.

- More than 50 percent of entrepreneurs in emerging economies who discontinued their businesses did so because of negative influences, usually lack of profitability or funding.

- Early-stage entrepreneurs are most often young to middle-age (25–44 years), although in many developing economies, there is a tendency toward younger entrepreneurs. In Switzerland and Japan, however, older entrepreneurs (44–54 years) are the most frequent participants in entrepreneurship.

- Eight out of 54 economies (Panama, Venezuela, Jamaica, Guatemala, Brazil, Thailand, Switzerland, and Singapore) have equal participation by men and women in entrepreneurship.

The GEM report concludes that "To create energy for making positive changes, societies must consider that entrepreneurship is not the heroic act of a few individuals, but the accomplishments of many people who pursue their ambitions in a supportive cultural and institutional environment."

Innovation   Finally, you can understand the especially important role of entrepreneurial ventures in innovation. Innovating is a process of creating, changing, experimenting, transforming, and revolutionizing. The "creative destruction" process of innovating leads to technological changes and employment growth.[8] Entrepreneurial firms are an essential source of new and unique ideas that might otherwise go untapped.[9] Statistics back this up. New entrepreneurial organizations generate 24 times more innovations per R&D dollar spent than *Fortune* 500 organizations, and they account for more than 95 percent of new and "radical" product developments.[10] In addition, the SBA's Office of Advocacy reports that small entrepreneurial firms produce 13 to 14 times more patents per employee than large patenting firms.[11] Innovation is important to entrepreneurial firms globally as well. The GEM 2006 study reported that 19 percent of early-stage entrepreneurs in middle-income countries and 15 percent of early-stage entrepreneurs in high-income countries indicated their product was new to all customers.[12]

There's no doubt that entrepreneurial ventures and small businesses play a significant role in the U.S. and global economies—and their economic importance will continue. That's why we need to look at what it means to manage strategically in these organizations. In addition, both face unique strategic challenges. Before we look at these, we need to explain how the strategic management process might be used.

The Strategic Management Process in Entrepreneurial Ventures and Small Businesses

How important is it to identify environmental opportunities? Consider the following: More than 4 million baby boomers turn 50 every year. Almost 10,000 turn 60 each day. More than 57.5 million baby boomers are projected to be alive in 2030, putting them between the ages of 66 to 84. The strategic decision makers at Zimmer Holding are well aware of those demographics. Why? Their company, which makes orthopedic products, including reconstructive implants for hips, knees, shoulders, and elbows, sees definite marketing opportunities.[13] Exploiting such opportunities and developing a sustainable competitive advantage are important for entrepreneurial ventures and small businesses. As we've discussed previously, getting a sustainable competitive advantage means developing organizational resources and capabilities into distinctive capabilities and core competencies that competitors can't duplicate and that provide customers with products they desire. However, getting to that point isn't easy. But, that's the intent behind managing strategically—using the strategic management process to identify and assess important internal and external factors that influence appropriate strategic choices and decisions. What's different or unique about the way in which strategic managers in entrepreneurial ventures and small businesses do this?

Value of Planning

We first need to look at whether strategic decision makers in these organizations should do strategic planning. Is such planning valuable? Research that's looked at the value of general planning, and pre-start-up planning in particular, has shown mixed results. Several studies have shown positive links between planning and business performance.[14] Others have found no such relationship between planning and performance or have shown that the relationship depends on the industry.[15] What's our conclusion? Many entrepreneurship researchers now believe that instead of spending months (or even years) developing elaborate business plans, a "more practical approach (especially if not seeking external start-up financing) is to write a 'back-of-the-envelope' plan with basic financial projections, such as cash flow, and fine-tune the business model after launching the business."[16] In other words, don't spend a lot of time writing a business plan without knowing whether you have actual customers. Also, a recent study that compared businesses that started with formal business plans and those that didn't, found no statistical difference in success.[17] Although spending a lot of time preparing a start-up business plan may not be as critical as once thought, strategic planning is. How should strategic planning be done?

The Overall Approach to the Strategic Planning Process

Most researchers generally agree that the strategic planning process in small organizations should be far less formal than in large organizations.[18] If the process becomes too formal, rigid, and cumbersome, an entrepreneurial venture or small business can lose the flexibility that's often crucial to its competitive success. In fact, the value of strategic planning for these organizations lies more in the "doing"—that is, in the process itself—than in the outcome of the process, a formal strategic "plan." And that value in "doing" comes from analyzing the external and internal environments—steps important to effective strategic planning.

External and Internal Analysis

Strategic decision makers in entrepreneurial ventures and small businesses need to know what's happening externally and internally. Why? One reason is that many aspects in an organization's external environment have been shown to influence performance, particularly in new entrepreneurial ventures.[19] However, even for established small businesses, external analysis provides important information for developing or exploiting a competitive advantage.

Another reason it's important to do an external analysis is to have information about changes in customer expectations, competitors and their actions, economic factors, technological advances, and other marketplace features.[20] As we discussed in Chapter 3, an external analysis provides information on potential opportunities and threats. If no external analysis is done, it's impossible to know what they are. The same thing holds true for an internal analysis. If employees don't assess an organization's strengths and weaknesses, it's difficult to know what strategies are needed to help develop or exploit the organization's competitive advantage. In other words, what resources, capabilities, and core competencies does the organization have and not have? Although it may be difficult for an entrepreneur or a small business owner to be totally objective in analyzing strengths and weaknesses, such an analysis *is* necessary.

Finally, the "boiled frog phenomenon," a classic psychological experiment, can help explain why environmental analysis is important to these organizations.[21] In the experiment, when a live frog is dropped in a pan of boiling water, it reacts instantaneously and jumps out. If a live frog instead is dropped into tepid water that's gradually heated to the boiling point, the frog doesn't react and so dies. The same concept can be seen in entrepreneurial ventures and small businesses. Research has shown that gradual negative changes in organizational performance don't trigger a serious response to do something or at least not until it's too late.[22] Therefore, both external and internal environments need to be analyzed in order to detect subtle, but potentially damaging, changes. Don't be like the frog that waits too long to jump out of the boiling water!

Strategy Choices

Entrepreneurial ventures and small businesses can use most of the same strategies that large firms do with just a few exceptions. Let's look at the three different strategy levels to see what these differences are.

The main difference in functional strategies between small and large businesses is the extent or range of possible strategies. These organizations are limited in terms of the resources and capabilities that are available to implement their strategies.

At the competitive level, the strategy choices for entrepreneurial ventures and small businesses often are limited to focus strategies because of their small size and narrow competitive scope. It would be extremely difficult, even with technological advances, for a smaller organization to compete head-to-head in a broad market with a large organization on the basis of low costs, and probably even on differentiation. However, these organizations can compete successfully in narrow market niches by developing a low-cost or differentiation competitive advantage. Which competitive advantage strategic decision makers choose to develop depends on the resources, capabilities, and core competencies present in the functional areas of the organization. One thing small firms want to avoid is pursuing both approaches. Research has shown that small firms that mixed efficiency (low-cost) and flexibility (differentiation) strategies significantly underperformed those firms that utilized one or the other.[23]

Finally, it may seem strange to talk about "corporate" strategies for an entrepreneurial venture or a small business, especially if you think of corporate strategy as encompassing a portfolio of businesses. However, strategic decision makers in these businesses do need a strategy that addresses the overall direction the organization wants to go. The possible strategic directions are the same as for a large organization: Is it going to grow, stabilize, or reverse a decline by renewing? Again, however, there are limits to the range of strategic options available to these organizations for each of these directions. For example, most entrepreneurial ventures will choose to grow using the concentration strategy because vertical integration, horizontal integration, or diversification may not be financially or operationally feasible. Organization renewal actions may be limited to cost cutting and simple restructuring activities. Despite the limited options, strategic decision makers still need a corporate strategy.

One final point we need to stress is that the whole process comes down to choosing what business to be in, the competitive advantages needed to be successful in that business, and the strategies necessary to get there. This encompasses the whole range of strategic activities from developing or exploiting organizational resources, capabilities, and core competencies to building or exploiting a sustainable competitive advantage in order to move the firm in the desired direction.

Strategy Evaluation

This phase of the strategic management process for entrepreneurial ventures and small businesses is similar to that in large organizations. The organization's strategies might be evaluated by measuring goal attainment at the various levels. Strategy evaluation might also include an assessment of certain performance trends and a comparison of the organization to its competitors. The organization's strategic decision makers need to know whether implemented strategies are working. If not, why not, and what changes might be necessary? The main difference between the strategy evaluation efforts of large and small organizations would be the extent of evaluation done.

All in all, the strategic management process in these organizations is similar to that used in larger organizations. Figure 1 illustrates this process. As we stated earlier, the main differences will be in terms of "how much" the small business or entrepreneurial venture can do these things. Because of limited resources and capabilities, strategic decision makers often find their options limited. This doesn't mean that they don't—or shouldn't—do these things, however; it just means they don't have the range or extent of alternatives to choose from.

Specific Strategic Issues Facing Entrepreneurial Ventures and Small Businesses

Although the strategic management process for entrepreneurial ventures and small businesses is virtually identical to that for larger organizations, these organizations do face some unique strategic issues, including human resource management and innovation and flexibility considerations. Let's take a closer look at each.

Human Resource Management Issues

One of the most valuable resources and competitive advantages a small organization has is its employees. Yet, research indicates that recruiting, motivating, and retaining employees is one of the biggest problems for small organizations.[24] Human resource management (HRM) issues

*Business plan is typically needed when business is first starting up.

are among the most significant ones for entrepreneurial ventures and small businesses. A large organization typically enjoys a wider range of HR strategy options than a smaller organization in terms of recruiting, selecting, training, appraising, and compensating employees. However, just because these organizations don't have the wide range of HR strategies doesn't mean they should just forget them. Quite the opposite, in fact! Strategic decision makers should recognize how important human resources are and commit whatever time and resources are necessary to develop appropriate strategies for attracting and keeping good people. It's something that entrepreneurial ventures and small businesses can't ignore.

Innovation and Flexibility Considerations

One of the primary competitive advantages that entrepreneurial ventures and small businesses can develop is being flexible and innovative.[25] Because large organizations are usually concerned with producing large quantities of products in order to take advantage of economies of scale, they often can't be as flexible. Their resource commitments often prevent them from responding to new and quickly changing markets as effectively as small, nimble businesses can. Therefore, strategic decision makers need to capitalize on this flexibility advantage and to be aware of and open to environmental changes (another good reason for doing an external analysis).

Also, these organizations have the potential—more so than large organizations—to come up with real innovations. Why? Larger organizations tend to concentrate on improving products they already have in order to justify large capital expenditures on facilities and equipment. Entrepreneurial ventures especially are in a better position to develop innovations in technology, markets, and products. Economist Joseph Schumpeter referred to this process in which existing products, processes, ideas, and businesses are replaced with better ones as **creative destruction.** These organizations are the driving force of change in the process of creative destruction. Developing and exploiting a sustainable competitive advantage may mean that strategic managers at these organizations need to be on the lookout for ways to "creatively destruct!"

- Contrast entrepreneurial ventures and small businesses.
- Why are these organizations important to U.S. and global economies?
- Describe the strategic management process for these organizations.
- Discuss the specific strategic issues facing entrepreneurial ventures and small businesses.

STRATEGIES FOR NOT-FOR-PROFIT AND PUBLIC SECTOR ORGANIZATIONS

In this section, we're going to look at strategic management in not-for-profit organizations. We'll start off by defining these organizational types and looking at how they're different from for-profit organizations. Then, we'll discuss the details of the strategic management process for these organizations and finish up with a discussion of some special strategic issues with which these organizations might have to contend.

What Are Not-for-Profit Organizations?

A **not-for-profit organization** is an organization whose purpose is to provide some service or good with no intention of earning a profit in order to meet the requirements of U.S. tax code Section 501(c)(3) as a tax-exempt organization. Note that "not-for-profit" doesn't mean "no revenue." Just because a not-for-profit (NFP) organization has no intention of earning a profit doesn't mean it needs no source of income. An organization can't exist without some means of covering the expenses associated with providing a good or service. Where can an NFP's revenues come from? Figure 2 shows typical sources of revenue: taxes; dues; donations; product sales; permits, fees, and charges; and grants. In many instances, an NFP gets its revenues from a combination of these sources. What happens if an NFP's revenues actually *exceed* its expenses?

FIGURE 2

Revenue Sources for Not-for-Profit Organizations

FIGURE 3

Types of Not-for-Profit
Organizations

Because an NFP can't earn a profit and retain its not-for-profit status, usually it will use any surplus to improve the goods or services it's providing or to reduce the price or fee charged for those goods or services. Also, it's not uncommon for an NFP to set aside a specified amount of funds in some type of reserve account to be used when revenues *don't* meet expenses.

Just as business (for-profit) organizations aren't all alike, neither are NFPs! There are a number of different types of NFP organizations. (See Figure 3.) One is the **public sector organization,** which is an NFP that's created, funded, and regulated by the public sector or government. These organizations include governmental units, offices, departments, agencies, and divisions at all levels—federal, state, and local. They provide public services a society needs to exist and operate, such as police protection, paved roads and other transportation needs, recreation facilities, care and help for needy and disabled citizens, laws and regulations to protect and enhance life, and so forth.

Other types of NFPs include educational (public schools, colleges, and universities); charitable (United Way, American Cancer Society, and Children's Miracle Network); religious (churches, synagogues, and other religious associations); social service (American Red Cross, Camp Fire, Habitat for Humanity, Big Brothers–Big Sisters, and Mothers Against Drunk Drivers); cultural and recreational (theaters, museums, dance troupes, symphonies, parks, zoos, and other arts or recreation-oriented organizations); health service (hospitals, medical clinics, and other health care-related organizations); professional membership associations (American Bar Association, American Medical Association, and Academy of Management); cause-related (Save the Whales, Republican or Democratic National Parties, Nature Conservancy, and American Association of Retired Persons); and foundations (Rockefeller Foundation, Bill and Melinda Gates Foundation, college-university alumni foundations, and Foundation for the Health and Safety of American Firefighters).

Both public sector organizations and other types of NFPs are important to society because they provide many of society's essential needs that either can't be or shouldn't be provided by for-profit businesses. For example, most individual citizens couldn't afford to pay for private police protection but instead rely on the government to provide this protection; the American Cancer Society provides funds for cancer research and to help educate people about cancer and its causes; and any child born with birth defects is eligible for help from the March of Dimes. Many of the services and goods that NFPs provide are important to the quality of life in society. NFPs also play a significant role in maintaining an economic, social, and political system that encourages, facilitates, and protects the development and continued existence of for-profit organizations. Although the vast array of laws and regulations may seem overly cumbersome and meaningless at times, most have been enacted with society's best interests in mind. Finally, NFPs are an important economic activity. These organizations contribute to the gross national product and employ a large number of individuals who, in turn, have income to pay taxes and to spend on goods and services.

You may not have realized the wide variety of NFPs, understood the extent of what they did, or recognized the economic significance of these types of organizations. These organizations *are* important to our society as well as to other societies around the world—one study of 37 nations found that the global nonprofit sector had total operating expenditures of over $1.6 trillion.[26] Other studies of the U.S. not-for-profit sector estimate that its total asset base "would make it the sixth largest economy in the world."[27] Strategically managing these organizations is also important and that's what we want to look at next.

The Strategic Management Process in NFPs

Because these types of organizations don't struggle to "make a profit," you may think that managing strategically isn't necessary or maybe even possible. However, developing and exploiting a competitive advantage *is* an important task for strategic decision makers. Why? Because NFPs also compete for resources and customers! For example, the American Heart Association competes with other social service, health service, and charitable and religious organizations for volunteers. A local community theater or symphony competes with other community arts organizations and with "entertainment" businesses for customers, volunteers, and corporate and private donations. A state university competes with countless other organizations for state funds, employees, and "customers" (that's you and the rest of your fellow students!). That means an NFP also needs to develop and exploit a competitive advantage—something that sets it apart and gives it a competitive edge. So, the strategic management process is clearly needed by these organizations.

Although most strategy research has been done in for-profit organizations, strategy researchers have recognized the need to look at strategic management in NFPs.[28] Just like for-profit organizations, there appears to be a positive link between strategic planning efforts in NFPs and organizational performance.[29] So, what *does* the strategic management process involve for NFPs?

External and Internal Environmental Analysis

Both external and internal analyses can reveal important information for strategically managing NFPs. These organizations are facing increasingly dynamic environments, just as business organizations are. An external analysis provides an assessment of the positive and negative trends that might affect the NFP's strategic decisions. For example, economic trends are likely to influence the amount of tax revenues or the level of private and corporate donations an NFP might expect. Changing societal attitudes toward respect for others and individual responsibility can influence the willingness of individuals to volunteer or to make contributions to a particular cause. A new community arts organization (a new "competitor") can affect the program offerings and revenues of other community arts organizations. Even a long-running governmental monopoly like the U.S. Postal Service faces intense competition from technological advances such as instant messaging, e-mail, fax machines, and overnight package delivery services. It should be quite evident that strategic decision makers in NFPs must analyze external factors in order to determine opportunities and threats.

An internal analysis provides an assessment of the organization's resources and capabilities and its strengths and weaknesses in specific areas. What resources and capabilities does it have? Which ones are inadequate or absent? With this information, strategic decision makers can see what distinctive capabilities, core competencies, and competitive advantage(s) an NFP might have or might need to develop. The functional areas of an NFP are probably not the same as those in a for-profit organization, but the process of analyzing the functional areas *is* similar. Even in an NFP, the product or service must be produced and delivered to the "customer" and revenues must be accounted for in some way. What an internal analysis shows, as we well know, is how efficient and effective the organization is at doing these things. An internal audit would be an appropriate tool for assessing an NFP's resources and capabilities and determining what the organization's strengths and weaknesses are. The information from the SWOT analysis is used to assess various strategy options and choices for creating or exploiting a competitive advantage.

Strategy Choices

The idea that NFPs have strategic choices may seem strange. After all, NFPs aren't "selling" anything and aren't competing with other organizations, and they certainly aren't motivated to be efficient and effective in developing a competitive advantage because they don't have to make a profit to stay in business. These statements definitely are *not* true! Strategic managers at NFPs *do* face similar constraints—limited resources, competition for customers and resources, performance measurement, and long-run survival—just as strategic managers at for-profit organizations do. Thus, at some point, an NFP's strategic decision makers must decide which strategies the organization is going to use to fulfill its vision and mission(s). The strategic options are similar in many respects to those available to businesses.

At the functional level, the NFP or public sector organization must have strategies that allow it to do what it's set up to do—whether that's collecting taxes; imprisoning or rehabilitating convicted felons; developing and showcasing community art, dance, and music; or providing regional home health care assistance to elderly individuals. Every NFP needs resources and capabilities to deliver its service or to provide its products. As we know, the functional strategies are the ways an organization might choose to do these things. The main difference between the functional strategies of business organizations and NFPs is that NFPs don't have the wide variety of alternatives from which to choose because of scarce and limited resources or because of external constraints. Scarce and limited resources affect both public sector organizations and other types of NFPs, but external constraints are most common in public sector organizations, particularly in functional areas such as purchasing or employee hiring or firing. These constraints may limit strategic decision makers' discretion in choosing appropriate and feasible functional strategies.

Competition still exists even if an organization isn't profit-oriented. As we stated earlier, NFPs *do* compete for resources (financial and human) and customers (clients, users, members, etc.) just like business organizations do. These NFPs are competing with each other and, in many instances, with business organizations for resources and customers. Very little research has been done on specific competitive strategies that NFPs and public sector organizations use. One study of community arts organizations did show that these organizations competed on the basis of keeping costs low, being different, or focusing on a specific niche—in other words, Porter's cost leadership, differentiation, and focus strategies.[30] Another study of competitive strategies of religious organizations focused on explaining how these organizations compete and elaborated specific strategic management issues facing these organizations.[31] Even without much research on specific competitive strategies in NFPs and public sector organizations, we know that these organizations must develop and exploit a sustainable competitive advantage to ensure their continued existence. How strategic decision makers choose to do that is the essence of their organization's competitive strategy.

Finally, NFPs face the same types of corporate strategy choices as businesses: Should it grow, and what are its options for growth? Does it need to stabilize its operations? Or, does it need to correct declining performance and renew itself? The main difference between corporate strategies for business organizations and for NFPs is the limited range of strategic options. For instance, concentration is a frequently used growth strategy for NFPs, but diversification would be unusual. For example, strategic managers at Rotary International had to use a turnaround strategy to address its declining performance. Strategic actions involved cost cutting, restructuring, and re-establishing good relationships with member chapters throughout the United States. However, even if strategic alternatives are somewhat limited, NFPs *do* look at ways to grow, stabilize, or renew. They're faced with the same kinds of broad, comprehensive, and long-run strategic decisions that for-profit organizations face.

Strategy Evaluation

Once a strategy has been implemented, strategic decision makers must evaluate whether it had the intended effect and, if not, to take corrective action. Even though we know it's important, this is the part of the strategic management process that's probably the most difficult for NFPs. Why? Primarily because there isn't a single performance measure, like profit, that accurately assesses success. Also, clearly stated performance standards (goals and objectives) aren't easy to develop for these types of organizations. Without clearly stated goals, strategy evaluation is more difficult. Instead, strategic managers may have to look at several measures of strategic performance. For example, what are some ways a church's strategic performance could be measured? One measure might be whether member contributions increased. Another might be the increase (or decrease) in the number of members. The fact that strategic decision makers may have to look for different performance measures makes the process of strategy evaluation and control more challenging. Also, because it's often easier for strategic managers of NFPs to measure the resources coming into the organization (inputs) rather than the services or goods being provided (outputs), they often tend to focus more on the resources coming into the organization than on how the resources are being used—that is, how the organization is performing.[32] Again, this reflects the difficulties associated with developing appropriate ways to evaluate the strategies. Despite the difficulties associated with strategy evaluation in these organizations, strategic decision makers must assess the strategies being used.

Specific Strategic Issues Facing NFPs

Because of their unique purposes, NFPs often must deal with some specific strategic issues such as the misperception that strategic management isn't needed in or can't be applied to these types of organizations, the challenges of managing multiple stakeholders, and some unique strategies that not-for-profits have developed in response to environmental pressures.

Misperception About the Usefulness of Strategic Management

You'd probably agree that strategic management is useful to and necessary in for-profit organizations. Somehow, when "profit" is involved, the benefits of the process are clear, and yet, many people question the usefulness of strategic management for NFPs. Also, many not-for-profit managers themselves aren't aware of what strategic management is and why it's important. They don't understand why and how it should be used. Some even go so far as to say that management, in general, isn't needed. Their rationale: We're not a business, so why should we be worried about managing the organization like a business?

Of course, we know that such attitudes are simply misunderstandings about strategic management and its purposes. Managing strategically in order to develop a sustainable competitive advantage is a task that *all* strategic decision makers face. Doing so requires tasks such as developing an organizational vision and mission(s), analyzing positive and negative external trends, assessing internal resources and capabilities, and designing appropriate programs and services. As academic research and media stories on well-managed and successful NFPs are published, these misperceptions about the usefulness of strategic management should change.

Multiple Stakeholders

We know that strategic decision makers in business organizations must cope with multiple stakeholders. However, this issue is magnified in not-for-profit organizations, and especially public sector organizations, which are closely intertwined with politics and the political process. Strategic managers in these organizations may find their plans and strategies ignored by political leaders who may be interested only in getting reelected. In addition, in the United States, our fundamental assumption about government is that individual citizens *are* the government—government of the people, by the people, and for the people, as our Constitution so eloquently states. Public sector organizations, then, are "owned" by all citizens, and strategic managers may find that their decisions and actions are more closely monitored. Public sector managers also may find their actions scrutinized by oversight agencies such as courts, legislative bodies, and political commissions. They may find their strategic decisions "second-guessed" by individuals who feel they have the right to voice their opinions.

Just as strategic managers in public sector organizations face multiple and often conflicting stakeholder demands, strategic managers in other types of NFPs may find themselves dealing with multiple stakeholders who have different agendas. For instance, think of a public school superintendent and the various stakeholder groups he or she must consider when making decisions and taking actions, or think of the executive director of a local Red Cross organization and the many stakeholders that might influence strategic decisions and actions. The challenge of coping with multiple stakeholders is compounded if the NFP relies on these stakeholders for revenues. You can begin to imagine how difficult that might be! Multiple stakeholders do represent a unique strategic issue with which NFP and public sector decision makers have to deal.

Unique Strategies Used by Not-for-Profit Organizations

Because NFPs often rely on variable and unpredictable revenue sources, they have developed some unique strategies to cope with changing environmental conditions—both external and internal. Three of these strategies are: (1) cause-related marketing, (2) marketing alliances, and (3) strategic piggybacking.

Many not-for-profit organizations use cause-related marketing activities. **Cause-related marketing** is a strategic practice in which for-profit businesses link up with a social cause that fits well with their products. For instance, Avon Products, Inc. (the cosmetics company) developed the Avon Breast Cancer Crusade [**www.avoncrusade.com**]. Its mission has been to provide women, particularly those who are medically underserved, with direct access to breast cancer education and early detection screening services. The Avon Breast Cancer Crusade in the United States is one of several Avon-sponsored programs in countries around the world that supports women's health. These programs are supported by the Avon Foundation, which has raised more than $860 million worldwide to "improve the lives of women, globally." The company sees these as a way to fund causes that are meaningful to its target customers. Cause-related marketing can, and does, benefit the NFP through public exposure and corporate donations, but the primary intent of the strategy is to enhance the image of the supporting company.[33] Although cause-related marketing may be designed for the strategic advantage of the sponsoring corporation, NFPs can also benefit from the marketing link, and many have chosen to participate in these types of activities.

Some NFPs have taken cause-related marketing a step further and actively pursue alliances between themselves and corporate partners. These **not-for-profit marketing alliances** are strategic partnerships between an NFP and one or more corporate partners in which the corporate partner(s) agrees to do marketing actions that will benefit both the NFP and the corporate

FIGURE 4

Types of NFP Marketing
Alliances

partner(s).[34] These marketing alliances are an extension of cause-related marketing, with the main difference being that the NFP is the one that proposes and initiates the alliance. Figure 4 illustrates the three different types of these marketing alliances.

The transaction-based promotion is an alliance in which the corporate partner donates a specific amount of cash, food, or equipment in direct proportion to sales revenues, typically up to a certain limit. The joint-issue promotion is an alliance in which the partners agree to tackle a social problem through actions such as advertising and distributing products and promotional materials. The last type of not-for-profit marketing alliance involves licensing names and logos of NFPs in return for a fee or percentage of revenues.

These marketing alliances can be an excellent way for NFPs to cope with uncertain revenue sources. However, strategic decision makers *do* need to ensure that the marketing alliance doesn't waste scarce organizational resources, reduce other types of donations, bring about restricted flexibility in decision making, or establish partnerships with unethical or questionable corporate partners.

The last unique strategy we want to look at is **strategic piggybacking,** or when an NFP develops a new activity to generate revenue.[35] For instance, when the Special Olympics organization sells clothing and other related merchandise, it's generating revenue through strategic piggybacking. A community symphony may decide to sell cookbooks or other types of merchandise to supplement revenue from symphony memberships. One cautionary note regarding strategy piggybacking is that the Internal Revenue Service watches these activities very closely. If an NFP engages in a business "not substantially related" to its exempt purposes, it may jeopardize its tax-exempt status. Obviously, strategic managers would want to monitor these activities closely.

LEARNING REVIEW

- List the typical sources of revenues for NFPs.
- What are the main types of NFPs?
- Describe the strategic management process for these organizations.
- Explain how functional, competitive, and corporate strategies might be used in NFPs and public sector organizations.
- Discuss the specific strategic issues that face NFPs.

Endnotes

1. F. Norris, "Small Companies Create More Jobs? Maybe Not," *New York Times Online,* February 24, 2012; "Frequently Asked Questions," *U.S. Small Business Administration* [www.sba.gov/advo], February 2012; L. W. Busenitz, "Research on Entrepreneurial Alertness," *Journal of Small Business Management,* October 1996, pp. 35–44; and J. W. Carland, F. Hoy, W. R. Boulton, and J. C. Carland, "Differentiating Entrepreneurs from Small Business Owners: A Conceptualization," *Academy of Management Review,* vol. 9, no. 2, 1984, pp. 354–359.

2. J. Hopkins, "Small Businesses Again Gain Ground in Overall U.S. Employment," *USA Today,* October 9, 2006, p. 2B; and "United States Business Facts, September 2006," *U.S. Chamber of Commerce Statistics and Research Center,* U.S. Chamber of Commerce Web site [www.uschamber.org], April 16, 2007.

3. News Release, "Small Business Creates America's Jobs," *U.S. Small Business Administration* [www.sba.gov/advo/press], October 25, 2007; "Frequently Asked Questions," *U.S. Small Business Administration* [www.sba.gov/advo], September 2008; and P. Coy, "Small Business: Right Place, Right Time," *BusinessWeek,* October 13, 2003, pp. 82–88.

4. Norris, "Small Companies Create More Jobs? Maybe Not;" and M. Craft, "Big Talk on Small Businesses Is Wrong," Associated Press, *Springfield, Missouri, News-Leader,* February 19, 2012, p. 1E.

5. M. Craft, "Big Talk on Small Businesses Is Wrong;" E. Caroom, "Dueling Statistics on Small Business Hiring," *Inc.com,* February 5, 2009; "The Third Millennium: Small Business and Entrepreneurship in the 21st Century," *U.S. Small Business Administration* [www.sba.gov/advo], April 16, 2007; and P. Hise, "Everyone Wants to Start a Business," *CNNMoney.com,* March 26, 2007.

6. "Frequently Asked Questions," *U.S. Small Business Administration* [www.sba.gov/advo], February 2012.

7. Based on Press Release, "Entrepreneurs Now Numbering Near 400 Million in 54 Countries According to GEM 2011 Global Report," [www.gemconsortium.org], January 19, 2012.

8. "The Third Millennium: Small Business and Entrepreneurship in the 21st Century."

9. P. Almeida and B. Kogut, "The Exploration of Technological Diversity and Geographic Localization in Innovation: Start-up Firms in the Semiconductor Industry," *Small Business Economics,* vol. 9, no. 1, 1997, pp. 21–31.

10. R. J. Arend, "Emergence of Entrepreneurs Following Exogenous Technological Change," *Strategic Management Journal,* January 1999, pp. 21–31.

11. U.S. Small Business Administration Office of Advocacy, "Frequently Asked Questions," *Small Business Administration* [www.sba.gov], April 16, 2007.

12. N. Bosma and R. Harding, *Global Entrepreneurship Monitor 2006 Results,* (Babson College and London Business School), p. 19.

13. J. W. Elphinstone, "Universal Home Design is Accessible for All Ages and Attitudes," *Dallas Morning News* [www.dallasnews.com], November 13, 2008; "Facts for Features," *U.S. Census Bureau Newsroom,* January 3, 2006; and M. Arndt, "Zimmer: Growing Older Gracefully," *BusinessWeek,* June 9, 2003.

14. C. Schwenk and C. B. Shrader, "Effects of Formal Strategic Planning on Financial Performance in Small Firms:" A Meta-Analysis," *Entrepreneurship Theory and Practice,* vol. 17, no. 3, 1993, pp. 53–64; J. Bracker, B. Keats, and J. Pearson, "Planning and Financial Performance Among Small Firms in a Growth Industry," *Strategic Management Journal,* vol. 9, 1988, pp. 591–603; J. Bracker and J. Pearson, "Planning and Financial Performance of Small, Mature Firms," *Strategic Management Journal,* vol. 7, 1986, pp. 503–522; R. Ackelsberg and P. Arlow, "Small Businesses Do Plan and It Pays Off," *Long Range Planning,* vol. 18, no. 3, 1985, pp. 61–67; C. Orpen, "The Effects of Long-Range Planning on Small Business Performance," *Journal of Small Business Management,* January 1985, pp. 16–23; R. Robinson and J. Pearce, "Research Thrusts in Small Firm Strategic Planning," *Academy of Management Review,* vol. 9, 1984, pp. 128–137; P. Wood and R. LaForge, "The Impact of Comprehensive Planning on Financial Performance," *Academy of Management Journal,* vol. 22, 1979, pp. 516–526; R. Robinson, "Forecasting and Small Business: A Study of the Strategic Planning Process," *Journal of Small Business Management,* vol. 17, no. 3, 1979, pp. 19–27; P. Karger and R. Mali, "Long Range Planning and Organizational Performance," *Long Range Planning,* vol. 8, no. 6, 1975, pp. 61–64; D. Herold, "Long Range Planning and Organizational Performance: A Cross-validation Study," *Academy of Management Journal,* vol. 15, 1972, pp. 91–102; and H. I. Ansoff, et. al., "Does Planning Pay? The Effect of Planning on Success of Acquisition in American Firms," *Long Range Planning,* vol. 3, no. 2, 1970, pp. 2–7.

15. K. K. Spors, "Do Start-Ups Really Need Formal Business Plans?" *Wall Street Journal,* January 9, 2007, p. B9; C. B. Shrader, C. Mulford, and V. Blackburn, "Strategic and Operational Planning, Uncertainty, and Performance in Small Firms," *Journal of Small Business Management,* October 1989, pp. 45–60; R. Robinson and J. Pearce, "The Impact of Formalized Strategic Planning on Financial Performance in Small Organizations," *Strategic Management Journal,* vol. 4, 1983, pp. 197–207; W. Lindsay and others, "Strategic Planning: Determining the Impact of Environmental Characteristics and Uncertainty," *Academy of Management Journal,* vol. 25, 1982, pp. 500–509; R. Hogarth and S. Makridakis, "Forecasting and Planning: An Evaluation," *Management Science,* vol. 27, no. 2, 1981, pp. 115–138; M. Leontiades and A. Tezel, "Planning Perceptions and Planning Results," *Strategic Management Journal,* vol. 1, 1980, pp. 65–76; R. Kudla, "The Effects of Strategic Planning on Common Stock Returns," *Academy of Management Journal,* vol. 23, 1980, pp. 5–20; R. Fulmer and L. Rue, "The Practice and Profitability of Long-Range Planning," *Managerial Planning,* May–June 1974, pp. 1–7; and S. Thune and R. House, "Where Long Range Planning Pays Off," *Business Horizons,* vol. 13, no. 4, 1970, pp. 81–87.

16. Spors, 2007.

17. Ibid.

18. T. J. Callahan and M. D. Cassar, "Small Business Owners' Assessment of Their Abilities to Perform and Interpret Formal Market Studies," *Journal of Small Business Management,* October 1995, pp. 1–9; C. B. Shrader and others, *Journal of Small Business Management,* 1989; L. R. Smeltzer, G. L. Fann, and V. N. Nikolaisen, "Environmental Scanning Practices in Small Businesses," *Journal of Small Business Management,* July 1988, pp. 56–62; S. W. McDaniel and A. Parasuraman, "Practical Guidelines for Small Business Marketing Research," *Journal of Small Business Management,* January 1986, pp. 1–9; and S. W. McDaniel and A. Parasuraman, "Small Business Experience With and Attitudes Toward Formal Marketing Research," *American Journal of Small Business,* Spring 1985, pp. 1–6.

19. S. Shane and L. Kolvereid, "National Environment, Strategy, and New Venture Performance: A Three-Country Study," *Journal of Small Business Management,* April 1995, pp. 37–50.

20. A. Bhide, "The Questions Every Entrepreneur Must Answer," *Harvard Business Review,* November–December 1996, pp. 120–130; S. I. Mohan-Neill, "The Influence of Firm's Age and Size on Its Environmental Scanning Activities," *Journal of Small Business Management,* October 1995, pp. 10–21; T. J. Callahan and M. D. Cassar, *Journal of Small Business Management,* October 1995; J. Masten, G. B. Hartmann, and A. Safari, "Small Business Strategic Planning and Technology Transfer: The Use of Publicly Supported Technology Assistance Agencies," *Journal of Small Business Management,* July 1995, pp. 26–37; and A. Shama, "Marketing Strategies During Recession: A Comparison of Small and Large Firms," *Journal of Small Business Management,* July 1993, pp. 62–72.

21. S. D. Chowdhury and J. R. Lang, "Crisis, Decline, and Turnaround: A Test of Competing Hypotheses for Short-Term Performance Improvement in Small Firms," *Journal of Small Business Management,* October 1993, pp. 8–17.

22. Ibid.

23. J. Ebben and A. C. Johnson, "Efficiency, Flexibility, or Both? Evidence Linking Strategy to Performance in Small Firms," *Strategic Management Journal,* December 2005, pp. 1249–1259.

24. S. P. Deshpande and D. Y. Golhar, "HRM Practices in Large and Small Manufacturing Firms: A Comparative Study," *Journal of Small Business Management,* April 1994, pp. 49–56.

25. See T. M. Hatten, *Small Business: Entrepreneurship and Beyond,* pp. 17–18.

26. R. Foroohar, "Where the Money Goes," *Newsweek,* October 31, 2006, pp. E18–E20.

27. Appraisal Institute Online, "FASB Issues Exposure Drafts on M&A for Not-for-Profit Organizations," *VFR in Focus,* October 2006.

28. S. L. Durst and C. Newell, "The Who, Why, and How of Reinvention in Nonprofit Organizations," *Nonprofit Management & Leadership,* Summer 2001, pp. 443–457; S. Espy, *Marketing Strategies for Nonprofit Organizations* (Chicago, IL: Lyceum Books, 1993); K. Ascher and B. Nare, "Strategic Planning in the Public Sector," in *International Review of Strategic Management,* vol. 1, 1988, D. E. Hussey (ed.) (New York: John Wiley and Sons), pp. 297–315; M. S. Wortman, Jr., "Strategic Management in Nonprofit Organizations: A Research Typology and Research Prospectus," in *Strategic Management Frontiers,* J. H. Grant (ed.) (Greenwich, CT: JAI Press, 1988), pp. 425–442; J. W. Harvey and K. F. McCrohan, "Strategic Issues for Charities and Philanthropies," *Long Range Planning,* December 1988, pp. 44–55; D. Harvey and J. D. Snyder, "Charities Need a Bottom

Line, Too," *Harvard Business Review,* January–February 1987, pp. 14–22; I. Unterman and R. H. Davis, *Strategic Management of Not-for-Profit Organizations* (New York: Praeger, 1984); J. M. Stevens and R. P. McGowan, "Managerial Strategies in Municipal Government Organizations," *Academy of Management Journal,* vol. 26, no. 3, pp. 527–534.

29. J. Collins, *Good to Great and the Social Sectors* (New York: HarperCollins, 2005); Durst and Newell, 2001; A. Howard and J. Magretta, "Surviving Success: An Interview with the Nature Conservancy's John Sawhill," *Harvard Business Review,* September–October 1995, pp. 108–118; P. V. Jenster and G. A. Overstreet, "Planning for a Non-Profit Service: A Study of U.S. Credit Unions," *Long Range Planning,* April 1990, pp. 103–111; and G. J. Medley, "Strategic Planning for the World Wildlife Fund," *Long Range Planning,* February 1988, pp. 46–54.

30. M. Coulter, "Competitive Strategies of Community Arts Organizations," working paper from a research study of community arts organizations in the Midwest, 1996.

31. F. Warner, "Prepare Thee for Some Serious Marketing," *New York Times Online,* October 22, 2006; W. C. Symonds, "Earthly Empires," *BusinessWeek,* May 23, 2005, pp. 78–87; and K. D. Miller, "Competitive Strategies of Religious Organizations," *Strategic Management Journal,* May 2002, pp. 435–456.

32. R. M. Kanter and D. V. Summers, "Doing Well While Doing Good: Dilemmas of Performance Measurement in Nonprofit Organizations and the Need for a Multiple-Constituency Approach," in *The Nonprofit Sector: A Research Handbook,* W. W. Powell, (ed.) (New Haven, CT: Yale University Press, 1987).

33. See, for example, N. Lublin, "Jurassic Park Syndrome," *Fast Company,* March 2009, p. 50; G. Smith and R. Stodghill II, "Are Good Causes Good Marketing?" *BusinessWeek,* March 21, 1994, pp. 64–65; G. Levin, "Green Marketing Gets Cautious," *Advertising Age,* July 5, 1993, p. 4; "Cause-Related Marketing," *Inc.,* July 1991, p. 72; and "Marketing: Cause-Related Marketing," *Wall Street Journal,* February 19, 1987, p. B1.

34. A. R. Andreason, "Profits for Nonprofits: Find a Corporate Partner," *Harvard Business Review,* November–December 1996, pp. 47–59.

35. R. P. Nielsen, "Piggybacking Strategies for Nonprofits: A Shared Costs Approach," *Strategic Management Journal,* May–June 1986, pp. 209–211; R. P. Nielsen, "Piggybacking for Business and Nonprofits: A Strategy for Hard Times," *Long Range Planning,* April 1984, pp. 96–102; and R. P. Nielsen, "SMR Forum: Strategic Piggybacking—A Self-Subsidizing Strategy for Nonprofit Institutions," *Sloan Management Review,* Summer 1982, pp. 65–69.

HOW TO DO A COMPREHENSIVE CASE ANALYSIS

Case analysis is a major component of the strategic management course at most schools. In this part of the text, we're going to look at how to do a comprehensive case analysis so that when it's time for you to do one, you'll feel comfortable with what's involved. One thing you need to understand is that a comprehensive case analysis is not like the end-of-chapter minicases you may have completed as you read the chapters in this text; that is, there are no discussion questions at the end of the case to guide you as to which strategic issues are important. Instead, you'll be using what you've learned by reading and studying the various aspects of strategic management in action to analyze the case.

What Is a Case?

A case is simply a story about a company and the strategic issues its strategic decision makers are facing. In order to identify and address those issues, you put yourself in the position of one of those decision makers. You analyze the information that's provided about the company in the case. In some instances, your professor may provide you with additional information that's not specifically provided in the case. With this information (from the case itself and any additional information that's provided), you'll do your SWOT analysis. Then, based on your analysis, you should be able to identify the major strategic issues facing the company and formulate the strategic alternatives you think would best address those issues. Going through the process of analyzing a case can be a wonderful way to "practice" the skills of a strategic decision maker, especially if you remember to put yourself in the role of that decision maker by asking the following questions: *What information do I have? What information do I need? Based on my analysis of that information, what do I need to do now?* Given this, what specifically should a case analysis include?

What Should a Case Analysis Include?

A case analysis typically includes six parts: external analysis, internal analysis (including financial analysis), strategic issues, strategic alternatives, recommendations, and implementation. Let's look at what's included in each of these areas.

External Analysis

The external analysis section includes a description of the opportunities and threats found in the specific and general external environmental sectors. The specific sector includes the industry and competitive forces. The general sectors include economic, demographic, sociocultural, political–legal, and technological forces. We discussed in Chapter 3 how you do an external analysis and what you look for in each of these sectors. Based on your analysis of these sectors, then, you should describe *what* opportunities and threats you see in each area and explain *why* you see these as opportunities and threats.

Internal Analysis

The internal analysis section includes a description of the strengths and weaknesses found in the organization's internal functional areas, which typically include production–operations, marketing, human resource management, research and development, information systems, and financial–accounting. The internal analysis should also include an assessment of other internal organizational aspects such as strategic managers (top management team and board of directors), organizational culture, and organizational structure. In Chapter 4, you learned how to do an internal analysis and what to look for in each of these areas. Based on your analysis of these internal areas, you should describe *what* strengths and weaknesses you see in each area and explain *why* you see these as strengths and weaknesses.

The internal analysis section also usually includes a thorough financial analysis. An organization's financial data represent the results or outcomes of its past or current strategies. Strategic decision makers must and do use some form of financial analysis to make good decisions. In preparing your financial analysis, be sure to examine and analyze any financial information that's included in the case material such as exhibits, tables, graphs, appendices, and so forth.

The financial analysis typically covers four parts: (1) ratio analysis and comparison to industry trends and company trends and an explanation of what is happening in the ratios (see Exhibit 1 for a description of the four major categories of ratios); (2) graphs and charts outlining the company's sales, profits, and other important financial measures and comparisons of the company's numbers to industry averages; (3) listing and explanation of company's financial strengths and weaknesses; and (4) a statement of the company's overall financial condition (weak, fair, or strong) and written support of how you came to that conclusion.

Strategic Issues

Once you've completed the SWOT analysis, you're ready to identify the critical strategic issues facing the company. What are "typical" issues? They're critical weaknesses that need to be

EXHIBIT 1 Financial Ratios

Category	Ratio	How Calculated	What It Measures
Liquidity	Current ratio	$\dfrac{\text{Current assets}}{\text{Current liabilities}}$	A measure of the organization's ability to meet short-term obligations
	Acid test	$\dfrac{\text{Current assets minus inventories}}{\text{Current liabilities}}$	A more accurate measure of liquidity when inventories turn over slowly or are more difficult to sell
Leverage	Debt ratio	$\dfrac{\text{Total debt}}{\text{Total assets}}$	Indicates what percentage of an organization's assets are financed by debt
	Debt–equity ratio	$\dfrac{\text{Total debt}}{\text{Total equity}}$	Indicates the organization's use of equity compared with its use of debt
	Times interest earned	$\dfrac{\text{Profits before interest and taxes}}{\text{Total interest charges}}$	Measures how many times the organization can cover its interest payments with its gross operating income
Activity	Inventory turnover	$\dfrac{\text{Sales}}{\text{Inventory}}$	A measure of efficiency that indicates how many times the organization has "sold" its inventory
	Total asset turnover	$\dfrac{\text{Sales}}{\text{Total assets}}$	A measure of how efficiently the organization is using its total assets to generate sales
	Fixed asset turnover	$\dfrac{\text{Sales}}{\text{Fixed assets}}$	A measure of how efficiently the organization is using its fixed assets to generate sales
Profitability	Profit margin	$\dfrac{\text{Net profit (after taxes)}}{\text{Sales}}$	Indicates the percentage of profit generated from each dollar of sales
	Return on assets (ROA) (also called return on investment, or ROI)	$\dfrac{\text{Net profit (after taxes)}}{\text{Total Assets}}$	Indicates the rate of return on organization is generating from its assets
	Return on equity	$\dfrac{\text{Net profit (after taxes)}}{\text{Total Equity}}$	Indicates the rate of return the organization is earning for its shareholders

corrected, opportunities that the company wants to take advantage of with its strengths, distinctive competencies the company wants or needs to develop from its strengths, or possibly threats the company wants to steer away from or buffer against. In describing the strategic issues, focus on describing *what* the issue is as well as *why* you see it as an issue. Supporting "why" you see something as an issue should come from the information you've included in your SWOT analysis.

Strategic Alternatives

Once you've identified the critical strategic issues, you'll need to develop strategic alternatives to address those issues. How many alternatives do you need to develop? Your professor may have guidelines for you on developing alternatives. If not, however, a general guideline is to propose at least two alternatives to address each issue. In fact, some issues may have only two alternatives—to either change or to stay as is. However, other issues may have numerous alternatives that could be proposed to resolve them.

What should your description of alternatives include? Again, your professor may have specific guidelines for you. But if not, one approach is to describe what, how, who, when, and where. *What* is the strategic alternative being proposed? The possible strategic alternatives are the functional, competitive, and corporate strategies we discussed in Chapters 5 and 6. *How* will the alternative be done? This is an important part of describing your proposed alternative and should explain in detail—step-by-step—what needs to happen in this alternative. *Who* will be responsible for doing the alternative? What individuals or groups will be involved in the alternative? *When* will the alternative need to be done? Is it something that needs to happen immediately, in the short run, or is it more long term? And finally, *where* will the alternative need to be done? Think in terms of the location(s) where the alternative will take place.

Recommendations

Once you've developed your issues and proposed strategic alternatives, you're ready to make some choices. Which alternatives are you choosing and why? Which alternatives are you rejecting and why? You can choose as many of your alternatives to "resolve" your issue as you want, as long as they're not mutually exclusive. You want to also explain how your chosen alternative(s) will resolve the strategic issue.

Implementation

One drawback of case analysis is that you can't really put your proposed ideas into action. To overcome this limitation, however, your case analysis should provide a description of what changes would have to take place if your chosen strategies were implemented. One approach to implementation involves describing the proposed changes in organizational structure, the proposed changes in organizational culture, and the source of funding for implementing the chosen strategies. In other words, how would the organization's structure and culture have to change if this alternative were implemented, and where would the money come from to implement the alternative?

Important Note: The format for a case analysis that we just described—external analysis, internal analysis, strategic issues, strategic alternatives, recommendations, and implementation—is just one approach. Keep in mind that your professor may have another specific format for you to follow rather than the approach that's described here.

Finding Information To Do a Case Analysis

Doing a case analysis involves getting and evaluating information. Where do you find the information to do a case analysis? The obvious place to start is the written case itself. You'll want to read through the case initially to familiarize yourself with the company and the situation.

Then, go back through the case and start noting certain statements and whether they describe internal or external factors. For instance, does the information relate to marketing, production–operations, research and development, and so forth? Or, does the information seem to describe the external sectors such as industry–competition, demographic, economic, and so forth? It may take you a couple of times reading through the case to determine the categories under which the information might eventually fit. And, keep in mind that not every piece of information included in the written case is going to be important to your analysis. But you won't be able to determine that unless you've studied the case by reading through it more than once.

If your professor allows it, you might also want to look at other sources of information about the company and the external environment it's facing (such as company Web sites, governmental Web sites, company and industry reference sources, and even general business and news periodicals). One precaution, however, is that you need to keep within the same time frame as the case. For instance, if your case ends in 2011, you couldn't use news events that happened after 2011 because those events wouldn't have happened at the time of the case. To get the most educational benefit from doing a case analysis, you have to "arm" yourself with the information the company's strategic decision makers would have had and address the case under those conditions. However, keep in mind that your professor may ask you to update the case to the present time period, which you would do by finding current information on the company, the industry, and the general external environment.

What then? Once you have your information, you're ready to evaluate it by identifying strengths, weaknesses, opportunities, and threats. The SWOT analysis should help you in identifying the relevant strategic issues facing the company and serve as the basis for formulating appropriate strategic responses to the issues.

Presenting Case Analysis Information

You've completed your analysis of the case information. Now what? You'll need to present the information in a written format, as an oral presentation, or maybe both. What do you need to know about presenting information as a written report or as an oral report?

Written Case Analysis

Your written report should cover the six parts of a case analysis. This information could be presented in a bulleted item format or in a paragraph format. Your professor will tell you what he or she prefers. Either way, label your case sections clearly and carefully check your spelling and grammar. If you have used information from another source, you will need to cite that information. Again, your professor will tell you the preferred format (e.g., as in the text itself, at the end of the report, or some other way) for doing this. Also, you should include a cover page with pertinent information. You may even want to include a table of contents (with page numbers) if your report is lengthy. Pay careful attention to what your professor outlines as the specific requirements for a written case analysis and follow those requirements to the letter!

Oral Presentation

You may also be required to present your case analysis information in an oral presentation. Again, your professor may have specific requirements for an oral presentation. Be sure that you prepare your materials in accordance with those specific requirements. Exhibit 2 offers some suggestions for good oral presentations.

EXHIBIT 2 Suggestions for Good Oral Presentations

- Get the audience's attention immediately by opening with, for instance, an interesting piece of information about the company, an audience participation survey, video clips, or examples of the company's products.
- Present all the required parts. Your professor will let you know what these are.
- Provide explanations of your analysis, but don't provide so much detail that you lose your audience.
- As each person starts his or her part, state your name and what you will be covering.
- Use good transitions between speakers.
- Stay within the allotted time frame.
- Use visuals to present information when appropriate; for example, audience members likely will better understand financial and other quantitative information when it is presented in a visual format.
- Make sure visuals have no grammatical or spelling errors.
- Make your visuals simple and attractive.
- Display examples or samples of the company's products, if appropriate.
- Make good eye contact with different members of the audience—you don't want to always look at your professor.
- Practice the presentation before actually doing it.
- Enjoy giving your presentation, or at least act like you're enjoying it. If you act bored or uninterested, your audience is likely to respond in the same way.
- Vary the tone of your voice so it doesn't sound like you're speaking in a monotone.
- Don't use "umm" or "uhh" as you speak.
- Wear appropriate business-professional dress.
- Use note cards or a professional-looking folder to hold your typed notes.
- If using a PowerPoint presentation, do not talk to the computer screen in front of you or to the display screen behind you.
- Be sure to turn off cell phones and any other personal electronic devices.

Here is a sample case analysis that one of my student groups prepared. This analysis covers the following: an executive summary; external analysis; internal analysis; financial analysis; and strategic issue, alternatives, recommendation, and implementation. The company has been disguised, and the analysis includes only *selected brief* portions of each section so that you can see content and format. Again, keep in mind that any case analysis you do should follow the format your professor requires.

Mary Coulter

Executive Summary

Big Loud Motorcycles Inc. (BLM) has had four consecutive years of revenue and profit increases. During the case years studied (2009–2012), revenue increased 8 percent each year and profits grew 12 percent. Although the company was able to maintain its dominant 42.1 percent share of the U.S. market during this period, its push into international markets has not been as effective as planned.

Company Vision/Mission

As stated on its Web site, BLM's vision is to "build the world's best motorcycle product so that customers can experience the joys of motorcycling." Its mission is to "continue expanding its extensive line of motorcycles and accessories and to continue developing product features that help make motorcycling enjoyable and safe."

Company Goals

- Achieve sales and profit growth of at least 4 percent a year.
- Foster a sense of connection and community among our dealers and customers.
- Continually innovate new safety features in our motorcycles and our motorcycling accessories.
- Increase global revenues from 8 to 10 percent of annual revenues.

Company Policies/Values

- Our employees are the reason behind our success, and we value their contributions.
- BLM is committed to environmental responsibility.
- We are dedicated to providing our customers with outstanding product value and product service.

Corporate and Competitive Strategies Used

BLM is pursuing a corporate growth strategy using concentration through product and market development. The company's competitive strategy can be described as a defender strategy. It's a well-established company with the dominant market share. However, in "defending" its market share, BLM also uses differentiation to provide its customers with the best products possible.

External Analysis

Industry/Competition—Five Forces

Current Rivalry Opportunities

- *Strong industry sales growth.* According to the Motorcycle Industry Council, motorcycle sales in the United States have been increasing steadily since 2007. This is an opportunity because competitors won't compete as fiercely for a share of the market.

Current Rivalry Threats

- *High exit barriers.* Manufacturing motorcycles to consumers' expectations requires specialized and expensive machinery and a skilled workforce. This is a threat because these specialized assets are tailored to this industry, making it difficult for competitors to leave the industry.

Potential Entrants Opportunities

- *Government regulation.* Many government entities have noise regulations governing the manufacture and sale of motorcycles. This is an opportunity because it creates a barrier for potential entrants into the industry.

Potential Entrants Threats

- None found.

Bargaining Power of Buyer Opportunities

- *Products purchased are differentiated and unique.* Consumers aren't making purchase decisions only on price. There are many different elements about motorcycles that make them unique and desirable to consumers. This is an opportunity for the industry to be innovative in creating new designs and features to attract consumers.

Bargaining Power of Buyer Threats

- *Buyers have full information.* The Internet has made information readily available to consumers. Each industry competitor has its own Web site to inform the public about its products. This is a threat to the industry because consumers can use this information to compare competitors' products and bargain for the best deal.

Bargaining Power of Supplier Opportunities

- *Suppliers do not have ability to do what buying industry does.* Suppliers of materials such as metal, rubber, and plastic do not have the ability to manufacture motorcycles. This is an opportunity because industry competitors do not have to fear that, if they don't agree to the suppliers' terms, the supplier will decide to manufacture the product.

Bargaining Power of Supplier Threats

- *Suppliers' products are an important input to industry.* Materials such as metal, rubber, and plastic are necessary inputs for the motorcycle manufacturing industry. This is a threat because without these resources, there would be no motorcycles.

Substitute Products Opportunities

- None found

Substitute Products Threats

- *There are several substitutes.* Consumers can satisfy their need for transportation in numerous ways: automobiles, carpooling, public transit, bicycles, walking, etc. As automobile manufacturers continue to focus on improving mileage efficiency and [overall] safety, the motorcycle industry may lose one of its major product selling points.

General External Environment

Economic Opportunities

- *Personal disposable income is around $37,682 and is forecasted to continue increasing.* This is an opportunity because it means consumers have more available funds to spend on products that are not necessities.

Economic Threats

- *Unemployment levels are currently rising and are forecasted to continue increasing as the economy slows down.* Although the U.S. unemployment level was at 8.2 percent, economic analysts are predicting it could rise to 9 percent as companies continue to downsize. This is a threat because unemployed individuals don't have enough disposable income to purchase nonnecessity products.

Demographic Opportunities

- *The U.S. population is increasingly diverse.* Data released by the U.S. Census Bureau in mid-2011 reported that about one-third of the U.S. population was a minority. Hispanics continued to be the largest minority group (43.6 percent of all minority groups) as well as the fastest-growing minority group (growing at a rate of 3.3 percent). This is an opportunity for motorcycle manufacturers to broaden their target market to encompass these minority groups. In addition, experience marketing to different minority groups could prove beneficial in the global market.

Demographic Threats

- *Cost of higher education continues to increase, as does the amount of student financial aid.* Information from The College Board indicated that the average tuition and fees at four-year public colleges was up 35 percent from 2008. Also, total student financial aid increased by 3.7 percent but that amount didn't keep pace with inflation. This is a threat because college graduates will be paying off their student loans, limiting the amount of disposable income they might have to spend on products such as motorcycles.

Sociocultural Opportunities

- *More "gold-collar" employees (knowledge workers) in the workforce.* Today's organizations are composed of more gold-collar workers (designers, researchers, analysts, engineers, etc.). These employees are highly skilled individuals who are creative and talented problem solvers. This is an opportunity because they represent a potential target market that's likely to have more disposable income.
- *The increasing popularity of "green" issues.* People are becoming more concerned with green issues, looking for ways to be more environmentally friendly. This is an opportunity for the industry to promote how its products are better for the environment.

Sociocultural Threats

- *Public image of motorcycle riders is not always positive.* The Hells Angels image still haunts the motorcycle industry. Motorcycle riders are often perceived as scary, black-leather- and chain-wearing reckless outlaws. Although this is far from reality, this is a threat the industry faces. It is a threat because this perceived image potentially could prevent people from buying motorcycles.

Political–Legal Opportunities

- *State helmet laws.* Only one state has no helmet restrictions. Twenty states have full helmet regulations. The remaining states say helmets must be worn with some exceptions; most typically the restriction deals with the age of the driver. This is an opportunity because people may be more likely to purchase a motorcycle depending on their state's helmet laws.

Political–Legal Threats

- *State helmet laws.* Helmet laws are also a threat because these laws may prevent some people from purchasing a motorcycle.

Technological Opportunities

- *Increased use of robotics in manufacturing.* Sales and shipments of robots for use in manufacturing have topped the $1 billion mark annually. Such robots can be used in many different situations. This is an opportunity because a manufacturer can use such technology to become more efficient.

- *Online purchasing.* The number of online purchases is skyrocketing. This is an opportunity because, as the number of customers looking for customized motorcycles continues to grow, the Internet can be a tool to help them try out different options and features.

Technological Threats

- None found.

Internal Analysis

Strategic Managers' Strengths

- *BLM's CEO is very hands-on.* Every week, the CEO meets with a small group of BLM employees to discuss the company's products and to hear what types of issues they're dealing with. This is a strength because it provides the top decision maker with employees who are dealing daily with products and customers.

Strategic Managers' Weaknesses

- *BLM's CEO is very hands-on.* The CEO is meeting weekly with employees. This is a weakness because these meetings take a lot of time that he could be using to address more important corporate strategic issues.

Corporate Structure Strengths

- *Organized into different product divisions.* BLM's structure is organized around two different divisions: motorcycles and accessories. This is a strength because it allows the company to develop resources and capabilities for each important product division.

Corporate Structure Weaknesses

- *Company is not organized around geographic markets.* Although BLM has said it wants to grow internationally, it doesn't have a structure in place that supports that [goal]. This is a weakness because the company may not be able to achieve its goal of expanding its global revenues.

Corporate Culture Strengths

- *BLM employees believe in the products.* More than 70 percent of the employees own one of the company's motorcycles. This is a strength because it shows that employees believe in and support the company and what it stands for.

- *Company is very people-oriented.* As stated in its company values, BLM values the contributions of its employees. This is a strength because it shows the company is aware of how important its people are to its success.

- *Company emphasizes open communication.* Managers are encouraged to maintain open lines of communication with their employees in all matters. In addition, the company uses its Web site, customer forums, and charity rides to communicate with its customers. This is a strength because good communication is essential to a company's ability to keep employees and customers.

Corporate Culture Weaknesses

- None found.

Production–Operations Strengths

- *Most of the company's production facilities are less than seven years old.* A major updating of the company's production facilities was completed within the last seven years. This is a strength because during this updating, the company reconfigured the layout to be more efficient.

Production–Operations Weaknesses

- *Company has a large number of suppliers.* BLM's supply network consists of well over 100 suppliers. This is a weakness because this network must be coordinated to ensure that materials are available when and where needed. In addition, a problem with any of the suppliers could result in a production slowdown.

Marketing Strengths

- *Company's logo.* BLM's open-road logo is well known and easily recognizable. This is a strength because it helps establish a strong brand identification for the company's products.

- *Repeat customers.* A high percentage (42 percent) of BLM customers are repeat customers. Such customer loyalty is a definite strength because it indicates that BLM knows its customers and what they want. Also, customer loyalty means customers are buying your product and not your competitors' products. This is a definite strength!

Marketing Weaknesses

- *Target market is narrow.* Marketing research has shown that BLM's average customer is a married white male in his mid-forties who makes around $79,000 a year. This is a weakness because the company has not been able to expand its product appeal to segments [in which] there may be additional opportunities, especially the female demographic group and a younger demographic group.

- *Global marketing has not been effective.* BLM has not been able to secure a larger share of the European or the Asian markets in which it is competing. This is a weakness because the company has set of goal of increasing its global revenues, but the marketing approach it is currently using does not appear to be effective.

R&D Strengths

- *Current expansion of R&D facility.* BLM is currently expanding its R&D facility by adding an additional 165,000 square feet to its 300,000-square-foot facility. This is a strength because R&D is critical to success in this industry. BLM recognizes this and has invested in ensuring that it continues to be on the cutting edge of innovations in motorcycling technology.

R&D Weaknesses

- *No global R&D facility.* Currently, BLM conducts all R&D in its facility in Tennessee. Although this keeps all R&D efforts under one roof, it is a weakness because it also means that global R&D efforts may not receive the amount of attention needed to know how those markets are changing.

Human Resource Management Strengths

- *Educational benefits offered to employees.* BLM employees can use tuition reimbursement to pursue additional educational training. This is a strength because BLM is investing in the knowledge, skills, and abilities of its employees. BLM plainly states on its Web site that "its employees are the reason behind our success." Thus, to continue being successful means investing in those employees, which BLM is doing.

Human Resource Management Weaknesses

*   *Assembly work on custom-ordered motorcycles is precise and demanding.* A large percentage of BLM's production is for custom orders. Producing these large numbers of custom-ordered products requires close attention to detail so that product quality remains high. This can be considered a weakness because employees may experience job stress from such precise work.

Information Systems Strengths

*   *Numerous forms of communication with employees and customers.* Employees have monthly work forums and access to a company intranet where information is updated weekly (or more often as needed). Customers have access to online catalogs, magazine catalogs, direct mail pieces, and company-sponsored events throughout the year. This is a strength because the company is committed to making sure that two important stakeholder groups—employees and customers—are well informed.

Information Systems Weaknesses

*   *Web site is only in English.* BLM's Web site currently can be viewed in only one language. This is a weakness because the company has committed to growing its international markets. If it wants to do this, its Web site needs to be offered in different languages.

Financial Analysis

Author's note: Appendix 1 (see p. 237) identified what a thorough financial analysis includes. Because your own professor is likely to have specific instructions on how the financial analysis should be done, I did not include financial analysis data in this sample case analysis.

Strategic Issues

Strategic Issue #1

What is the issue?

One important issue facing BLM is the fact that **its target market is very narrow**. The company's research shows that its average customer is a married white male in his mid-forties who makes around $79,000 a year.

Why is this an issue?

BLM is missing out on significant marketing opportunities as the U. S. Census shows that about 51 percent of the population is female. There are some significant marketing opportunities being missed. BLM needs to come up with strategies to attract this potential target group.

Strategic Alternatives

Alternative #1

What: Offer more bikes tailored to fit women. Most of the company's bikes are heavy and designed to fit men. We need to design and develop completely new products designed for women.

How: The first step in this alternative is to find out what female riders want in a motorcycle. We propose they do this in a couple of ways. First, do an online survey of a selected sample of its current female customers. Ask them several questions about their experiences with our products. Then, conduct a focus group survey of a selected sample of women who are not currently customers. This research should look at what product features these women would look for in purchasing a motorcycle.

Once this information has been gathered and analyzed, a cross-functional group will be formed with seven employees—two each from R&D, production, and marketing and one from the financial area. This group will be asked to study the information and develop a list of possible product ideas that BLM might pursue. Once this group has completed its task, the information will be presented to BLM's top management team who will make the final decision regarding which ideas are the most feasible.

When that idea (or ideas) has been selected, the top management team will develop a plan for implementing the idea. This plan will cover product R&D (researching all aspects of design, building prototypes, product testing), production-operations (preparing to launch production of the new product), marketing (creating a total marketing campaign for the new product), human resource management (determining [whether] additional employees will be needed or if current employees will need additional production training), and financial (putting together the financials for this product).

Who: Individuals from the marketing area will be responsible for creating and administering the surveys. The analysis of the information will be done by the marketing research department. The cross-functional team will be formed by the director of marketing. BLM's top management team will be involved with assessing the team's ideas selecting which one(s) will be pursued and developing the implementation plan.

When: This alternative should be started immediately. The demographic opportunities are there, and we need to exploit those opportunities. The total time frame for doing this alternative is expected to be 18 months.

Where: This alternative will be done in the U.S. market and will involve input from headquarters staff in Tennessee. The implementation plan will indicate whether the new product will be produced at the Tennessee or the Arkansas facility.

Alternative #2

What: BLM should advertise and promote its current line of motorcycles to women.

How:

Who:

When:

Where:

Alternative #3

What: Acquire an established motor scooter manufacturer. A motor scooter is a two-wheeled vehicle with a step-through frame. They are typically lighter weight and highly maneuverable with styles and designs that might have strong appeal to women.

How:

Who:

When:

Where:

Recommendation

We are recommending that BLM pursue Alternative #3. Several small motor scooter manufacturers have developed products that have proven quite popular. An added benefit to this alternative is that it has the potential to not only attract women but an older demographic as well. As the average age of baby boomers continues to increase, a smaller, lighter-weight motorized product such as a motor scooter might appeal to them. Such an arrangement could be beneficial to both BLM and the motor scooter manufacturer. BLM would have ready access to R&D and production. The motor scooter manufacturer would have access to a wider market. This alternative will resolve this strategic issue because it allows BLM to add products to its line that are more suitable for the female market. With such products, BLM should see its sales revenues increase.

We are recommending that BLM reject Alternatives #1 and #2. Although Alternative #1 would provide BLM with complete control of the product from design to sale, too many uncertainties are associated with this alternative. Alternative #2 has some serious drawbacks because even by developing a targeted marketing campaign, the current products still have some drawbacks for the female customer.

Implementation

Changes in Organizational Structure: BLM's organizational structure will change when this motor scooter company is acquired. Those employees will now be part of BLM's employee team. In addition, BLM may need to add some additional employees to its marketing staff as they make this push into the female market.

Changes in Organizational Culture: The company's culture is not likely to change all that much although there will now be an emphasis on the female customer perspective. The cultural challenge is likely to be in ensuring that the employees of the newly acquired company are welcomed as employees of BLM and are made aware of the values and philosophies that have made BLM so successful.

Funding: Funds will be needed for the actual acquisition of the motor scooter company as well as the transition of that company as a subsidiary of BLM. These funds will come from two sources. The funds needed for the actual acquisition will come from long-term debt. Because BLM's debt ratio is favorable (50 percent), getting that funding should be no problem. The funds needed for the transition will come from BLM's $500 million cash reserves. As revenues increase (as expected), the long-term debt will be paid off.

Strategic Issue #2
What is the issue?

Why is this an issue?

Strategic Alternatives
Alternative #1
What:

How:

Who:

When:

Where:

Alternative #2
What:

How:

Who:

When:

Where:

Recommendation

Implementation

COMPREHENSIVE CASES FOR ANALYSIS

APPENDIX
3

In this section, you'll find three comprehensive cases for analysis. These cases—McDonald's, Southwest Airlines, and Ford Motor Company—cover a range of industries and strategic issues to consider. Although a significant amount of information is provided, you may want to find and use additional outside information, *if* your professor allows you to do so. After gathering your information, use the guidelines outlined in Appendix 1 for doing a comprehensive case analysis, unless your professor has specific directions for you to follow. I hope you have as much fun reading and analyzing these cases as I did writing them!

Mary Coulter

McDonald's Corporation

The first decade of the twenty-first century was one of ups and downs for McDonald's Corporation. In the early part of the decade, bad and poorly executed strategic decisions and the untimely consecutive deaths of two competent, experienced, and passionate CEOs (Jim Cantalupo in April 2004 and Charlie Bell in January 2005) led to a number of strategic challenges. The company got through those with its golden arches shining bright—then the worldwide economic crisis hit. But with the no-nonsense leadership of the company's CEO, Jim Skinner, McDonald's is doing better than ever.

A LOOK BACK

What happened at the world's number one fast-food company when things weren't looking so good? For years, McDonald's had been at the forefront of the fast-food industry (or as it's also known, the quick-service restaurant industry). It was the best known of the fast-food chains and changed the way Americans ate (issues of healthy eating aside). Millions of teenagers got their first taste of working for a paycheck at a McDonald's restaurant. The company prided itself on its consistent product and restaurant experience. Customers knew what to expect. They knew they would have the same product quality and restaurant experience at a McDonald's in downtown Detroit as one in Birmingham, Alabama, or Birmingham, England. However, the company's golden arches had become a little tarnished by 2000. A brand that was synonymous with fast and friendly service and consistent product quality had become known more for slow, surly service and poor product quality. In fact, McDonald's ranked last in a national survey done in 2001 of nearly 50,000 customers who ate frequently at fast-food chains. As one of the researchers said, "Most consumers have a pretty low perception about food at McDonald's." In another survey of repeat customers, many respondents said they ate at McDonald's simply because there wasn't a better alternative. That survey also showed that for the first time in 15 years, more people disliked

the brand than liked it. As if the company's own problems weren't enough of a strategic challenge, the industry also faced some major issues during this time period. A price war with a "how-low-can-you-go" approach had taken a toll on all fast-food restaurants. Savvy, value-seeking consumers recognized that they could get a really cheap meal by purchasing a full-size burger or sandwich for a dollar and stopped buying the value meal deals, which typically required purchasing the more profitable fries and soft drink.

What had gone wrong at McDonald's, and how did it respond? Poorly planned product changes, ineffective marketing plans, and changing consumer attitudes toward fast food forced a major restructuring of its U.S. operations in 2001. During this restructuring, corporate jobs were eliminated and service regions consolidated. But even those drastic steps didn't lead to desired performance improvements. So in 2002, additional corporate jobs were cut, and some 175 underperforming stores closed. The corporate performance tipping point came at the end of 2002 when the company had its first quarterly profit loss ever. That was a huge wake-up call for the company. So by early 2003, the CEO was out and longtime veteran company employee Jim Cantalupo was brought in as CEO. He took over a company with serious problems. However, McDonald's board of directors felt that Cantalupo's 30 years of experience in the company as well as his hands-on, back-to-basics leadership style was exactly what was needed to fix things and fix them fast.

Cantalupo obsessed over the basics—fast service, hot food, and clean restaurants. He was known for walking into any of the chain's stores unannounced, and after looking around, handing the store manager a scorecard that just happened to be printed on the back of his business card. And quite often, that score was frank and critical. He said, "When I see something wrong, someone's gonna hear about it." Cantalupo had a plan for turning around the company he loved, a plan he dubbed the Plan to Win. His plan for refocusing and redirecting the company's strategies was built on three components.

245

The first component was operational excellence. The company implemented this through a consistent restaurant-specific review and measurement process, including mystery diners. It also made changes to increase the speed of service by taking actions such as better organizing the kitchen, front counter, and drive-through areas and simplifying the restaurant environment by eliminating certain sizes and slow-selling items. In addition, the company reemphasized hospitality, accuracy, and cleanliness through new employee training and incentive programs.

The second component in the Plan to Win was to retake the lead in marketing, which McDonald's did by reconnecting with customers using a more hip and contemporary global marketing direction. The company chose to use a global brand message in advertising, packaging, and restaurant experiences, instead of having different messages for different locations. What it developed was the popular Justin Timberlake "I'm lovin' it" campaign (which it still uses). That campaign was more than a global marketing effort. It reflected an attitude that employees were to embrace and display as they served customers.

The final component in the Plan to Win was innovation. The company refocused its efforts on being an innovator. Its goal was to feature a variety of value, premium, and wholesome product options and to deliver the right products at the right price to customers.

In addition to its Plan to Win, McDonald's worked hard to improve individual restaurant profitability by leveraging economies of scale and by being more efficient. To this end, it expanded the use of labor-saving equipment and it streamlined processes.

All these strategic changes had a positive effect on performance. The company posted steady sales increases through most of 2003 and early 2004. Then, tragedy struck. In April 2004, at a worldwide convention for McDonald's franchisees in Orlando, Florida, Cantalupo died unexpectedly of an apparent heart attack. The company's board met and quickly named Charlie Bell as CEO. Bell was Cantalupo's right-hand man and one of the most forceful proponents of change at McDonald's. Bell continued the strategic realignment that he and Cantalupo had started. However, one month after being named CEO, another tragedy hit. Bell was diagnosed with cancer and underwent radical surgery. A recurrence of the cancer led to Bell's resigning his CEO position in November 2004. Not long after (January 2005), Bell lost his battle with cancer. Jim Skinner, the company's vice chairperson, was named CEO. Today, Skinner is building on the foundation put in place by both Jim Cantalupo and Charlie Bell. The Plan to Win is still the strategic cornerstone of McDonald's business today.

MCDONALD'S TODAY

"Our Plan to Win, with its strategic focus on 'being better, not just bigger,' has delivered even better restaurant experiences to customers and superior value to shareholders." The company's commitment to its strategic plan—the Plan to Win—summarizes the results of McDonald's varied strategic efforts. In a recent annual report, CEO Skinner stated, "Our success remains global, with all areas of the world contributing significantly to our results. We achieved all of this through our Plan to Win, which has served as our strategic blueprint for the past eight years."

It's clear that McDonald's strategic plan with its emphasis on the key business drivers—people, products, place, price, and promotion—is the foundation for its future strategic choices. What are some of the strategies the company, which now has almost 33,000 outlets worldwide, is pursuing today?

Marketing

McDonald's has long recognized the importance of promoting its brand and has one of the world's best-known and most valuable brands. In the 2011 ranking of best global brands by *BusinessWeek* and Interbrand Corporation, it ranked sixth on the list of the top 100 brands, the position it also held in 2010. In another global survey of the 100 most valuable brands by market research firm Millward Brown, McDonald's was ranked as the fourth most valuable brand, although it was rated number one in the fast-food segment. In 2011, the company was honored as the world's most effective brand by Effie Worldwide.

As far as company advertising, one promotional approach the company used was putting real people on its packaging. The company's chief marketing officer said, "People are really interested in reality. It's about real people connecting with our brand." Advertising industry experts say that for companies like McDonald's, "packaging has become an increasingly important opportunity to connect with consumers who may not be spending as much time watching television commercials." In today's economic environment, however, the company's promotional push has focused on value. McDonald's has relentlessly reminded consumers about its dollar menu, which has been around for a number of years. Although the company has been careful "not to overuse value messaging," it added the tagline "Now more than ever" to its ads during the second half of 2008 as the economic recession took hold. McDonald's promotional strategies appear to be hitting the mark, but the company's marketing strategies don't just revolve around promoting their brand.

The company always has been and continues to be on the forefront of product innovations. McDonald's basic product strategy is to "offer relevant menu variety to appeal to a broad range of customers." It carefully searches the market for new products and spends months testing those products in heavily monitored field tests to ensure that customers will purchase its new products. Some recent menu additions include Chicken McBites, Cherry Berry Chiller (slushie), frozen lemonade, blueberry banana nut oatmeal, and additional flavors to current menu items. The company is currently testing Fish McBites. Sensing a market opportunity, the company continues to push its McCafe coffees. A company spokeswoman said, "We are very aggressive and very bullishly adding this new line of coffees to all of our existing restaurants."

Although new product development is an important strategy, the company also relies heavily on old classics like the Big Mac and French fries. These products are on company menus around the world and account for a large chunk of annual revenues. In addition, McDonald's recognizes the importance of appealing to local tastes and offers a broad selection of food and beverages tailored to those preferences. For instance, in Japan, it offers the Ebi Filet-O (a shrimp burger similar to the Filet-O-Fish). In the Middle East, there's the McArabia (available with either grilled chicken or grilled kofta). Aussies can order a McOz (similar to a Quarter Pounder with beetroot, tomato, lettuce, and fresh onions). And doughnuts are a fixture on menus at British, Dutch, and German McDonald's locations. As the company states, it has "a global commitment, but a local approach."

One issue that McDonald's has been addressing is that its products have been the target of an ongoing negative publicity campaign aimed at what critics call its low nutritional quality (films and books such as *Super Size Me* and *Fast Food Nation*). However, as one analyst said, "McDonald's is not responsible for the way Americans eat. But the inescapable fact is that it serves an enormous number of them every day." That's why it's likely to remain the "top target for the food police." And that's why the company announced in mid-2011 a new initiative to offer healthier items on its menus over the next decade. McDonald's USA president Jan Fields said, "The commitments we're announcing today will guide the future evolution of our menu and marketing." It has pledged to continue to introduce healthier menu items and work to meet changing consumer expectations and needs as far as nutrition and balanced lifestyles. Fields said, "From a business standpoint, it is something we need to do to protect that business. Clearly, this is the way people are moving—we have a health-conscious society. We're in business for the long term, so we have to evolve." One focus has been its Balanced, Active Lifestyles (BAL) efforts that are designed to provide customers with tools to help them make informed lifestyle choices. For instance, it was the first restaurant chain to place nutrition information in an easy-to-read graphic format on product packaging. It also introduced high-tech, minigyms for kids called R Gyms (named for Ronald McDonald) to replace the familiar PlayPlaces. These gyms encourage kids to be physically active and feature everything from stationary bicycles with kid-friendly video screens to mini–basketball courts that give electronic feedback to participants to video dance pads where kids dance to moves programmed on video screens. One restaurant owner/operator located in California who installed an R Gym said that business at his store was up considerably and he planned to install them at his other stores. In fall 2011, McDonald's started adding apple slices and smaller portions of fries to its Happy Meal boxes. The company also relies on a Global Advisory Council of top academic researchers and fitness experts from around the world to give advice on a diverse range of BAL issues. Despite the company's efforts with its Happy Meals, the Center for Science in the Public Interest, an advocacy group that has pressured McDonalds' in the past, says "McDonald's clearly has a lot more to do, for both kids and adults."

Beyond Burgers

In an attempt to move beyond its reliance on burgers, McDonald's has tried different strategies. For instance, it developed a McKids line of clothing and toys to build on its strong brand name. However, only a few products remain in this line including toys, interactive videos, and books, some of which can be found online at Amazon.com, Wal-Mart.com, and Target.com. A more significant push beyond burgers was the company's investment in different restaurant formats including the Chipotle Mexican Grill (in 1998) and the Boston Market chains (in 2000). In 2006, it spun off Chipotle through an initial public offering (IPO). Then, in 2007, it sold its Boston Market U.S. locations, and in 2008, sold its minority interests in the United Kingdom–based Pret A Manger. These strategic actions should allow McDonald's to concentrate on its flagship brand.

Taking Care of Its People

McDonald's commitment to its employees has been a focus since Ray Kroc founded the company in 1955. He said, "Take good care of those who work for you, and you will float to greatness on their achievements." The company's belief is that "only satisfied people can satisfy our customers."

Despite its stated commitment to its employees, McDonald's has been criticized for its "dead-end McJobs" work environment and its high employee turnover (restaurant crews turn over entirely within a year, on average). In response, the company says, "Work at McDonald's meets various needs. For some people, it's a starting point…for others, it's a way to earn money while pursuing other interests." Forty percent of the top management team (20 of 50) started in a McDonald's restaurant, including the CEO, who joined the company in 1971 as a manager trainee. For the company to achieve its goal of being the world's best quick-service restaurant, it realizes the importance of providing the best experience for all McDonald's employees. These beliefs have been formalized into its strategic initiative called People: Learning for Life. At the heart of this initiative are its five people principles, as follows: (1) resources and recognition—managers treating employees as they would want to be treated; respecting and valuing employees; and formally recognizing employees for good work performance, extra effort, teamwork, and customer service; (2) values and leadership behavior—all acting in the best interest of the company; all communicating openly and valuing diverse opinions; all accepting personal responsibility; and all engaging in coaching and learning; (3) competitive pay and benefits—paying at or above local market salary levels; and having employees value their pay and benefits; (4) learning, development, and personal growth—giving employees work experiences that teach skills and values that last a lifetime; and providing employees the tools they need to develop personally and professionally; and (5) resources to get the job done—giving employees the resources they need to serve the customer; and adequately staffing restaurants to allow for a good customer experience and to provide schedule flexibility, work–life balance, and time for training.

Training is at the core of McDonald's people strategies. It wants its employees worldwide to be committed to quality, service, cleanliness, and value. The company and its owners/operators spend more than $1 billion a year on training and development programs worldwide. More than 300,000 people have graduated from Hamburger University (U), the company's Center of Training Excellence. At Hamburger U, employees are immersed in training on restaurant operations procedures, service, quality, and cleanliness. When they complete their Hamburger U training, they are said to leave with "ketchup in their veins."

The company has been recognized worldwide for its workforce practices. In 2008, the Great Place to Work Institute® ranked McDonald's as one of the best places to work in Latin America. It has received similar honors in more than 20 countries, including Australia, Canada, France, Germany, Hong Kong, and the United Kingdom. Also, the company trains more women and minorities than any other U.S. employer. In recognition of this, McDonald's received the Freedom to Compete Award from the U.S. Equal Employment Opportunity Commission in 2006 for its diversity and inclusion initiatives. And the company continues to receive awards for its diversity efforts.

Operational Excellence

CEO Jim Skinner is a fanatic about operations. When out in the field, he's known for inspecting the kitchens with a "rigor that many of his peers might reserve for financial reports." He's intensely focused on the efficiency and performance of the company's 33,000 restaurants worldwide. "Luckily for McDonald's, Skinner is an operations whiz who has turned the restaurant giant into a well-oiled machine, insisting on planning and accountability throughout the company." One analyst used the term "execution wonder" to describe McDonald's focus on restaurant operations.

"Serving customers is job #1 at McDonald's." Doing so efficiently and effectively is the goal of every single restaurant throughout the company. That's why McDonald's relentlessly focuses on all details of its restaurant operations. Many of the operational strategic initiatives introduced in the Plan to Win continue today. For instance, the Global Restaurant Operations Improvement Process evaluates how effectively company restaurants are meeting McDonald's standards and identifies opportunities to improve performance. Also, since more than half of its revenues come from its drive-through windows, the company continually upgrades and improves that product delivery format by using things such as double drive-through lanes. And it continues to develop products that are easy to eat, easy to prepare so they can be made quickly, and appealing to customers. But McDonald's also is implementing some new operational strategies. Recognizing the 24/7 lifestyles of many consumers, one major strategic shift has been the move to a round-the-clock schedule. There was a time when lunch used to be the busiest time at a McDonald's restaurant. However, when the Egg McMuffin was introduced in 1975, the breakfast hours (typically 6 a.m.–10:30 a.m.) became the big revenue generator. The company is evaluating the possibility of offering breakfast items at any time during the day. And it wants to be there for customers the rest of the day as well! Today, nearly 40 percent of the company's U.S. outlets are open around the clock, up from about 30 percent seven years ago. The midnight to 5 a.m. hours of operation are the fastest-growing time segment for the company. Now, both the night owls and the early birds can indulge their McDonald's cravings! And in Singapore, Egypt, and several countries in Asia and the Middle East, customers can get food orders delivered to their homes or offices.

Another operational strategy initiative has been a total redesign of its restaurant format. "The last major change at McDonald's restaurants was the introduction of PlayPlaces for children in the early 1980s." The company focused on two aspects with this redesign. One was an operational system encompassing production, customer service, and support with flexible components that could be "plugged in" to customize the operations and menu to specific restaurant needs. Even with this customization, the critical need for standardization wasn't ignored. Every component of the production system has been designed to ensure that products are easy to prepare and can be prepared fast. The other aspect of the redesign was "the look." Although coming up with an efficient design was critical, the company didn't overlook the importance of visual appeal. It eliminated the "heavy, plastic look" and replaced it with a more "clean and simple design"—something that it feels matches the new "contemporary, welcoming image the company wants to present."

The uncertain economic environment has led company executives to prepare for the "what ifs" that come with uncertainty. One thing it's doing is installing computerized systems in more locations that allow price adjustment based on consumer demand. For instance, in China, some restaurants cut the price of certain combo meals at lunch by as much as one-third. This increasing focus on customer data "measuring everything from whether customers are trading down to smaller value meals or dropping Cokes from their order to exactly how much they're willing to pay for a Big Mac" can only help McDonald's. As the company's president, Ralph Alvarez, said, "I love numbers. I think data used well really tells a story."

Other operational strategies include the company's emphasis on energy efficiency and an efficient supply chain. McDonald's has implemented a global energy management strategy to optimize energy use. In a pilot program in North and Latin America, restaurants were able to cut their energy consumption by more than 10 percent. This program is now being introduced to other locations. In 2007, the U.S. Environmental Protection Agency named McDonald's an Energy Star Partner of the year for its energy efficiency program. The company also realizes how important an efficient supply chain is to its ability to provide customer value. To that end, it collaborates with suppliers to ensure a "reliable supply of high-quality food at predictable, competitive prices."

Doing Business Responsibly

"For us at McDonald's, corporate responsibility is about who we are and how we operate in the diverse communities we serve." The philosophy of doing good and giving back is an important part of the company's heritage. It's always been at the heart and soul of McDonald's business. And with its Worldwide Corporate Responsibility Report, McDonald's "opens the doors to share what's behind the Golden Arches … not just what we do well, but our challenges too." McDonald's commitment to corporate responsibility can be seen in four areas: community, environment, marketplace, and people.

Its community responsibilities focus on local development by supporting local schools, youth sports, and other community programs. For example, one of its most widely known programs, the Ronald McDonald House charities, provides health care and help to children and families around the world. Its environmental responsibilities reflect its long-standing commitment to environmental protection. They have developed innovative programs for recycling, resource conservation, waste reduction, and now, energy conservation. The company's marketplace responsibilities involve working with suppliers and expert advisers to improve animal handling practices, helping preserving the effectiveness of antibiotics, ensuring the safety and quality of products and restaurant environments, and promoting the protection of workers' health, safety, and human rights. In early 2012, McDonald's announced it would begin working with its pork suppliers to begin phasing out "the use of so-called gestational crates, the tiny stalls in which sows are housed while pregnant." McDonald's has asked its five direct suppliers of pork products to provide their plans for reducing reliance on sow stalls. It will then assess those plans and announce what plans it might take in response. The company's senior vice president for supply chain management said, "McDonald's believes gestation stalls are not a sustainable production system for the future. There are alternatives we think are better for the welfare of sows." Finally, McDonald's people responsibilities, as shown by its workforce management policies and practices, revolve around integrating diversity in business operations and planning.

INDUSTRY CHARACTERISTICS

The restaurant industry is an interesting one. It's highly competitive, although there is significant growth potential as an increasing portion of consumers' food dollars is being spent on eating out, both in the United States and globally. According to industry analysts, the global fast-food market is forecast to increase by 27.7 percent through 2016. And the U.S. Department of Agriculture reports that consumption of food away from home accounted for 47.9 percent of total food expenditures in 2010. With the increase in dual-income families, single-parent families, and numerous moderately priced restaurant choices, dining out is a convenient option. Although the casual dining sector had been profiting from this trend, the declining global economic environment has seemed to favor the fast-food industry as consumers look for ways to stretch their dollars. In addition, fast-food chains must continue to cater to consumers' demands for healthier food alternatives. Not only will this help attract customers, it's important for deflecting potential obesity-related lawsuits.

Another trend affecting the fast-food industry is the rapidly fragmenting market with different ethnicities that have made once-exotic foods like sushi and burritos everyday meal options. In addition, quick meals of all kinds can be found in many locations, including supermarkets, convenience stores, and even vending machines. Another aspect of this trend is menu-item customization—tailoring a restaurant menu to meet customers' needs. Offering a variety of options to "have it your way" can be both a challenge and an opportunity.

Another trend affecting all areas of the "food" industry is consumer concern over food safety. News reports of customers eating unsafe food and getting sick or even worse, dying, have captured the attention of the public. Industry participants have to take this concern seriously.

Finally, the fast-food industry is coping with other companies trying to slice away pieces of its market, especially the lucrative breakfast market. According to a fast-food research firm, 11 percent of business is done at breakfast. That's why Starbucks, Panera, and Subway have introduced hot breakfast sandwiches.

WHAT NOW?

McDonald's golden arches continue to gleam brightly. Amazingly, the company serves nearly 68 million customers in 119 countries every single day. Ever since posting that first-ever quarterly loss in 2002, the company has logged 115 months of global comparable consecutive quarterly sales increases (through the end of the first quarter of 2012). Results for 2011 showed systemwide sales of $27.5 billion, up 12 percent globally and net income of more than $4.9 billion, up over 11 percent. However, where does McDonald's go from here? Its Plan to Win is driving results and has played a primary role in the company's strategic direction. Now, the strategic imperative is "to be better, not just bigger." CEO Skinner stated, "Our customer-centric Plan to Win continues to drive sustained momentum and is generating broad-based growth in our business. Our performance confirms that our emphasis on improving the McDonald's restaurant experience on the 5 P's of People, Products, Place, Price, and Promotion is the right strategy for our customers and McDonald's. One of our two separate but equally important goals is to stay sharply focused on the here and now and to run day-to-day operations with maximum efficiency and productivity. The other is to ensure that the right people and processes are concentrating on the future and developing new innovations that can sustain profitable growth over the long haul."

Sources: Based on McDonald's [www.mcdonalds.com], May 31, 2012; L. Burkitt, "McDonald's Pushes for More Gains in China," *Wall Street Journal,* February 29, 2012, p. B7; "Food CPI and Expenditures," *USDA Economic Research Service,* [www.ers.usda.gov], February 29, 2012; "Fish McBites, McDonald's Newest Snack, Makes It to Select Stores in Time for Lent," *Huffington Post,* [www.huffingtonpost.com], February 23, 2012; S. Strom, "McDonald's Set to Phase Out Suppliers' Use of Sow Crates," *New York Times Online,* February 13, 2012; N. Kruse, "Tailoring the Menu to Meet Customers' Needs," *Nation's Restaurant News,* February 6, 2012, p. 8; J. Jargon, "Late-Night Sales on a Roll For U.S. Fast-Food Outlets," *Wall Street Journal,* January 25, 2012, pp. B1+; "Fast Food Industry Profile: Global," Datamonitor Plc, January 2012, pp. 12+; A. Gasparro and M. Warner, "McDonald's Sells, 24/7," *Wall Street Journal,* December 9, 2011, p. B2; B. Kowitt, "Why McDonald's Wins in Any Economy," *Fortune,* September 5, 2011, pp. 70-78; J. Jargon, "Under Pressure, McDonald's Adds Apples to Kids Meals," *Wall Street Journal,* July 27, 2011, pp. B1+; S. Strom, "McDonald's Trims Its Happy Meal," *New York Times Online,* July 26, 2011; A. Schachtel, "McDonald's New Menu to Focus on Healthy Options," [http://wallstcheatsheet.com], July 26, 2011; Press Release, "Effie Worldwide and Warc Reveal First Global Effectiveness Rankings: The Most Effective Agencies, Advertisers and Brands," *Effie Worldwide,* [www.effie.org], June 23, 2011.

Southwest Airlines

Simple, fun, and *profitable.* These three words sum up Southwest Airlines. Yet, behind these words lies the heart and soul of a company's strategies that have helped it achieve an enviable record in the intensely competitive airline industry—39 consecutive years of profitability. As Southwest continues to do what it's in business to do, can it maintain that commitment to simplicity, fun, and profitability?

BACKGROUND

Southwest Airlines began service in June 1971, with three planes flying between three Texas cities: Houston, Dallas, and San Antonio. Herb Kelleher, the colorful character who cofounded the company and who now serves as chairman emeritus, recalls, "A lot of people figured us for road kill at that time." Why? Because the company's strategic approach was unlike anything the other major airlines were doing at that time. Air service in the early 1970s could best be characterized by high airfares, inconvenient flight schedules, complicated ticketing, and long and inconvenient flying experiences (from driving to the airport, parking, and finally reaching your destination). Southwest wanted to change that! It began with a simple notion—get your passengers to their destinations when they want to get there, on time, at the lowest possible fares, and make sure they have a good time doing it. To deliver this type of service, Southwest's strategy was to fly short-haul routes where the fares were competitive with driving. In these short-haul markets, speed and convenience would be essential to marketplace success. Therefore, Southwest's overall strategy was to minimize total travel time for customers, including ticketing and boarding, and to provide service out of airports convenient to doing business or vacationing in a city. Simple, yet effective, even today. Southwest has had a dynamic and impressive corporate history. The company has earned the respect of other airline competitors as well as other businesses around the world. An entertaining description of various highlights in the company's history can be found on its Web site **[www.southwest.com]**.

CURRENT OPERATIONS

Southwest Airlines bills itself as the nation's low-fare, high customer satisfaction airline. It serves primarily short- and medium-haul routes with single-class service targeted at business and leisure travelers. Its approach has been to focus primarily on point-to-point, rather than hub-and-spoke, service in markets. This point-to-point system provides for more direct nonstop flights for customers and minimizes connections, delays, and total trip time. Approximately 79 percent of Southwest's customers fly nonstop, with an average passenger trip length of about 658 miles. Despite the challenges facing the airline industry—high fuel costs, uncertain economic conditions, and enhanced security measures—2011 was another year of accomplishments for Southwest, including its 39th consecutive year of profitability (an airline-industry record) and continued leadership in customer satisfaction as it once again received the fewest customer complaints of all airlines. Several strategic factors can be identified as the keys to Southwest's success.

Low-Cost Advantage

Historically, Southwest has enjoyed a significant cost advantage compared to other traditional carriers, and low operating costs continue to be one of its competitive strengths. How does Southwest keep its costs low? One important element is its use of a single type of aircraft—the Boeing 737—that allows for simplified scheduling, operations, maintenance, and training. The planes have identical configurations, making them easy for crews to operate, maintain, and service. In 2011, Southwest operated a total of 559 Boeing aircraft with an average age of approximately 11.5 years. Planes on order through 2024 will replace older ones in the fleet and will add additional capacity as needed. Each plane flies an average of about six flights per day, with an average daily utilization of about 12-1/2 hours. The company also has outfitted its fleet with fuel-saving, performance-enhancing blended winglets (appendages on the wings). These winglets extend flight range, save fuel, and reduce engine maintenance costs and takeoff noise.

For several years, Southwest benefited from fuel hedging in which it paid upfront for the right to buy fuel at certain (in this instance, lower) prices. Although it still pays less for fuel than its competitors, Southwest's average fuel price rose from an average of $2.44 per gallon in 2008 to $3.25 in the 4th quarter of 2011. (An average 737 plane can hold about 7,000 gallons.) Southwest's fuel costs add up to about 37.7 percent of operating profits. To cut fuel costs, the company is power-washing jet engines to get rid of grime, carrying less water for bathroom faucets and toilets, and replacing passenger seats with lighter models.

Early in 2012, Southwest's CEO Gary Kelly announced the delivery of "a game-changer"—the Boeing 737-800. This aircraft will accommodate more passengers (175), but will require a fourth flight attendant. It also features a quieter cabin, increased overhead bin space, improved operational security features, LED reading and ceiling, and more durable/comfortable/eco-friendly seat. This aircraft is better suited for long-haul flying opportunities and will give Southwest more scheduling efficiency by "allowing for additional seats per departure in high-demand, slot-controlled, or gate-restricted markets." And this aircraft will allow Southwest to more profitably serve in the future more distant markets such as Hawaii, Alaska, Canada, Mexico, and the Caribbean. Kelly says, "We are building Southwest for the future, and the -800 will play a crucial role in getting us there."

Another operational strategy that has allowed Southwest to keep costs low is the use of technology, especially automated processes. Early on, Southwest recognized the benefits of automation. It was the first airline to offer a ticketless travel option (in 1994), eliminating the need to process and then print a paper ticket. It was the first airline to establish a home page on the Internet. In 2011, some 84 percent of Southwest's passenger revenues were booked via their Web site **[www.southwest. com]**. In 2005, Southwest further exploited technology by introducing DING!—a downloadable desktop application that alerts customers to exclusive deals. And now, Southwest is the first airline to offer this application on all three mobile platforms (iPhone, Blackberry®, and Android™).

Southwest also has relied on automation to facilitate the implementation of increased security requirements. It also has invested significant sums in facilities, equipment, and technology to efficiently process customers, who now have plenty of options to acquire boarding passes and who don't have to wait in lines at ticket and gate counters. Baggage tags are computer generated, as are automated boarding passes, and customers can access both at multiple points throughout the airport. Southwest also has self-service, rapid check-in boarding pass kiosks where customers can check their bags and obtain transfer boarding passes. Customers can also check in and get their boarding passes online at Southwest's Web site. In 2011, approximately 80 percent of Southwest customers checked in online or at a kiosk. Not only do such options benefit the customer, they benefit the company as well, because fewer employees are needed to provide these services. In December 2011, the company announced that it would be the first U.S. airline to equip ramp employees systemwide with hands-free wireless headsets that enable the ground crew and pilots to verbally coordinate the pushback of planes from the concourse gates. These new devices are expected to add another level of safety to potentially dangerous situations and could potentially help improve departure times and fuel efficiency.

The company's information technology strategies have benefited it in other ways, as well. As one of the first airlines to establish a Web site, southwest.com is the third largest travel site and continues to be the largest airline site in terms of unique visitors. It's clear that the Web site has been and will continue to be a vital part of Southwest's strategy for generating passenger revenue.

Southwest also has chosen to operate out of conveniently located satellite or downtown airports, which are typically smaller and less congested than other airlines' hub airports that are usually located quite a distance from a city's main business district. This operating strategy allows for high asset utilization because gate turnaround is quick (currently, Southwest's turnaround time is approximately 25 minutes), and the planes can get back in the air transporting more customers to their destination. As Kelleher used to point out, you don't make money sitting on the ground. Quick turnaround also means that the company doesn't need as many aircraft or gate facilities. Southwest has veered away from this strategy by flying out of New York's LaGuardia and Boston's Logan airports. However, this strategic shift is part of the company's plan to target new markets. CEO Gary Kelly says, "There are opportunities to tap that we haven't taken advantage of." And with the company's acquisition of Atlanta-based AirTran AirWays, Southwest will soon be dealing with the challenges of the busiest airport in the United States, Hartsfield-Jackson Atlanta International Airport.

Legendary Customer Service

Southwest gives customers what they want—great service at low prices. Southwest isn't just attracting large numbers of passengers—according to U.S. Department of Transportation (DOT) numbers, it's the largest domestic air carrier in the United States—it's keeping them happy. For 17 years running, the American Customer Satisfaction Index has ranked Southwest

first among airlines for highest customer service satisfaction. In 2011, Southwest rated highest among all major airlines in the DOT in terms of lowest rate of passenger complaints. In addition, another industry survey, the Airline Quality Rating report, said that Southwest is "consistently the company with the lowest customer complaint rate in the industry."

Southwest has formalized its dedication to customer satisfaction by adopting a comprehensive plan called Customer Service Commitment, which outlines actions the company is taking to promote the highest quality of customer service. This plan covers the gamut of possible customer concerns from baggage handling and passenger safety to delays and cancellations and getting a refund. The company is so committed to customer service that it has a person whose formal job title is senior manager of proactive customer communications. This person spends his or her "12-hour work days finding out how Southwest disappointed its customers and then firing off homespun letters of apology."

The company's mission (as found on its Web site) establishes the foundation for its commitment to serving customers: "The mission of Southwest Airlines is dedication to the highest quality of Customer Service delivered with a sense of warmth, friendliness, individual pride, and Company Spirit." This mission statement influences the way Southwest employees do their work. It emphasizes the company's strong desire to serve its customers and provides guidance to employees when they make service-related decisions. In fact, employees are continually reminded that Southwest is in the customer service business—and its business just happens to be airline transportation. The goal is getting customers from Point A to Point B and doing so in a way that is simple and fun for the customers and profitable for the company.

Southwest currently flies to 72 destinations in 37 states throughout the United States with more than 3,300 flights a day. With the high frequencies of flights and extensive route system that's continuing to expand, customers have convenience and reliability with lots of options to get where they want to go, when they want to go. The combination of low fares, convenient and frequent schedules, and friendly customer service means that Southwest dominates the majority of the markets it serves. And with the acquisition of AirTran, Southwest immediately and significantly expanded and diversified its overall route network.

A Black Eye for the Company—Plane Maintenance and Inspection Troubles

In the first quarter of 2008, Southwest faced serious allegations about its plane maintenance program. Two Federal Aviation Administration (FAA) officials who had noticed problems with the company's planes and Southwest's failure to do required inspections said they were pressured by Southwest executives to keep the serious problems hidden. In the wake of these allegations, the company grounded 8 percent of its fleet due to safety concerns until required inspections of the planes could be completed. In addition, Southwest suspended three employees and pledged to "fix any deficiencies in its internal controls." After receiving the results of an internal investigation, CEO Kelly said he "was concerned with some of our findings related to maintenance compliance." He went on to say that he has "insisted that we have the appropriate maintenance organizational and governance structures in place to ensure that the right decisions are being made." In March 2009, Southwest Airlines announced that it had resolved all outstanding issues with the FAA and would continue to work together with the agency to ensure the highest degree of flight safety for the public.

SOUTHWEST'S CULTURE AND PEOPLE

A major reason behind Southwest's success has been its culture and its people. Southwest has one of the most unique cultures among those of all major U.S. corporations. It's a high-spirited, often irreverent culture, much like its legendary cofounder Herb Kelleher. At company headquarters, the walls are covered with more than 10,000 picture frames containing photos of employees' pets, of Herb dressed like Elvis or in drag, of flight attendants in miniskirts, and caricatures of Southwest planes gnawing on competitors' aircraft. There are teddy bears and pink flamingoes. There's lots of laughter, and few, if any, neckties to be found. Even the CEO, Gary C. Kelly, normally a mild-mannered former accountant, shocked coworkers by showing up at a company Halloween party dressed—makeup and all—as Gene Simmons, front man for the rock group Kiss. On flights, flight attendants have been known to dress up as the Easter Bunny or to wear Halloween masks on those respective holidays. They've hidden in the overhead baggage compartments and jumped out at passengers who first opened them. However, no matter how fun and goofy it may get, no one at Southwest loses sight of the fact that the focus is on customers. This was plainly evident in the weeks after 9/11 when the laughter stopped. And it didn't take a memo from company headquarters to tell employees how to handle themselves during this difficult period. Employees understood that the normal gags played on passengers and the jokes and Halloween costumes were inappropriate. However, after about six months, passengers indicated through e-mails and comments that they were once again ready for Southwest's brand of fun. But even now, employees are sensitive to customers' concerns and know when to tone it down.

On its company's Web site, the company describes its culture from the perspective of "living the Southwest way, which involves a warrior spirit, a servant's heart, and a fun-LUVing attitude." In addition, employees are expected to get excellent results by focusing on safety, low costs, and high customer service and by demonstrating integrity in all actions.

In April 2006, Southwest went where no other airline had gone—the blogosphere. Playing the role of maverick once again, it launched its blog, Nuts About Southwest, "which allows customers to take a peek inside the culture and operations of Southwest Airlines." The corporate blog has employee bloggers representing a mix of frontline and behind-the-scenes employees—flight attendants, pilots, schedule planners, mechanics, and more. The blog offers customers a great venue for open dialogue. Southwest Air's now-retired president, Colleen Barrett, said, "When we first started the blog, I often told folks that I considered it to be a great customer service laboratory, if you will, but it has evolved into much more than that." Check it out at **[www.blogsouthwest. com]**. Southwest also has been tweeting since July 2007 and was recently named one of the Top 10 Best Twitter Brands. The company's social media specialist says that success in the micro-blogging arena requires being "honest, real, quick, and FUN."

Southwest recognizes that its success is due to its people and emphasizes that its people are its most valuable asset. The company has deep concern for its employees and seeks to provide fun and challenging jobs. It also takes care of its employees. Southwest was the first U.S. airline to offer a profit-sharing plan (in 1974). Employees own approximately 10 percent of the company's stock. Southwest's employees are known for their commitment to the company and to the Southwest spirit, which isn't surprising considering that the company has a reputation as a great place to work. The number of resumés it receives every year (more than 143,000 in 2010) is further proof that Southwest is perceived as a great place to work. At the end of 2011, Southwest (including AirTran) had almost 46,000 employees with more than 43 percent in flight operations; almost 7 percent in maintenance; more than 44 percent in ground, customer, and fleet service; and 5 percent in management, accounting, marketing, and office support positions.

The company, of course, wants the best of the best. Job applicants endure a rigorous interview process that can take as long as six weeks. Once hired, about 20 percent of new hires fail to make it through the training period. "We don't keep them if they don't fit into our culture. A lot of people think we're just relaxed, loosey-goosey, but we have a lot of discipline." Those employees who do make it are provided the support they need to succeed. Southwest has always had the approach of trusting employees and empowering them to make decisions effectively as they perform their jobs.

Many people assume that Southwest's outstanding relationship with its people is because it's nonunion but nothing could be further from the truth. More than four out of five employees at Southwest (approximately 82 percent) are union members. However, even during the times when other heavily unionized airlines were laying off employees and asking for sizable pay cuts from their employees, Southwest was negotiating new contracts and trying to keep its strategy of no layoffs and using employee furloughs as "a last resort." The company is proud of its reputation as a great place to work and acknowledges that its people are wonderful. They want to honor them, to treat them with respect, and to reward their productivity. However, Southwest also understands the importance of maintaining its low-cost structure. If that is lost, the company's future could be jeopardized.

FINANCIAL HIGHLIGHTS

To achieve 39 consecutive years of profitability in an industry that's known to be challenging and competitive is quite an accomplishment. During 2011, revenues were up 29.4 percent to almost $15.7 billion, but net income was down 61.2 percent to $178 million. (This financial information includes the operations of AirTran since the May 2, 2011 acquisition date, but only includes the operations of Southwest prior to that.) Considering the state of the economy, however, the ability to even post a net income is a testament to Southwest's strategies. Complete financial information can be found on the company's Web site **[www.southwest.com]**.

COMPANY AWARDS AND RECOGNITIONS

When you do outstanding work, you get recognized and Southwest Airlines is no exception. Here are a few of the company's many awards from 2011 and 2012:

- One of the most admired companies in *Fortune* magazine's annual ranking of Most Admired Companies for the 16th year in a row. In 2012, it ranked number ten.

- Named the Stevie Award Winner for the Company of the Year—Transportation by the International Business Awards for outstanding performance and customer service.

- Recognized as one of the top 10 safest airlines in the Holistic Safety Rating 2011 by the Air Transport Rating Agency.

- Ranked first in the 2011 Air Cargo Excellence Survey by *Air Cargo World* in the "up to 199,000 tonnes" category.

- Named the Number One Airline Brand by The Harris Poll in March 2011.

- Featured in J.D. Powers list of 2011 Customer Service Champions.

THE AIRLINE INDUSTRY AND MAJOR COMPETITORS

The airline industry is intensely competitive and highly unpredictable. Numerous external factors influence each competitor's profitability. One major uncertainty now facing the industry is fuel prices. Airlines need fuel to operate and are severely impacted by changes in jet fuel prices. Southwest has substantial fuel-hedging positions until 2013, but the company continues to actively manage its fuel hedge portfolio to address volatile fuel prices.

Other industry uncertainties included economic conditions in the United States and the resulting customer demand and continued vulnerability to exogenous events (such as a terrorist attack) that had the potential to adversely affect air travel. Other characteristics that make the airline industry vulnerable include:

- It is tremendously capital intensive.

- There are enormous fixed costs.

- It is fuel intensive, and with alternative energy sources unlikely, is subject to global political events.

- It is labor intensive, and there are fewer and less experienced workers available to fill jobs.

- There is no product inventory or shelf life—an unfilled seat on a flight can't be put in inventory and sold later.

- It is quite cyclical as much of passenger travel demand is discretionary.

- It is heavily regulated and taxed.

Competitors continue to nip at Southwest's wings. JetBlue and Spirit Airlines, especially, are strong, innovative, and low-cost. Other mainline carriers (e.g., American, Delta, and United) have been addressing many of their fundamental problems by consolidating with other air carriers. Delta combined with Northwest in 2008; United and Continental became one in 2011; and American filed for Chapter 11 bankruptcy in late 2011. Although these carriers are large, they still have a long way to go to pose a major threat.

THE FUTURE

Southwest Airlines has been an anomaly among airlines. Its performance has consistently been among the industry's best. However, Southwest faces some serious challenges as it seeks to maintain its competitive leadership position. Severe cost pressures have led the company to implement some aggressive measures to improve productivity. These measures included no longer paying commissions on flights booked by traditional travel agents, consolidating its reservations operations centers, and motivating employees to continue to look for innovative ways to better run the business. Even though Southwest continues to have some of the lowest costs in the industry, costs continue to climb. Keeping costs under control and keeping its culture alive are just two of the key challenges facing Southwest as it continues to consolidate operations with AirTran and to expand and reinforce its role as a leading prime-time industry player.

Sources: Based on "Most Admired Companies, 2012," *Fortune Online,* [money.cnn.com/magazines/fortune], March 5, 2012; Southwest Airlines [www.southwest.com], March 1, 2012; N. Trejos, "Southwest-AirTran Deal Cuts Service to Some Cities," *USA Today,* March 1, 2012, p. 1B+; S. Carey and D. Cameron, "Southwest Takes a Breather," *Wall Street Journal,* February 27, 2012, p. B3; "Southwest Airlines Form 10-K," *EDGAR Online,* [www.edgar-online.com], February 9, 2012; American Customer Satisfaction Index [http://www.theacsi.org], June 21, 2011; S. McCartney, "Can't Call Southwest a Discount Airline These Days," *Wall Street Journal,* June 2, 2011, pp. D1+; T. W. Martin, "Southwest Eager for a Seat in Atlanta," *Wall Street Journal,* May 10, 2011, pp. B1+; D. Koeni, "Southwest Takes Aim at Business Travelers," The Associated Press, *Springfield, Missouri, News-Leader,* May 3, 2011, p. 7A; and B. D. Bowen and D. E. Headley, "2011 Airline Quality Rating," [http://aqr.aero/aqrreports], April 2011.

Ford Motor Company

Ford Motor Company (Ford), like other global car manufacturers, is facing a challenging environment. Although it had a net income of $20.2 billion in 2011 ($12.4 billion of that from a one-time tax allowance), it faces economic troubles in Europe, growing pains in Asia, and intensifying competition in the United States. Once the world's third largest automaker (in terms of cars sold), Ford is now number four behind General Motors, Volkswagen, and Toyota. The first decade of the twenty-first century was a tough one for Ford. The company faced declining market share, an industry going through dramatic changes, and an uncertain future. CEO and president Alan Mulally faced a challenge in turning around this corporate icon. His plan can be summed up by the following statements: "Although business conditions have deteriorated rapidly on a global scale, our ONE FORD plan is more right than ever; we are focused on swift and decisive actions to stay on course with the four elements of our plan; and we are working on longer term restructuring actions on a global basis and managing all of the elements that we control to respond to changing economic conditions."

HISTORY

With much sentimental fanfare and hoopla, Ford celebrated its 100-year anniversary in June 2003. In the early 1900s, Ford "began a manufacturing revolution with its mass production assembly lines." From the production of the first Model T in 1908 to the 500hp GT racer with a price tag of $150,000, Ford has had some fabulous successes in product design. The Mustang, first introduced in 1964, is one of the company's best ever products. The car made the company a lot of money as it ignited Detroit's obsession with the baby boomer market, a preoccupation that has been difficult to let go. Ford sold one million Mustangs in 24 months, an incredible product launch for a new model, even by today's standards. Then, there was the Ford Explorer, the first sport utility vehicle (SUV) designed for the consumer market. It proved extremely popular and started a product craze that other car manufacturers soon followed as consumers clamored for more. Other big product successes for Ford Motor included the Taurus and the popular and best-selling F-Series truck. But it's also had some notable failures as well. For example, there was the Pinto and its exploding gas tanks. And the Edsel (1958–1960) was a car with an unusual design that never really caught on with consumers. More recent (2000–2001) was the Firestone tires–Ford Explorer fiasco, which some have suggested may have been the start of the company's current struggles.

In 1998, when family member William Clay Ford Jr. (who prefers to be called Bill) became chairman of the company (a position in which he wouldn't have to be heavily involved with the "strategy stuff"), Ford was riding high. Sales and market share were strong and the company was well positioned to exploit its strengths. However, the CEO at that time, Jacques Nasser, had grand plans to transform Ford from a simple car manufacturer to a consumer brand company. He planned to take the company into diverse businesses such as Internet ventures, car retailing, repair shops, and even junkyards. Not surprisingly, these businesses flopped and, perhaps even more damaging, distracted Ford executives from their core business of designing, building, and selling cars. Then, the Firestone tire recall spun out of control. With the company's worldwide operations floundering, the board of directors fired Nasser in October 2001 and Bill took on the additional responsibility of CEO, a position he was reluctant to assume. However, as the great-grandson of founder Henry Ford and the fourth generation of his family to lead the company, Bill understood and accepted his family responsibility. The burden was on him to fix the company and drive it into its second century. And this was a company in crisis, having lost close to $6.4 billion total in 2001 and 2002. Although the company posted a profit of $495 million in 2003 and $1.4 billion in 2005, Bill felt it was time to turn over the leadership reins to someone else. Former Boeing executive Alan Mulally was named president and CEO in 2006. And Mulally had his work cut out for him. Ford posted losses in the billions for 2006 to 2008. The company seems to have turned a corner, although it faces many challenges.

INDUSTRY AND COMPETITORS

The global car industry is one characterized by fierce competition; fickle customers; manufacturing overcapacity worldwide; maturity stage of the industry life cycle, especially in the large industrialized countries; and declining demand for cars in an anemic global economy. Technology continues to drive rapid change in products and processes. In addition, more market segments and new products are leading to intensified competition. The once-dominant U.S. car manufacturers have been displaced by strong, smart, and aggressive global competitors. In 2008, Toyota took over the title of the world's number one automaker from General Motors. It held that position until 2011 when natural disaster disrupted many of that company's operations. Toyota and the other Japanese car companies have made an all-out assault on the European market—a market that had been dominated by the U.S. car companies. In May 2007, DaimlerChrysler sold a controlling interest in its struggling Chrysler Group to a private equity firm, Cerberus Capital Management of New York. In early 2008, Ford announced the sale of its Land Rover and Jaguar lines to India-based Tata Motors. Then, in late 2008, as the economy situation worsened and car sales volumes continued to decline, both Chrysler and General Motors took bailout money from the U.S. government. Ford was the only U.S. car manufacturer that did not take any government monies, saying that it had enough cash on hand to get through 2009. Also, in 2009, the Chrysler Group formed a global strategic alliance with Fiat and now produces Chrysler, Jeep, Dodge, Ram, SRT, Fiat, and Mopar vehicles and products.

Consumer demand for cars, especially in the U.S. and European markets, tends to follow the state of the economy. During good economic times, consumers are more willing to buy cars and other durable and expensive products. However, uncertainty—economic, social, global, or political—makes consumers more hesitant to buy new cars. To stimulate demand, car companies often try incentives such as rebates, no money down, and free financing for extended time periods to pull customers into dealers' showrooms. Although these incentives can be good for consumers, they tend to have a disastrous effect on a car company's bottom line. Because of the intense competition in the industry, when one car company introduces an incentive, others usually must follow suit or risk losing potential buyers. Also, U.S. car manufacturers have had to deal with the threat of the ever-strengthening foreign car companies, especially the Japanese.

For years, the Japanese car manufacturers have used flexible manufacturing systems, which allow multiple models to be built on the same assembly line and enable faster product changeovers. Although U.S. car manufacturers had lagged behind Japanese competitors in terms of manufacturing costs and efficiency, they are making progress. A key annual manufacturing efficiency study (the Harbour Report) showed that in 2008, Chrysler and Toyota both had an average 30.37 manufacturing labor hours per vehicle; GM averaged 32.29 hours per vehicle and Ford was at 33.88 hours. Another area where Ford was outpaced by foreign auto companies was in labor costs. Ford's union labor costs were about $22 an hour more than nonunion labor at U.S. plants of foreign makers. These manufacturing realities have made it difficult for U.S. car companies, especially Ford, to be competitive. However, Ford remained committed to transforming its assembly plants into lean and flexible centers of manufacturing excellence, although it was still trying to catch up.

FORD MOTOR COMPANY TODAY

Alan Mulally's team-building skills and industrial savvy have inspired and emboldened employees enough to revive the automaker. Mulally joined Ford Motor in September 2006 from Boeing, where he also led a successful turnaround effort. Mulally's first move was to "immediately dust off his Boeing playbook" as he looked to implement many of the same strategies that had worked in turning around Boeing. Although he recognized the massive problems facing the company in achieving strategic competitiveness and profitability, he was determined to take the dramatic, painful steps and to "plow through gut-wrenching change" to transform the company and return it to global prominence. Guiding his initial efforts was the Way Forward plan that was first announced in January 2006 and the implementation of which was accelerated in September 2006 when Mulally was appointed CEO. This comprehensive plan addressed seven areas where strategic changes would be focused: bold leadership; customer focus; strong brands; bold, innovative products; great quality; clear pricing; and competitive costs and capacity. Mulally also identified four key priorities: (1) aggressively restructure the company to operate profitably at the current real demand and changing model mix; (2) accelerate product development with new products that customers really want and value while achieving manufacturing excellence by reducing complexity and improving quality; (3) obtain financing to do these things and improve the balance sheet; and (4) work together with accountability with all partners. In addition to the Way Forward plan, Mulally fashioned a strategic effort dubbed ONE FORD in an attempt to "fully leverage the tremendous worldwide resources of Ford." In his remarks to shareholders at the 2008 annual meeting, Mulally

had this to say: "We operate in a fiercely competitive global industry. To achieve profitable growth, we have to make the best use of our human resources and take advantage of every potential economy of scale and best practice we can find. That means operating as one team around the world, with one plan and one goal…ONE FORD…profitable growth for all." These efforts and priorities affect several functional areas within the company.

Manufacturing and Product Design

Ford is first and foremost a manufacturing company. However, the stark reality is that the Japanese and Korean car companies outearn Ford on each car made by delivering more features for lower cost. To have any chance of turning its business around, Ford would have to focus on its manufacturing strategies.

As the Way Forward plan indicated, Ford's goals in manufacturing were competitive costs and capacity. A central part of the strategy for achieving those goals was the decision to close 16 plants and eliminate 44,000 jobs by 2012, with nine of the plants closed by 2008. But Ford also had to continue to make its remaining manufacturing plants as efficient and effective as possible by stressing manufacturing strategies and processes to maximize operational quality and efficiency.

Ford already had several strategic initiatives in place to reduce costs. During 2003, for instance, it achieved cost reductions of $3.2 billion, part of which came from its quality improvement and waste elimination methodology called consumer-driven Six Sigma. Since the implementation of this quality improvement program, Ford completed more than 9,500 projects that saved a total of $1.7 billion worldwide. These quality improvements also led to a dramatic reduction in the number of car recalls and drove down warranty spending by 18 percent. In 2010, Ford began adding touch-screen control systems to some of its most popular models as a way to stand out from competitors and hopefully draw in new customers. Unfortunately, MyFordTouch had some flaws, frustrating many buyers. "Ford's quality ratings plunged and a feature meant to increase loyalty instead damaged perceptions of the company." In response, Ford issued a major upgrade that redesigns much of what customers see on the screen and addresses problems with the system crashing and rebooting while the vehicle is being driven. Ford's group vice president for global product development says, "We expect that these improvements will put us back on track in the quality ratings. It's more than just an update. This is a substantial upgrade."

In addition to the quality improvements, Ford also is working on improving its safety ratings. At one time, it was the industry safety leader, with more five-star crash ratings than any other brand or company. However, in 2011, Hyundai/Kia and Volkswagen/Audi led the pack, each with nine models that earned "top safety pick." In 2012, Toyota Motor North America got the most "top safety picks" with 15 of its models. Ford also is working collaboratively with suppliers to find additional areas for performance improvement. Another challenge that Ford has is with its unions. Although the company loudly proclaimed the fact that it was the only U.S. auto company to get through the recession without help from the government or a bankruptcy judge, it also lost two weapons that its competitors have: binding-arbitration clauses in its labor contracts and a ban on strikes. However, Mulally says that the focus should be on competitiveness. "We have gone from not being able to compete in the U.S. to where we are now competitive. Our cost structure, including wages and benefits, is competitive with the best in the world." The agreement with the United Automobile Workers union announced in mid-March 2009 reduced workers' hourly rate (including salary and benefits) to $55, an amount that is saving the company at least $500 million a year and bringing its labor costs more in line with that of foreign competitors' plants in the United States.

Under the Way Forward plan, Ford continued efforts to reduce material costs by at least $6 billion by 2010. Achieving such cost reductions required continued efforts to reduce manufacturing complexity and to improve quality in products and in processes. Although the company made progress, it hasn't been an easy thing to do.

When Mulally came on board, he scrambled to familiarize himself with Ford's vehicles. He began driving a different Ford car to and from work each day. He discovered that the switches for lights, wipers, and so on, were often in different locations. Such variations are unnecessary and costly. Mulally "demanded that product engineers create uniform parts that most Fords can share," an action he believed would lead to leaner and more reliable production. At another meeting, Mulally laid out 12 different metal rods used to hold up a vehicle's hood. "He wanted to demonstrate that this kind of variation is costly but doesn't matter to consumers." By sharing vehicle architecture, components, and best practices from around the world, the company could leverage its scarce resources for the greater good of the entire company.

Another element in changing Ford's manufacturing strategy was to right-size its capacity. Although the announced plant closings played a major role, Mulally also wanted to emphasize a capacity strategy that was in line with customer demand—a more "customer-driven strategy versus a fill-the-plant strategy." Although the goal was to reduce capacity by 26 percent by the end of 2008, the dire economic situation and plummeting demand for cars forced an unplanned reduction in capacity.

Mulally also realigned the organizational structure to put additional focus on markets and customers and to better leverage global assets and capabilities. The automotive operations, which include Ford North America, Ford Europe, Ford South America, and Ford Asia/Pacific & Africa, now report directly to him. In 2010, Ford sold its Volvo unit to China's Geely Holding Group in a $1.5 billion deal.

Mulally also created a single global product development organization. This new structure enabled the company to "work together more effectively to continuously improve quality, productivity, and speed of product development." The global product head was working to create a "Ford feel" for all its vehicles, much like BMW. He said, "When you get into a Ford vehicle, you should know immediately it's a Ford by the feel." Many of these strategic changes are impacting the company's marketing strategies as well.

Marketing

Great automotive products have always been important to Ford. The company's auto brands include Ford and Lincoln. Many of its brands are quite successful. For instance, in 2011, the Ford F-series was the best-selling truck in America—a feat it's achieved for more than 35 years. It currently has about 100 nameplates, but wants to reduce that number to around 13 by 2014. Economic troubles in Europe and Asia are of major concern to the company. And 2012 was going to be a challenging year.

Ford's marketing strategies will again play an important role in turnaround efforts. Mulally hired James Farley, a former Toyota executive, as Ford's chief global marketing executive. They decided that the company's brands needed to be more focused. Thus, Lincoln now will focus on premium sedans and SUV and the Ford brand will continue to offer the broadest range of products and options.

In continuing its aggressive move to global vehicles, Elena Ford (great-great-granddaughter of company founder Henry Ford) was hired for the newly created position of director of Global Marketing, Sales, and Service Operations. In this position, she will implement the company's "ONE FORD" marketing vision. Enhancing the global marketing efforts is the next step in the ONE FORD plan to integrate Ford's worldwide operations and leverage its scale and expertise. This marketing approach follows the company's consolidation of global product development in 2006 and global purchasing operations in 2008. Within the next five years, the plan is to have common Ford vehicles competing in global segments. The launch of these global products will be built on lessons learned from the launch of the Fiesta, the company's first global product under its ONE FORD vision. Farley said, "Our new products are being recognized for excellence around the world, and they are leading the competition in quality, fuel efficiency, safety, and smart technologies. Now, our job is to more effectively and efficiently connect these great products with our customers and build on Ford's strength as one of the world's most admired companies and brands. In early 2011, Ford introduced a worldwide line of compact cars under the Ford Focus name. Ford called the Focus its first truly global product—that is, created from scratch to share as many parts as possible wherever it is built or sold. The company recently unveiled a new SUV, the 2012 Escape, that also showcases the company's world car strategy. The car is made from a common set of parts and components that Ford will use to make its Focus compact car, two future minivans, and at least six other models.

Another marketing change Ford made was to its advertising. The company used a "more combative strategy that it hoped would put its vehicles back on America's shopping list." The Ford Challenge advertising campaign asked consumers to compare Ford vehicles to their toughest competitors. The first ads showed consumers favorably comparing the Ford Fusion midsize sedan against a Toyota Camry and a Honda Accord. This "push" accelerated the model's sales by almost 33 percent. Ford also ran ads that compared the safety record of its popular F-150 truck with that of competitors, especially taking a jab at Toyota's Tundra truck that received only a four-star safety rating. The Focus campaign is zeroing in on what Ford Motor considers to be the technological advantages of the car—features like assisted parking and Wi-Fi hot-spot capability that are typically found only in larger, more expensive cars. "That democratizing of technology is a strategy by Mulally, to add value to smaller cars to convince consumers that they are worth paying more for than previous pared-down models with dismissive descriptors like econo-boxes."

Ford is committed to its products and customers. The company's vision, mission, and values can be found on its Web site **[www.ford.com]**. Its values statement is particularly enlightening: "The customer is Job 1." Ford understands how important strong customer relationships and innovative, high-quality, high-value products are to its business and its ultimate success.

Ford's dealers—almost 12,000 of them in 2011—are an important element in the success of the company's marketing efforts. Together, the dealers and the company must provide customers (current and potential) with products and a buying and service experience that meet and exceed their expectations. It's a relationship that hasn't always been pleasant—especially now, as Ford and the auto industry face challenging circumstances. However, one automotive magazine writer stated that "Ford dealers I've talked with show a pride of dealership that belies some of the troubles they and Ford have seen lately from sluggish sales and lost market share." Ford is committed to working together closely as partners and providing dealers with outstanding new products and trucks so everyone experiences a successful and profitable outcome.

In addition to its automotive products, Ford's other main business is its finance subsidiary, Ford Motor Credit, which provides financial services and is the number one auto finance company in the United States. Also, until 2005, it owned Hertz, the rental car company, but sold it to focus on its automotive divisions.

Employees

The struggles Ford is facing have not been easy for its employees. Despite the difficult conditions, Ford cares about its people. The top management team is experienced and firmly committed to turning around this proud company. Its workforce is dedicated and talented. The company understands that its future success depends on its people. As it says in its Code of Basic Working Conditions (which can be found on the company's Web site), "The diverse group of men and women who work for Ford are our most important resource." This code outlines universal values that serve as the cornerstone of the company's relationship with employees and covers important people issues such as child labor, compensation, forced labor, collective bargaining, harassment and discrimination, healthy and safety, and work hours.

As stated earlier, a major component of the Way Forward plan was the elimination of 44,000 jobs by 2012. To accomplish this, Ford used buyout offers to persuade hourly workers to retire early or to give up their jobs, hoping to get 35,000 hourly workers to leave. More than 37,000 accepted the deals, but Ford announced in April 2007 that about 2,000 hourly workers had changed their minds about accepting incentives to leave. But that merely put Ford back to its original goal. Additional workforce reductions are coming from the elimination of salaried positions through early retirements, voluntary separations, and even involuntary separations, as needed. Ford is at the point now where, over the next two years, it's going to be adding about 7,000 new jobs.

Another major personnel problem Ford faced was increasing health care-related expenses. For instance, in 2006, its health care expenses for U.S. employees, retirees, and their dependents were $3.1 billion, 58 percent of that going to retirees' health care costs. Ford, like many other companies, has shifted a higher portion of health care costs to its employees and retirees, but still expects its health care costs to continue to increase. This commitment will continue to affect the company's ability to meet its profitability goals. Agreements between the company and its union should go a long way to helping the company better control its total labor costs.

Corporate Culture

Having a CEO with no experience in the industry is always a gamble. However, even Bill Ford says that Mulally's progress in "shaking up a calcified culture has thus far kept Ford independent and away from" the government's bailout. Another industry consultant said that, "The speed with which Mulally has transformed Ford into a more nimble and healthy operation has been one of the more impressive jobs I've seen. It probably would have been game over for Ford already but for the changes he has brought."

With its long and exceptional heritage, Ford believes strongly in the values that have guided the company over the years. But that heritage also made needed changes more difficult. A professor of management at Wharton said he was "concerned that Ford's corporate culture might be getting in the way of Mr. Mulally. As you walk into Ford or even General Motors these days, the culture feels different. It does not have that drive for perfection, the focus on continuous improvement, the attention paid to the small things that Toyota does." Ford employees may be finding it difficult to change their "mental mapping" instilled when the company was reaping millions in profits from its SUVs and pickup trucks and not wanting to recognize the dire circumstances and tough choices faced today. The new message at Ford is that "the bigger-is-better worldview that had defined it is being replaced with a new approach: less is more."

What did Mulally have to deal with? Initial discussions between Bill Ford and Mulally were pretty candid. Bill shared one key insight: "Ford is a place where they wait for the leader to tell them what to do." His point? Ford executives weren't sufficiently involved in the decision making. By the time Mulally came on board, he had met with every senior executive and asked a lot of questions. Not all of them liked the "Way Forward Plan," especially the part that had the company moving to vehicles that could be sold in different markets. Mulally knew that to work the plan, he would have to change Ford's culture.

The changes haven't been easy for Ford's hourly workers or for its management team. One of Mulally's first moves when he came onboard was instituting the same Thursday meetings he had used at Boeing. These meetings were a tool for formulating business plans. "At those weekly meetings, cell phones, BlackBerrys, side conversations, mean jokes, personal opinions, turf battles, and bathroom breaks (unless urgent and quick) were out. In were candor, data, results, more data, and applause for executives who showed progress." The first Thursday meeting, as expected, went badly. When Mulally asked each division head to present his or her results and forecasts, he said that the numbers didn't make sense. He asked, "Why don't all the pieces add up for the total corporate financials?" One manager replied, "We don't share everything." Instead, executives had run their units without integrating with other divisions, even occasionally holding back information. Mulally was astounded. He told the associates, "Data can set you free. You can't manage a secret."

After that first disastrous meeting, one thing Mulally tackled was a culture that "loved to meet and where managers commonly held 'pre-meetings' where they schemed how to get their stories straight for higher-ups." Mulally was determined to have a constant stream of current data that would give his team a "weekly snapshot of Ford's global operations and hold executives' performance against profit targets." Now it's become difficult for managers to hide unpleasant facts because numbers are being constantly updated. In the data operation rooms at Ford's headquarters, the walls are covered with color-coded tables, bar charts, and line graphs that represent what's going on in every corner of Ford's world. Divisions not living up to profit projections are red; those hitting their numbers are green; and yellow means results could go either way. Even though executives were held accountable, most began believing in the power of information when they saw how Mulally used the data. For instance, the executive team decided to delay the launch of the F-Series truck by about six weeks, cycle down fourth-quarter production, and clear out last year's F-Series trucks when inventory had piled up.

Another thing Mulally changed was Ford's approach to grooming managers. Previously, Ford executives were cycled into new jobs every few years. No one was ever in a job long enough to feel accountable or like they could make a difference. Under Mulally, executives were kept in jobs and as one said, "I've never had such a consistency of purpose before." A big test for Ford will be Mulally's successor. Analysts expect Mr. Mulally to give up the top spot before 2013. "Ford has begun considering potential successors and ways of handling the transition, including the appointment of a chief operating officer who would work alongside Mr. Mulally before taking the helm."

One final important aspect of Ford's culture is something that Bill Ford is known for: his strong and unwavering commitment to environmental responsibility. And Mulally supports those efforts. He said, "Bill Ford and I share the same vision of building fuel efficient, environmentally friendly vehicles that protect their passengers and our planet." Although the company backed off its headline-grabbing promise in 2000 to improve the fuel economy of its SUVs by 25 percent in five years, its commitment to the environment hasn't wavered. In fact, Bill likes to point out his pet project—an eco-friendly manufacturing plant that opened in Dearborn, Michigan, in 2004. As fuel oil prices continue to be an issue for consumers, environmentally friendly products will continue to be attractive options. Ford maintains its commitment to being a green company. Descriptions of its environmental efforts can be found in the 2010 Sustainability Report. As government-mandated, fuel-economy standards continue to get tougher, Ford is looking at several ideas from the past for boosting gas mileage and slashing emissions. Ford was recognized in early 2012 for its environmental efforts with a Climate Leadership Award from the United States Environmental Protection Agency.

Financial

Ford's executives are well aware that the company has a difficult road ahead and that its financial health is not guaranteed. The company has forecasted 2012 earnings to be flat, compared to 2011's strong profits. However, at the best, this may suggest a period of stable profitability. Complete company financial information can be found on its Web site **[www.ford.com]**.

FORD MOTOR COMPANY—THE FUTURE

In the company's 2012 Outlook, Alan Mulally reiterated his commitment to delivering the key aspects of the One Ford plan. "In a global market, success flows from having ONE TEAM working on ONE PLAN with ONE GOAL in mind." The ONE TEAM concept means including everyone with a stake in the outcome in the decision-making process. The ONE PLAN concept means changing the way the company has been run as largely autonomous business units to a more aligned and globally integrated organization and leveraging worldwide resources. The ONE GOAL is to build more of the products that people really want and value. Is Ford going down the right road with its Way Forward plan? How will a prolonged global economic downturn affect Mulally's ability to continue the company on its profitable path? Mulally says, "We are making consistent progress on our commitment to deliver great products, invest for global growth, build a strong business and provide profitable growth for all. We recognize we have challenges and opportunities ahead. We are excited about realizing the full potential of the global scale and operating margin benefits inherent in our One Ford plan. We also are excited about what leveraging our global assets ultimately will deliver for everyone associated with our business."

Sources: Based on Ford Motor Company [www.ford.com], March 5, 2012; N. Bunkley, "After Ratings Drop, Ford Reworks Touch Screens," *New York Times Online*, March 5, 2012; "Ford Motor Company, 10-K," Thomas Reuters Accelus, pp. 1–22; J. Bennett, "Ford Cruises, But Woes Loom," *Wall Street Journal*, January 28/29, 2012, p. B3; N. Bunkley, "G.M. Regains the Top Spot in Global Automaking," *New York Times Online*, January 19, 2012; M. Ramsey, "Ford Aims to Shake Up Family Car Market," *Wall Street Journal*, January 6, 2012, p. B4; J. Edgerton, "IIHS Rates the Safest Cars of 2012," *CBS Money Watch*, December 16, 2011; M. Ramsey and J. S. Lublin, "Ford Succession Will Test Mettle," *Wall Street Journal*, December 7, 2011, pp. B1+; M. Ramsey, "Ford SUV Marks New World Car Strategy," *Wall Street Journal*, November 16, 2011, pp. B1+; "Charlie Rose Talks to Alan Mulally," *Bloomberg BusinessWeek*, August 1–August 7, 2011, p. 27; K. Naughton, T. Higgins, D. Welch, and C. Trudell, "At Ford, Staying Solvent Has Its Costs," *Bloomberg BusinessWeek*, August 1–August 7, 2011, pp. 24+; J. R. Healey, "Ford Leads A Detroit 3 Surge," *USA Today*, July 27, 2011, pp. 1B+; and S. Elliott, "Ford Tries a Global Campaign for Its Global Car," *New York Times Online*, February 24, 2011.

Index

Note: Letters n, f, and t denote notes, figures, and tables, respectively.